MW01626375

Laws of Pesaḥ

Rabbi Eliezer Melamed

PENINEI HALAKHA

פניני הלכה

LAWS OF PESAḤ

Yeshivat Har Bracha Maggid Books

Laws of Pesaḥ

First Maggid Edition, 2014

Maggid Books
An imprint of Koren Publishers Jerusalem Ltd.

POB 8531, New Milford, CT 06776-8531, USA
& POB 4044, Jerusalem 91040, Israel
www.korenpub.com

Translation from Hebrew: Yehoshua Wertheimer and Moshe Rapps
Series Editor: Rabbi Elli Fischer
Editors: Elli Fischer, Nechama Unterman

Published in Cooperation with Yeshivat Har Bracha

The publication of this book was made possible through
the generous support of *Torah Education in Israel.*

ISBN 978 159 264 380 6, *hardcover*

A CIP catalogue record for this title is
available from the British Library

Printed and bound in the United States

This book is dedicated to Rabbi Eliezer Melamed
and all the wonderful people of Har Bracha.

May their commitment to Yishuv Haaretz
be an inspiration to us all.

Moshe Bronner and Yoram Katz

RABBI DR. TZVI HERSH WEINREB
Executive Vice President, Emeritus

212.613.8264 *tel*
212.613.0635 *fax*
execthw@ou.org *email*

LETTER BY RABBI DR. TZVI HERSH WEINREB

Kislev, 5774

The contemporary Jew who wishes to live a life of religious observance needs a variety of resources. One such resource is a guidebook to follow as he struggles to abide by *halakha* in the modern world. He cannot function religiously in the context of contemporary social and technological reality without such a resource.

For some years now, Rav Eliezer Melamed, the spiritual leader of the yeshiva and community of Har Bracha in Israel, has been publishing guidebooks which enable Jews with a very wide range of religious backgrounds to better observe halakhic practice.

At this point in time there are thirteen such volumes, covering a great diversity of topics. These volumes have a number of unique features, all of which contribute to the usefulness of the series. For starters, the author demonstrates literary skill and human sensitivity in rendering complex topics clearly intelligible to the novice practitioner but still gratifying to advanced students. Secondly, for a work to qualify as a practical guidebook, it must be authoritative. Rav Melamed is thoroughly familiar with the entire realm of applied *halakha* and is able to offer definitive rules and regulations. Finally, Rav Melamed excels in providing ideological rationales for the dos and don'ts of *halakha*. The background he provides as he introduces each new topic is consistently enlightening and uplifting. Charging the fine details of *halakha* with spiritual significance is a daunting objective, but it is one that Rav Melamed unfailingly achieves.

Until now, this series had but one shortcoming: it was inaccessible to audiences that are proficient only in English. That shortcoming is being rectified by the publication of this English translation of the series, beginning with Volume One, the Laws of Pesaḥ.

The team charged with translating this work into English includes Moshe Rapps, Nechama Unterman, and Yehoshua Wertheimer, and is headed by Rabbi Elli Fischer. This thoroughly experienced and talented team ensures that the English rendering retains all of the qualities that make this necessary work so precious.

It is therefore with great enthusiasm that I recommend this translation to the English-reading public. This series will educate and inspire the reader and help achieve a higher level of meaningful religious observance.

Sincerely,

Tzvi Hersh Weinreb

Rabbi Dr. Tzvi Hersh Weinreb
Executive Vice President, Emeritus
Orthodox Union

Contents

Chapter Nine: *Kitniyot*

Chapter Ten: The Principles of *Hagalat Kelim*

Chapter Eleven: Koshering the Kitchen

Chapter Fifteen: The Hagada

Chapter Sixteen: Seder Night

List of Abbreviations

Note: Throughout this volume, unless otherwise indicated, citations of *Tur, Shulḥan Arukh,* and Rema refer to the *Oraḥ Ḥayim* section

AHS	*Arukh Ha-shulḥan*	OḤ	*Oraḥ Hayim*
AZ	*Avoda Zara*	RH	*Rosh Ha-shana*
Baḥ	*Bayit Ḥadash*	SA	*Shulḥan Arukh*
BB	*Bava Batra*	SAH	*Shulḥan Arukh Ha-Rav*
Behag	*Halakhot Gedolot*	*San.*	*Sanhedrin*
BHL	*Bi'ur Halakha*	*Shakh*	*Siftei Kohen*
BK	*Bava Kama*	*Shev.*	*Shevu'ot*
BM	*Bava Metzi'a*	SHT	*Sha'ar Ha-tziyun*
EH	*Even Ha-ezer*	*Smag*	*Sefer Mitzvot Gadol*
ḤM	*Ḥoshen Mishpat*	*Smak*	*Sefer Mitzvot Katan*
MA	*Magen Avraham*	SSK	*Shemirat Shabbat Ke-hilkhata*
MB	*Mishna Berura*		
MK	*Mo'ed Katan*	*Taz*	*Turei Zahav*
MT	*Mishneh Torah*	YD	*Yoreh De'a*

Preface

It was taught in the academy of Eliyahu: One who reviews halakhot *every day is assured a place in the Next World, as it states: "His ways are forever"* [Habakkuk 3:6]. *Do not read this "ways"* ["halikhot"], *rather "laws"* ["halakhot"]. (Nida 73a)

Daily study of halakha *demonstrates that every facet and epoch of one's life is connected to the godly ideals whose parameters are described by* halakha. *One who studies* halakha *daily connects his temporal, mundane activities to the world of eternal truth. Thus he will be part of the Next World.* (Rav Eliezer Melamed, Preface to the Hebrew *Peninei Halakha* Series)

Over the course of the past two decades, Rav Eliezer Melamed's *Peninei Halakha* has evolved from a radio program into a well-known and widely accepted Israeli halakhic code. Its thirteen volumes (and counting) adorn the shelves of countless shuls and *batei midrash*, and are the textbook of choice for teaching *halakha* in dozens of schools. In all, over 300,000 individual volumes of *Peninei Halakha* have been sold.

Peninei Halakha owes its success in large part to three guidelines that shape Rav Melamed's writing. First, he begins each topic by defining and elucidating its basic principles before moving on to the practical details. He thus distinguishes between the general and the specific, between the primary and the secondary. Second, he anchors his discussions in relevant contemporary issues, thus demonstrating how theoretical ideas impact the details of halakhic practice. Finally, he uses clear and accessible language to explain the theoretical and theological roots of *halakha*.

The result of these guidelines is a code of law that is crystal clear in its presentation, concise in its formulation, and well-organized. These qualities are attested to by the approbations of many leading Torah scholars and former chief rabbis of Israel:

> It is composed in a manner that makes for easy comprehension and is made concrete through the use of examples from contemporary reality. This is accompanied by explanations that make the material beloved by its audience and that teach the love of God and man. (Rav Shaul Yisraeli *z"l*, *Rosh Yeshiva* of Merkaz Harav and author of *Eretz Ḥemda* and other works)

> I attest that Rav Eliezer Melamed invests days and nights clarifying the *halakha* and its rationale logically and with great erudition. (Rav Shlomo Goren *z"l*, Chief Rabbi of the IDF, Tel Aviv, and the State of Israel)

> Rav Melamed's book is of great value. He adroitly elucidates and illustrates the principles and reasons for the *mitzvot* and laws he addresses, encompassing the vast details of the issue at hand, and presenting both its principles and its specifics in a clear light. (Rav Avraham Shapira *z"l*, *Rosh Yeshiva* of Merkaz Harav and Ashkenazic Chief Rabbi of the State of Israel)

> The content is written well and organized beautifully. Each word is spoken skillfully, so that the reader may read it quickly. (Rav Mordechai Eliyahu *z"l*, Sephardic Chief Rabbi of the State of Israel)

> I am impressed by his clear and readable style. He wisely chose relevant halakhic issues and problems of paramount importance to contemporary students of the Torah. He presents the foundations and basics in an organized fashion, to the point that his conclusions are virtually self-evident. (Rav Nachum Eliezer Rabinovitch, *Rosh Yeshiva* of Birkat Moshe, Maale Adumim)

> The effort invested by Rav Melamed in assembling and reworking the material so that it is of use to those who populate the study halls as well as those who love and support Torah and wish to base lives of sanctity on a halakhic foundation, can be discerned between the lines of the work. (Rav Dov Lior, Rabbi and *Rosh Yeshiva* of Kiryat Arba – Ḥevron)

> You have blazed a singular trail in elucidating the depth and breadth of *halakha* by first considering the basis of each matter. By explaining the fundamental parameters and rationale of the *halakha*, you treat each issue with great clarity, down to the last detail. (Rav Zalman Baruch Melamed, Rabbi and *Rosh Yeshiva* of Beit El, and father of Rav Eliezer Melamed)

Rav Melamed's rulings relate to both Ashkenazic and Sephardic practice and chart a mainstream course, rooted in practical common sense, even while presenting other positions, whether lenient or stringent, and treating them with due respect.

Yeshivat Har Bracha is proud to present this translation of Rav Eliezer Melamed's work on the laws of Pesaḥ, the first volume of the eventual translation of the entire series, to the English-speaking world. Although various portions of Rav Melamed's halakhic writings have appeared in English in the past, online and in print, the reader will find that the present re-launch of the series will standardize style and usage and exhibit the accuracy, clarity, and concision typical of the Hebrew version of *Peninei Halakha* (for example, the list of *kitniyot* species that appears in section 4 of chapter 9 is the result of hours of research, including consultation with linguists and botanists). We hope that our efforts yield a clear, readable, and thorough presentation of the laws of Pesaḥ.

Many people contributed to the preparation of this volume for publication, and we would like to express our gratitude to them. The initial impetus to translate *Peninei Halakha* into English came from Yonatan Behar, and Rabbi Maor Cayam was instrumental in transforming the idea into a reality and first publishing Rav Melamed's works in English. The present volume was first translated by Yehoshua Wertheimer and Moshe Rapps. After undergoing editing, it was proofread by Nechama Unterman who, together with Dr. Yocheved Cohen, has been indispensable to the difficult and occasionally frustrating task of formulating stylistic guidelines for rendering a halakhic work into English. The editorial team at Maggid Books, particularly Tomi Mager, gave this volume its current form and design. Their invaluable guidance ensured that the final product meets the needs and tastes of its English-speaking audience. The creation and presentation of high-quality, compelling Torah content is part and parcel of the vision of Koren and its publisher, Matthew Miller. We hope that *Peninei Halakha* takes its place on Maggid's ever-expanding and increasingly comprehensive bookshelf.

Rabbi Yogev Cohen
Director, the *Peninei Halakha* Project

Rabbi Elli Fischer
Editor, the English *Peninei Halakha* Series
Tishrei, 5774

Chapter One

The Meaning of the Holiday

1. THE FESTIVAL OF *MATZOT* AND THE FESTIVAL OF PESAḤ

The holiday of Pesaḥ has two different names in the Torah: *Ḥag Ha-matzot* (the Festival of *Matzot*)[1] and *Ḥag Ha-Pesaḥ* (the Paschal festival, or Passover).[2] These two names express two different meanings of the holiday: *Ḥag Ha-matzot* represents the revelation of God's providence, and *Ḥag Ha-Pesaḥ* represents Israel's unique spiritual capacity.

At the Exodus from Egypt, God's sovereignty over the world was given its most apparent and concrete manifestation. Thus, our faith in God is fundamentally rooted in the Exodus. The matza symbolizes this aspect of our holiday, as we read in the Hagada: "This matza that we eat – what is the reason? Because our forefathers' dough did not have time to rise before the holy Supreme King of kings **revealed** Himself to them and redeemed them."

The unique mission and destiny of the people of Israel was also revealed at the time of the Exodus. The distinction between the Egyptians and the Israelites was conspicuous in all of the plagues, as the

1. Shemot 23:15 *et al.*
2. Shemot 34:25.

Egyptians were struck and the Israelites were saved. This culminated with the Plague of the Firstborn, when the Destroyer struck every Egyptian household but passed over (*pasaḥ*) Israelite homes. Israel's uniqueness is expressed through and symbolized by the Paschal sacrifice.

These two fundamental principles – faith and Israel – are linked together and interdependent. Unlike the other nations, which are formed through human endeavor, the nation of Israel was forged through divine miracles and wonders at the time of the Exodus for the purpose of receiving God's Torah. Israel's status entirely depends on their connection with God: when Israel does God's will and makes God's name manifest in the world, they earn all the blessings promised in the Torah. But when they do not fulfill God's will, all of the curses written in the Torah are visited upon them.

The revelation of God's name in the world, i.e., the manifestation of divine values on earth, depends upon Israel, as Scripture states: "I created this nation for My sake; they will tell My praise" (Yeshayahu 43:21). For this reason, the Sages stated (*Bereishit Rabba* 1:4) that the idea of Israel preceded the creation of the world, for it is through Israel that the purpose of the world is revealed. This is what the Sages meant when they said, "God set a condition with Creation: 'If Israel accepts the Torah, you will continue to exist, but if not, then I will return you to being formless and void'" (*Shabbat* 88a). Israel's unique capabilities were further made manifest in that God chose us to be His nation and children, in spite of the fact that we were lowly slaves, stuck in the morass of impurity in Egypt.

Thus the two biblical names of the holiday express two aspects of one matter, namely, the revelation of God's name in the world through Israel.

2. THE FESTIVAL OF FREEDOM – THE REVELATION OF MORALITY

Why did the people of Israel, before their appearance as a nation, first have to endure such terrible slavery in Egypt? The simple explanation is that Israel's mission is to rectify the moral state of the world, and in order to do so, it must experience firsthand the suffering and the pain that human beings can cause to one another.

Thus, we find several instances where the Torah invokes our experiences in Egypt when instructing us about interpersonal relationships. For example: "You shall not oppress a stranger – for you know the soul of a stranger, since you were strangers in the land of Egypt" (Shemot 23:9) and "If a stranger resides with you in your land, you shall not wrong him. The stranger who resides with you shall be to you as one born among you, and you shall love him as yourself, for you were strangers in the land of Egypt; I am the Lord your God" (Vayikra 19:33-34).

Similarly, the Sages said that before God began to smite the Egyptians, He instructed Moshe to command Israel concerning the mitzva of releasing slaves. Thus, even before they gained their freedom from Egypt they resolved that once they become free and have slaves of their own, they would never torment them. On the contrary, after six years they would send slaves free and grant them generous gifts (*y.* RH 3:5).

Indeed, an amazing thing happened at the Exodus. All other peoples who overthrew their enslavers became haughty and enslaved their former masters. Israel, however, did not try to enslave the Egyptians, even after completely defeating them; they only sought their own freedom. This was the first time that freedom appeared in the world as a moral value.

This is why Pesaḥ is called the Festival of Freedom, or, as the Sages termed it in the liturgy, "*zman ḥerutenu,*" "the season of our freedom." It is no coincidence that Pesaḥ is the first of the pilgrimage festivals: it embodies the foundation of human freedom and consequently of moral responsibility for every individual and societal act. Perhaps this is also why the years of Israelite kings' reigns were counted from the beginning the month of Nisan, so that the idea of freedom be fundamental to Israelite sovereignty.

3. SPIRITUAL LIBERATION FROM MATERIAL ENSLAVEMENT

Israel and Egypt are diametrically opposed. Egypt was an extremely materialistic society with a pagan worldview. The nation of Israel, on the other hand, is unique with its spiritual and abstract worldview. Thus, only Israel was able to accept the abstract belief in one incorporeal and non-physical God. Consequently, Israel's relationship to the material world is also pure and refined, and Jews are thus naturally modest and circumscribed in their sexual mores. The Egyptians, on the other hand, due to their emphasis on the physical and their materialistic worldview, were strongly attracted to promiscuity and sexual transgression. Thus, the Torah commands: "You shall not do like the deeds of the land of Egypt, in which you dwelt" (Vayikra 18:3). The Sages interpreted this to mean that no nation committed deeds more abominable than the Egyptians did (*Torat Kohanim ad loc.*), especially the last generation that enslaved Israel (based on Maharal's *Gevurot Hashem* ch. 4).

The Egyptians of that period indeed accomplished some amazing material and administrative feats by creating a stable regime, an advanced irrigation system, and a sophisticated economy (in part due to the help of Yosef, Yaakov's son). However, these material accomplishments were disconnected from the spiritual world and even opposed to it. Their worldview was extremely idolatrous. They did not believe in the existence of an independent, spiritual soul, but thought that the soul is contingent on and subservient to the existence of the physical body. This is why the Egyptians went to such great lengths to embalm corpses; they thought that one's existence hinges solely on his physical reality. Death, in their view, merely means that one is no longer able to move or speak, but still exists in every other respect. Accordingly, they also invested enormous effort in building the pyramids, which are glorified cemeteries for the body.

To be sure, the material world has an important place in Judaism as well. However, a worldview based solely on physical existence will necessarily be idolatrous and amoral. This is because all of the paradigms provided by nature are amoral. There may be beauty and wisdom reflected in the amazing regularity of the laws of nature, but they do not possess morality. The strong prey on the weak just as the powerful enslave the poor. The pagan worldview, instead of striving toward a higher level, sanctifies material existence with all its brutality and injustice. In contrast, a faith-based and spiritual worldview is characterized by constant striving toward improving the world, fighting evil and empowering justice. This is how the prophet Yeshayahu described the ultimate redemption and the *Mashi'aḥ*'s leadership:

> But with righteousness shall he judge the poor, and decide with equity for the meek of the land; he shall smite the land with the rod of his mouth, and with the breath of his lips he shall slay the wicked. Righteousness shall be the girdle of his waist, and faithfulness the girdle of his loins. The wolf shall dwell with the lamb, and the leopard shall lie down with the kid... the cow and the bear shall graze, together their young shall lie down. The lion shall eat straw like cattle... They shall not hurt nor destroy in all My holy mountain, for the earth shall be full of the knowledge of the Lord, as the waters cover the sea. (Yeshayahu 11:4-9)

Thus, the Exodus from Egypt was not merely the emancipation of the Israelites enslaved in Egypt. Rather, it was the liberation of all mankind from the chains of materialism. This is why it is so important to delve into the Exodus, to the extent that we are commanded to see ourselves, every year on the Seder night, as though we ourselves left Egypt. We have also been commanded to remember the Exodus every day and every night. To a certain extent, Shabbat and all holidays were established to commemorate the Exodus, for at the Exodus the spirit of man was freed from the bonds of material existence. Since we have not finished liberating ourselves from the bonds of the material world – the chains of the evil impulse and its lusts – from a spiritual perspective, we still need to continue leaving Egypt. Hence, it is a mitzva to delve into the Exodus.

4. AT THE EXODUS, THE MATERIAL WORLD BECAME A VEHICLE FOR GOD'S *SHEKHINA*

The way this world is ordered, its material aspects gain prominence first and easily reach their complete, powerful expression. Spiritual elements, however, remain hidden; it takes a long time before their significance becomes discernible. It was thus natural that the Egyptians initially overpowered Israel, for Egyptian might had already come to full fruition, while Israel was still like an unborn embryo. Since Israel's strength could not be yet expressed, the Egyptians exploited Israel's weakness and enslaved them to fuel their glory and their lusts.

But this was also for the best. Spirituality cannot be expressed in the world without a material basis, and this is exactly what we gained from being enslaved in Egypt. During the entire period that the Egyptians enslaved Israel and thought that they were overpowering us completely, in reality we were drawing and absorbing their power, as it is written: "The Israelites were fruitful, and increased abundantly, and multiplied, and waxed exceedingly mighty; and the land was filled with them" (Shemot 1:7). The more the Egyptians tried to enslave and subdue us, the more we increased, as it is written: "But the more they tormented them, the more they multiplied, and the more they proliferated" (*ibid.* 12) until we numbered 600,000 adult men. Maharal explains (*Gevurot Hashem* chs. 4 and 12) that this was the number necessary for the establishment of the nation of Israel. Once we numbered 600,000, an aspect of the divine was revealed within us, the Egyptian empire collapsed, and we left Egypt to receive the Torah at Sinai.

Not only were we blessed with fertility in Egypt, we also left Egypt with great wealth, compensation for many years of slavery. Thus, Israel began its course with a solid material foundation. This is the meaning of:

> When you go, you shall not go empty-handed; rather, every woman shall ask of her neighbor and of she who lives in her house silver and gold vessels and clothes; and you shall put them upon your sons and your daughters, and thus you shall despoil Egypt. (Shemot 3:21-22)

The Egyptians got their just desserts; had they chosen to be righteous, they would have taken care of the Israelites and helped them multiply and prosper. They would have benefited from this doubly, as they did when Yosef contributed to Egypt's success during the difficult years of famine. But they chose evil, cruelly enslaving Israel, and consequently they were punished with ten plagues. The name of God was thus sanctified in the world, for the wicked were brought to justice and Israel left to eternal freedom.

5. THE MEANING OF THE PROHIBITION AGAINST *ḤAMETZ* – PRIDE IN RELATION TO GOD

The prohibition against *ḥametz* on Pesaḥ is especially stringent, for the Torah not only forbade eating it, but commanded that it not be seen nor found in our possession. Our Sages further forbade eating any food with even the slightest amount of *ḥametz* mixed in. Thus the avoidance of *ḥametz* on Pesaḥ is absolute. This is because *ḥametz* symbolizes evil, as it says in the *Zohar* (2:40b) that *ḥametz* is the evil impulse. Specifically, it alludes to the impulse of pride. Fermentation causes dough to rise – it looks as though the dough is inflating itself and puffing up with pride, as an arrogant person would. In contrast, matza, which remains in its original size, as it was when God created it, symbolizes the trait of humility.

At first glance, this is difficult to understand. If *ḥametz* represents the evil inclination, then why is there no commandment or custom to avoid it throughout the year? On the contrary, man is praised for knowing how to make wheat into tasty *ḥametz* cakes (see *Tanḥuma Tazri'a* 5). This was the Creator's purpose in endowing man with the wisdom and practical skills to engage in developing the world. God created an imperfect world intentionally, so that man could imitate His deeds and participate in improving the world through scientific and technological development.

The answer is that there are two types of pride: One is that man exaggerates his own praiseworthiness and thinks he is wiser, stronger, and better than he really is. Any intelligent person understands that such pride harms one's ability to actualize his potential for the betterment of the world. His ability to judge is completely impaired, and he cannot conduct his life properly. Clearly, such pride is inappropriate all year long and has nothing to do with the prohibition of *ḥametz*. On the contrary, such pride detracts from one's good works and thus harms the good, year-round *ḥametz*.

The second type of pride, which corresponds to *ḥametz* on Pesaḥ, is man's pride vis-à-vis his Creator, his God. Jewish faith is predicated on the acknowledgment that God created the world and determined its destiny, and that the roots of all things depend on Him alone. Although God gave man the ability to improve and to develop the world, this is limited to manipulating and developing the outgrowths of the root elements of creation; man has no power over the root elements, which are divine creations. God created the world, chose the people of Israel to be His *am segula*, His treasured nation, and gave them the Torah. Man has no authority to call these fundamental principles into question.

Therefore, when one stands before his Creator, he must envelop himself in humility and make every effort not mix his petty human thoughts with the fundamental principles of creation. Such confusion, like *ḥametz* on Pesaḥ, is forbidden.

Pesaḥ, and especially the Seder, is designed to instill in us the fundamentals of faith: that the world has a Creator, that He watches over His creatures, and that He chose the people of Israel to reveal His name in the world. Whenever there is revelation of an aspect of the divine in the world, it appears in a completely miraculous fashion, to show that it is not a human endeavor. Thus, the Exodus was accompanied by signs and wonders, to make public that the election of Israel was a divine matter. Similarly, the Torah was given with obvious miracles, to a generation that lived miraculously for forty years in the desert, in order to make it known that this was an entirely divine matter. In other words, we **receive** the fundamental principles of faith from God – we do not invent them. Whoever mixes some human aspect into these basic principles of faith is guilty of idolatry. This is alluded to in *Zohar*'s statement that *ḥametz* on Pesaḥ is idolatry (2:182a).

Therefore, on Pesaḥ, the holiday geared toward imparting the fundamentals of faith, we are commanded to be extremely cautious to avoid eating and possessing even a smidgen of *ḥametz*, which symbolizes our human aspects that must not get mixed in when we speak about the roots and foundations of faith. During the rest of the year, however, when we nurture and improve the branches that develop from those roots, *ḥametz* is allowed and even desirable.

6. THE MEANING OF MATZA

Matza, symbolizing our recognition that the spiritual roots of things are beyond our grasp even though God granted us the ability to operate within and improve the world, is the opposite of *ḥametz*. Therefore, on Pesaḥ, when we are engaged with the most fundamental elements of faith, we do not mix even one iota of *ḥametz* in our food. We eat only matza, which remains simple and thin throughout its baking, without going through any additional process of swelling.

Through our humility before God, expressed in the matza, we internalize the faith, first revealed at the Exodus from Egypt, that God actively watches over the world and elected Israel. To be sure, there were elite individuals who believed in God even before the Exodus, but their connection with the divine was of a personal nature. The wholeness of faith was first revealed only at the Exodus, with the formation of a complete nation containing all strata of society destined to manifest God's name in the world.

Matza comes to remind us of faith and is therefore called the "food of faith" (*meikhla de-mehemnuta*) by the *Zohar* (2:183b). By eating matza on the Seder night with the proper intent, one achieves faith, and by eating matza all seven days of Pesaḥ, one implants that faith firmly in one's heart (*Pri Tzadik*, Pesaḥ 9).

Since matza signifies faith, it is understandable that its entire manufacturing process must be performed very meticulously, as we will learn below (ch. 12, p. 200 ff.). This is because the roots of all things depend on faith, and any small flaw in faith can cause tremendous destruction in the world.

We can thus understand why the nation of Israel came into being as slaves in Egypt. All other nations develop naturally, from the ground up, from family to clan to tribe to nation. As they grow, they develop cultures that evolve out of the circumstances of their lives, the climate of their territories, and their conflicts with their neighbors. As part of the emergence of their culture, they develop some type of deistic belief. Since human beings are involved in their invention, such beliefs are idolatrous.

In contrast, Israel became a nation as slaves, devoid of any culture. They could not develop their own culture while enslaved and lacking national self-esteem. At the same time, Egyptian culture was foreign to them and possibly despised by them, as it was associated with their tormentors. Israel was thus a *tabula rasa*, free of preconceived notions, and perfectly capable of absorbing the true faith based on divine revelation and accepting the Torah without introducing human considerations into its fundamental principles. The impoverished, unembellished matza alludes to the condition of the Israelites at that time.

7. ONE WHO DEMEANS THE HOLY DAYS

An important principle is articulated in *Mishna Avot* (3:11): "Rabbi Elazar Ha-Moda'i says: 'One who desecrates holy foods, one who demeans the holy days… and one who expounds the Torah not in accordance with *halakha,* even if he has Torah study and good deeds to his credit, has no share in the World to Come.'"

My teacher, R. Zvi Yehuda Kook, would ask how one with Torah study and good deeds to his credit could not have a share in the World to Come. Moreover, since the *mishna* does not specify how much Torah study and good deeds this person has to his credit, it is implied that even if the person is a great Torah scholar, highly scrupulous in his observance of *mitzvot,* and a doer of many good deeds, he has no share in the World to Come since he demeans the holy days and expounds the Torah not in accordance with the *halakha.*

R. Zvi Yehuda went on to describe one who greatly respects tradition and is meticulous about fulfilling the halakhic requirements of the Seder, but considers it all the product of human intelligence. He explains that the importance of the Pesaḥ holiday and the Seder lies in the parents passing their traditions on to the next generations, imparting to them the moral principles of human liberty and a sense of mission to improve the world. The matza merely concretizes Israel's historical consciousness, and the four cups of wine simply add a dimension of joy. Even though all of these lovely ideas are true, the central fundamental principle is missing: that God chose us from among all nations, gave us the Torah, and commanded us to celebrate Pesaḥ and eat matza on the Seder night.

R. Zvi Yehuda's hypothetical Jew similarly honors Shabbat as a day when the family spends time together and grows closer, and when hardworking people can rest and engage in spiritual pursuits. He even adds that "Shabbat kept the Jews more than the Jews kept Shabbat." He forgets only one thing: that God commanded us to observe Shabbat, down to its finest detail.

This is what the *mishna* meant by "one who expounds the Torah not in accordance with *halakha.*" Even though he studies it diligently, to him it is not God's Torah but merely human wisdom, so he allows himself to interpret it any way that comes to mind. Thus he demeans the holy days; he thinks they are customs and traditions that human beings invented to give expression to all sorts of spiritual notions, thereby denying that they are God-given *mitzvot* of the Torah. Therefore, even though he may have studied much Torah and performed many good deeds, and he is thought of as a good, honorable man in this world – he has no connection with holiness. He has no share in the eternal historical mission of the Jewish people, and thus has no share in the World to Come.

8. ONE INQUIRES ABOUT THE LAWS OF PESAḤ BEGINNING THIRTY DAYS BEFORE PESAḤ

We inquire about and expound upon the laws of Pesaḥ beginning thirty days before Pesaḥ. We learn this from Moshe, who on Pesaḥ itself explained the matter of *Pesaḥ Sheni*, the make-up date for those unable to bring the Paschal offering, which takes place thirty days later. The main reason for this is that all of Israel had to prepare animal sacrifices as Pesaḥ approached, examining them to be certain that they were free of disqualifying blemishes (*Pesaḥim* 6a; AZ 5b).

This enactment was not canceled even after the Temple was destroyed; it is proper to study the laws of Pesaḥ thirty days before the holiday arrives. As is well known, Pesaḥ has very many laws, pertaining to preparing the home for Pesaḥ, seeking and destroying *ḥametz*, baking the matza, and the Seder. Some Rishonim maintain that the enactment applies specifically to Torah scholars, enjoining them to prioritize answering practical questions about the upcoming holiday. According to this view, there is no universal obligation to set a fixed time for studying the laws of Pesaḥ (Ran and Rashba). Nevertheless, since many Rishonim maintain that it is indeed obligatory to set a fixed time for studying the laws of Pesaḥ beginning thirty days before Pesaḥ, it is proper that every individual do so, beginning on the fourteenth of Adar (Purim). It is also proper for schools and *yeshivot* to set a fixed time for studying the laws of Pesaḥ during this period.

There is a dispute amongst halakhic authorities about whether one is obliged to study the laws of the other holidays thirty days in advance. Some say that since this enactment was established primarily for preparing the animal sacrifices, and such sacrifices were in fact brought on the three pilgrimage festivals – the *olat re'iyah* (pilgrimage burnt-offering), *shalmei ḥagiga* (pilgrimage peace offerings), and *shalmei simḥa* (festival peace offerings) – therefore it is proper to study the laws of each festival thirty days in advance. Others say that the practice today primarily concerns Pesaḥ, since its laws are so numerous and strict (MB 429:1).[3]

These differences of opinion and distinctions concern advance preparations for the holidays. During the course of the holidays, however, there is an ancient enactment, ordained by Moshe, for people to study the laws and spiritual meanings of that holiday (*Megilla* 32a, MA 429:1).

3. *Tosafot* AZ 5b, s.v. "ve-hatnan" states that even after the destruction of the Temple this decree was not nullified. MB 429:1 (see also BHL *ad loc.*) reinforces the opinion that one must learn the laws of Pesaḥ thirty days before, and rejects Ran's opinion since most Rishonim disagree with him. This is also the opinion of many Aḥaronim, including SAH 429:1-3, which explains the issue thoroughly and states that this is a rabbinic decree (as opposed to the opinion of *Baḥ*, which states that it is a Torah law). Conversely, see *Yabi'a Omer* 2:222, which explains that Ran and Rashba maintain that the essence of the decree is to first answer a person who asks about the laws of Pesaḥ, since he is asking about a pertinent issue, and that this is the opinion of most Rishonim. (There is also debate about the position of *Shulḥan Arukh* itself: some infer that it concurs with Ran from the fact that it only mentions the term "inquire"; others reject this inference.) In practice, I used the terms "mitzva" and "proper" since not everyone agrees that this is an obligation. Moreover, even though according to *Baḥ* this is in fact a Torah obligation, most authorities view it only as a rabbinic decree.

It is also worth noting that there are authorities who maintain that the main obligation is for rabbis and Torah teachers to begin teaching the laws of Pesaḥ thirty days before the festival, but there is no obligation on each individual. This is what *Ḥok Yaakov* states in 429:1, 3, adding in the name of *Rokei'aḥ*, Raavan, and *Kol Bo* that even the reading of *Parshat Para* right after Purim was established to remind the people to purify themselves for the upcoming Pesaḥ. Similarly, many Aḥaronim write that this is the reason for the establishment of the custom to teach the laws of Pesaḥ on *Shabbat Ha-gadol*, as recorded in SAH and MB 429:2. Nevertheless, according to most authorities there is still a mitzva for every individual to delve into the laws of Pesaḥ during the thirty days prior to the festival. BHL rules accordingly. However, there is arguably a greater obligation for rabbis and teachers.

Chapter Two

General Rules of the Prohibition against *Ḥametz*

1. FOUR *MITZVOT* CONCERNING THE PROHIBITION AGAINST *ḤAMETZ*

Four Torah commandments deal with the prohibition against *ḥametz* on Pesaḥ: three negative and one positive.

The first prohibition is to refrain from eating *ḥametz*, as it is written: "And *ḥametz* shall not be eaten" (Shemot 13:3). Our Sages taught that the prohibition against eating *ḥametz* on Pesaḥ includes not deriving any kind of benefit from the *ḥametz*. The Torah also says, "You shall not eat anything leavened; in all of your settlements you shall eat *matzot*" (Shemot 12:20). Our Sages concluded from this verse that not only some thing that had fermented on its own is prohibited, but even food t' had been leavened by some external agent may not be eaten on P It must be noted that the Torah was particularly stringent cor the prohibition against eating *ḥametz*. Almost all of the Tr prohibitions are punishable by lashes, while eating *ḥamet* punishable by *karet* (extirpation), as it is written: "Whoe from the first day until the seventh day, that soul sh Israel" (Shemot 12:15).

The second prohibition is that no *ḥamet* possession, as it is written: "Seven days there your homes" (Shemot 12:19). *Se'or* is the leavening agent that one uses to make dough ferment. This verse means not only that *se'or* is forbidden, but also that no *ḥametz* may be found in our possession on Pesaḥ. This prohibition is often called *bal yimatzei.*

The third prohibition is that no *ḥametz* may be seen in our possession, as it is written: "*Matzot* shall be eaten seven days; and no *ḥametz* of yours shall be seen, and no *se'or* of yours shall be seen within all your borders" (Shemot 13:7). One violates the second prohibition (*bal yimatzei*) and this third prohibition (called *bal yera'eh*) only if one has in his possession on Pesaḥ at least one olive's bulk (*kezayit*) of *ḥametz.* If the volume of the *ḥametz* that remained in one's possession was less than a *kezayit,* he does not violate *bal yera'eh* and *bal yimatzei* on account of that *ḥametz.*

The fourth mitzva – a positive commandment – is to get rid of *ḥametz* and *se'or* in advance of Pesaḥ, as it is written: "Seven days you shall eat *matzot*; however, on the first day you shall remove the *se'or* from your houses" (Shemot 12:15).

2. THE TIMES WHEN *ḤAMETZ* IS PROHIBITED BY TORAH LAW AND BY RABBINIC LAW

Although the prohibition against *ḥametz* applies primarily during the seven days of *Ḥag Ha-matzot,* from the fifteenth through the twenty-first of Nisan, nevertheless we are commanded to remove *ḥametz* from our homes at midday on the fourteenth of Nisan, Erev Pesaḥ.

The prohibition against eating *ḥametz* also begins at midday on the fourteenth, as is written: "And you shall sacrifice the *Pesaḥ* [offering] to G-d ... you shall not eat *ḥametz* with it" (Devarim 16:2-3). This prohibits the eating of *ḥametz* from the time fit for bringing the *Pesaḥ* sacrifice, i.e., at midday on the fourteenth of Nisan. This prohibition against eating *ḥametz* includes the prohibition against deriving any benefit from it.[1]

1. The mitzva of removing the *ḥametz* applies from midday on the fourteenth, as it is written: "However, on the first day you shall remove the *se'or* from your houses" (Shemot 12:15). The Sages demonstrated from other verses that "the first day" refers to Erev Pesaḥ. Since the *ḥametz* must already have been removed by the onset of the holiday self so as not to violate *bal yera'eh* and *bal yimatzei,* the mitzva of removing the *ḥametz* ust be in the middle of the day preceding Pesaḥ, that is, at midday (*Pesaḥim* 4b).

In order to distance one further from possibly violating commandments, the Sages added to the prohibitions and forbade gaining benefit from *ḥametz* for an additional hour. They also forbade eating *ḥametz* for two extra hours, since on a cloudy day people are likely to err by as much as two hours.

These times are calculated by dividing the day into twelve equal parts, each of which is called "a seasonal hour" ("*sha'ah zmanit*"). Thus, one may eat *ḥametz* for the first four seasonal hours of the fourteenth. During the fifth hour it is rabbinically forbidden to eat *ḥametz*, but it is permissible to derive benefit from it by, for example, feeding it to an animal or selling it to a gentile. When the sixth hour of the day begins, possession of *ḥametz* becomes prohibited rabbinically, and if one forgot to sell it to a gentile, it must be destroyed. When midday arrives, that is, after the sixth hour ends, *ḥametz* is forbidden by Torah law both for consumption and for deriving any benefit, and one must dispose of it as soon as possible. Every moment that one does not get rid of it, he violates the positive commandment to remove the *ḥametz* (see below 3:6 concerning the mitzva of removing the *ḥametz*).

The prohibition against eating *ḥametz* and obtaining any benefit from it applies from midday on the fourteenth, according to R. Yehuda, as explained in *Pesaḥim* 28a. Rambam, as well as R. Yitzḥak ibn Gi'at, Rosh, and most Rishonim, ruled in accordance with this view. R. Shimon's view is that the prohibition against eating *ḥametz* begins with the holiday itself, and it is only the mitzva of removing the *ḥametz* that comes into effect at midday on the fourteenth. Some Rishonim rule in accordance with this view, although they disagreed about what the mitzva of getting rid of *ḥametz* entails according to R. Shimon. Let us mention two approaches. According to Ramban and Raavad, since one must get rid of the *ḥametz*, he is also not allowed to eat it; yet Torah law permits him to benefit from it in the course of its being burned. Only the Sages prohibited deriving any benefit from the *ḥametz* from the beginning of the sixth hour of the day. According to *Ha-ma'or*, the mitzva of disposing of the *ḥametz* does not imply a prohibition against eating it, since by eating it, one is, in fact, disposing of it (see *Encyclopedia Talmudit*, vol. 16, s.v. "*ḥametz*", p. 66; *Hilkhot Ḥag Be-ḥag*, p. 8, n. 3). Again, the view of most *poskim* is that the *halakha* follows R. Yehuda's view that the prohibition against eating *ḥametz* and the prohibition against deriving any benefit from *ḥametz* are of Torah origin, and apply from midday. This is how the *halakha* is decided in SA (443:1).

Once the holiday begins, two additional prohibitions apply: *bal yera'eh* and *bal yimatzei*.[2] The prohibition against eating *ḥametz* also becomes more severe: one who willfully eats *ḥametz* after midday on the fourteenth is punishable by lashes only, whereas one who willfully eats *ḥametz* after the holiday begins is punishable by *karet*. This is based on the verse: "Whoever eats *ḥametz*, from the first day until the seventh day, that soul shall be cut off from Israel" (Shemot 12:15).

Ḥametz becomes permissible once again after Pesaḥ, except that our Sages forbade *ḥametz* that belonged to a Jew during the holiday ("*ḥametz she-avar alav ha-Pesaḥ*"). Since by keeping the *ḥametz* on Pesaḥ he violated the prohibitions of *bal yera'eh* and *bal yimatzei*, the Sages prohibited eating or gaining benefit from that *ḥametz* even after Pesaḥ. *Ḥametz* that was in the possession of a gentile during Pesaḥ, however, is permissible; a Jew may buy it and eat it (SA 448:1-3).

3. WHAT IS *ḤAMETZ* AND WHAT IS *SE'OR*?

The *ḥametz* that is prohibited by the Torah on Pesaḥ is any one of the five species of cereal grains that came into contact with water and fermented. The five species are wheat (*ḥitta*), barley (*se'ora*), oats (*shibolet shu'al*), rye (*shifon*), and spelt (*kusmin*). These species are used to make bread, the staple food of mankind. The Sages ordained a special blessing to be recited before eating bread – "Who brings forth bread from the earth" ("*ha-motzi leḥem min ha-aretz*"). After eating bread, the Torah commanded us to recite *Birkat Ha-mazon*. So that bread will be tasty and easy to digest, its dough is fermented and made to rise.

There are two types of leaven products: *ḥametz* and *se'or*. Both are produced by mixing flour and water. *Ḥametz* is the regular leavening of dough to bake bread and cakes. The fermentation is accomplished by leaving the dough at rest without handling it. If one wants the leavening to be faster and of higher quality, one mixes *se'or* (sourdough) into the

2. This is the opinion of most *poskim*, since for these prohibitions the term "seven days" is stated explicitly; see MB 443:1 in the name of MA and others. However, SHT 443:2 states that not everyone agrees to this, and according to Rashi the prohibition starts on midday of the fourteenth. This also seems to be the opinion of Rabbeinu Ḥananel and *Itur*, namely, that according to R. Yehuda these prohibitions are like the prohibition of eating and begin at midday.

dough. *Se'or* is the second type of leavening. It is produced by leaving *ḥametz* for a long time, so that it continues to effervesce and ferment, until it tastes so sour that people cannot eat it. As noted, the purpose of *se'or* is to hasten and improve the quality of the leavening process of various types of dough, for the preparation of breads and cakes. More specifically, *ḥametz* is intended for eating while *se'or* is a leavening agent in preparing *ḥametz* foods. The Torah prohibited both, and the law is the same regarding both. One who leaves a *kezayit* of either of them in his possession during Pesaḥ violates *bal yera'eh* and *bal yimatzei* (*Beitza* 7b).

But if flour of the five cereal grains is mixed with water, kneaded rapidly, and put it into an oven immediately, then the dough will not have enough time to rise. This is the matza that we are commanded to eat on the first night of Pesaḥ, as a remembrance of the Exodus from Egypt, as is written: "And the people picked up their dough before it fermented" (Shemot 12:34). Thus, specifically those species of grain that may become *ḥametz* are the species from which one makes matza for the mitzva (*Pesaḥim* 35a).

Although rice and millet are similar to the five species of cereal grain, and although they rise, they do not undergo a complete fermentation process as the five cereal species do. Therefore, the prohibition against *ḥametz* does not apply to them, and if one made matza out of one of them, one does not fulfill any mitzva with it on Pesaḥ.

Note that *kusmin* (spelt) is not the same as *kusemet* (buckwheat). The former is one of the five species of cereal grain, whereas the latter is a type of legume and may be eaten on Pesaḥ by those who eat *kitniyot*; even among those who do not eat *kitniyot*, it is permitted for sick people (MB 453:4, 7. Note that some mix up the names and call spelt *kusemet*).

4. THE DEFINITION OF LEAVENING DOUGH

As we have learned, the difference between bread and matza is that the dough used for making bread has undergone a leavening process resulting from the fermentation of ingredients within the flour that have come into contact with water. In order to augment the leavening process, bakers customarily mix *se'or* into the dough, causing the dough to ferment more thoroughly and quickly. However, even without the leavening agent, if dough were left without kneading, it would ferment and rise.

Therefore, when preparing *matzot* one must work quickly to ensure that the leavening process within the dough does not begin.

As long as the dough is in motion, being kneaded, it does not become *ḥametz*. Even if the kneading were to continue an entire day, the dough would not become *ḥametz*, since kneading inhibits the leavening process. However, if the dough sat motionless for eighteen minutes, the leavening process has begun and all the prohibitions concerning *ḥametz* apply to it. This applies to normal conditions, but where it is hotter, the leavening process is accelerated, and the dough becomes *ḥametz* in even less than eighteen minutes.

Cracks appearing in the dough are a physical indication that the dough has become *ḥametz*. Even if eighteen minutes without kneading had not yet passed, since there are cracks in the dough, it has certainly become *ḥametz*; apparently conditions were warm and so it took less time to become *ḥametz*. Moreover, the kneading may have been inadequate, so that certain parts of the dough were neglected, causing those areas to become *ḥametz*. Even if there are only a few cracks, and they appeared only in part of the dough, the entire dough is *ḥametz*. If no cracks appeared but the dough blanched, it is *ḥametz nuksheh* (hardened *ḥametz*; see next section), which is rabbinically forbidden (SA 459:2).[3]

---

3. The rising of the dough indicates that it has become *ḥametz* (Me'iri), and other symptoms, namely, cracks in the dough, a blanched appearance, and the time that has elapsed, are only relevant in a case where the dough did not begin to rise. However, there are situations in which the dough rises but this does not indicate that it has become *ḥametz*; rather, it has undergone what the Sages call "*sirḥon*" (spoilage). This applies to the case of rice, or of flour mixed with fruit juice, according to most *poskim*. However, when wheat flour mixes with water and begins to rise, this is in fact a sign that the mixture has become *ḥametz*. If the dough sat and was not kneaded for the time that it takes to walk one *mil*, it has become *ḥametz* even if there is no visible indication, as explained in the Mishna and Gemara in *Pesaḥim* 46a. SA 459:2 explains that this amount of time is eighteen minutes, although Rambam and R. Ovadia of Bertinoro maintain that it is twenty-four minutes. BHL *ad loc.* rules that these lenient positions may be relied upon to prevent a significant loss of money, and that the authorities rule according to the *Shulḥan Arukh* without even mentioning the more lenient opinion because of the strict nature of the prohibition of *ḥametz*.

According to Rashi and Me'iri, however, one must check the amount of time that the dough has been sitting only when it is unclear whether or not the leavening process

5. ḤAMETZ NUKSHEH

The *ḥametz* that the Torah forbade is *ḥametz gamur* (absolute *ḥametz*), meaning that the leavening process has been completed, and the food has become edible. But if fermentation had begun but not concluded, and from the outset the food was barely edible, then it is called "*ḥametz nuksheh*." According to most *poskim*, *ḥametz nuksheh* is not forbidden by Torah law, but the Sages prohibited it so that people would not err and come to eat or keep real *ḥametz*.

---

has begun: if more than the time it takes to walk one *mil* has elapsed, the dough is *ḥametz*. If one is certain that the dough is not *ḥametz*, even if it has been sitting for longer than the time that it takes to walk one *mil*, it is not considered *ḥametz*. Nonetheless, according to most Rishonim in any situation where the dough has sat for longer than it takes to walk one *mil*, the dough is *ḥametz*. See, for example, MT, Laws of *Ḥametz* and Matza 5:13; SA 459:2. *Pri Megadim*'s introduction to §467 contends that such dough is complete *ḥametz*; eating it on Pesaḥ incurs the punishment of *karet*. Rashbatz writes that one must suspect that such dough has become *ḥametz*. In a warm place, dough becomes *ḥametz* in less than the time it takes to walk a *mil*, as written in *Aguda* in the name of the Ge'onim. This is the halakhic consensus, as it is also the ruling of *Yerei'im*, *Mordechai*, and *Hagahot Maimoniyot*. Additionally, Rosh writes that even if the dough became warm in one's hands, the dough will become *ḥametz* more quickly. This is cited in SA and Rema 459:2 (see also *Berur Halakha on Pesaḥim* 46a). Although there is dispute as to whether or not the "sitting times" of the dough are combined, *Terumat Ha-deshen* rules that a full kneading of the dough cancels the previous sitting time, though merely poking the dough would not be effective. This is cited in MB 459:16.

Pesaḥim 48b states: "As long as the dough is being worked it cannot become *ḥametz*." The vast majority of Rishonim, including Rambam in *Laws of Ḥametz and Matza* 5:3 and *Tur* and SA 459:2, explain that as long as one keeps kneading the dough it will not become *ḥametz*, even if he does so for the entire day. Yet it appears that the Yerushalmi disagrees with the Bavli and says that if one kneaded the dough for the amount of time that it takes to walk four *mil*, the dough is considered *ḥametz*. *Baḥ* cites Ri'az that ideally we should act in accordance with the Yerushalmi. There is an even more stringent opinion – Ritva's – according to which as long as one kneads the dough at the appropriate pace so that he will complete the kneading in less time than it would take to walk one *mil*, the dough does not become *ḥametz*. However, if the kneading goes on for longer than this time, the dough is considered *ḥametz* (see *Berur Halakha* on *Pesaḥim* 48b; *Encyclopedia Talmudit*, s.v. "*ḥametz*," §5, pp. 74-75). Even though the vast majority of *poskim* disagree with Ritva, they rule that it is still preferable to be stringent and complete the kneading process within eighteen minutes, as explained in AHS 459:7.

An example of *ḥametz nuksheh* is the glue that scribes used to prepare from flour and water for gluing paper. Since its leavening process was never completed, and it is barely edible, it is *ḥametz nuksheh*, and the Sages forbade eating it or keeping it on Pesaḥ (MB 442:2). If its form was changed, as when the glue is used to stick papers together, then one is allowed to keep it. Others are more stringent and maintain that if the glue protrudes from between the pages, then it is considered as if it has maintained its same form, and it is forbidden to keep it on Pesaḥ (SA and Rema 242:3).

Similarly, dough that began to ferment to the point that its surface blanched, but the surface was not cracked as with true leavening, is considered *ḥametz nuksheh*, and it is forbidden by rabbinic law to eat or keep it on Pesaḥ (SA 459:2).[4]

6. ḤAMETZ SO SPOILED THAT A DOG WOULD NOT EAT IT

Ḥametz that was originally fit for eating, but that became moldy or spoiled to the point that it is not fit for human consumption, is still considered *ḥametz gamur*, since it can still be used as a leavening agent. In other words, even though, in general, all forbidden foods become no longer forbidden once they are no longer fit for human consumption, *ḥametz* is different. Since it can still help in the preparation of food, it is like *se'or*, which serves as a leavening agent and is therefore considered *ḥametz*. However, if it became so spoiled that it is not fit for consumption by a dog, then it is not considered food at all. Therefore, the law of *ḥametz* does not apply to it and it is permissible to keep it during Pesaḥ and to gain benefit from it (SA 442:2; MB *ad loc.* 10). By rabbinic decree,

4. The opinion of SA 447:12 is that *ḥametz nuksheh* is only rabbinically forbidden, and therefore, *ḥametz nuksheh* that existed over Pesaḥ is not forbidden after Pesaḥ. This is also the opinion of SAH 442:20-21 and MB 442:2, based on the opinion of most Rishonim. However, several Rishonim are of the opinion that *ḥametz nuksheh* is forbidden by Torah law. There are two related issues: the prohibition of eating *ḥametz nuksheh* and the prohibition of keeping *ḥametz nuksheh* (see *Berur Halakha* on *Pesaḥim* 48b regarding the issue of eating, and 42a regarding the issue of keeping it over Pesaḥ). See also the *Encyclopedia Talmudit* entry "*Ḥametz Nuksheh*" p. 108 (definition) and pp. 110-115 (extent of the prohibition). According to Rabbeinu Tam and many other *poskim*, flour that is mixed with fruit juice and a little bit of water is also considered *ḥametz nuksheh*. See below (8:1) regarding *matza ashira*.

however, it is still forbidden to eat it on its own, for one who eats it – even though he is doing something very unusual – demonstrates that he still considers this *ḥametz* to be food (MB 442, 43).

The yardstick of being fit for a dog's consumption is relevant only for measuring the spoilage of *ḥametz* or *se'or*. But if *se'or* was not spoiled, but only became so sour that it is not fit even for a dog, since it is good *se'or* (that functions as a leavening agent and is usable like regular yeast), all the laws of *ḥametz* apply to it, and one is required by Torah law to destroy it (BHL 442:9).

This law – that one does not have to burn *ḥametz* that was spoiled to the point of not being fit for a dog's consumption – applies only if it became spoiled before the time that *ḥametz* becomes prohibited. But if it was fit to be eaten by a dog when the prohibition of *ḥametz* began, then even if it became spoiled later, to the point of not being fit for a dog's consumption, one must burn it. Once the mitzva of eliminating the *ḥametz* is in effect, one does not discharge his obligation until he has destroyed the *ḥametz* completely (MB 442:9; see below, ch. 5, n. 5).[5]

Note that all of these laws are conditional on the *ḥametz* having initially been fit for human consumption, or for preparing food for humans as *se'or*. If, however, it was not fit for human consumption at all from the beginning, then even if it was fit to be eaten by a dog, no prohibition applies to it. If from the beginning it was not intended for consumption, but it was in fact barely fit for human consumption, then it is *ḥametz nuksheh*, as described above.

5. MB 442:44 cites *Ḥok Yaakov*, which quotes *Terumat Ha-deshen* that if a gentile prepared *ḥametz* on Pesaḥ and then made it inedible even for dogs, it is prohibited for a Jew to gain any benefit from it, since it had been proper *ḥametz* during a time when *ḥametz* was forbidden. See also *Igrot Moshe* OḤ 3:62, which is lenient in this matter. *Yeḥaveh Da'at* 2:60 summarizes the opinions regarding this issue. See also *Bedikat Ḥametz U-vi'uro* 2:27-32, which explains this topic at length, and in n. 87 explains that according to Rambam and Rosh, *ḥametz* that became inedible for humans and is still edible for dogs but would not cause any other dough to become *ḥametz* need not be burned; Raavad disagrees. See AHS YD 103:1-5 regarding other forbidden foods that are no longer prohibited when they become unfit for human consumption.

7. WAYS IN WHICH THERE IS NO LEAVENING

As noted, there are five types of grain that can become *ḥametz* after touching water. However, if they are roasted in fire, they can no longer become *ḥametz,* and in principle they may be mixed with water. Nevertheless, the Sages were concerned lest the roasting not be thorough, and thus the grain would become *ḥametz* when coming into contact with water. Therefore, one must treat them just as one treats regular cereal grains. If they became wet and eighteen minutes passed, we suspect they may have become *ḥametz,* and it is forbidden to gain any benefit from them; one must destroy them (SA 463:3; MB *ad loc* 7).

The above concerns kernels of grain that were roasted in fire, but if it was flour that was roasted, there are Rishonim who are lenient, maintaining that one need not suspect that the flour was not roasted well. Thus, it is permissible to mix such flour with water or in a cooked food without concern for *ḥametz* (Rashi, Rambam). However, many Rishonim hold that in the case of flour, as well, one must be concerned that it may have not been roasted thoroughly (Rabbeinu Yeruḥam, *Hagahot Sefer Mitzvot Katan, Hagahot Maimoniyot,* and others). The Aḥaronim rule that one must not mix roasted flour with water or in a cooked food, lest it become *ḥametz.* Nevertheless, if one did make such a mixture, even though it is forbidden to eat it, it is permissible to keep it until after Pesaḥ and to eat it then (MB 463:8; *Kaf Ha-ḥayim ad loc.* 13).

However, concerning matza that was properly baked, it is agreed that it cannot become leavened again. Accordingly, it is permissible to soak matza and matza meal in water, and, indeed, this is what most people do. Ḥasidim, however, customarily do not eat soaked matza (see below 8:2).

Scalding the grains or the flour in boiling water also destroys the capacity for becoming *ḥametz.* However, the Ge'onim prohibited doing so, for today no one knows how to do this scalding, and if the boiling does not destroy the potential for becoming *ḥametz,* an opposite process of rapid fermentation may be generated, as heat may hasten fermentation. Therefore, scalded grains or flour are treated just like *ḥametz*: it is forbidden to gain any benefit from them and one must burn them (SA 454:3; MB 13).

Flour on which water dripped, drop by drop, continuously, even all day long, does not become *ḥametz*, since the falling of the drops disturbs the flour and shakes it, and does not allow the leavening process to develop. Immediately upon cessation of the dripping, one should knead the dough and bake it. If there is doubt that some of the dripping may not have been continuous, then this is a doubt concerning a law of Torah, and one must relate to that flour as *ḥametz* and burn it (*Pesaḥim* 39b; SA 466:6).

Another way to prevent the dough from fermenting is by soaking it in cold water (*Pesaḥim* 46a; SA 457:2). Preferably, one should not do so, lest the water not be cold enough, allowing the dough to ferment (Rosh, MB 454:18).[6]

Flour that was kneaded with fruit juice does not become leavened at all, but if even a little water was added to the mixture, then it will become leavened (*matza ashira* will be explained below [8:1]).

6. Does freezing the dough halt the leavening process? *Igrot Moshe* OḤ 3:59 states that one may not assume that freezing halts the process, since perhaps the cold just slows down the leavening process but does not stop it completely. On the other hand, *Ḥelkat Yaakov* 3:166 and *Devar Yehoshua* 2:58 are lenient based on the fact that freezing the dough stops the leavening process completely. Nevertheless, one should not purposely prepare dough to freeze and bake on Pesaḥ, but if one prepared dough before Pesaḥ and did not have a chance to bake it before Pesaḥ, as long as the dough has not yet risen, he may freeze the dough and bake it after Pesaḥ.

All of the processes that slow the leavening process are summarized in the *Encyclopedia Talmudit* entry "*Ḥametz*" pp. 83-89. And even though we generally are not lenient when it comes to scalding the dough, there are practical applications when dealing with a dangerously sick person, where it is better to minimize the number of prohibitions involved, as explained in MB 454:13.

Chapter Three

The Mitzva of Getting Rid of *Ḥametz*

1. THE *MITZVOT* ASSOCIATED WITH GETTING RID OF *ḤAMETZ*

It is a positive Torah commandment to eliminate all *ḥametz* from our possession before Pesaḥ, as it is written: "Yet on the first day you must remove the *se'or* from your homes" (Shemot 12:15). The oral tradition teaches that we are to clear out the *ḥametz* by midday of the fourteenth of Nisan, Erev Pesaḥ. This ruling is supported by the verse, "You shall not slaughter the blood of My sacrifice over *ḥametz*" (*ibid.* 34:25), which is interpreted to mean that one may not slaughter the Paschal sacrifice while there is still *ḥametz* in his possession, and the time for slaughtering the Paschal sacrifice begins at midday on the fourteenth of Nisan (see *Pesaḥim* 4b; MT, Laws of *Ḥametz* 2:1). Men and women are equally obligated in this mitzva, as they are concerning all of the *mitzvot* of Pesaḥ.

Whoever did not remove the *ḥametz* from his home by midday of the fourteenth of Nisan is in violation – every single moment that he delays – of the positive commandment of removing the *ḥametz* (MB 443:1). Furthermore, from the moment the Pesaḥ holiday begins, he is in violation of two prohibitions: *bal yimatzei*, as it is written: "Seven days there shall be no *se'or* found in your homes" (Shemot 12:19), and *bal yera'eh*, as the Torah declares, "*Matzot* shall be eaten seven days;

and no *ḥametz* of yours shall be seen, and no *se'or* of yours shall be seen within all your borders" (*ibid.* 13:7). Thus, by fulfilling the mitzva of getting rid of the *ḥametz* we are saved from two prohibitions: *bal yera'eh* and *bal yimatzei* – that *ḥametz* should be neither seen nor found in our possession.[1]

The mitzva of removing the *ḥametz* is the first in a series of *mitzvot* connected with Pesaḥ. As noted, *ḥametz* on Pesaḥ is a metaphor for the evil inclination, and one has to clear out the *ḥametz* from the house in order to experience the sanctity of the *Pesaḥ* sacrifice and the eating of the matza properly. Therefore, the first of the preparations for Pesaḥ is removal of the *ḥametz*.

2. THE PROHIBITION AGAINST *ḤAMETZ* ONE OWNS

The prohibition against *ḥametz* on Pesaḥ is unique in that it is not only forbidden to eat it, but it is forbidden even to keep; whoever keeps it in his home violates the two prohibitions of *bal yera'eh* and *bal yimatzei*.[2]

---

1. Let us summarize the opinions regarding the times of the onset of the *ḥametz* prohibitions. The removal and destruction of the *ḥametz* must be done by midday of the fourteenth (perhaps according to *Ha-ma'or* the mitzva begins at midday, but according to the rest of the Rishonim, on the Torah level the removal and destruction of the *ḥametz* must be completed by midday). There is a dispute regarding the starting times of the other *mitzvot* connected to *ḥametz*. Regarding the prohibition of eating *ḥametz*, R. Yehuda maintains that the prohibition begins at midday of the fourteenth, and R. Shimon maintains that the prohibition of eating *ḥametz*, on the Torah level, begins at the onset of the Pesaḥ festival. Most Rishonim adopt the view of R. Yehuda that the eating prohibition begins at midday of the fourteenth, but there are those who adopt the view of R. Shimon that the eating prohibition begins at the start of the holiday. Regarding the prohibitions of *bal yera'eh and bal yimatzei*, most Rishonim are of the opinion that these prohibitions begin at the onset of the Pesaḥ festival, while a minority hold that these prohibitions begin at midday of the fourteenth.

   Additionally, note that one who participated in the Paschal sacrifice (*korban Pesaḥ*) while he still had at least a *kezayit* of *ḥametz* in his possession, violated a Torah prohibition, as it says: "You shall not slaughter the blood of My sacrifice over *ḥametz*" (Shemot 34:25). If he was warned about this and still did it on purpose, he incurs the penalty of lashes (MT, Laws of *Korban Pesaḥ* 1:5).
2. R. Zevin explains in *Ha-mo'adim Be-halakha* (chapter on *ḥametz* and matza) that there is a dispute about the parameters of these negative commandments. According to

The Torah's language, "no *ḥametz* **of yours** shall be seen, and no *se'or* **of yours** shall be seen within all your borders" (Shemot 13:7), shows that there is no prohibition against a Jew having a gentile's *ḥametz* or ownerless *ḥametz* in his domain. It says "**of yours**" – you are not allowed to see *ḥametz* that belongs to you specifically, implying that the *ḥametz* of gentiles and *ḥametz* that is ownerless are permissible.

Therefore, if a gentile lives in a Jew's courtyard, even if the Jew owns the courtyard and the gentile works for the Jew, the Jew does not have to clear out the gentile's *ḥametz*. Similarly, if a gentile deposited *ḥametz* in a Jew's house for safekeeping before Pesaḥ, the Jew need not clear it out, as long as he is not responsible for the *ḥametz*. However, he must erect a partition at least ten *tefaḥim* (handbreadths) high in front of the *ḥametz*, to make certain that he does not forget and eat of it (SA 440:2). Alternatively, he may lock it up and hide the key, or close it in a cabinet and tape the doors shut, so that if someone opens them, he will be reminded of the prohibition against *ḥametz*.

Similarly, a Jew may let a gentile enter his home on Pesaḥ, carrying his *ḥametz* with him. It is forbidden, though, for the Jew to eat with the gentile at the same table, lest the Jew forget and eat of the gentile's *ḥametz*. Even if he puts something on the table to remind himself not to take *ḥametz* from the gentile, there is still concern that a crumb of *ḥametz* may get mixed into the Jew's food. However, if the gentile eats at the table first, a Jew may clean the table thoroughly of all the *ḥametz* crumbs and then eat matza there (SA 440:3; MB *ad loc.* 18).

3. ḤAMETZ THAT HAS BEEN GUARANTEED BY A JEW AND THE STATUS OF STOCKS

We have learned that one violates the prohibitions of *bal yera'eh* and *bal yimatzei* only by possessing *ḥametz* that is the property of a Jew,

---

Rosh (*Pesaḥim* 1:9), any *ḥametz* that can possibly be seen, even if in reality it is not seen, would cause a person to violate *bal yera'eh*. It turns out then, that anyone who is in possession of at least an olive-sized piece of *ḥametz* violates two prohibitions: *bal yera'eh* and *bal yimatzei*. However, according to *Kessef Mishneh* (on MT, Laws of Ḥametz and Matza 1:3), one who keeps any type of *ḥametz* in his possession violates *bal yimatzei*, but he would only violate *bal yera'eh* if he actually sees the *ḥametz*. See also *Bedikat Ḥametz U-vi'uro* ch. 1 n. 16.

as it is written, "no *ḥametz* **of yours** shall be seen" (Shemot 13:7). Yet, at first glance, there is a difficulty here, for it is written, "there shall be no *se'or* found in your homes" (*ibid.* 12:19), implying that it is forbidden to have *ḥametz* in a Jewish home under any circumstances. The Sages explained that, indeed, if the *ḥametz* belongs to a gentile, and the Jew has not undertaken the responsibility of its safekeeping and guaranteeing its return, then it is not forbidden to have it in the Jew's domain, as it is written, "and no *ḥametz* **of yours** shall be seen." If, however, the Jew accepted responsibility for the item, then it is considered like his own, and the prohibition applies. This is what the Torah intended when commanding: "there shall be no *se'or* found in your homes" (*Pesaḥim* 5b).

Therefore, if a Jew guaranteed the return of *ḥametz* that was deposited with him, it becomes like his, and he is not allowed to keep it in his home or courtyard, but must return it to the gentile or clear it out. In a situation where he cannot return it to the gentile and clearing it out will cause him a loss, he should sell the *ḥametz* together with the place it is stored, to a different gentile (SA 440:1; MB *ad loc.* 4). However, if the Jew undertook the protection of a gentile's *ḥametz* that remains in the gentile's possession, then the Jew does not violate any prohibition (MB 440:7).[3] Thus an insurance company owned by a Jew may insure gentiles' *ḥametz,* because it remains in their possession (*She'arim Metzuyanim Be-halakha* 114:29).

3. The Rishonim disagree about these laws. According to Ri, the *ḥametz* is considered to be in a person's possession only if he accepted the responsibilities of a paid custodian. According to *Behag,* however, he is considered the owner of the *ḥametz* – and thus in violation of the *halakha* – even if he only accepted the responsibilities of an unpaid custodian. SA rules in accordance with Ri and cites *Behag* as "others say." MB (8) states that it is preferable to follow the opinion of *Behag.* According to Rambam, even if one did not accept any responsibility for the *ḥametz,* if the gentile is powerful and will forcibly extract compensation for the Jew destroying the *ḥametz,* the *ḥametz* is considered owned by the Jew, and he would be considered in violation. According to Raavad, he is not in violation, but the predominant view is that of Rambam. In all these cases, if the *ḥametz* remained over Pesaḥ, one may eat it *be-di'avad,* since the prohibition of using *ḥametz* that existed on Pesaḥ is only rabbinic, and in an uncertain situation we are lenient.

Furthermore, if a Jew deposited *ḥametz* with a fellow Jew for safekeeping, each of them is under obligation to clear it out – the depositor, since he owns the *ḥametz*, and the recipient of the deposit, since by undertaking to safeguard it he becomes like an owner (SA 440:4). Even if he did not undertake its safekeeping, he is required to clear it out.[4]

If one bought stock in a company that owns *ḥametz*, and Pesaḥ arrived, if he has the authority to express his view about how to manage the company's affairs – what to sell and what to buy – then it is considered as if he owns the *ḥametz*, and he violates *bal yera'eh* and *bal yimatzei* on account of it. But if he is not authorized to express an opinion, then he is like everyone who invests in stocks – the company owes him a percentage of its value, but its property is not considered his, and he does not violate any prohibitions on account of its *ḥametz* holdings. Accordingly, those who invest money in mutual funds or pension funds do not violate any *ḥametz* prohibitions, even though the managers of the funds may invest part of the money in a company that owns *ḥametz*, since this *ḥametz* is not considered the property of the investor (*She'arim Metzuyanim Be-halakha* 114:28).[5]

---

4. Regarding a Jew who deposited his *ḥametz* with another person, SA 440:4 rules in accordance with R. Yona that even if the custodian accepts responsibility over the *ḥametz*, since the *ḥametz* still belongs to the owner, it is the owner's responsibility to destroy it. This is the opinion of other *poskim* as well. According to Ramban and Ran, since the *ḥametz* is not in the owner's possession and the custodian accepted responsibility for it, the owner of the *ḥametz* does not transgress any prohibition. As for the custodian, SA 443:2 states that if the owner of the *ḥametz* did not come to collect it before Pesaḥ, the custodian should preferably sell the *ḥametz* to a gentile in order to preserve its value. If he did not do so, the custodian is obligated to destroy the *ḥametz*. MB *ad loc.* (14) explains that according to *Baḥ* and MA, the reason for this obligation is that every Jew is responsible for his fellow Jew ("*kol Yisrael areivim zeh la-zeh*"). Gra's opinion on the matter is that even if the custodian did not accept responsibility for the *ḥametz*, he still has a Torah obligation to destroy it, as it is forbidden to harbor a Jew's *ḥametz* in one's home. This is also the opinion of *Tzlaḥ* and *Beit Meir*.
5. There are those who are stringent in this matter and sell their shares of *ḥametz*-owning companies and companies that insure *ḥametz*, and many *ḥametz*-sale documents contain a clause that includes these types of situations (see *Piskei Teshuvot* 440:1).

4. HOW ONE FULFILLS THE MITZVA OF REMOVING THE ḤAMETZ

We clear the *ḥametz* out of our homes in two ways: in thought and in deed, that is, spiritually and in practice. The removal in thought is done through nullification (*bitul*) of the *ḥametz*, declaring it ownerless and considered as mere dust. We do this nullification because we violate the prohibitions of *bal yera'eh* and *bal yimatzei* only with *ḥametz* that belongs to us and that we consider valuable. One who nullifies his *ḥametz* and considers it to be as dust does not violate any prohibitions on its account. Similarly, if he declares it ownerless, he commits no violation on its account.

In addition to *bitul*, we also get rid of our *ḥametz* in fact. The evening of the fourteenth, we search the entire house for *ḥametz*, and on the day of the fourteenth we eliminate it from our homes.

Although each method independently is sufficient to fulfill the requirements of Torah law, the Sages required that we remove the *ḥametz* using both methods, to be on the safe side. Thus, we annul the *ḥametz* verbally and clear it out of the house physically.[6]

On the one hand, the Sages did not want to rely on the nullification alone, lest some Jews not annul the *ḥametz* wholeheartedly and subsequently keep it in their homes to eat after Pesaḥ. Since they had not annulled the *ḥametz* wholeheartedly, they would violate the prohibitions of *bal yera'eh* and *bal yimatzei* by keeping it at home (Rashi, *Pesaḥim* 2a). Moreover, they were concerned lest, if *ḥametz* remained in the house, people might eat it by mistake. Therefore they also required removing it from the house physically (*Tosafot ad loc.*).

Similarly, the Sages did not want to rely on the search alone, lest some Jews not succeed in finding all of the *ḥametz* in their homes, but then find it on Pesaḥ. In that event, there is a chance that they might wait briefly before burning it – because they would feel badly for a moment

6. According to the majority of *poskim*, on the Torah level one method of destroying the *ḥametz* is sufficient: either by nullifying the *ḥametz* or by searching for and destroying the *ḥametz*. The Sages decreed that one must use both methods, as I wrote above (1:1), in the name of Ran and as cited in *Beit Yosef* §432. However, it seems that according to *Tur*, the Torah's primary method is *bitul*, and the Sages added that one must also search for and destroy all *ḥametz*, because of the reasons presented above.

about losing their *ḥametz* – and, in that moment, they would violate the prohibitions of *bal yera'eh* and *bal yimatzei*. By nullifying the *ḥametz* before Pesaḥ, however, they would not violate the prohibitions, even if they hesitated a little before burning the *ḥametz* (MB 434:6).[7]

5. THE ESSENCE OF THE MITZVA

A fundamental question arose concerning the essence of the mitzva of removing the *ḥametz*: is the mitzva essentially to eliminate the *ḥametz* actively or is the main principle that no *ḥametz* remains in a Jew's possession?

According to the view accepted by most Rishonim (Maharik, Ramban, and others), the mitzva is primarily that one's domain be free of *ḥametz*. One who has *ḥametz* must clear it out, and one who has no *ḥametz* in his domain has already fulfilled the mitzva.

However, some Rishonim (Ran, *Tosafot*) imply that only someone who has *ḥametz* becomes obliged to fulfill the mitzva, and he fulfills it by clearing the *ḥametz* out of his house. One who has no *ḥametz* is exempt from the mitzva. Yet even according to this approach, we do not find that the Rishonim recommended acquiring *ḥametz* in order to fulfill the mitzva of removing the *ḥametz*. Nevertheless, there are Aḥaronim who wrote that it is appropriate for one who has no *ḥametz* in his possession before Pesaḥ to go beyond the letter of the law and buy some *ḥametz*, so that he may fulfill the mitzva of removing the *ḥametz* according to those who hold that one must actively remove *ḥametz*.[8]

---

7. To expand on this topic: According to Rema in 434:5 in the name of *Tur*, if one thoroughly checks his house and yet still an olive-sized piece of *ḥametz* remains, he violates the prohibition of *bal yera'eh* and *bal yimatzei*. (This is why, according to Rema, the main and most important "removal" of *ḥametz* in the Torah's eyes is mental nullification.) However, according to many other *poskim*, including Rambam and Rosh, anyone who checks his house properly, even if he does not succeed in finding every last bit of *ḥametz*, does not violate any prohibitions for unintentionally having *ḥametz* in his house, since he did a proper and thorough check. Only if one finds *ḥametz* in his house on Pesaḥ and intentionally leaves it in his house because he wants the *ḥametz*, would he violate any prohibition. Moreover, according to *Taz*, even *Tur* is of this opinion, as I have written above.
8. *Minḥat Ḥinukh* §9 discusses the different sides of the issue at length and notes that according to Rashi, Rambam, and *Sefer Ha-ḥinukh*, the mitzva is passive (this is also

In practice, Jews are a holy people and strive to perform the *mitzvot* in the most praiseworthy fashion, including making sure that they have *ḥametz* on the fourteenth of Nisan, which they use to fulfill the mitzva of removing the *ḥametz* in a way that satisfies all views. Moreover, they are so scrupulous as to remove the *ḥametz* specifically by burning it, for, according to many *poskim*, burning is the preferred way to destroy the *ḥametz* (see below 5:4).

---

the opinion of Maharik in §174 and Ramban at the beginning of *Pesaḥim*). According to *Tosafot* and Ran, however, the mitzva is an active one, and so according to this opinion, one who has no *ḥametz* in his possession should purchase *ḥametz* in order to fulfill the mitzva of destroying it. R. Ḥayim Soloveitchik offered a novel interpretation, namely, that this dispute hinges upon the dispute between the Sages and R. Yehuda regarding the method of destroying the *ḥametz*: according to R. Yehuda, the mitzva is specifically to burn the *ḥametz*, whereas according to the Sages, any act of destruction works. Those who follow R. Yehuda's opinion, therefore, would hold that one must do a positive action to fulfill the mitzva of destroying the *ḥametz*; and this needs further study. See also *Piskei Teshuvot* 445:6 which mentions several Aḥaronim, among them the authors of *Ḥelkat Yo'av* and *Mekor Ḥayim*, and Maharash Engel, who maintain that there is a mitzva for every person to own *ḥametz* in order to destroy it; conversely, SAH (436:21), *Divrei Ḥayim* (1:9), *Ḥavot Ya'ir* (§4), and *Avnei Nezer* (OḤ 318) maintain that there is no mitzva to obtain *ḥametz* in order to destroy it. As mentioned, the custom is to actively destroy some *ḥametz* to fulfill this mitzva according to all opinions. Indeed, MB (445:10) states that it is proper to leave a *kezayit* of *ḥametz* in order to destroy it actively and fulfill the mitzva of destroying the *ḥametz*.

The reason we have written that one needs a *kezayit* of *ḥametz* to fulfill this mitzva is that according to many *poskim* only an olive's bulk must be destroyed (see MB 442:33). Even according to those who adopt the stringent view that less than a *kezayit* must be destroyed, this is probably because of the concern that one may come to eat it and violate the prohibition of eating *ḥametz*, which applies even to a piece smaller than an olive. According to the overwhelming majority of *poskim*, however, there is no Torah prohibition of *bal yera'eh* and *bal yimatzei* on a piece of *ḥametz* smaller than an olive (see *Dagul Mei-rvava* §442, *Ḥakham Zvi* §86, and *Sha'agat Aryeh* §81). This is significant since most authorities believe that the mitzva to destroy the *ḥametz* is connected to the prohibition of *bal yera'eh* and *bal yimatzei*, not the prohibition of eating the *ḥametz*. See also *Sidur Pesaḥ Ke-hilkhato* 15:4, which states that one should not pour lighter fluid on the *ḥametz* itself at the time of burning; rather, he should pour it onto the wood, so that the *ḥametz* is destroyed by fire itself and not ruined by the lighter fluid. *Hilkhot Ḥag Be-ḥag* 8:10 n. 17 explains that there is no reason to be stringent about this, since the main point of the burning is to turn the *ḥametz* into ashes, regardless of whether or not the taste of the *ḥametz* is ruined.

6. WHEN THE PROHIBITIONS OF EATING AND BENEFITING FROM *ḤAMETZ* BEGIN

The mitzva of getting rid of the *ḥametz* must be carried out by midday of the fourteenth of Nisan. Every instant that a Jew keeps his *ḥametz* after that time he is in violation of the positive commandment to remove the *ḥametz*. Beginning at midday, the Torah prohibition against eating and gaining benefit from *ḥametz* begins as well (MT, Laws of *Ḥametz* and Matza 1:8; see also section 1 of the present chapter).

As discussed above (2:2), in order to distance one further from possibly violating commandments, the Sages added to the prohibitions and forbade gaining benefit from *ḥametz* for an additional hour. They also forbade eating *ḥametz* for two extra hours, since on a cloudy day people are likely to err by as much as two hours.

These times are calculated by dividing the day into twelve equal parts, each of which is called "a seasonal hour" ("*sha'ah zmanit*"). It is forbidden to eat *ḥametz* from the beginning of the fifth hour; it is forbidden to gain any benefit from the *ḥametz* from the beginning of the sixth hour; and the Torah prohibition against eating and benefiting from *ḥametz* begins from the beginning of the seventh hour.

Thus, in practice, it is permissible to eat *ḥametz* throughout the first four hours of the fourteenth day of Nisan. During the fifth hour, it is forbidden to eat *ḥametz* by rabbinic decree, but it is still permissible to benefit from the *ḥametz* – for example, one may feed it to an animal or sell it to a gentile. From the beginning of the sixth hour of the day, it is forbidden by rabbinic decree to gain benefit from the *ḥametz*. From the time that it is forbidden for a Jew to gain benefit from the *ḥametz* it is considered as if it does not belong to him, so that he is no longer able to sell it to a gentile or to nullify it. The only way to get rid of it then is to burn it, crumble it and throw it into the sea, or scatter it to the wind (SA 443:1).

However, the *poskim* disagree about when the day begins. *Magen Avraham* maintains that it begins at dawn, that is, from when the first light becomes visible in the east. The Vilna Gaon maintains that it begins at sunrise, that is, from the time when the sun itself becomes visible in the east. The difference between dawn and sunrise is more than an hour; thus, for every *halakha* contingent on the hours of the day, calendars list two times. The earlier one in the morning is based on the approach of *Magen Avraham,* and the later one accords with the Vilna Gaon's approach. This is true concerning the recitation of the morning *Shema,* which must be done by the end of the first three hours of the day, and it is also true of the *Shaḥarit* prayer, whose set time is until the end of the fourth hour (for more detail, see *Peninei Halakha: Prayer* 11:10 n. 14).

In practice, since the final times for eating and benefiting from *ḥametz* are of rabbinic origin, as are the sale and *bitul* of *ḥametz,* the *halakha* follows the more lenient view, since in cases of doubt on matters of rabbinic origin the *halakha* follows the lenient view. Nevertheless, it is better to be stringent when possible (MB 443:8).[9]

7. THE PROCEDURE FOR GETTING RID OF *ḤAMETZ*

As we have learned, we clear the *ḥametz* out of our homes both in deed and in thought. The process of removal consists of four stages: search (*bedika*), nullification (*bitul*), elimination (*bi'ur*), and nullification once again. The process begins with the *bedika* on the evening of the fourteenth. The search is aimed at ensuring that we have no more *ḥametz* in our home other than the *ḥametz* that we are keeping to eat and to destroy. Immediately after the search, we nullify the *ḥametz* for the first time; this is the removal in thought. The next morning we physically

9. A question arises regarding one who is in Israel and owns *ḥametz* in America, and he wants to sell his *ḥametz.* The issue is whether the end of the fifth hour (until when the *ḥametz* can be sold) is determined according to the location of the person or the location of the *ḥametz,* a discrepancy in this case of around seven hours after the end of the time for nullification (and selling) in Israel. According to most *poskim,* we follow the location of the person, although there are some who maintain that one should follow the location of the *ḥametz.* Preferably, one should follow the earlier time, but if this is not possible, we follow the location of the person. This is the view of *Igrot Moshe* OḤ 4:94-95. See also the *Piskei Teshuvot* 443:1 which summarizes the opinions.

The first opinion is quoted in the name of MA, even though the author himself was unsure. *Hilkhot Ḥag Be-ḥag* ch. 8 n. 4 summarizes the topic of the Jewish time calculations. See also Rema 443:1 and MB *ad loc.* 9, stating that according to *Terumat Ha-deshen* this particular issue is assessed using fixed hours, not seasonal hours, and in a situation of large losses, it is permissible to rely on this opinion. In *Hilkhot Ḥag Be-ḥag* 8:4 in the notes, the author explains what to do in extenuating circumstances where a person forgot to sell or nullify his *ḥametz* by the end of the fifth hour.

destroy the remaining *ḥametz* in our possession in deed. It is customary to destroy it by burning it. After the burning, one again declares null any *ḥametz* in his possession.

There are two more possible ways of disposing of *ḥametz*: selling it to a gentile and declaring it ownerless. As noted, one violates *bal yera'eh* and *bal yimatzei* only for *ḥametz* in his possession, and it is only *ḥametz* that is in his possession that he is commanded to eliminate. Thus, if he sells the *ḥametz* to a gentile or declares it ownerless, he does not violate any prohibition on its account.

Thus, search, disposal, and nullification are actions directed against the *ḥametz* with the aim of eliminating it. In contrast, declaring the *ḥametz* ownerless and selling are not directed against the *ḥametz* to destroy it, but rather their aim is to remove the *ḥametz* from our possession so that we do not violate the *ḥametz* prohibitions. With the search, the disposal, and the nullification, we wage war against the *ḥametz,* whereas by selling it or declaring it ownerless, we evade the responsibility it places upon us. These are all ways to remove the *ḥametz.*

Now that we have learned the principles of the mitzva of removing the *ḥametz,* in the coming *halakhot* we will explain the laws of removal of *ḥametz* in detail. We will begin with the *halakhot* of the search for *ḥametz,* with which we begin our campaign against *ḥametz.* We will then continue on to the *halakhot* of nullifying and destroying *ḥametz.* Then we will address the laws of selling *ḥametz* to a gentile for one who wishes to preserve the value of his *ḥametz* and free himself from the need to destroy it.

Chapter Four

Bedikat Ḥametz – The Search for *Ḥametz*

1. THE TIME FOR *BEDIKAT ḤAMETZ*

As we learned in the previous chapter, one who possesses *ḥametz* on Pesaḥ transgresses two prohibitions: "no *ḥametz* of yours shall be seen" (Shemot 13:7), and "there shall be no *se'or* found in your homes" (*ibid.* 12:19). In order not to violate these Torah prohibitions, one must eliminate all *ḥametz* from his possession. According to the Torah, it is possible to dispose of the *ḥametz* by nullifying it verbally, because when one nullifies the *ḥametz* in his possession, it becomes like dust, no longer belonging to him, and consequently, it does not cause him to transgress the prohibition of *bal yera'eh* and *bal yimatzei.*

Nonetheless, the Sages ruled that we must not rely on this nullification (*bitul*) alone; rather, one must also physically remove *ḥametz* from his possession. There are two reasons for this: firstly, they feared that people would nullify *ḥametz* insincerely, intending to benefit from it after Pesaḥ, and this would result in their transgressing the prohibition of *bal yera'eh* and *bal yimatzei.* Secondly, they feared that after nullifying the *ḥametz,* one might see an enticing piece of pastry and eat it, forgetting that it is Pesaḥ. The Sages therefore ordained that, in addition to *bitul ḥametz,* one must search out *ḥametz* in order to eliminate it from his possession.

At first glance, the appropriate time for *bedikat ḥametz* should be just before midday on the day of the fourteenth of Nisan, the deadline for removing *ḥametz*. However, the Sages ordained that we search for *ḥametz* at nightfall of the fourteenth, because during the day people are busy with their affairs, and if one waits until the day of the fourteenth to do *bedikat ḥametz* he is liable to forget it altogether. Furthermore, candlelight is especially effective for checking the cracks and crevices of the house. But during the day, candles do not illuminate well, since sunlight prevents the eye from focusing on the weaker light of the candle. Therefore, the Sages instituted *bedikat ḥametz* at nightfall of the fourteenth, because at night, people are usually at home and candlelight is effective at this time (SAH 431:5).

Since people normally pray *Ma'ariv* at the beginning of the night, one should do so prior to the *bedika*, as a more frequent mitzva takes precedence. One should then proceed quickly to *bedikat ḥametz* (MB 431:8). One who is accustomed to praying with a *minyan* later in the evening should search for *ḥametz* at *tzeit ha-kokhavim* (the appearance of three distinct stars) and then pray at his usual hour.

The obligation to search for *ḥametz* rests primarily upon the father. However, if he must return home late on this day, it is better that he appoint his wife or another adult family member to search in his stead at the appointed hour, when nighttime arrives. Regarding this mitzva there is no difference between men and women, and one should choose as a *shali'aḥ* (proxy) a person who can be trusted to carry out the search properly and responsibly (see AHS 437:7). If it is difficult to appoint a *shali'aḥ*, then *be-di'avad* one should perform the search himself later in the evening, when he gets home.[1]

1. Some have suggested that one who wishes to engage in the search himself should appoint one of his family members to search the house at the proper time and leave one room unchecked; when he returns later that night he can search the unchecked room. He should be sure to ask them to remind him to check the room when he returns, or if he does not return, to check the room themselves (*Teshuvot Ve-hanhagot* 2:214). However, it seems to me that if there is someone in the house who can perform the search instead, it is better to appoint this person as a *shali'aḥ* to conduct the search of the entire house at the appropriate time. This issue is dependent upon a fundamental question: did the Sages decree that the *bedika* should be conducted

2. ACTIVITIES RABBINICALLY FORBIDDEN BEFORE *BEDIKAT ḤAMETZ*

The Sages prohibited starting a task or a meal during the half hour before the time of *bedikat ḥametz*, out of concern that one might become caught up in these activities and forget to search for *ḥametz*. It is permitted, however, to snack on fruit or pastry, or to perform light work that can be finished quickly.

Once the time for *bedikat ḥametz* arrives, it is improper to start any sort of work or eat fruit, even as a quick snack, for it might impede the fulfillment of the mitzva at its proper time (BHL §431).

One should not even begin studying Torah once the time for *bedikat ḥametz* has arrived. If one began studying Torah beforehand, some *poskim* rule that he may continue studying (*Beit Yosef*). Nonetheless, according to many *poskim*, even in this situation it is best to stop studying at *tzeit ha-kokhavim*, in order to fulfill the mitzva of *bedikat ḥametz* at its proper time (MB 431:11; *Kaf Ha-ḥayim ad loc.* 23).

It is best not to cancel a regular, public Torah lecture at this time. Proceeding with the study will not cause participants to neglect the mitzva of *bedikat ḥametz*, for the search can be performed after the lesson, but canceling the lecture will result in the loss of group Torah study (SAH 431:9). However, the participants should remind each other after the lesson to be prompt about searching for *ḥametz*.

3. THE *BERAKHA*

Before beginning to search for *ḥametz*, one recites the *berakha* "Who sanctified us with His *mitzvot* and commanded us concerning *bi'ur*

---

specifically at the beginning of the night, or is the entire night acceptable for *bedika* since the candlelight is more visible at night, but in order to prevent a person from forgetting to check, they forbade working and eating before the *bedika*? According to most *poskim*, the primary time for the *bedika* is at the beginning of the night. This is the opinion of *Taz, Pri Ḥadash*, Gra, and SAH in 431:5. Conversely, Rema and *Mekor Ḥayim* maintain that the *bedika* can be done throughout the entire night. Thus according to them, one may be more lenient about postponing the *bedika* as long as there is someone who will remind him to check later on. I have written in accordance with the view of most *poskim*, and in the next section, I have written that it is proper to refrain from eating even casually once the time for *bedikat ḥametz* has arrived, so as not to delay the *bedika*.

ḥametz" ("*asher kideshanu be-mitzvotav ve-tzivanu al bi'ur ḥametz*"). Though the actual *bi'ur ḥametz* will not take place until the following morning with the burning and nullification of *ḥametz,* we nonetheless recite "*al bi'ur ḥametz*" before the search on the night of the fourteenth, because *bedikat ḥametz* is the first step in the process of eliminating *ḥametz* from the home.[2]

After the *berakha,* it is forbidden to talk before beginning the search. If at this point one talks about matters unrelated to *bedikat ḥametz,* he has abandoned that *berakha* and must recite another. If, however, one talks about unrelated matters *after* beginning the search, his *berakha* remains valid, for it applies to the portion of the search that was already carried out. One should preferably avoid talking about unrelated matters during the search, in order not to become distracted (SA 432:1; MB *ad loc.* 5, 6).

One who owns several houses must search them all. He recites the *berakha* before searching in the first location. He recites it only once, even if the houses are located a distance from one another.[3]

2. If one forgot to make the *berakha* before the *bedika* and remembered while in the middle, as long as he has other areas to check, he may still make the *berakha.* However, if he remembered after the completion of the *bedika,* the *poskim* disagree about whether he can make the *berakha* before burning the *ḥametz* the following day. According to MB 432:4, we do not prevent someone from making the *berakha* in this situation, since the *berakha* is on the burning of the *ḥametz*; thus, as long as he has not yet burned the *ḥametz,* he can make the *berakha.* On the other hand, there are those who hold that the Sages enacted the *berakha* on the *bedika* and not on the burning, and therefore if one forgot to make the *berakha* by the end of the *bedika,* he has lost his opportunity to do so. This is the opinion of *Baḥ,* SAH, and others. When in doubt about whether or not to make a *berakha,* we are lenient, and so one should not make the *berakha.* One should not make a *berakha* on *bitul ḥametz* alone, since we do not make *berakhot* on mere words or thoughts.
3. The authorities disagree about this, as noted in MB 432:7. According to *Pri Ḥadash* and *Ḥayei Adam,* walking a far distance is considered a significant interruption, and he would have to make a new *berakha.* Conversely, according to *Ḥok Yaakov* and *Ma'amar Mordechai,* walking is not considered a significant interruption. This is also the opinion of *Kaf Ha-ḥayim* 432:22. When in doubt about whether or not to make a *berakha,* we are lenient. The Aḥaronim also disagree about whether a *shali'aḥ* appointed to search part of a house who did not hear the owner's *berakha* must make his own *berakha*; see SHT 432:9.

If one must travel, and therefore performed *bedikat ḥametz* before the fourteenth of Nisan, even though his search is valid, he does not recite the *berakha*. One only recites the *berakha* over a search performed from the night of the fourteenth onward, because such a search is adjacent to *bi'ur ḥametz*. Any *ḥametz* found on the evening of the fourteenth will be destroyed the next morning. If one was unable to search on the evening of the fourteenth, and instead searched the following day, or during Pesaḥ, he recites the *berakha*, because he will immediately destroy any *ḥametz* he finds, and it is appropriate to recite "*al bi'ur ḥametz*" over such a search. But if one searches before the fourteenth, he does not recite the *berakha* (Rema 436:1 and BHL *ad loc.*; MB 435:5).[4]

4. PLACES THAT MUST BE SEARCHED

Any property owned by a Jew that might contain a *kezayit* of *ḥametz* must be searched. Therefore, the kitchen and the dining room where people eat must be searched, and any room, storage space, or porch where people sometimes bring *ḥametz* must also be searched (SA 433:3-4).

Clothing closets that are not generally used during the course of a meal need not be searched. However, if there are children in the house, closets must be searched, because the children may have opened

4. Indeed according to Ra'ah and *Pri Ḥadash*, one who is halakhically required to check should make a *berakha*, since the purpose of the *bedika* is to ensure that he does not violate *bal yera'eh/bal yimatzei* afterward; since the Sages decreed that one who leaves his house before the night of the fourteenth should check before he leaves, he should also make a *berakha*. According to Ritva and *Baḥ*, he should make the *berakha* as long as he checks within the thirty days before Pesaḥ. But, as noted, *Kol Bo* and Rema (436:1) are of the opinion that the *berakha* is also on the burning that takes place the following morning. This is also the opinion of Gra, and seems to be the conclusion of MA, *Taz*, and others. If one is uncertain about the *berakha*, we are lenient, and this seems to be the opinion of BHL *ad loc.*

   Itur states that there are those who maintain that one must also make the *berakha* of "*she-heḥeyanu*" prior to the *bedika*, since it is a mitzva that comes periodically, and there are those who say not to recite this *berakha*. Rosh rules that one should not make this *berakha*, since the *bedika* is connected to the Pesaḥ holiday, when anyway he will recite *she-heḥeyanu*. *Shulḥan Arukh* does not even mention the idea of *she-heḥeyanu* on the *bedika*. However, some Aḥaronim suggest, as a nice custom, that one take a new fruit or new garment and recite *she-heḥeyanu* on it before the *bedika* (*Kaf Ha-ḥayim* 432:9).

them while handling *ḥametz,* or may have even hidden *ḥametz* in them. Closets that are too high for children to reach need not be searched.

One must also search cars and carrying bags in which he sometimes puts food. Adults who generally do not put food in their pockets need not search them. However, the pockets of children must be searched. Garments that were washed and had their pockets emptied out beforehand need not be searched on the night of the fourteenth (see section 8 of the present chapter). One who does not have a home does not recite the *berakha* when searching his car or pockets, for the Sages instituted saying a *berakha* only when searching a house (*Kaf Ha-ḥayim* 433:91).

The stairwell of an apartment building or condominium is shared by all of the building's occupants, and therefore they have a collective obligation to search it. In such a case, one of the occupants should be given the responsibility of performing *bedikat ḥametz.* Open yards need not be searched because we can reasonably assume that animals ate any *ḥametz* that might have been there. However, if there are alcoves in the yard that might contain *ḥametz,* they must be searched, because animals may not have crawled into them to eat the *ḥametz.* Likewise, if one knows for certain that there was *ḥametz* in his yard on the night of the fourteenth, he must search it, because he cannot be certain that animals will eat it by midday of the fourteenth (MB 433:27, citing *Mekor Ḥayim*). An enclosed porch, even if it opens into a yard, must be searched.

Ownerless public domains need not be searched, for even if they contain *ḥametz,* no violation has been committed. This is because such *ḥametz* is not in the possession of any particular Jew, and the *ḥametz* prohibition only applies where *ḥametz* is in the possession of a Jew, and not in an ownerless domain (SA 445:3; MB *ad loc.* 18. Garbage bins are discussed below, 5:5).

5. THE CANDLE AND THE FLASHLIGHT

The Sages ordained that *bedikat ḥametz* be performed by candlelight, because candlelight is focused and effective for searching. During the day, the light of the sun detracts from the brightness of the candle, and it is difficult for the eye to focus on its weak light. Therefore, the Sages ordained searching at night, because at night candlelight is more brilliant and does a good job of illuminating holes and crevices, where the essence of the search is carried out.

One may not search for *ḥametz* by torchlight, i.e., with a candle that has two or more separate wicks. There are several reasons for this, the main one being that the large flame will cause the searcher to worry about burning something, and as a result not be able to concentrate on the search. If one erred and searched by torchlight, he did not fulfill his obligation. Additionally, one may not search by the light of an oil lamp, because the fear of spilling oil and staining his belongings will deter him from maneuvering the lamp into narrow spaces to get a good look at cracks and crevices. Likewise, one should not use a paraffin candle for *bedikat ḥametz*. Therefore, the widespread custom is to prefer wax candles, because they do not drip excessively (SA and MB 433:2).

In principle, it is permissible to use a flashlight for *bedikat ḥametz*; the Sages ordained using a candle because its light is focused, and the light of a flashlight is focused. Moreover, a flashlight has an advantage in that one need not worry about burning things or spilling wax and oil, and if it is a good flashlight, its light is stronger and more focused than a candle's. Nonetheless, some people are strict and do not search with a flashlight because the Sages derived from Scriptural verses that the search for *ḥametz* should be performed with a candle (*Pesaḥim* 7b). Yet a flashlight can also be considered a kind of candle, for the filament is like the flame and the battery is like the oil (*She'arim Metzuyanim Be-halakha* 111:4).

In practice, the prevailing custom is to search by candlelight, in keeping with the practice of the Sages. However, one who wishes to search with a flashlight may do so with a *berakha*, and in places where the searcher is concerned that the candle will cause a fire, it is preferable to search with a flashlight (see *Sidur Pesaḥ Ke-hilkhato* 13:10; *Yeḥaveh Da'at* 1:4).

6. MUST ONE SEARCH FOR LESS THAN A *KEZAYIT* OF *ḤAMETZ*?

The purpose of *bedikat ḥametz* is to find pieces of *ḥametz* that are a *kezayit* or larger, for one only violates *bal yera'eh* and *bal yimatzei* if there is a *kezayit* or more of *ḥametz* in one place in his home. Therefore, any part of the house into which people sometimes bring *ḥametz* must be searched. In a house where children are present, one must search all of the places that children enter; however, one need not search closets or shelves that are out of the reach of children.

Some *poskim* take the stringent position that the purpose of the search is to ensure that not a single edible crumb of *ḥametz* remains in one's possession, for if even one crumb remains, somebody might mistakenly eat it during Pesaḥ and thus transgress a Torah prohibition. Even though there is no punishment for eating less than a *kezayit* of *ḥametz*, the Torah nonetheless prohibits it. According to this position, one must search the entire house meticulously and keep an eye out for even small crumbs that might be *ḥametz*. Such a search in a normal house should take at least two hours. However, even according to stringent opinions, one need not search for crumbs so small that they are not recognizable as food. Likewise, there is no need to search for crumbs so filthy that they are inedible. For example, it is not necessary to inspect the cracks between floor tiles, because the crumbs there are repulsive and not fit to be eaten.

In practice, one who chooses to be stringent and search for crumbs smaller than a *kezayit* is praiseworthy, but the *halakha* follows the lenient opinion. The reason is that the obligation to search for *ḥametz* is rabbinically ordained. According to the Torah, one who mentally nullifies his *ḥametz* has already avoided the prohibition of *ḥametz* and need not search his home. It is the Sages who ordained that, in addition to the *bitul*, we must seek and destroy *ḥametz*. Whenever there is a disagreement about a rabbinic enactment, the lenient opinion is generally preferred.

All this applies to the house in general, but it goes without saying that any object that will come into contact with food during Pesaḥ must be thoroughly cleaned, for even the slightest amount of *ḥametz* renders food forbidden on Pesaḥ. Therefore, the dining table, countertops, and cabinets must all be cleaned so well that not a single crumb of *ḥametz* remains.[5]

5. SAH explains in 446, *Kuntrus Aḥaron* 1, that according to most Rishonim, there is no need to burn a piece of *ḥametz* smaller than a *kezayit* (see *Berur Halakha* on Pesahim 45a regarding 45:1: dough in the cracks of a kneading tub). MB 442:33 cites

a dispute about whether one must destroy a piece of *ḥametz* smaller than a *kezayit*: some say that since one transgresses a prohibition by eating it on Pesaḥ, he must burn it beforehand; others are more lenient and would not require him to burn it.

SHT *ad loc.* mentions that the practice is to be stringent and burn this *ḥametz*, but does not discuss whether one must search for crumbs smaller than a *kezayit* during *bedikat ḥametz*. However, it seems from the comments in 442:60 that the main point of the *bedikat ḥametz* is specifically to find *ḥametz* that is larger than a *kezayit*, and indeed this is the opinion of *Pri Ḥadash* and many other halakhic authorities. On the other hand, *Ḥayei Adam* (109:6) rules stringently that one must search even for small crumbs. This is also the view of *Ḥazon Ish* (OḤ 116:13, 17).

Ostensibly, it is possible to connect this dispute to a disagreement about the purpose of *bedikat ḥametz*. According to Rashi, the purpose of *bedikat ḥametz* is to prevent one from transgressing the Torah prohibitions of *bal yera'eh* and *bal yimatzei*, which, according to almost all authorities, one does not violate with less than a *kezayit* of *ḥametz*. *Sha'agat Aryeh* explains that small amounts of *ḥametz* do not combine ("*lo ḥazi le-itztarufei*") to cause one to transgress *bal yera'eh* and *bal yimatzei*, unlike small amounts of forbidden foods, which combine to the size of a *kezayit* (according to *Ḥakham Zvi*, since there is no action involved in the violation of *bal yera'eh* and *bal yimatzei*, the principle of "*aḥshevei*" does not apply).

On the other hand, according to *Tosafot*, since the purpose of *bedikat ḥametz* is to prevent one from eating any *ḥametz* that remains in his house on Pesaḥ, one would thus be required to check for even small crumbs of edible *ḥametz* (and remove them from his home). Since we follow both Rashi's and *Tosafot*'s reasons, as Ran records both, perhaps one must be stringent in this matter. However, it seems that even according to *Tosafot*, despite the fact that one would violate a Torah prohibition by eating less than a *kezayit* of *ḥametz*, the Sages did not require one to check for such crumbs, since eating a piece of *ḥametz* this size does not incur a penalty of *karet*. Additionally, *Tosafot*'s concern about one finding *ḥametz* in his house on Pesaḥ and eating it applies mainly to a nice, substantial piece of *ḥametz*; regarding a small crumb of *ḥametz*, the concern is not as severe. Even if one were to find, say, a small crouton somewhere in his house, it is not likely that he will eat it, since it was found where food is not normally stored. Furthermore, even if he does eat this small crouton, he arguably did not intend to eat it; rather, he was cleaning, and instead of throwing the crouton in the garbage, he put it in his mouth. Such an action is not a Torah prohibition, and not something for which the Sages would mandate *bedikat ḥametz*. Nevertheless, perhaps one who normally eats these types of crumbs should be stringent in accordance with the ruling of *Ḥazon Ish*.

See also *Hilkhot Ḥag Be-ḥag* ch. 6 n. 2, which discusses the two opinions in this matter and proves the lenient approach from the implication of *Pesaḥim* 4a that *bedikat ḥametz* lasts for less than an hour.

See also *Sidur Pesaḥ Ke-hilkhato* §13 n. 39, which rules according to the stringent opinion that one must check for crumbs, and *Bedikat Ḥametz U-vi'uro* 2:1, which is

7. DO BOOKS REQUIRE *BEDIKAT ḤAMETZ*?

According to several Aḥaronim, one is required to search all of his books, page by page, because a crumb of *ḥametz* might have fallen into one of them. These authorities maintain that the objective of *bedikat ḥametz* is to remove every crumb of *ḥametz* from one's possession, and this was the practice of Ḥazon Ish: he would check page by page the books he planned to read on Pesaḥ and then sell the rest of his books to a gentile and put a partition in front of them. In this manner, he exempted himself from the obligation to search them all.

However, according to those *poskim* who maintain that the purpose of *bedikat ḥametz* is to find pieces of *ḥametz* the size of a *kezayit*, clearly there is no need for such a thorough search of books, for it is inconceivable that there could be a *kezayit* of *ḥametz* between the pages of a book. In fact, even some of the stringent *poskim* who say that all *ḥametz* must be sought out maintain that one is not required to search for the sort of tiny crumbs one is liable to find in books, because even if one sees them on Pesaḥ, there is little concern that one will want to eat them.

Therefore, one should not search his books page by page, because this is overly stringent behavior and is even liable to result in a waste of Torah-study time. Indeed, the accepted practice is not to be stringent in this regard.

Nevertheless, one should not put books on the dining table during Pesaḥ unless he was careful to distance them from *ḥametz* throughout the year. Such books might contain a crumb of *ḥametz*, which could fall into some food on Pesaḥ, and any amount of *ḥametz* on Pesaḥ is forbidden, even if it is mixed with a much greater quantity of other foodstuffs. It is permissible, though, to read such books on a table at which one does not eat.

If during the year one places such books on the dining table between meals, he must be careful to clean the table well after eating, so that not a single crumb remains. Even the stringent *poskim* maintain

---

very strict about crumbs. However, since this is a dispute about a rabbinic injunction, practice follows the lenient approach. Nevertheless, one must differentiate between places to which he brings *ḥametz* and the rest of the house, similar to the distinction made regarding koshering utensils and *bedikat ḥametz*.

that one who is careful all year long to distance his books from *ḥametz,* and when bringing them to the dining table is careful that no crumbs of *ḥametz* fall into them, is not required to search his books, because they are already considered *ḥametz*-free.[6]

The status of the bookcase itself depends upon the household. If there are no children, and the adults are careful not to put any food on the bookshelves, no search is required. If there are children in the house who may have placed food there, one is required to search among the books and behind them. If the bookshelf was cleaned well beforehand, a casual search is sufficient.

8. DO WE RELY UPON THE CLEANING DONE BEFORE PESAḤ?

Most Jewish families clean their homes thoroughly before Pesaḥ. Any part of the house that was cleaned well, and into which people were careful not to bring *ḥametz* afterward, does not require a thorough search (*Sha'arei Teshuva* 433:1; *Da'at Torah* 433:2).

However, some *poskim* take a stringent position in this regard and assert that the cleaning does not change a thing, for the Sages ordained searching the cracks and crevices of one's entire home on the night of the fourteenth. Other *poskim* are stringent on the grounds that one cannot rely upon previous cleaning unless it was carried out at night by the light of a candle. Only in this manner, they maintain, is it possible to discern the *ḥametz* in the cracks and crevices.

In practice, though, the custom is to follow the lenient approach and to perform a relatively cursory search of all those places that were cleaned beforehand. This makes sense, for if a room has been cleaned

---

6. The opinion of Ḥazon Ish appears in *Ḥazon Ish* OḤ 116:18. *Bedikat Ḥametz U-vi'uro* 2:1 is very strict about small crumbs, but regarding the issue of checking books, states in 3:24 that the custom is not to be strict like *Ḥazon Ish,* since the crumbs in books are extremely small and insignificant. *Responsa Or Le-Tziyon* 1:32 disagrees with *Ḥazon Ish* and proves from Rambam that one need not be concerned with *ḥametz* that is smaller than a *kezayit.* However, as noted in the previous section, whenever there is a concern that a small crumb might mix into food, one must be stringent, and as such, one should not bring books that may have crumbs in them into contact with food on Pesaḥ.

well, and afterward, people were careful not to enter with *ḥametz,* it has the status of a place into which no *ḥametz* was ever brought, which in principle does not need to be searched. Although a search is not effective unless it was carried out at night by the light of a candle, a thorough cleaning is more effective than searching. For example, when one cleans a clothing closet, he takes out all of its contents and wipes off all of the shelves. After this, the chances of *ḥametz* remaining are less than the chances of finding *ḥametz* remaining there after a thorough search on the night of the fourteenth by candlelight.

Nonetheless, even after such a thorough cleaning one must search for *ḥametz* with a *berakha* on the night of the fourteenth, because the dining area certainly needs to be searched. In addition, one may have forgotten to clean a closet, drawer, or corner. Thus, when performing *bedikat ḥametz,* one must search the entire house and confirm that everything has indeed been cleaned well. If the one performing the search did not participate in the cleaning, he must ask those who cleaned to search with him so that he may ask them if each part of the house he inspects was properly cleaned. Alternatively, they can mark all properly cleaned places with stickers, and all such places need only be given a cursory search.[7]

---

7. See *Sidur Pesaḥ Ke-hilkhato* 13 (n. 1) which tends toward stringency, citing *Derekh Pekudekha* that those who do *bedikat ḥametz* superficially are in violation of the rabbinic enactment, and their *berakhot* may be considered in vain. See also *Hilkhot Ḥag Be-ḥag* 2:5 and *Bedikat Ḥametz U-vi'uro* 3:16. However, as I have written, the custom is to be lenient in this matter, as *Kaf Ha-ḥayim* 433:85 states. This is true even though *bedikat ḥametz* with a candle during the day is not effective, as per MB 433:1, and even though a proper house cleaning does not exempt one from conducting *bedikat ḥametz,* as per SA 433:11 and MA *ad loc.* 20. There are two reasons mentioned (concerning the ineffectiveness of checking during the day): firstly, because only at night does the candle illuminate the small cracks and crevices properly, and secondly, because the Sages decreed that the *bedika* be done on the fourteenth of Nisan at night. Clearly, our customary checks fulfill both aspects: firstly, a full cleaning of the house accomplishes more than a daytime *bedikat ḥametz,* and since we check on the night of the fourteenth, we also fulfill the second aspect of the Sages' decree. Accordingly, one may not claim that he is exempt from the *bedika* after cleaning his house, or that he cannot make a *berakha* on the *bedika,* for the reasons I have just mentioned. (Moreover, see the next section, which will explain that according to most authorities there is no need to place small pieces of bread around the house for the *bedika* even though it is clear that no *ḥametz* remains.) Since, as we have learned,

However, even when performing a casual search, one must check every corner of the room, along the walls, and between the furniture, and one must open every closet and drawer that could possibly contain *ḥametz*, in order to assure that they are indeed clean and remain so. Searching a room in this manner should take no more than a few minutes.

9. HIDING PIECES OF BREAD AND RECEIVING HELP FROM FAMILY MEMBERS

It is customary hide pieces of bread before *bedikat ḥametz*, so that the person performing the search will have to discover them. Some maintain that this custom is meant to ensure that the searcher finds *ḥametz*, because if he does not his *berakha* may have been in vain. In truth, though, this is not the case, for even if no *ḥametz* was discovered, there is no *berakha le-vatala*, since the objective of the search is to ensure that there is no *ḥametz* in the house, and this objective is achieved even if no *ḥametz* is found. In addition, the *berakha* is not on the search alone; rather, it covers the entire process of *ḥametz* removal, which begins with the *bedika* and ends with the *bi'ur* and *bitul* of the *ḥametz* the following day. This is evident from the fact that the *berakha* is "*al bi'ur ḥametz*," and not "*al bedikat ḥametz*." Thus, even if one does not find *ḥametz* in his search, he continues the process of removing the *ḥametz* the next morning, and hence his *berakha* in not in vain (Rema 432:2; MB *ad loc.* 13).

Nonetheless, this Jewish custom should not be discontinued. Arizal himself had a custom to scatter ten pieces of bread before his search. Some *poskim* explain that the reason for this practice is so that some *ḥametz* will remain after the search, and thus one will not forget to nullify his *ḥametz*. Another explanation is that these pieces will ensure that one is not negligent in his search (*Ḥok Yaakov* 432:14). Therefore, where the house has received a thorough cleaning, and in principle a casual search is sufficient, the pieces of bread should be put in places where they can be found without much trouble; but where the house

---

bedikat ḥametz is a rabbinic decree and according to many authorities one must only search for pieces of *ḥametz* that are larger than a *kezayit*, it is certainly permissible to be lenient and rely on a cursory *bedika*, provided that one has already cleaned his house very well.

has not been cleaned well, they should be hidden more carefully. At any rate, it is a good idea for the person who scatters them to make a list of where he hid them, so that if they are not found initially, it will still be possible to locate and remove them.

After the search, one should nullify the *ḥametz* that he did not find and that might remain in the house (as will be explained in 5:1). One must exercise extreme caution with the *ḥametz* that was found and the *ḥametz* that he plans to eat until the following morning, making sure that they not become scattered about the house.

If it is difficult for one to search the entire house on his own, he may ask family members to help him. In this case, they should stand next to him while he recites the *berakha* and answer "amen." Then they should spread out in the house to search it. If the homeowner is unable to perform the search, he should ask somebody else to search for him, and the searcher says the *berakha* (SA 432:2; MB *ad loc.* 10).

10. ONE WHO TRAVELS

If one travels abroad before Pesaḥ and plans to return home after Pesaḥ, his performance of *bedikat ḥametz* depends on when he departs: if he departs within thirty days of Pesaḥ, i.e., from Purim onward, he must search his home for *ḥametz* before leaving. That he will certainly nullify his *ḥametz* has no bearing, because, as we have learned, the Sages ordained that in addition to *bitul ḥametz,* one must perform *bedikat ḥametz,* and since he is still at home within the thirty days before Pesaḥ, the mitzva of *bedikat ḥametz* already applies to him. Therefore, he must perform *bedikat ḥametz* on his last night at home. However, he does not say a *berakha* over this search because it is conducted before the time the Sages ordained for searching (as explained in 3:4 above).

If one leaves home more than thirty days before Pesaḥ, i.e., before Purim, he need not perform a search before he leaves. Then, on Erev Pesaḥ, he must nullify all of the *ḥametz* in his possession so that he does not transgress by possessing *ḥametz.* When he returns home after Pesaḥ, he must physically dispose of all of the *ḥametz* in his home.

However, if at the time of departure one intended to return to his home before Pesaḥ, the Sages ordained that he must perform *bedikat ḥametz* before leaving, even if he sets out at the beginning of the year.

This is because something could go wrong on his journey, preventing him from returning in time for *bedikat ḥametz* (*Pesaḥim* 6a, according to Rambam). However, if one appoints a *shali'aḥ* to search on his behalf on the night of the fourteenth in case he is unable to return in time, he is not required to search before his departure. Nowadays, when one can make a phone call from anywhere in the world, one need not search before setting out on a trip because even if he is unable to return in time for *bedikat ḥametz*, he can ask a friend or relative to search on his behalf (see *Sidur Pesaḥ Ke-hilkhato* 12:13).

The *poskim* differ over what should be done when one was supposed to perform *bedikat ḥametz* before traveling but forgot to do so. Some say he must return and others say he need not. Therefore, if it is very difficult for him to return, and he cannot find a *shali'aḥ* to perform *bedikat ḥametz* for him, he may rely upon his *bitul ḥametz* (BHL 436:1, s.v. "zakuk"). Then, after Pesaḥ, he must burn or destroy the *ḥametz* he nullified, because if he derives benefit from it after Pesaḥ, he demonstrates that his nullification was insincere. The same applies any time one nullifies *ḥametz* but does not remove it – the Sages forbid eating or deriving benefit from it after Pesaḥ (SA 448:5). The best thing to do when one forgot to search his house before traveling is to rent it to a gentile and sell him all of the *ḥametz*.

11. DOES RENTING ONE'S ENTIRE HOUSE TO A GENTILE EXEMPT IT FROM *BEDIKAT ḤAMETZ*?

Some families leave home for the entire Pesaḥ holiday, and the question arises: Can these people exempt themselves from cleaning and searching for *ḥametz* by selling or renting their entire house to a gentile?

The *poskim* differ on this issue. Some take the lenient position that since the house is not actually in the owner's possession on Erev Pesaḥ, he is not obligated to search it (*Ḥok Yaakov*; Gra's understanding of *Tur* and Rema). Many others, however, take the stringent position that since the owner lives in this house during the thirty days prior to Pesaḥ, it becomes incumbent upon him to perform *bedikat ḥametz* there. Only if he moves to another house in which he will become obligated to search for *ḥametz* will he be exempt from searching the house he rented or sold to the gentile (SA 436:3, MA *ad loc.*, and SAH's understanding of *Tur* and Rema). In addition, it is inappropriate for one to avoid performing the mitzva of *bedikat ḥametz.*

In practice, in order to satisfy all opinions, one should sell or rent his entire house except for one room, and in it he fulfills the mitzva of *bedikat ḥametz.* Once one has fulfilled the mitzva of *bedikat ḥametz* in this room, all *poskim* agree that there is no need to search the rooms that have been sold or rented to a gentile.

In Eretz Yisrael, it is forbidden to sell a house to a gentile (SA YD 151:8), and it must therefore be made clear in the sale of *ḥametz* contract that a rental is being transacted. In addition, the homeowner must sell the *ḥametz* in all of the rented rooms, and by doing this, he becomes exempt from searching these rooms.[8]

When possible, it is best to rent one's house before the night of the fourteenth, because some *poskim* maintain that if, on the night of the fourteenth, the rooms are still in the homeowner's possession, he becomes obligated to search them (*Mekor Ḥayim* and *Ḥayei Adam*). When it is difficult to rent out the house before the night of the fourteenth, as most rabbinical authorities execute the sale (and rental) on the morning of the fourteenth, one may rely on the lenient opinions. Since he intends to rent out these rooms, there is no longer a fear that he will violate *bal yera'eh* and *bal yimatzei,* and he therefore need not search them (*Binyan Olam, Ḥatam Sofer,* as cited in MB 436:2).

---

8. SA expresses the same opinion as *Avi Ezri.* The Aḥaronim disagreed regarding the opinion of *Tur* and Rema. According to MA (436:17) and SAH, one is only exempt from the *bedika* if the gentile will actually enter his house before Pesaḥ. According to *Ḥok Yaakov* and Gra, even if the gentile will not actually enter the house, since the Jewish owner declared the *ḥametz* in it ownerless, there is no need for *bedikat ḥametz.* MB 436:32 seems to lean toward a strict ruling (see SHT *ad loc.* 31-32).

In Israel, where it is forbidden to sell a house to a gentile, one is permitted to rent his house. However, *Mekor Ḥayim* 437:4 and *Ḥayei Adam* 119:18 in the name of *Eliya Rabba* state that one who rents his house to a gentile still must conduct *bedikat ḥametz.* Nonetheless, it seems that if one sells all of the *ḥametz* in his house, even these *poskim* would agree that no *bedika* is required. This is the opinion of *Ḥatam Sofer* §136 and *Hilkhot Ḥag Be-ḥag* 6:20 (pp. 103-104), *Noda Bi-Yehuda,* SAH, and *Kitzur* SA. Another benefit of renting one's house is that it is done wholeheartedly, as is written in *Beit Shlomo* §91 and *Zekher Yehosef* §138.

The utensils and the stove should be cleaned of all substantial *ḥametz* before Pesaḥ, for if this is not done, it will be necessary to clean them after Pesaḥ in order to avoid eating *ḥametz she-avar alav ha-Pesaḥ* (*ḥametz* that remained in a Jew's possession during Pesaḥ). However, it is not advisable to sell the utensils to a gentile, because this will necessitate immersing them in a *mikveh* after Pesaḥ, in keeping with the law regarding utensils bought from a gentile. To sell the *ḥametz* on them, or absorbed into them, makes no sense at all, as will be explained in 6:4 below.

12. *BEDIKAT ḤAMETZ* AFTER THE PROPER TIME AND THE STATUS OF ONE WHO RENTS A HOTEL ROOM

The Sages ordained searching for *ḥametz* on the night of the fourteenth of Nisan. If one did not search at this time, he is required to do so on the fourteenth by day, and to say a *berakha* over the search. If one did not search before Pesaḥ at all, he must search on Pesaḥ, with a *berakha*. The fact that he nullified his *ḥametz* before Pesaḥ does not change this, because he is still required to fulfill the Sages' enactment, and secondly, because there is a possibility that he will come across some *ḥametz* during Pesaḥ and, forgetting the prohibition, eat it. If, after Pesaḥ, one suddenly realizes that he did not perform *bedikat ḥametz*, he must do so, in order not to violate the rabbinic prohibition of *ḥametz she-avar alav ha-Pesaḥ*. This search, however, requires no blessing (SA §435).

One who rents a hotel room has the status of a tenant. This is because he pays for the room, it is at his disposal, he receives a key to lock and unlock it, and strangers and hotel personnel are only allowed to enter with his permission. Therefore, he is commanded to recite a *berakha* and search his room on the night of the fourteenth, and afterward he must nullify any *ḥametz* in his possession that may have gone undiscovered. One who checks into a hotel during Pesaḥ must inquire whether the rooms were searched for *ḥametz*. If they were not searched for *ḥametz*, but were merely cleaned in the routine manner, the guest himself is obligated to search. In this case, no *berakha* is required.

A hospital patient is required to search his room and his closet on the night of the fourteenth. However, no *berakha* is said over this search, since the room is not at his disposal; at any time he can be moved to a different room, and other patients can be moved into his room.[9]

A hotel owner is required to perform *bedikat ḥametz* in every room of his hotel, and if it is difficult for him to do this himself, he can hire a *shali'aḥ*. Regarding rooms rented to gentiles, or to Jews who do not perform *bedikat ḥametz* on the night of the fourteenth, a problem arises. On the one hand, the rooms are rented to them, and the owner cannot force them to keep *halakha* and search for *ḥametz*. On the other hand, if they vacate during the holiday, he will have to search their rooms immediately and remove any *ḥametz* left behind, and he might not have time to do this. The solution, therefore, is to sell or rent all the hotel rooms to a gentile before Pesaḥ, and to have the hotel owner serve as an intermediary during Pesaḥ between the gentile and the guests.

13. SYNAGOGUE, DORMITORY, AND YESHIVA

Synagogues and *batei midrash* (Torah study halls) require *bedikat ḥametz* on the night of the fourteenth, because people sometimes eat *ḥametz* in them. This is true even of synagogues where people generally do not eat, for children sometimes enter them with *ḥametz* (SA 433:10). However, when it comes to saying a *berakha* over this search, there is some uncertainty. Therefore, it is best that the person responsible for searching the *beit knesset* first search his own home, and when saying the *berakha* there, intend to include the synagogue.[10]

---

9. This is what *Sidur Pesaḥ Ke-hilkhato* 12:8 states regarding a hotel, and this is what *Torat Ha-yoledet* 43:1 states regarding a hospital. See also *Piskei Teshuvot* 437:1-2, which brings other sources regarding this matter.

10. The opinion of most *poskim* is that he should recite the *berakha*, since it is a mitzva. See MB 433:43 in the name of SAH. But AHS 433:12 states that one of the reasons for *bedikat ḥametz* is to prevent violation of *bal yera'eh*, and since a synagogue does not belong to any one individual, no one would violate *bal yera'eh* on any *ḥametz* that remains there. Accordingly, there is no mitzva to check the synagogue, and thus no *berakha* should be recited. See Maharsham 5:49. Nonetheless, if the synagogue or *beit midrash* belongs to one particular individual or to several partners, according to all authorities he/they must check it with a *berakha*. However, if the synagogue owner had already recited the *berakha* in his house, he need not recite another *berakha* in the synagogue.

Boys or girls living in a dormitory and paying for this facility have the status of tenants, and if a *kezayit* of *ḥametz* remains in their room during Pesaḥ they violate *bal yera'eh* and *bal yimatzei*. Therefore, they are obligated to search their rooms before Pesaḥ, and if they will be staying there during Pesaḥ, they are required to search on the night of the fourteenth with a *berakha*. If they leave the dormitory a number of days before Pesaḥ, they are required to search on the night before they leave, without reciting a *berakha*.[11]

The responsibility for searching the rest of the rooms and halls in the yeshiva belongs to the yeshiva administration. It is also possible for them to sell the rooms to a gentile and thus exempt themselves from the obligation to search.

One who buys or begins renting a home before Pesaḥ must search it even if he has not yet occupied it, because the previous resident may have left some *ḥametz* there. Since the house is in his possession, this *ḥametz* will cause him to violate *bal yera'eh* and *bal yimatzei*. If he owns another house where he will be fulfilling the mitzva of *bedikat ḥametz*, he can sell or rent out the new home to a gentile and thus exempt himself from the obligation to search it (see section 11 of this chapter above).

14. *ḤAMETZ* BURIED UNDER A PILE OF DIRT AND SEARCHING A STOREROOM

If *ḥametz* is buried under less than three *tefaḥim* (24 cm) of stones, dirt, and the like, it is not considered to have been disposed of, and it must be uncovered and disposed of before Pesaḥ. This is because it is possible for a dog to smell it and dig it up.

11. Ḥazon Ish states that even if yeshiva students will not be in their rooms over Pesaḥ, it is preferable for them to check their rooms on the night of the fourteenth with a *berakha*. This opinion is quoted in *Sidur Pesaḥ Ke-hilkhato* 12:9. Some authorities debate whether the yeshiva student is considered a renter, since the yeshiva administration can switch him to a new room at a whim (see *Piskei Teshuvot* 437:4). However, it appears that yeshiva administrations generally do not transfer older students to new rooms without prior agreement. Therefore, this is similar to a standard rental agreement where there are conditions that if breached result in the cancellation or abrogation of the rental agreement. Thus, older yeshiva students are considered renters of their rooms.

However, if the *ḥametz* is covered by more than three *tefaḥim*, it is considered to have been disposed of and does not cause one to transgress *bal yera'eh* and *bal yimatzei*. Therefore, it need not be dug up and disposed of. *Bitul ḥametz* is nonetheless required, because it is possible that some of the stones will be moved during Pesaḥ, and the *ḥametz* will no longer be covered by three *tefaḥim*, causing the person to violate *bal yera'eh* and *bal yimatzei*.[12] Likewise, in a case where *ḥametz* falls into a pit in one's yard, if it is the sort of pit one does not generally enter, one may nullify the *ḥametz* without extracting and disposing it.

Accordingly, if *ḥametz* is stuck behind a wall cabinet and impossible to remove without first taking the cabinet apart or emptying it out and moving it, one need not remove the *ḥametz*. In this case, one may rely upon its *bitul* (SAH 333:19). If *ḥametz* is located where it can only be removed with some difficulty, one may pour bleach or soapy water on it until it is no longer fit for consumption, and hence no longer considered food (not even for an animal). Once this has been done, it need not be removed.

A storage room where one keeps articles not in use or merchandise that he does not intend to use until after Pesaḥ need not be searched for *ḥametz*. It is sufficient to nullify any *ḥametz* that might be there. However, if one wishes to fill the storage room during the thirty days prior

12. I have written in accordance with the opinion of Rashi, Ran, and the majority of *poskim* that if the *ḥametz* is covered by more than three *tefaḥim* it is considered destroyed, and one would not violate *bal yimatzei* with this *ḥametz*. However, the opinion of *Sefer Mitzvot Katan* is that if it is covered by something that is generally moved, the *ḥametz* would indeed be considered in the owner's possession and he would violate *bal yimatzei*. In such a case, he would only be exempt from destroying the *ḥametz* if he nullified it verbally.

In a case where the *ḥametz* is covered by less than three *tefaḥim*, one would be required to remove the *ḥametz*, as I have written, but only if one is certain that there is *ḥametz* under this particular covering. Even if there is a danger of snakes and scorpions, he still must take a shovel and remove the covering to expose and destroy the *ḥametz*. However, if one merely suspects that there is *ḥametz* under the covering but is not certain, he is not required to check for the *ḥametz* if there is a danger of snakes and scorpions, and is only required to nullify the *ḥametz* verbally. If there is no danger, though, he is required to check (SA 433:8, MB *ad loc.* 35). In any situation where one is required to check, he can exempt himself from checking by selling the item to a gentile.

to Pesaḥ, he must search it first, because the obligation to prepare for Pesaḥ has already taken effect. If one did not search it beforehand, it must be thoroughly searched for *ḥametz* on the night of the fourteenth (SA 336:1). If it is difficult to move all of the storeroom's contents in order to carry out the search, one may sell or rent it to a gentile and thus exempt oneself from the obligation to perform *bedikat ḥametz* there.

Chapter Five

Bitul and *Bi'ur Ḥametz*

1. *BITUL ḤAMETZ* IN THE EVENING AND MORNING

As we learned (above 3:4), one fulfills the mitzva of *bi'ur ḥametz* (disposing of *ḥametz*) in two ways, in action and in thought. The process of *bi'ur ḥametz* involves four stages. The first two, *bedika* and the first *bitul*, are performed on the evening of the fourteenth of Nisan. The second two stages, *bi'ur* and the second *bitul*, take place the following morning. Having discussed the laws relating to *bedikat ḥametz* in the previous chapter, we shall now address *bitul ḥametz*.

After *bedikat ḥametz*, we immediately rid ourselves of the *ḥametz* by nullifying it mentally. To make this process easier, a formal declaration of nullification – *bitul ḥametz* – was composed. This declaration is in Aramaic, because, at the time of its formulation, most Jews understood only Aramaic. It reads (according to the Ashkenazic rite):

כל חמירא וחמיעא דאיכא ברשותי, דלא חזיתיה ודלא בערתיה, לבטיל ולהוי הפקר כעפרא דארעא.

Kol ḥamira ve-ḥami'a de-ika bi-rshuti, de-lo ḥazitei u-delo bi'artei, li-vtil u-lehavi hefker ke-afra de-ar'a.

This declaration can also be said in Hebrew:

> כל חמץ ושאור שיש ברשותי, שלא ראיתיו ושלא ביערתיו, יבטל ויהא הפקר כעפר הארץ.
>
> *Kol ḥametz u-se'or she-yesh bi-rshuti, she-lo re'itiv ve-shelo bi'artiv, yivatel ve-yehei hefker ke-afar ha-aretz.*

In English:

> All *ḥametz* and leaven in my possession that I have not seen and have not eliminated shall be nullified and become ownerless, like the dust of the earth.

The Sephardic version mentions only *ḥametz*, which includes leaven, and only nullification, which includes renunciation of ownership (see *Ḥazon Ovadia*, p. 32).

Following the actual *bi'ur ḥametz* on the morning of the fourteenth (see below, part 3 of this chapter), we perform a second *bitul ḥametz*. This is because the evening *bitul ḥametz* applies only to *ḥametz* we did not find in our search, and of which we remain unaware. It cannot, however, apply to the *ḥametz* we still intend to eat, since such *ḥametz* is important to us. We likewise cannot nullify the *ḥametz* we found in our search, because we intend to dispose of this by burning. Moreover, applying our evening *bitul ḥametz* to the *ḥametz* we still plan to eat would reveal the insincerity of our *bitul* and render it ineffective.

Therefore, in the evening we nullify only the *ḥametz* we did not find in our search; we do not intend to include the *ḥametz* we set aside to be eaten or burned. The problem is that if we misplace or overlook some of this remaining *ḥametz*, we are liable to violate the law of *bal yera'eh* and *bal yimatzei*. To prevent this from happening, we nullify the *ḥametz* a second time. One must be careful to nullify the *ḥametz* by the end of the fifth seasonal hour of the day, for with the onset of the sixth seasonal hour it is forbidden to derive any benefit from *ḥametz*, and it can no longer be nullified (SA 434:2).

The wording of the morning nullification is slightly different from that of the evening. In the evening we nullify only the *ḥametz* that was not found during the search, while in the morning we nullify the *ḥametz* in its entirety. It reads:

> **כל חמירא וחמיעא דאיכא ברשותי, דחזיתיה ודלא חזיתיה, דבערתיה ודלא בערתיה, לבטיל ולהוי הפקר כעפרא דארעא.**
>
> *Kol ḥamira ve-ḥami'a de-ika bi-rshuti, de-ḥazitei u-delo ḥazitei, de-bi'artei u-delo bi'artei, li-vtil u-lehavi hefker ke-afra de-ar'a.*

This declaration can also be said in Hebrew:

> **כל חמץ ושאור שיש ברשותי, שראיתיו ושלא ראיתיו, שביערתיו ושלא ביערתיו, יבטל ויהא הפקר כעפר הארץ.**
>
> *Kol ḥametz u-se'or she-yesh bi-rshuti, she-re'itiv ve-shelo re'itiv, she-bi'artiv ve-shelo bi'artiv, yivatel ve-yehei hefker ke-afar ha-aretz.*

Or in English:

> All *ḥametz* and leaven in my possession that I have seen and that I have not seen, that I have destroyed and that I have not destroyed, shall be nullified and become ownerless, like the dust of the earth.

2. THE SIGNIFICANCE OF *BITUL ḤAMETZ*

As noted, the wording of our *bitul ḥametz* is in Aramaic because it was composed in an era when this was the vernacular. Yet one is free to recite it in Hebrew or any language he understands. If one utters the declaration in Aramaic without understanding its general significance as an act of *bitul*, thinking instead that it is an Erev Pesaḥ prayer, he has not nullified his *ḥametz* (MB 434:9).

The Rishonim explain the significance of the *bitul* (nullification) in two ways. Rashi and Ramban explain that man has the power to nullify *ḥametz*. This capacity is unique to the context of *ḥametz*, since according to the Torah *ḥametz* is entirely insignificant during Pesaḥ. It is forbidden to derive benefit from it, and consequently it is like the dust of the earth, lacking all importance. In one respect alone does *ḥametz* retain significance during Pesaḥ: if it remains in one's house, he transgresses the law of *bal yera'eh* and *bal yimatzei*. However, if one nullifies his *ḥametz* before it becomes forbidden, he has fulfilled the intention of the Torah, and if such a person keeps *ḥametz* in his possession during Pesaḥ, he will not have violated *bal yera'eh* and *bal yimatzei.*

Tosafot explain that the *bitul* is effective because it renders the *ḥametz* ownerless (*hefker*), and the Sages teach that *bal yera'eh* and *bal yimatzei* apply only to *ḥametz* one owns, not to ownerless *ḥametz.*

Thus, according to the first explanation, the nullification focuses on the *ḥametz* itself, while according to the second explanation, the nullification is directed at the owner, who relinquishes his ownership over the *ḥametz.*

The Ashkenazic version of the declaration takes both explanations into account, and therefore mentions both nullification and renunciation of ownership. The Sephardic version mentions only nullification, which includes renunciation, for if something is nullified it consequently becomes ownerless.

3. LAWS REGARDING *BITUL ḤAMETZ*

Most Rishonim agree that, in principle, it is not necessary to recite the *bitul ḥametz* aloud. It is possible to nullify the *ḥametz* "in one's heart," i.e., to mentally regard his *ḥametz* as null and consider it as the dust of the earth. Preferably, however, one should express the *bitul* verbally, because this makes it clear and explicit. Moreover, some Rishonim maintain that the *bitul* must indeed be pronounced aloud (see SAH 434:7). All *poskim* agree that it is not necessary to pronounce the *bitul* in the presence of others. Nonetheless, some people enhance the mitzva by reciting the *bitul* in the presence of their family, to remind them that there is such a mitzva.[1]

1. *Bedikat Ḥametz U-vi'uro* (6:4) which cites *Tur* §436, Ramban, Ran, and Maharam Ḥalawa that *bitul* in one's mind is sufficient. SAH (434:7 and *Kuntrus Aḥaron*) explains that even though these authorities believe that nonverbal nullification suffices on a Torah level, they still maintain that on a rabbinic level preferably one should nullify the *ḥametz* verbally. According to Ritva and *Beit Yosef*, based on the Yerushalmi, one must verbalize the *bitul*. However, SA 437:2 states: "He nullifies it in his heart and this is sufficient." BHL 437:2 states that there are two opinions in the matter, and Gra agreed that nullification in one's mind is sufficient. Whatever one nullifies to himself is considered *hefker*, as per *Tosafot*'s explanation that the purpose of the nullification of *ḥametz* is to deem it ownerless. Even though generally if one wants to declare his property ownerless he must do so in front of three others, as per rabbinic injunction, in this case the Sages deferred to the Torah standards of *hefker* and allowed one to make the declaration to himself.

The *bitul* must be sincere. One must agree in his mind that the *ḥametz* is null and void forever, and that he will not use it even after Pesaḥ. If one intends to use the *ḥametz* after Pesaḥ, the *bitul* is not effective, and he violates *bal yera'eh* and *bal yimatzei*. Likewise, even if one renounces ownership of his *ḥametz* and places it in a completely open domain, he must not intend to reclaim it after Pesaḥ, for if he does, his *bitul* is not wholehearted (MB 445:18).[2]

As mentioned above (3:4), according to the Torah, one can dispose of his *ḥametz* by merely nullifying it, and even if one were to keep *ḥametz* of great value in his possession, he may nullify it and would not transgress *bal yera'eh* and *bal yimatzei* as long as he makes a firm mental commitment that the *bitul* is absolute and that he will never again derive benefit from the *ḥametz*.

However, the Sages ordained that we not rely upon the *bitul* alone. Rather, one must also physically remove the *ḥametz* from his possession. They did this because they feared that the *bitul* might not be performed wholeheartedly. However, if one forgets to eliminate his *ḥametz*, and when Erev Pesaḥ arrives he is far from his home, he may rely on the *bitul* alone – but as soon as he returns home he must destroy the *ḥametz*. Even if he returns after Pesaḥ, he must remove the *ḥametz*, for if he fails to remove it, he proves that his *bitul* was not wholehearted (SA 448:5; MB *ad loc.* 25).

In principle, it is possible to nullify *ḥametz* through a *shali'aḥs*. However, preferably the owner of the *ḥametz* should perform the *bitul* himself, because some authorities maintain that only the owner of the *ḥametz* has the power to nullify his *ḥametz* (SA 434:4; MB *ad loc.* 15).

---

2. See *Bedikat Ḥametz U-vi'uro* 6, n. 7, which cites *Responsa Akiva Eger* that if one verbalized the declaration to make his *ḥametz* ownerless, it becomes ownerless, even if he did not make the declaration wholeheartedly. Thus, anyone can claim his *ḥametz*, and the former owner is not able to claim that he did not mean what he said. Perhaps, according to MB in the name of SAH, although legally another individual can acquire the *ḥametz*, if the original owner did not nullify his *ḥametz* wholeheartedly, the *ḥametz* remains in his possession until someone else actually claims it (as opposed to becoming ownerless right away).

4. THE CUSTOM OF *BI'UR ḤAMETZ* BY BURNING

As we have learned, in addition to *bitul ḥametz*, the Sages ordained the active elimination of all *ḥametz* remaining after breakfast on the morning of the fourteenth, and any *ḥametz* that was found during *bedikat ḥametz* (including the ten pieces of bread that were hidden before the search). In principle, one may eliminate the *ḥametz* in various ways: by crumbling it and throwing it into the wind, the sea, or a river (SA 445:1); by pouring bleach or some other substance on it, rendering it unfit to be eaten by a dog, since if it is not considered *ḥametz* food, it need not be eliminated (SA 442:9); by placing it in an ownerless public domain before it becomes forbidden (MB 445:18); or by flushing it down the toilet, whereby it no longer remains in the house.

Nonetheless, the holy people of Israel customarily enhance the mitzva of eliminating the *ḥametz* via burning it. Nothing eliminates *ḥametz* better than fire. Furthermore, there are *poskim* who maintain that the mitzva to dispose of *ḥametz* must be fulfilled by burning.

Those who wish to enhance this mitzva further must make sure to nullify the *ḥametz* after burning it, since if they nullify it beforehand, the *ḥametz* will no longer be considered theirs, and they will lose the enhancement of *bi'ur* by burning. One must therefore be careful to leave enough time after burning the *ḥametz* to nullify it, for after the fifth hour of the day it is no longer possible to nullify *ḥametz* (as we learned above 3:6). Hence, as soon as a *kezayit* of *ḥametz* has been burned, the enhancement of *bi'ur ḥametz* by burning has been achieved, and the *bitul* can be recited.

Some people, when using kerosene to light the fire, are careful not to pour it directly on the *ḥametz*. They do this so that the fire alone destroys the *ḥametz*, and the kerosene does not render it unfit for consumption by a dog before it is burned.[3]

---

3. There is a dispute in *Pesaḥim* 27b regarding the mitzva of destroying the *ḥametz*: R. Yehuda says it must specifically be burned, and the Sages say it can be destroyed in any fashion. According to the majority of Rishonim, including Rambam, Rosh, Ritva, and Ran, the *halakha* follows the Sages; this is also the ruling of SA 445:1. A minority of authorities, including *Tosafot* and *Sefer Mitzvot Katan*, follows R. Yehuda. *Baḥ* and Gra add that even the Sages believe that the preferred method is burning, just that it is also possible to destroy the *ḥametz* in other ways. Other Aḥaronim

5. ḤAMETZ IN THE GARBAGE

On the morning of the fourteenth of Nisan the question arises: Must *ḥametz* that has been placed in the garbage also be destroyed?

If the garbage bin belongs to a Jew or is located on his property, he is obligated by rabbinical ordinance to remove the *ḥametz* before it

---

disagree and feel that according to the Sages there is nothing special or preferable about burning, and one may destroy his *ḥametz* in any way.

Most Rishonim feel that even according to R. Yehuda, the mitzva to burn *ḥametz* only applies to *ḥametz* that is left over past midday of the fourteenth, when it becomes forbidden, similar to the law of *notar* (uneaten portions of a sacrifice left over until the morning), which must also be burned. However, before midday of the fourteenth, it is possible that even R. Yehuda would agree that one may destroy the *ḥametz* any way he wants; this is the opinion of Rabbeinu Tam and Maharam Halawa. On the other hand, Rashi explains that according to R. Yehuda the mitzva is to burn the *ḥametz* before midday. According to Rosh's understanding of Rashi, the mitzva to burn the *ḥametz* only applies during the sixth hour of the day, but according to *Tur*'s understanding of Rashi, the mitzva to burn the *ḥametz* applies even prior to the sixth hour. If this opinion is correct, the mitzva to destroy the *ḥametz* is specifically by burning it. See *Berur Halakha Pesaḥim* 27b for a summary of the topic. Even though it is clear according to almost all *poskim* that there is no mitzva to burn the *ḥametz* before it becomes forbidden, Rema 434:2 and 445:1 writes that the custom is to burn the *ḥametz* even earlier. See *Or Le-Tziyon* 2:33, which explains that the stringency of burning the *ḥametz* is dependent upon the combination of several opinions: firstly, the authorities who follow R. Yehuda; secondly, *Tur*'s understanding of Rashi that the mitzva to burn the *ḥametz* applies even before the *ḥametz* becomes forbidden; and thirdly, *Tosafot*'s opinion that the act of nullification renders the *ḥametz* ownerless, as opposed to Rashi's understanding that nullification accomplishes the mitzva of destroying the *ḥametz* (and thus the only way to fulfill the mitzva of destroying the *ḥametz* according to *Tosafot* is by burning it). See also *Bedikat Ḥametz U-vi'uro* 7:5-7 and *Hilkhot Ḥag Be-ḥag* 8:7-8.

It is also worth noting that, according to a simple reading, the mitzva of removing *ḥametz* (in Shemot 12:15) is to dispose of the *ḥametz* before it becomes forbidden, as most Rishonim write. Ran and Ritva also write that one fulfills this mitzva by conducting *bedikat ḥametz*. Rambam writes that the mitzva of removing *ḥametz* begins on the night of the fourteenth (MT, Laws of *Ḥametz* and Matza 3:1). However, Rosh maintains that the mitzva only begins once the *ḥametz* becomes forbidden. *Hilkhot Ḥag Be-ḥag* 8:8 summarizes this topic.

Sidur Pesaḥ Ke-hilkhato 15:4 states that one should be careful not to pour lighter fluid on the *ḥametz* itself, and see *Hilkhot Ḥag Be-ḥag* 8:10 n. 17, which disagrees, since the main objective is to turn the *ḥametz* into ashes, regardless of whether or not its taste remains intact. See above ch. 3 n. 8.

becomes prohibited. The owner may pour bleach or some other foul substance on the *ḥametz* rendering it unfit for consumption by a dog.

If the garbage container is the property of the local authority and is located in the public domain, one need not destroy the *ḥametz* he placed in it before the *ḥametz* becomes prohibited. The local authority is not obligated to destroy it because it was not interested in acquiring the *ḥametz* to begin with. Its only aim was to remove it to a garbage dump.[4]

6. *ḤAMETZ* FOUND AFTER THE ONSET OF THE PROHIBITION

If one finds *ḥametz* in his possession after the sixth hour of the day, he must dispose of it immediately. After midday, if one forgot to nullify the *ḥametz* in his possession, he is obligated by Torah law to eliminate it. The most preferable form of the mitzva is to burn the *ḥametz*, but one may eliminate it in a number of ways, as we have learned. For example, one may crumble the *ḥametz* and cast it into the wind, or break up the *ḥametz* and flush it down the toilet.

However, if one throws his *ḥametz* into an ownerless public domain, he has accomplished nothing. Although one may renounce ownership of his *ḥametz* before it becomes prohibited and thus avoid the obligation to remove it, if one still possesses *ḥametz* when the prohibition takes effect, the only way he can get rid of it is by destroying it completely.

---

4. *Igrot Moshe* OḤ 3:57 states that the mere act of placing the *ḥametz* in the trash clearly shows that one's intentions were to rid himself of the *ḥametz*. However, if the trash can belongs to him, according to *Taz* and MA 445:3 he has a rabbinic obligation to burn the *ḥametz*. However, if the trash can is in the public domain, he does not have to burn any *ḥametz* he placed inside the trash can. *Bedikat Ḥametz U-vi'uro* 3:45 adds that if the *ḥametz* is so filthy that clearly no person would use it for any purpose, it is considered destroyed. It also adds a novel idea in n. 130: *ḥametz* that is unfit for humans but suitable for dogs only must be destroyed if the *ḥametz* is able to cause other dough to become *ḥametz*. However, if the *ḥametz* is so filthy that it is no longer suitable to any person for any purpose, it is considered nullified and need not be destroyed (see also *Piskei Teshuvot* 445:7, which cites other opinions). Nevertheless, when one discards his trash into a bag, as is the modern custom, the *ḥametz* does not always become that dirty. Thus, if the trash can is in his domain, it is best to dispel all doubt and refrain from discarding *ḥametz* that is still suitable for dogs into that particular trash can in the days leading up to Pesaḥ.

Similarly, once the prohibition has taken effect, it is no longer possible to remove *ḥametz* simply by pouring a foul substance like bleach on it to make it unfit to be eaten by a dog. Only before the *ḥametz* becomes prohibited is it possible to do so. If the *ḥametz* was fit for consumption when the prohibition took effect, one is obligated to dispose of it completely. Therefore, if one finds such *ḥametz* in his possession, he must burn it, scatter it in the wind, or crumble it into pieces and flush it down the toilet, in order to eliminate it. As stated, the best way to fulfill this mitzva is by burning the *ḥametz*. Moreover, even after the *ḥametz* has been burned, it is forbidden to derive benefit from its ashes.[5]

---

5. See n. 3, where we learned that the main dispute between R. Yehuda and the Sages is about *ḥametz* that one finds after it has already become forbidden. According to the Rishonim who follow R. Yehuda, one has a mitzva to burn this *ḥametz*. Even though most *poskim* follow the Sages, as quoted in SA 445:1, burning the *ḥametz* is an acceptable method, especially according to R. Yoel Sirkis (*Baḥ*) and Gra, who maintain that the Sages agree that the preferable method to destroy the *ḥametz* is burning. This is what MB states in 445:6.

Once the *ḥametz* becomes forbidden, there is an obligation to destroy the *ḥametz* completely, as cited in SA 442:9 and MB *ad loc.* 40. Even declaring the *ḥametz* ownerless does not work at this point; it only works before the *ḥametz* becomes forbidden, as explained in MB 445:18. Even after the *ḥametz* is burned, one is forbidden to benefit from the ashes, as explained in SA 445:2. MB 445:5 states that if one throws *ḥametz* into an outhouse, it is considered destroyed. However, the outhouses in the times of MB were exceptionally filthy, and anything that was thrown there became so repulsive that it would no longer be usable in any capacity. Conversely, bread that has been discarded in a modern toilet is likely to emerge intact from the drainpipes, and would likely be fit for a dog; therefore, if one were to discard bread this way, he should first break up the bread into smaller crumbs. See also *Bedikat Ḥametz U-vi'uro* 7:24 n. 56 for more on this topic, and see 7:1-2 and the corresponding footnotes. In n. 7, the author writes that if one finds *ḥametz* on Pesaḥ and spoils it so that it is no longer fit for a dog, he still violates *bal yera'eh* and *bal yimatzei* according to SAH, but according to *Ḥazon Ish* he is required to destroy the *ḥametz*, but does not violate *bal yera'eh* or *bal yimatzei*. According *Pri Megadim*, he only has a rabbinic obligation to destroy the *ḥametz*, since by not completely destroying the *ḥametz* before Pesaḥ he missed the Torah-level mitzva (the opinions of SAH and *Pri Megadim* are cited in SHT 442:19).

Although in general any *ḥametz* found on Pesaḥ has already been nullified and would therefore only be rabbinically forbidden, the *ḥametz* must still be destroyed, as would any *ḥametz* that had not been nullified, since, as noted, the rabbis decreed that all *ḥametz* must be nullified and eliminated. SAH (435:4) adds that if one did not

If one finds *ḥametz* on the first or last day(s) of Pesaḥ or on Shabbat of *Ḥol Ha-mo'ed,* he may not burn it or even carry it to the bathroom to flush it down the toilet, as *ḥametz* is *muktzeh* and may not be handled. Rather, one must cover it with a container so that nobody accidentally eats it, and it must be burned as soon as possible after the Shabbat or holiday. If the same person forgot to nullify his *ḥametz* before Pesaḥ, he violates two Torah prohibitions – *bal yera'eh* and *bal yimatzei* – every moment the *ḥametz* remains in his possession. In order for one to spare himself from these transgressions, according to many *poskim* he may pick up the *ḥametz,* break it up somewhat, and throw it into the toilet; these *poskim* permit violating the laws of *muktzeh,* which are of rabbinic origin, in order to avoid Torah prohibitions. Nonetheless, some *poskim* take the stringent position that he should wait until Shabbat is over before getting rid of the *ḥametz* (MB 446:6).

Regarding the *berakha,* if one finds *ḥametz* during Pesaḥ, even though it is a mitzva to dispose of it, he does not recite a *berakha* before the *bi'ur,* because the blessing he said before *bedikat ḥametz* included all *ḥametz* in his possession that required removal. However, if one kneads dough during Pesaḥ and it becomes *ḥametz,* he must say the *berakha* over its disposal since this *ḥametz* was not in his possession before Pesaḥ, at the time of his *bedika,* and thus the *berakha* he said then did not apply to it (MB 435:5).

---

burn his *ḥametz,* he violates *bal yera'eh* and *bal yimatzei* on the rabbinic level and is subject to the rabbinic obligation of *tashbitu.* See also *Bedikat Ḥametz U-vi'uro* 7 n. 40 for other sources. Additionally, see chapter 8, 24, which says that if one finds *ḥametz* on Pesaḥ, there are ways that he can avoid *bal yera'eh* and *bal yimatzei,* although he cannot fulfill the active mitzva of *tashbitu.* For example, he can heave the *ḥametz* into the sea in a manner that the *ḥametz* would be impossible to retrieve. The mitzva, however, which he cannot fulfill, is to burn the *ḥametz.*

Regarding the time for burning the *ḥametz*: if one finds *ḥametz* in his possession after the beginning of the sixth hour of the day, he has a rabbinic obligation to burn it, and if he found *ḥametz* that he did not nullify, he has a Torah obligation to destroy it. If he does not, he violates *bal yera'eh* and *bal yimatzei* as soon as the festival begins. If he nullified his *ḥametz,* he does not violate *bal yera'eh* and *bal yimatzei* on the Torah level, but he still has a rabbinic obligation to burn it.

Chapter Six

Mekhirat Ḥametz – The Sale of *Ḥametz*

1. SPARING *ḤAMETZ* FROM DESTRUCTION BY SELLING IT TO A GENTILE

By midday of the fourteenth of Nisan, every Jew must have disposed of the *ḥametz* in his possession. In the past, Jews would plan their food purchases and their meals so that by Pesaḥ they would have finished consuming any *ḥametz* foods and thus not have to dispose of large quantities. They would leave only a small amount of *ḥametz* with which to fulfill the mitzva of *bi'ur ḥametz* in the best possible manner: by burning it.

However, occasionally one's plan would backfire and he would find himself possessing a large quantity of *ḥametz* when Pesaḥ arrived. In such a case, if he did not mind losing the *ḥametz*, he could burn it or give it as a gift to a decent and deserving gentile. If he did not want to lose the value of his *ḥametz*, he could sell it to a gentile before Pesaḥ, since, as long as the prohibition has not gone into effect, it is permissible to sell the *ḥametz* and receive its full value. The prohibition against deriving benefit from *ḥametz* goes into effect on the sixth hour on the day of the fourteenth of Nisan, and until that time it is permissible to sell the *ḥametz*.

This was especially important for food merchants who would remain with large stocks of *ḥametz* before Pesaḥ and had no choice but to sell to a gentile, in order to avoid great financial loss. Even if a gentile could not be found who was sincerely interested in buying all of the *ḥametz*, the Sages teach that it is permissible for a Jew to say to a gentile, "Even though you do not need so much *ḥametz*, buy all of my *ḥametz* for the full price, and if you want, I will buy it back from you after Pesaḥ" (based on *t. Pesaḥim* 2:7).

2. HOW THE PRACTICE OF SELLING *ḤAMETZ* SPREAD

About 400 years ago, many Jews living in Europe began to support themselves through the production and sale of whiskey. This was because the barons, the landowners, would often contract Jews to manage their affairs, and it was common for them to lease their distilleries and inns to Jews in exchange for a fixed price and/or a percentage of sales. This whiskey, which was made from barley and wheat, is considered *ḥametz gamur*. To prevent the great financial loss that would come each year with its disposal before Pesaḥ, it became necessary to sell it to a gentile before Pesaḥ and buy it back again immediately thereafter, in order to continue selling the whiskey as usual.

Over time, rabbinic leaders noticed that the sale was sometimes carried out improperly, leading to serious problems. If the sale is improper, the *ḥametz* remains in the possession of the Jew, and with every hour that passes he violates *bal yera'eh* and *bal yimatzei*. Additionally, it is forbidden to derive benefit from such *ḥametz* after Pesaḥ, and it must all be completely destroyed. Therefore, rabbinic authorities began to oversee the sale of *ḥametz*, in order to ensure its proper sale. Seeing that the sale was being carried out in an orderly manner, other Jews began to participate in the transaction, in order to save their own *ḥametz* from being lost. This is how *mekhirat ḥametz* began to spread and become increasingly common.

However, a number of prominent rabbis claimed that *mekhirat ḥametz* was not a real sale, but merely a fiction. In the first place, it is clear that after Pesaḥ the *ḥametz* will return to the Jew. Moreover, no sales tax is paid to the government on this sale. Thirdly, in a normal sale the buyer pays for all of the *ḥametz* and physically takes it into his possession, but here the gentile neither pays the full price, nor takes the *ḥametz* with him.[1]

---

1. *Tevu'ot Shor*, a commentary on *Pesaḥim*, is hesitant about the idea of selling *ḥametz*, since it might be considered a fiction. *Baḥ, Eliya Rabba,* and *Maḥatzit Ha-shekel*

Nevertheless, the opinion of the vast majority of *poskim* is that *mekhirat ḥametz* may be relied upon and is as valid as any sale. By law, the gentile can refuse to sell the *ḥametz* back to the Jew after Pesaḥ. It is a bona fide sale, not a fiction. Nevertheless, in order to avoid even the appearance of a fiction, the rabbis made a practice of being very meticulous about all details of the sale. Since there are different halakhic opinions regarding the proper mode of purchase when a gentile buys from a Jew, the rabbis are careful to execute the sale using all forms of acquisition, so that it is clear that the sale is effective according to all opinions. In addition, they make sure that the sale is effective according to state laws as well (see MB 448:17, 19, and BHL *ad loc.*).

Regarding payment, a bill of sale is formulated to reflect the actual value of the *ḥametz*, and the gentile pays a cash deposit, as merchants are wont to do. The remainder of the sum is charged to him as a debt, but this does not prevent the completion of the purchase. After Pesaḥ, the gentile can decide: if he wants to keep the *ḥametz*, he must pay the debt; if he wants to sell the *ḥametz* back to the Jew, the Jew repays the cash deposit, and in return for the *ḥametz*, he pardons the gentile's debt from before Pesaḥ. The reason no tax is paid on *mekhirat ḥametz* is that the king, or government, understands that this sale is carried out for religious, not commercial purposes, and therefore waives the tax.

(§448) state that one should not rely on *mekhirat ḥametz* except in extreme situations, to prevent a significant loss. In *Ma'aseh Rav* (a compendium of the Vilna Gaon's customs) it is written that one should only sell *ḥametz gamur* in an irrevocable sale, and after Pesaḥ one should not purchase *ḥametz* that had been sold in a standard *ḥametz* sale. This was also the practice of Rabbi Akiva Eger. See *Sidur Pesaḥ Kehilkhato* 11, n. 38 and *Hilkhot Ḥag Be-ḥag* 10:14 and 11:31. Over time several of the concerns of those opposed to selling *ḥametz* have been allayed by the addition of specific clauses to the sale. For example, *Bekhor Shor* claimed that the gentile buying the *ḥametz* does not understand the details of a legal sale, but nowadays, we sell our *ḥametz* to knowledgeable gentiles who certainly understand the legal ramifications of the sale. Another allegation was that the *ḥametz* was sold for a symbolic sum, as written in SA 448:3, and those opposed to the sale claimed that the seller in such a case does not have full intention to sell. The answer to this problem was that the Jewish seller would certainly agree to sell his *ḥametz* for a nominal fee in order to save himself from violating the prohibition of owning *ḥametz*, as is written in *Ḥok Yaakov*. Nowadays, however, our custom is to sell the *ḥametz* for its full value, as per MB and BHL 448:19, which effectively eliminates this issue.

In order to reinforce the sale, so that it resembles any other sale in which the buyer takes the purchased item into his possession, the rabbis ordained that the Jew sell to the gentile the ground on which the *ḥametz* rests, thereby transferring the *ḥametz* into the gentile's possession (MB 448:12). In Eretz Yisrael, where it is forbidden to sell land to a gentile, the area is rented, and some *poskim* say that even outside Eretz Yisrael it is best to rent the area instead of selling it.[2]

3. FOR WHOM IS THE *ḤAMETZ* SALE INTENDED TODAY?

In recent generations, new storage methods have been introduced that allow us to preserve food products for long periods of time. As a result, food manufacturers and dealers are in constant possession of large inventories of food, and they need to sell their *ḥametz* before Pesaḥ in order not to lose the value of their stock. Moreover, if food manufacturers were to make a point of exhausting their entire inventory before Pesaḥ, it would take days and even weeks to restock and market their products, and in the mean time, they would lose business. Even if no competitors were to seize the opportunity, it would cause a great inconvenience to buyers, who would be unable to purchase *ḥametz* foods during the weeks after Pesaḥ. Therefore, factory owners, food chains, and stores sell all of their *ḥametz* to a gentile before Pesaḥ, and as soon as Pesaḥ passes, they buy it back again and remarket it.

In principle, anyone may sell his *ḥametz* to a gentile via the *mekhirat ḥametz* organized by his local rabbis. He may do so even if he only wishes to sell a small amount of *ḥametz* – for example, a package

2. It is impossible to list all of the *poskim* who permit the sale of *ḥametz,* since there are too many, but I will mention several of them: *Noda Bi-Yehuda* 141:8, *Ḥatam Sofer* OḤ §62 and §113, *Oneg Yom Tov* §28, and *Sdei Ḥemed* 8:9, which discusses the opposition to the sale at length. See also R. Zevin's *Ha-mo'adim Be-halakha* in the chapter about selling *ḥametz* and its evolution. *Igrot Moshe* OḤ 2:95 states that the sale works even if the seller is not an observant Jew. MB 448:12 discusses the optimal procedure of selling the area where the *ḥametz* sits as well. There are those who prefer to rent their rooms or houses that contain *ḥametz,* since they themselves are only renting and therefore cannot sell the house. Additionally, *Avnei Nezer* §345 states that renting is preferable, since it seems less fictitious, as one certainly does not really want to sell his house. See *Hilkhot Ḥag Be-ḥag* 11:10 in the notes.

of pasta – because once it has been sold, the Jew no longer violates the prohibitions relating to *ḥametz*.

Some are stringent and prefer not to rely on *mekhirat ḥametz* since it appears fictitious: the *ḥametz* remains in the Jew's house, the gentile will almost certainly not come to take it, and the Jew resumes eating the very same *ḥametz* as soon as Pesaḥ is over. According to these *poskim*, it is only possible to sell *ḥametz* in order to prevent a great loss; concerning a small loss, one should not sell his *ḥametz*, in order to avoid possible transgression.

Nowadays, all are advised to participate in *mekhirat ḥametz*, because some food products and flavored medicines may contain small amounts of *ḥametz*, and they should not be destroyed just because of this possibility. On the other hand, these must not be kept because they may actually contain *ḥametz*. Therefore, to avoid all doubt, the best thing to do is to sell them.[3]

---

3. *Sidur Pesaḥ Ke-hilkhato* 11:5 states that there are those who maintain that one who has money invested directly or indirectly in stock of companies that produce *ḥametz* must sell these shares before Pesaḥ. Consequently, all *ḥametz* sale documents include clauses regarding stocks and shares in these types of companies. However, according to the letter of the law, if one does not have any decision-making power in the company, he is considered a creditor, not a partner, and he would not be required to sell his shares, as explained above in 3:3. Thus, one who sells his shares in this particular company does so merely to satisfy all opinions. Above at 4:11 we cited a dispute between *poskim* regarding whether or not one can exempt himself from *bedikat ḥametz* by selling his home to a gentile. According to all opinions, however, if the Jewish owner leaves one room in the house for himself, he can perform *bedikat ḥametz* in that room and exempt himself from *bedikat ḥametz* in the rest of the house. *Bedikat Ḥametz U-vi'uro* 8:17 states that in addition to *bitul*, one should sell all of the *ḥametz* in his possession, since if he was unaware of a certain piece of *ḥametz* during the time of nullification and did not nullify it properly, the *ḥametz* sale will certainly protect him from violating any prohibition. Even though he sold his *ḥametz*, if he finds the *ḥametz* on Pesaḥ he is permitted to burn it. This is not considered stealing from the gentile, since he is not causing the gentile any monetary loss. However, it seems to me that it is better not to sell all the *ḥametz* that one has in his possession, since this makes the whole sale look fictitious, because every buyer wants to know where his purchase is without having to look for it all over the house. Therefore, one must decide where to place his *ḥametz*, and it is preferable to specify the location in the authorization contract. Regarding *ḥametz* that may have remained in the house, *bitul* is sufficient.

Concerning *ḥametz gamur*, people are advised not to sell insignificant amounts of *ḥametz*, so as not to use the *mekhirat ḥametz* for small needs. However, when a significant loss is involved, it is permitted, even *le-khatḥila*, to sell the *ḥametz*. Each individual should decide for himself what he considers a significant or small loss. Nonetheless, one is permitted to sell his *ḥametz* even if he only wants to prevent a small loss, for *mekhirat ḥametz* is fundamentally halakhically valid, and one may be confident that the rabbis conducting the sale do so in full compliance with *halakha*.[4]

Because the sold *ḥametz* remains in the Jew's house, there is a risk that he will forget that it is prohibited and eat it during Pesaḥ. Therefore, one must set up a partition at least ten *tefaḥim* high (80 cm) to act as a barrier between himself and the *ḥametz*, or lock the *ḥametz* in a cupboard and hide the key. One may also tape up the cupboard. It is advisable to write "sold *ḥametz*" on it so that one does not accidentally open it on Pesaḥ (see SA 440:2).

4. THE LAWS OF THE SALE

Every Jew, before selling *ḥametz*, should read the authorization contract he will be signing, so that he understands that he is empowering the rabbi to sell his *ḥametz*, and that the sale is absolute. Nonetheless, if instead of reading the contract one simply relied on the rabbi, the sale is valid, for, if the gentile comes during Pesaḥ to take the *ḥametz*, and the rabbi

4. *Hilkhot Ḥag Be-ḥag* 10:14 and 11:9 and in the notes states that the sale of *ḥametz gamur* should be limited to owners of large businesses, but individuals must take care, as much as possible, to only sell uncertain *ḥametz*. So states *Bedikat Ḥametz U-vi'uro* 8:9.

According to the letter of the law, every individual has the right to rely on the sale, since the sale is valid according to the majority of *poskim*. Even if the seller feels that the sale is somewhat fictitious, if the gentile wishes to do so, he could take the seller to court and legally claim the purchased *ḥametz*, which proves that the *ḥametz* indeed belongs to the gentile. Additionally, since every person nullifies his *ḥametz*, and subsequently there is no Torah prohibition on this *ḥametz* (there is only a rabbinic injunction that requires destroying or selling the *ḥametz* in addition to *bitul*), the *ḥametz* assumes the status of a *safek de-rabanan* (an uncertainly about a rabbinic prohibition). Thus, one may certainly rely on the lenient opinions that permit the sale.

tells the Jew that the *ḥametz* indeed belongs to the gentile, and that he must give it to him, the Jew will do so.

The seller should write his name and address in clear script on the contract of sale so that the gentile knows who he is and where he lives. In this manner, the gentile buyer will be able, if he wants, to go to the seller's house and take the *ḥametz* (see *Sidur Pesaḥ Ke-hilkhato* 11:7-8, and in the notes).

It is most preferable to give the gentile the key to the place where the *ḥametz* is located so that he can enter and take it at any time. In practice, though, it is sufficient to give the gentile the seller's phone number so that when the gentile wants the *ḥametz,* he can call to come and take it. The most important principle is that sellers of *ḥametz* should be aware that after the sale, the *ḥametz* indeed belongs to the gentile, and the seller must allow him to enter the house and take his *ḥametz* (MB 448:12).

Ideally, the seller should indicate the various types of *ḥametz,* and their prices, on the contract the rabbi gives him to sign, and some people are meticulous about this. In practice, though, this is very difficult to carry out. Therefore, the custom is to write that all *ḥametz* in one's possession is included in the sale, and that the price is in accordance with the accepted market price, as determined by appraisers (see BHL 448:3, s.v. "be-davar mu'at").

It is best to write in the contract where exactly the *ḥametz* is located, for example: "In the upper left kitchen cupboard," or "in the room on the right, in the box so marked." Several places may be listed. Even without this, the sale is still valid, though all *ḥametz* should be gathered to one place and labeled. Everything gathered to the place determined for the sale by two hours before the onset of the prohibition against deriving benefit from *ḥametz* is included in the sale.

As noted, the preferred custom is to sell or rent to the gentile the place upon which the *ḥametz* rests, so that the *ḥametz* will be in the possession of the gentile, and the sale will appear to be like any other sale in which the buyer transfers possession.

One may sell *ḥametz* through a proxy who writes all relevant details and signs on the owner's behalf. One may also sell *ḥametz* over the phone, by fax, or via the Internet. Usually, the person selling *ḥametz* signs and performs a *kinyan* (act of acquisition) in order to empower the rabbi as a *shali'aḥ*. Nonetheless, the *kinyan* is not crucial, as the most important thing is the transaction between the rabbi and the gentile, which is effective for everyone who has appointed the rabbi to sell his *ḥametz* (*Sidur Pesaḥ Ke-hilkhato* 19:4, 9-10).[5]

In kitchens that belong to public institutions, the manager or his representative sells the *ḥametz*.

One should not sell the *ḥametz* that is absorbed into utensils. Quite a few laws relating to *mekhirat ḥametz* were introduced in order to make it clear to all that it is an actual sale, but if one writes that he is selling the *ḥametz* absorbed in his utensils, the sale will appear to be lacking seriousness, since *ḥametz* absorbed in utensils has no value and nobody is interested in buying *ḥametz* absorbed in utensils. The same applies to *ḥametz* stuck to utensils. Therefore, one should not indicate this in the sale contract.[6]

---

5. *Sidur Pesaḥ Ke-hilkhato* 11:12 states that one is permitted to enter into a *ḥametz* sale agreement with multiple rabbis. Even if each rabbi sells to a different gentile, the sale completed first takes effect. Preferably, one should not do this, since it seems deceitful, unless he is worried that one rabbi may not sell his *ḥametz*, and he wants to ensure that his *ḥametz* is sold one way or another.

   Additionally, *Sidur Pesaḥ Ke-hilkhato* 11:20 states that if one was unable to sell his *ḥametz* due to some unavoidable reason, his friend may sell the *ḥametz* for him even without permission, since it is beneficial to the owner of the *ḥametz*, and one may act to benefit another even without permission. This is the opinion of many *poskim*, as cited in *Piskei Teshuvot* 448:21.

6. Selling the utensils themselves to a gentile is not worthwhile, since after Pesaḥ one would be required to immerse the utensils in a *mikveh*, like any eating implement bought from a gentile (*Ḥatam Sofer* OḤ §109 and most *poskim*; however, AHS YD 108:52, states that one may be lenient). Therefore, some *poskim* write that it is preferable to sell the *ḥametz* that is absorbed in or stuck to the utensils, as written in *Bedikat Ḥametz U-vi'uro* 8:18-21. It is also written that one should only sell the utensils that have small holes or grooves, which make them difficult to clean, and that some are careful to sell the *ḥametz* that is absorbed in these utensils. The truth is, though, that this is unnecessary, because the *ḥametz* was already nullified. Even if there is substance remaining on the utensils, as long as there is less than a *kezayit* cumulatively, according to the majority of *poskim* there is no need to burn it (SAH 446 and *Kuntrus Aḥaron* 1). One must store these utensils in an enclosed area so that he does not accidentally use them on Pesaḥ, and after Pesaḥ one must remove any substance that remained on the utensils before using them, because of the rule that one may not benefit from *ḥametz* that he owned over Pesaḥ. Preferably, in order to satisfy those who maintain that one

5. THE DEADLINE FOR SELLING *ḤAMETZ* AND THE STATUS OF THE TRAVELER

The sale must take place while it is still permitted to derive benefit from *ḥametz,* for when the sixth hour of the day of the fourteenth of Nisan arrives, and it becomes forbidden to derive benefit from *ḥametz,* it likewise becomes forbidden to sell it. Instead, it must be destroyed. In order to allow people to sell their *ḥametz* until the very last minute, *mekhirat ḥametz* takes place on the fourteenth, just before the end of the time that it is permissible to derive benefit from *ḥametz.*

The prohibition takes effect according to one's location. In Israel, the sixth hour arrives approximately seven hours before the East Coast of the United States. Therefore, a U.S. resident who is in Israel must sell his *ḥametz* in Israel, because if he sells his *ḥametz* according to the deadline in the United States, the sale will take place after the onset of the prohibition incumbent upon him. The end of Pesaḥ also poses a problem for such a person, because he must observe *yom tov sheni shel galuyot* (the extra day of Yom Tov observed in the Diaspora), which means that the prohibition of *ḥametz* applies to him until the end of the eighth day, while in Israel the *ḥametz* is bought back from the gentile after the seventh day. However, in fact, it is not a problem for him to sell his *ḥametz* in Israel. Even though the gentile sells the *ḥametz* back at the end of seven days, since the U.S. resident is still observing Pesaḥ according to the custom of Jews in *ḥutz la-aretz,* and he is not yet interested in buying the *ḥametz* back, the *ḥametz* remains *hefker* or in the possession of the *beit din* (rabbinical court). Only after *yom tov sheni shel galuyot* has passed does the *ḥametz* return to his possession.

If his family remains in the United States, and they plan to eat the *ḥametz* after the prohibition has commenced in Eretz Yisrael, he must renounce ownership of his portion in that *ḥametz,* and his family sells the *ḥametz* there (*Sidur Pesaḥ Ke-hilkhato* 11:14).

---

is required to burn even less than a *kezayit* of *ḥametz* (MA 442:12), one should remove any trace of *ḥametz* from the utensils before Pesaḥ or ruin the residue with detergents until they are no longer fit for a dog's consumption.

If this is the case, even if there is more than a *kezayit,* there is no obligation to burn it. Therefore, there is no need to sell the *ḥametz* that is stuck to the utensils, and even more so one should not sell the *ḥametz* that is absorbed in the utensils.

A resident of Israel who travels to the U.S. may, in principle, sell his *ḥametz* in the United States, for, according to most *poskim*, the obligation to eliminate *ḥametz* depends on the owner's location, not the location of the *ḥametz*. Nevertheless, one should preferably sell it in Eretz Yisrael, in order to satisfy the opinions of all *poskim*, for some maintain that one must eliminate *ḥametz* according to its location, and, if this is the case, one must sell the *ḥametz* before the onset of the prohibition in Eretz Yisrael.[7]

Additionally, a resident of Israel who is visiting a Diaspora community should not eat *ḥametz* on the eighth day of Pesaḥ, just as he should not do any other activity forbidden on Yom Tov, even in private (AHS 596:5). If such a person has his own place of residence, he need not partake in a second Seder. However, if he is being hosted by people who live abroad, he should participate in the second Seder. He should not recite *berakhot* on *mitzvot*, but instead should answer "Amen" to the *berakhot* of others.[8]

6. *ḤAMETZ* THAT WAS SOLD – ITS STATUS AFTER PESAḤ

After Pesaḥ, it is best not to use the *ḥametz* that was sold until one can assume that the rabbi has bought it all back. When necessary, though, one may take out some *ḥametz* immediately after Pesaḥ with a willingness

7. *Oneg Yom Tov* (§36) states that we follow the location of the *ḥametz*. Many disagree with this ruling and maintain that the prohibition takes effect according to the location of the owner. This is the opinion of *Ḥessed Le-Avraham* §35, *Eretz Zvi* 1:83, *Mikra'ei Kodesh* Pesaḥ 1:55, and other *poskim* quoted in *Piskei Teshuva* 443:1. *Le-khatḥila*, we take both opinions into consideration and follow whichever time is earlier, as is written in *Igrot Moshe* OḤ 4:94-95.

   A Diaspora resident who is presently in Israel and sells his *ḥametz* in Israel should have in mind not to reacquire this *ḥametz* until after the festival ends in the Diaspora, as written above. Even if he did not have this intent, *Sidur Pesaḥ Ke-hilkhato* 11:35 states that presumably he does not want to reacquire the *ḥametz* before the festival ends, so he does not reacquire it until it becomes permissible. *Mikra'ei Kodesh* Pesaḥ 1:76 states that even if one acquired *ḥametz* on the eighth day of Pesaḥ in the Diaspora, the *ḥametz* may be eaten after Pesaḥ, since there are *poskim* who maintain that a Diaspora resident in Israel is not required to observe two days of Yom Tov. Therefore, since this is an uncertain situation on the rabbinic level, we are lenient.
8. A thorough treatment of *yom tov sheini shel galuyot*, including the status of travelers and temporary residents, appears in *Peninei Halakha: Holidays* ch. 9.

to pay the gentile for it were he to request this. It is best that the *beit din* make an explicit condition with the gentile that the Jew will be obligated to pay for any sold *ḥametz* he takes, if the gentile so desires. Thus, there will be no question about the Jew taking *ḥametz* immediately after Pesaḥ (see *Sidur Pesaḥ Ke-hilkhato* 11:22).

Some people are strict and do not eat *ḥametz* that was sold because, according to stringent *poskim*, such a sale is not legitimate and this *ḥametz* has the status of *ḥametz she-avar alav ha-Pesaḥ*, which one may neither eat nor derive benefit from.

In practice, however, one need not be concerned about complying with this stringency, because the prohibition of *ḥametz she-avar alav ha-Pesaḥ* is rabbinic, and whenever there is uncertainty about a rabbinic law, *halakha* follows the lenient opinion. This is all the more true where only a small number of *poskim* are strict, while the overwhelming majority permit. Indeed, there were great rabbis who, after Pesaḥ, would make a point of eating *ḥametz* that had been sold through *mekhirat ḥametz*, in order to demonstrate that the sale was done in keeping with *halakha*.[9]

When shopping for food after Pesaḥ, one must make sure that the seller has a certificate verifying that he sold his *ḥametz* in keeping with the *halakha* so that one does not buy *ḥametz she-avar alav ha-Pesaḥ*. Even more caution is needed if the seller is not religious, because if he did not understand the significance of the sale and continued to sell *ḥametz* in his store during Pesaḥ, a few *poskim* (*Sdei Ḥemed*, Maharam Schick) maintain that the sale was not legitimate, and that it is forbidden to eat or derive benefit from any *ḥametz* in his store. In this case, one must preferably follow the stringent *poskim* and wait for goods produced after Pesaḥ to arrive. If, however, it is clear that the seller performed *bedikat ḥametz* in keeping with the *halakha*, and was careful not to let anybody go near the *ḥametz* that was sold, it is permissible to buy *ḥametz* from him as soon as Pesaḥ has ended (*Sidur Pesaḥ Ke-hilkhato* 11:13, 23).

---

9. See n. 1 where we listed those who adopt stringent opinions, including Gra, who refrained from eating *ḥametz* that had been sold. In n. 2 we listed those who adopt lenient opinions (the majority of authorities).

Chapter Seven

Ḥametz Mixtures

1. EVEN A DROP OF *ḤAMETZ* RENDERS FOOD FORBIDDEN

In general, when a forbidden food becomes mixed with a permitted food, it is *batel be-shishim* (rendered insignificant if the forbidden food constitutes less than one sixtieth of the mixture); in such small quantities, it does not contribute flavor. At the level of Torah law, *ḥametz* is also *batel be-shishim*. The Sages, however, ordained that even a drop of *ḥametz* render a permitted food forbidden when mixed with it. Even if the quantity of permitted food is a thousand or ten thousand times greater than the *ḥametz*, the entire mixture becomes forbidden.

The Sages added this stringency because the Torah itself is more stringent about *ḥametz* than other forbidden foods. This is true in two respects: 1) generally, if one consumes a Torah-forbidden food, the punishment is *malkot* (lashes), but one who eats *ḥametz* incurs the more severe punishment of *karet* (extirpation); 2) whereas all other forbidden foods may be kept in one's home, *ḥametz* can neither be seen nor be found in our homes throughout Pesaḥ. The Sages therefore continued in this direction by establishing a safeguard: even if a drop of *ḥametz* falls into a food, it is forbidden to consume or derive benefit from it. Another reason for this stringency is that all other forbidden foods are prohibited throughout the year, and we are therefore accustomed to distancing ourselves from them, but since we eat *ḥametz* all year long, we are liable to forget that it is forbidden on Pesaḥ. The Sages, therefore, are more stringent about *ḥametz,* so that everybody remembers to be careful about it.

This law, that even a drop of *ḥametz* renders a mixture forbidden, goes into effect with the onset of Pesaḥ. Before Pesaḥ, *ḥametz* is *batel be-shishim* like all other forbidden foods. Although the prohibition against eating *ḥametz* and the mitzva to dispose of *ḥametz* go into effect at midday on the fourteenth of Nisan, the law that *ḥametz* is not *batel be-shishim* does not take effect until Pesaḥ begins. This is because one who consumes *ḥametz* incurs *karet* only once Pesaḥ has begun, when the prohibitions of *bal yera'eh* and *bal yimatzei* take effect (SA 447:2).[1]

---

1. According to *She'iltot,* Rabbeinu Tam, and Ri'az, *ḥametz* is similar to other forbidden foods and is *batel be-shishim.* All other *poskim* (including Rif, Rosh, and Rambam) maintain that *ḥametz* is not *batel* even in a thousand-to-one ratio, as per the opinion of Rava, following Rav, in *Pesaḥim* 30a. Even Rabbeinu Tam and Ri'az refrained from acting leniently (see *Berur Halakha ad loc.*). However, MB 447:2 states, citing Aḥaronim, that in a case where there are other factors that support a lenient ruling, *She'iltot* and Rabbeinu Tam can also be taken into consideration.

   The aforementioned reasons for the strict nature of *ḥametz* are from Rashi, Rosh, *Smak,* Rabbeinu Yona, and many others. The first reason is the principal one, and therefore *ḥametz* becomes forbidden in the most minuscule quantities only once Pesaḥ begins. However, Rambam and Ramban explain that the reason a tiny amount of *ḥametz* is forbidden is that after Pesaḥ it will again become permitted, since on the Torah level *ḥametz she-avar alav ha-Pesaḥ* is permissible, and anything that will become permissible in the future (*davar she-yesh lo matirin*) is not *batel* in any mixture. According to this opinion, the tiniest amounts of *ḥametz* are forbidden as early as midday of the fourteenth, and this is indeed what *Magid Mishneh* claims is Rambam's opinion. This is also the opinion of several Rishonim and Aḥaronim. It is possible, however, that according to this, *ḥametz* is not *batel* after midday on the fourteenth unless it is mixed with the same sort of food item (*min be-mino*). *Kaf Ha-ḥayim* 447:46 and *Hilkhot Ḥag Be-ḥag* 9:23 quote those who adopt this opinion. Nonetheless, even based on the rationale that we are used to eating *ḥametz,* there are still grounds to forbid even the tiniest amounts of *ḥametz* starting from midday of the fourteenth, as Ran writes.

   SA adopts the opinion that tiny amounts of *ḥametz* only become forbidden once Pesaḥ begins, and most Aḥaronim accept this view.

2. CAN A MIXTURE CONTAINING A DROP OF ḤAMETZ BE SALVAGED?

As we have learned, the laws of *ḥametz* are uniquely strict: even a miniscule amount of *ḥametz* mixed with a permitted food renders the entire mixture forbidden for consumption or benefit. However, most *poskim* maintain that if the *ḥametz* is less than one sixtieth of the mixture, one may salvage its monetary value by selling it to a gentile. For example, if a kilogram of *ḥametz* falls into a metric ton of another food, it is permitted to sell the mixture to a gentile as long as one first throws away a kilogram of the mixture in order to avoid benefiting from the added *ḥametz*. This is because when the Sages forbade benefiting from such mixtures, their intention was to forbid benefiting from the *ḥametz* as well. Thus, if one disposes of a quantity of the mixture equaling the amount of *ḥametz* that was added, he does not benefit from the *ḥametz*, and he can then sell the mixture to a gentile. If a single wheat grain of *ḥametz* fell into a large amount of cooked food, it all becomes forbidden to eat and benefit from as long as it remains in a Jew's hands, but one may sell it to a gentile. It is not necessary to dispose of any of the mixture, because the wheat did not cause the price to rise (SA 467:10).

Rema (447:1), however, rules stringently in accordance with the opinion of a few Rishonim who maintain that since it is forbidden to derive benefit from the mixture, it is likewise forbidden to sell it to a gentile. Instead, the entire mixture must be destroyed. This is the practice of Ashkenazic Jews. However, if this will result in a very great loss, even those who follow the Ashkenazic custom may rely upon the opinion of those who permit selling the mixture to a gentile (MB 447:3).[2]

2. There is a dispute as to whether or not one is forbidden to derive benefit from a mixture of *ḥametz* and non-*ḥametz*. According to Rif, Rosh, and the majority of *poskim*, *ḥametz* causes the entire mixture to become forbidden, whereas Ramban and Raavad maintain that the mixture is only prohibited for eating, but it is permissible to derive benefit from it. SA 447:1 adopts the former view.

However, according to Rif and Rosh, if one would discard the value of the *ḥametz* in the mixture, he would be permitted to sell the mixture to a gentile, since ultimately he obtains no benefit from the *ḥametz*; rather, he merely receives payment for the portion of the mixture that is not *ḥametz*. The overwhelming majority of *poskim*, including SA 467:10, agree with this. However, Rema writes in *Darkhei Moshe* 447:2 that *Mordechai, Terumat Ha-deshen*, and Mahari Brin all adopt a stringent approach – that

3. CAN *ḤAMETZ* THAT WAS NULLIFIED BEFORE PESAḤ REGAIN ITS STATUS ON PESAḤ?

The Rishonim disagree over this fundamental question: Is *ḥametz* that was *batel be-shishim* before Pesaḥ *ḥozer ve-ne'or* ("reawakened." i.e., its nullification is reversed) when Pesaḥ arrives, or does its *bitul* before Pesaḥ mean that it cannot be *ḥozer ve-ne'or*? If it is *ḥozer ve-ne'or*, the entire mixture is rendered forbidden, because during Pesaḥ even a drop of *ḥametz* is not nullified in any mixture. For example, a crumb of *ḥametz* that falls into a large dish of cooked meat before Pesaḥ is obviously *batel*, and this food may even be consumed after midday on the fourteenth of Nisan. The question is whether it is still permissible to eat it after Pesaḥ begins.

Some *poskim* rule that if *ḥametz* was *batel be-shishim* before Pesaḥ, it is considered completely eradicated, and it cannot be *ḥozer ve-ne'or* on Pesaḥ. Therefore, the entire mixture is permitted for consumption (Rosh, *Smag*, *Tur*, and others). Other *poskim* say that the annulment that takes place before Pesaḥ is not effective; as soon as Pesaḥ begins the *ḥametz* reawakens, and the entire mixture is rendered forbidden (Rambam, Rashba).

This question has implications for the status of *matzot*. Occasionally, some water drips on a mound of wheat grains, causing a few of the grains to leaven. It is very difficult to find these grains and remove them from the pile, but it is clear that the kosher wheat grains that did not become *ḥametz* out number the leavened grains by more than sixty-to-one. According to the opinion that *ḥametz* is *ḥozer ve-ne'or*, if all the wheat is ground together and *matzot* are baked from its flour, it will be forbidden to eat them on Pesaḥ, because the drop of *ḥametz* in it renders all of the *matzot* forbidden. It is therefore important to make sure that there is not even a single leavened grain in the wheat from which matza is made. However, according to the opinion that *ḥametz* that is nullified before Pesaḥ is not *ḥozer ve-ne'or*, the *matzot* are kosher for Pesaḥ. There

---

the entire mixture must be burned. MB 447:3 states in the name of Aḥaronim that in a situation of potential severe monetary loss one may sell such a mixture to a gentile. Additionally, SHT 467:74 in the name of *Beit Meir* states that if one will suffer severe monetary losses despite selling the mixture to a gentile, he may even keep the mixture until after Pesaḥ, and then eat it or sell it to a Jew.

is no need to check the wheat kernels one by one in order to remove the leavened ones, because they were already *batel be-shishim* before Pesaḥ.

4. *ḤOZER VE-NE'OR* IN PRACTICE

SA 447:4 rules that when *ḥametz* is *batel be-shishim* before Pesaḥ it is not *ḥozer ve-ne'or,* and therefore it is permissible to eat such a mixture on Pesaḥ. This is because, according to the Torah, *ḥametz* is *batel be-shishim* even during Pesaḥ. The Sages added the stringency of rendering a mixture forbidden because of even a drop of *ḥametz.* This means that the dispute about *ḥozer ve-ne'or* relates to a rabbinic prohibition, and when in doubt about a rabbinic dispute, the *halakha* follows the lenient opinion. This is the position adopted by most Sephardic Jews.

Rema (*ad loc.*) rules in accordance with *Terumat Ha-deshen* (1:124), that if *ḥametz* that was *batel be-shishim* before Pesaḥ was a fluid mixture (*laḥ*), the *halakha* follows the lenient opinion, and the *ḥametz* is not *ḥozer ve-ne'or.* If, however, it was a solid (*yavesh*), the law follows the stringent opinion, and it is *ḥozer ve-ne'or.* For example, if a drop of beer falls into another beverage, it blends with the liquid and ceases to exist independently. As a result, after being nullified, it is not *ḥozer ve-ne'or* and does not render the mixture forbidden. However, if a crumb of *ḥametz* falls into a solid food, because it continues to exist independently and does not blend with the mixture, it has a degree of significance. Therefore, when Pesaḥ arrives it is *ḥozer ve-ne'or* and renders the entire mixture forbidden. This is the approach adopted by Ashkenazic Jews and some Sephardic Jews.[3]

3. **The custom of the Sephardim:** *Kaf Ha-ḥayim* 447:76-78 states that many Sephardim have the custom to be stringent about *ḥozer ve-ne'or,* and this is the opinion of *Pri Ḥadash* and Ḥida in *Birkei Yosef* 447:14. It seems that these authorities were also stringent about liquid mixtures. *Kaf Ha-ḥayim* adds that Sephardim have the custom to be as strict as Rema, but no more. This is similar to what *Zekhor Le-Avraham* states: Sephardim on Pesaḥ follow Rema. Nonetheless, SA cites the lenient position anonymously, which indicates that it is completely lenient in this matter. Additionally, *Yabi'a Omer* OḤ 2:23 expands on the topic and reinforces the lenient opinions, arguing that most Rishonim are lenient about *ḥozer ve-ne'or*. Moreover, according to *She'iltot ḥametz* is *batel be-shishim* even on Pesaḥ, and even those who are stringent maintain that this prohibition is rabbinic, and in a dispute about rabbinic law we are lenient.

Flour, because of its fineness, is considered a fluid mixture. This is because the distinction between fluid and solid depends principally upon whether or not the forbidden food blends completely with the permitted food. In a fluid mixture, the forbidden food blends completely with the permitted food, and in a solid mixture the forbidden food remains independent. Accordingly, there is no need to check the wheat grains before they are ground and baked into *matzot,* because after the wheat is ground, the flour produced from the leavened grains will be nullified and blend completely with the rest of the flour, and when Pesaḥ arrives it will not reawaken to render the mixture forbidden (SA and Rema 453:3).

Based on this principle, some *poskim* say that it is best to bake *matzot* before Pesaḥ so that if some flour or dough becomes *ḥametz* during the kneading process, it will blend with the rest of the dough and be *batel be-shishim* before Pesaḥ. This assures that it will not reawaken and render the *matzot* forbidden during Pesaḥ. Sometimes, when machine *matzot* are being baked, particles of dough get stuck in the tines of the machine and remain there long enough to become *ḥametz,* whereupon they fall back

---

SA (442:4) cites Rambam that "*tiryaka*" (a type of edible medicine) is prohibited on Pesaḥ since it contains a drop of *ḥametz* that becomes reawakened once Pesaḥ begins, and renders the entire mixture forbidden. This seems to contradict what SA stated in 447:4. According to Rema, SA retracted what was written in §442 and permitted *ḥozer ve-ne'or. Pri Ḥadash* explains that *ḥozer ve-ne'or* applies in a case where one intentionally mixed *ḥametz* into the mixture. *Taz* states that *tiryaka* is forbidden because the *ḥametz* in it acts as a stabilizer (*davar ha-ma'amid*) in the mixture.

It is also important to note that even according to the lenient opinions that *ḥozer ve-ne'or* is permitted (according to SA – in all cases; according to Rema – in liquid mixtures), it is forbidden to intentionally blend *ḥametz* into a mixture before Pesaḥ and annul it in a sixty-to-one ratio in order to eat the mixture on Pesaḥ (as per *Pri Ḥadash*'s explanation of SA and MB 447:102 at the end). The only time such a mixture is permissible is if the *ḥametz* was mixed in unintentionally. According to the stringent opinions, since the mixture may not be eaten, it also may not be kept in one's house, though if one kept the mixture in his house over Pesaḥ anyway, he is permitted to eat it after Pesaḥ (MB 447:102).

MB 453:32 states that according to *Taz,* if a bit of *ḥametz* was already mixed in before Pesaḥ and there are less than sixty parts of permissible food in the mixture to annul the *ḥametz,* one is permitted to add more permissible food to the mixture to nullify the *ḥametz.* However, MA and most *poskim* maintain that this is forbidden, since it appears that he is intentionally trying to nullify a forbidden food. In extreme situations one may rely on the lenient opinions.

into the dough. However, because the pieces of dough that became *ḥametz* blend completely with the rest of the dough, it is considered a fluid mixture, and since the *ḥametz* is *batel be-shishim* before Pesaḥ, it is not *ḥozer ve-ne'or*.

All of this is *be-di'avad*, but one should preferably take care to bake *matzot* from wheat that certainly has not become *ḥametz* and guard against the smallest crumb of flour or dough becoming *ḥametz*.[4]

5. DOES ḤAMETZ THAT IMPARTS FOUL TASTE RENDER A MIXTURE FORBIDDEN?

There is a well-known rule that something that imparts foul taste ("*noten ta'am li-fgam*") does not render a mixture forbidden. For example, if non-kosher meat falls into a pot of kosher food, and the quantity of kosher food is sixty times that of the non-kosher meat, the taste of the non-kosher meat is nullified, and it is permitted to eat the food. On the other hand, if the kosher food is not sixty times the quantity of the non-kosher meat, it is forbidden to eat the food, because the taste of the non-kosher meat is discernible in the mixture. If, however, the taste of the non-kosher meat is foul ("*pagum*"), since it spoils the cooked dish, it does not render it non-kosher. Therefore, as long as the kosher food constitutes the majority of the mixture, it is permitted to eat it (SA YD §103).

What about a *ḥametz* mixture on Pesaḥ? Some *poskim* (Rashbam, Rashba) say that the fact that the Sages, due to the gravity of the

4. *Terumat Ha-deshen* 1:114 states that flour is considered a fluid mixture, and this is the opinion of the majority of *poskim*, as MB states in 447:32. However, *Baḥ* states that according to *Smak* and Raavya, flour mixed with flour is considered a solid mixture; therefore, one should preferably take care that no leavened flour mixes with the matza flour. This is also the opinion cited in MB 453:17 and SHT 25. Additionally, it is clear that one should preferably take into consideration the opinions that all *ḥametz* reawakens on Pesaḥ, whether solid or liquid.

Let us note three opinions regarding the rationale for the law of *ḥozer ve-ne'or*. According to the most stringent opinion, *ḥozer ve-ne'or* applies even in a fluid mixture, even if the *ḥametz* itself has been removed and only a minuscule amount of taste was absorbed into the mixture, and even though this taste is not discernible. The second opinion, cited in MB 453:17 in the name of *Olat Shabbat* and *Eliya Rabba*, is that *ḥozer ve-ne'or* only applies if one re-cooks the mixture, which would cause the *ḥametz* to add taste to the mixture. The third opinion is that of MA, quoted by MB *ad loc.*, that *ḥozer ve-ne'or* applies only to solid foods and only when there is still actual *ḥametz* remaining in the mixture.

ḥametz prohibition, ordained that even a drop of *ḥametz* renders any mixture forbidden indicates that the matter does not depend upon the taste it gives to the mixture. Therefore, even when it contributes a foul taste, it is no different than a drop of *ḥametz* that renders its entire mixture forbidden.

The opinion of most Rishonim (Rabbeinu Tam, Ri, Rosh, and *Mordechai*) is that *ḥametz* is like other prohibited foods except with regard to *bitul be-shishim*. Where other forbidden foods do not render a mixture forbidden, however, like in cases of *noten ta'am li-fgam*, *ḥametz* also does not render a mixture forbidden.

In practice, SA 447:10 rules leniently whereas Rema writes that in Ashkenazic communities the custom is to follow the stringent ruling that even a drop of foul-tasting *ḥametz* renders an entire mixture forbidden.

Let us clarify this disagreement by way of an example: a pot in which non-kosher meat is cooked absorbs the taste of the non-kosher meat. If the same pot is then used to cook kosher food, the kosher food will absorb the taste of non-kosher meat exuded by the pot, rendering it forbidden. However, if more than twenty-four hours passed since the cooking of the non-kosher meat, the taste absorbed by the pot is *pagum*, and if some other food is cooked in it, it will not be rendered forbidden, because the pot is *noten ta'am li-fgam*.

Similarly, if one inadvertently cooks in a *ḥametz* pot during Pesaḥ, according to *Shulḥan Arukh* and most *poskim* since more than twenty-four hours have passed since *ḥametz* was cooked in the pot, the food is kosher. However, according to Ashkenazic custom, although the taste of *ḥametz* absorbed into the pot is foul, it renders the food forbidden, because during Pesaḥ we take the stringent position that even *noten ta'am li-fgam* renders a food forbidden.[5]

---

5. The custom of the Ashkenazic community is to be stringent, as we have said; however, MB 447:98 states (citing *Terumat Ha-deshen*) that where there is no established custom, one may act leniently, though one who acts stringently is commended. Sephardic custom follows SA, although some are stringent (*Kaf Ha-ḥayim* 447:228). Rema 447:2 states that the custom to be stringent about *ḥametz pagum* only applies once Pesaḥ begins, but before the onset of the holiday, the *ḥametz* is nullified even in less than a sixty-to-one ratio, like the normal case of foods that spoil the taste of a mixture into which they fall.

6. THE TORAH LAW CONCERNING *ḤAMETZ* MIXTURES

The Torah law concerning a *ḥametz* mixture is complicated and subject to dispute among Tanna'im, Amora'im, Rishonim, and Aḥaronim. We shall summarize its laws here succinctly.

The Torah declares that one who eats a *kezayit* of *ḥametz* on Pesaḥ incurs *karet*. If the *ḥametz* is mixed with other foods and the mixture contains a *kezayit* of *ḥametz* in a *shi'ur akhilat pras* of kosher food (an olive's bulk of *ḥametz* in three or four eggs' bulk of kosher food), Ramban and other Rishonim rule that his punishment is *karet*, while Rif and Rambam maintain that his punishment is only *malkot* (lashes).

If *ḥametz* mixes with the same type of food, for example, leavened flour with unleavened flour, most *poskim* maintain that since they taste the same, the *ḥametz* flour is nullified by the majority (*batel be-rov*) at the Torah level, though there is still a rabbinic prohibition against eating it.

When it comes to the prohibition against keeping *ḥametz* on Pesaḥ, if a *kezayit* of *ḥametz* becomes mixed with permitted food, and the permitted food is less than sixty times the quantity of the *ḥametz*, one violates both *bal yera'eh* and *bal yimatzei*. According to Torah law, if the mixture is more than sixty times the quantity of the *ḥametz*, the *ḥametz* is *batel*. If the *ḥametz* becomes mixed with its own kind – for example, leavened flour with unleavened flour – and there is more of the kosher ingredient than the non-kosher, according to Torah law the *ḥametz* is *batel* and no prohibition is violated. Nevertheless, the Sages ordained that the mixture must be disposed of, lest one end up eating it on Pesaḥ.[6]

It is also important to stress that according to all opinions, one is not permitted to use a utensil that absorbed the taste of a forbidden food, even more than twenty-four hours after absorption. This is because the Sages were concerned that if they permitted the use of such utensils after twenty-four hours, people would make mistakes and use them even within twenty-four hours and would end up eating forbidden foods. Understandably, this is also the *halakha* on Pesaḥ. If one violated this prohibition and intentionally used a utensil that had absorbed forbidden foods more than twenty-four hours prior, most *poskim* maintain that he is not permitted to eat the food due to a rabbinic penalty imposed on him (MB 442:1; *Knesset Ha-gedola* YD §122, *Hagahot Ha-Tur* §26).

6. If one did not dispose of it, since he did not violate *bal yera'eh* or *bal yimatzei* he is permitted to benefit from the *ḥametz* after Pesaḥ. Regarding eating the *ḥametz* after Pesaḥ, *Eliya Rabba* claims that since he violated a rabbinic prohibition by keeping it over Pesaḥ, he may not eat it, although according to MA, cited in MB 447:102, he is allowed to eat it.

Chapter Eight

Pesaḥ *Kashrut*

1. *MATZA ASHIRA* ("EGG MATZA")

The *ḥametz* that the Torah forbids is comprised of flour and water. If flour was kneaded with fruit juice – even if the dough sits a full day and rises – it is not considered *ḥametz* since rising of this kind is different from the type forbidden by the Torah. The category of "fruit juice" ("*mei peirot*") includes wine, honey, milk, oil, and egg, in addition to all juices squeezed from a fruit, like apple or berry juice. Since fruit juice does not cause dough to become *ḥametz*, one may knead, bake, and eat such dough on Pesaḥ. Nevertheless, one would not fulfill the mitzva of matza on the first night of Pesaḥ with it, because the Torah calls matza "*leḥem oni*" ("poor man's bread"), and matza made from fruit juice is "*matza ashira*" ("rich matza" – colloquially known in English as "egg matza"), since it possesses more than the taste of just flour and water.

If a drop of water gets mixed in with the fruit juice, it can cause the dough to become *ḥametz*. Moreover, according to many *poskim*, the combination of water and fruit juice actually expedites the leavening process. Thus, in order to avoid such doubts, the Sages prohibited kneading dough with a mixture of fruit juice and water during Pesaḥ (SA 462:1-3).

The Ashkenazic custom is to avoid eating anything made of dough kneaded with fruit juice out of concern that water mixed with the fruit juice causes the dough to become *ḥametz*. Furthermore, it takes into account the opinion of Rashi, who disagrees with most Rishonim and maintains that fruit juice alone can cause something to become *ḥametz* on the rabbinic level. Although in principle it is possible to follow the lenient ruling of the vast majority of *poskim*, Ashkenazic custom, which should not be altered, is nevertheless strict, except in the case of the elderly and ill, where the custom is to be lenient (Rema 462:4). Nowadays, many Sephardic *poskim* also rule stringently, because it is known that water and other ingredients are generally added to fruit juice, increasing the likelihood that the egg matza became *ḥametz* (R. Mordechai Eliyahu).[1]

---

1. There are two issues here: The first is whether flour mixed with fruit juice can become *ḥametz*, and the second is whether, in a case where water was added to the dough, one may knead the dough while being careful that it does not become *ḥametz*.

The first issue is summarized in *Berur Halakha* on *Pesaḥim* 35a, s.v. "mei peirot ein maḥmitzin." According to Rashi and those who agree with him, a flour and fruit juice mixture can become *ḥametz nuksheh* (see above 2:5), which is rabbinically forbidden. Conversely, most Rishonim maintain that flour mixed with fruit juice alone never becomes *ḥametz*, but if any water got into the mixture, the mixture can become *ḥametz*. There is a dispute about the severity of this *ḥametz*: According to Rambam, it is *ḥametz gamur*, and according to Rabbeinu Tam it is *ḥametz nuksheh*. *Pri Megadim* states that all agree it becomes *ḥametz gamur* when the majority of liquid in the mixture is water (BHL 462:2 s.v. "memaharim"). See the book *Matza Ashira* 5:7-8.

The second issue is explained in *Berur Halakha* on *Pesaḥim* 36a, which cites a tannaitic dispute about *matza ashira* on Pesaḥ. According to Rif and Rambam, the *halakha* follows Rabbi Akiva that one is permitted to knead flour in a mix of fruit juice and water provided that one takes caution to prevent the mixture from becoming *ḥametz*, just as one would with a standard flour-water mixture. This is also the opinion of R. Natronai Gaon and Me'iri. On the other hand, many Rishonim maintain that one should not knead flour with fruit juice and water, since it turns into *ḥametz* faster than does flour and water. There is a dispute about what to do *be-di'avad*. According to R. Hai Gaon and *Behag*, the *halakha* follows Rabban Gamliel that one is required to burn the kneaded dough. According to Rabbeinu Ḥananel, Ritz Gi'at, and Rosh, the *halakha* follows the Sages that if one bakes the dough very quickly, he is permitted to eat it. This is the opinion that SA accepts (462:2). The Ashkenazic custom is to be strict out of concern for Rashi's opinion that flour and fruit juice alone can become *ḥametz*, or out of concern that some water will mix with the fruit juice.

The parameters of what is considered water and what is considered fruit juice are discussed in SA 462:3 and 7 and §466. The entire topic is summarized in detail in *Encyclopedia Talmudit* entry "*Ḥametz*" pp. 89-99.

Regarding the Sephardic custom, R. Mordechai Eliyahu had a long-standing opposition to certifying *matza ashira* as kosher for Pesaḥ out of concern that the fruit juice

2. BECOMING *ḤAMETZ* ONCE IT HAS BEEN BAKED, AND THE STATUS OF *MATZA SHERUYA* ("*GEBROKTS*")

Once matza has been completely baked, the flour in it loses the capacity to become *ḥametz,* even if it is soaked in water for a long time. An indication that the matza is fully baked is that a crust has formed on its surface and that it breaks cleanly, with no threads of unbaked dough extending from it. Thus, it is permitted to soak matza in soup, and an elderly or sick person who cannot eat dry matza on the Seder night may soften matza by soaking it in water (SA 461:4 and below 16:29). Likewise, if the matza was ground into flour, it is permitted to knead it with water; one need not worry about it becoming *ḥametz* because, as mentioned, once it has been thoroughly baked, it cannot (SA 463:3). Therefore, one may bake cakes from the five species of grain during Pesaḥ, or cook various dishes – such as gefilte fish and matza balls – that contain matza meal.

Yet there are some who avoid soaking fully-baked matza in water, lest some of the flour was not kneaded properly and remained unbaked, and soaking the matza will cause the unbaked dough to become *ḥametz.* They likewise fear that some flour may have stuck to the matza after the baking process, and if the matza is soaked in water, this flour will become *ḥametz.* There is yet another reason to be strict about matza meal: an unlearned person might confuse matza meal with real flour and end up violating the prohibition of *ḥametz* on Pesaḥ. Ḥasidim accept this stringency and refrain from eating matza that has been soaked, or "*gebrokts.*"

The *poskim,* however, nearly unanimously agree that one need not be stringent, since it can be assumed that the kneading was thorough, leaving no flour unkneaded or unbaked. This is the custom of Sephardic and non-Ḥasidic Ashkenazic Jews. Today, even some Ḥasidic Jews are

---

has been mixed with water or a leavening agent. (There are also grounds to forbid this because it generates activity that mimics the process of becoming *ḥametz,* as explained by Maharam Ḥalawa on *Pesaḥim* 28a and *Matza Ashira* p. 178.) Over time, it became apparent that this concern was justified, and water and occasionally leavening agents are added to fruit juice. Nevertheless, some authorities rule leniently; according to them, these leavening agents do not cause the dough to become *ḥametz.* This ruling appears in *Yabi'a Omer* 9:42 and *Shema Shlomo* 4:13-17. However, according to many authorities these leavening agents are forbidden by the Torah, or at least rabbinically, and therefore they prohibit Sephardim from eating factory-produced *matza ashira* on Pesaḥ.

lenient because, due to the popular practice of baking thin *matzot*, there is no longer any concern that some of the flour was not properly baked. Likewise, there is no concern that flour may have gotten stuck to the matza, since matza bakeries are careful to separate the area where flour is handled from the area where the matza comes out of the oven. MB 458:4 states: "Although in principle there is no reason for concern about this, and it is permitted to eat soaked matza, one should not mock conscientious people who choose to be stringent."[2]

2. *Pesaḥim* 39b states: "These are the things that cannot become *ḥametz*: baked items..." Rambam rules accordingly in MT, Laws of *Ḥametz* and Matza 5:5, and this is the consensus of the Rishonim. The sign that something is completely baked is that it has a crust on the outside and that it breaks cleanly, with no threads of dough extending (these two standards are identical, as per MB 461:15 and SHT 23 *ad loc.*). SAH 463:3 states that a baked item cannot become *ḥametz* and one may cook with matza meal. However, responsum §6 at the end of SAH states that matza meal is only permissible if one is absolutely certain that all of the flour was fully baked, and one should be concerned that perhaps not all of the flour was fully baked or that some flour stuck to the *matzot* after baking. SAH concludes that one should not reprimand the masses who are lenient since they have acceptable authorities on which to rely, but one who is stringent is commendable. Regarding matza meal, *Knesset Ha-gedola* §461 recounts that a woman once saw her neighbor, the rabbi's wife, cooking and frying with matza meal and mistakenly assumed that it was permissible to use actual flour on Pesaḥ. When the town's rabbis heard what had happened, they banned matza meal because of *marit ayin* (see *Tur* §463). *Pri Ḥadash* and many other Aḥaronim disagreed with this ban; see also *She'elat Yaavetz* 2:65 citing the author's father (Ḥakham Zvi) and *Sha'arei Teshuva* §460, cited in MB 458:4. In *Ma'aseh Rav* §183 it is written that one is permitted to make *kufta'ot* (dumplings). See *Encyclopedia Talmudit* entry "*Ḥametz*" pp. 83-84. *Kaf Ha-ḥayim* 461:31 mentions the different opinions of the Aḥaronim, and concludes: "Where the custom is to be lenient, one may be lenient, since there is basis for this opinion, but where there is no custom, one should be stringent." It adds: "There is no concern about *rekikim* ("flatbreads")." Our *matzot* are "*rekikim.*" *Yeḥaveh Da'at* 1:21 rules leniently *le-khatḥila* and states that one who was stringent because he thought that this is the *halakha* erred and may switch to the lenient practice without performing *hatarat nedarim* (the annulment of vows). However, one who accepted the stringency (without saying "*bli neder*") because he wanted to go beyond the letter of the law and now wishes to be lenient should first perform *hatarat nedarim*.

In practice, many people of Ḥasidic descent no longer observe the stringency of *gebrokts*. This is because contemporary *matzot* are very thin and our ovens are very strong. If one's father was lenient in this matter, one need not perform *hatarat nedarim*, even if he is from a Ḥasidic family. However, if one's father was stringent

3. SEPHARDIC AND ASHKENAZIC APPROACHES TO KEEPING KOSHER ON PESAḤ

In general, there are two fundamental approaches to *kashrut* on Pesaḥ. According to most *poskim*, the laws of *ḥametz* on Pesaḥ are no different than the laws of all other forbidden foods, with one exception: all other forbidden foods are *batel be-shishim* (rendered insignificant when constituting less than one sixtieth of the volume of a mixture), whereas *ḥametz* is not. However, all other laws of mixtures apply to *ḥametz* on Pesaḥ. Therefore, when there is no halakhic reason to suspect that a food mixture has absorbed the taste of *ḥametz*, it is kosher for Pesaḥ. Likewise, where an individual *posek* is stringent and the great majority of *poskim* are lenient, *halakha* follows the lenient opinion.

However, Ashkenazic Jews are customarily very strict about *ḥametz*, often showing concern for a stringent opinion even against the lenient majority and practicing caution where general halakhic principles indicate no reason to do so. Nevertheless, Ashkenazic custom also places a limit to its stringencies, and *poskim* are careful not to pile restrictions upon existing restrictions. The general tendency,

---

and he wants to be lenient, he should perform *hatarat nedarim* and make sure not to insult his father.

The details of practicing the stringency of *gebrokts*: Those who do not eat *gebrokts* may be lenient when it comes to children or sick people, since soaking matza is not considered making *ḥametz* on Pesaḥ. Additionally, Jews in the Diaspora who keep *gebrokts* customarily make matza balls on the eighth day of Pesaḥ to show that *matza sheruya* is not fully prohibited. They prepare the matza balls on *Ḥol Ha-mo'ed* but do not otherwise eat off the dishes used to prepare the *gebrokts*. *She'arim Metzuyanim Be-halakha* 113:7 allows using utensils in which matza was soaked. On the other hand, *Responsa Kinyan Torah Ba-halakha* 2:87 states that one may not even soak matza for children or sick people.

As far as soaking the matza in fruit juice, SAH (*op cit.*) states that one need not be stringent, and indeed the widespread custom is to soak matza in wine and spread various spreads on matza. *Responsa Kinyan Torah Ba-halakha* 2:87 is stringent regarding this as well. See the extended discussion in *Piskei Teshuvot* 458:5-7.

Sha'arei Teshuva 460:10 states that even according to those who keep *gebrokts* one may dip the matza in water and eat it immediately, before it could conceivably become *ḥametz*. Those who are stringent about dipping matza in fruit juice are stringent about this as well.

though, is to show concern for every uncertainty. The basis for this approach is the Sages' ruling that even a drop of *ḥametz* is forbidden; thus, if a mere crumb of *ḥametz* renders its entire mixture forbidden, so too individual halakhic opinions should be taken into account.

This explains the consistent difference between the rulings of *Shulḥan Arukh*, which follow general halakhic principles, and those of Rema, which account, *le-khatḥila*, for the stringent opinions. Nonetheless, in cases of pressing need Rema adopts the lenient approach, since *halakha* fundamentally accords with most *poskim*.[3]

---

3. Here is brief overview of the major disputes between SA and Rema: 1) In 447:4, regarding the dispute among the Rishonim about *ḥozer ve-ne'or* (see above 7:4), SA rules that the *ḥametz* does not "reawaken," taking the lenient approach in the case of a rabbinic law, whereas Rema rules strictly that *ḥametz* in a dry mixture "reawakens," though not in a fluid mixture. 2) In 447:5, regarding a food that was not guarded for Pesaḥ but there is no indication that it may have become forbidden for Pesaḥ: according to SA it is kosher, and according to Rema it is not. 3) In 447:10, regarding *ḥametz* that is *noten ta'am li-fgam*: according to SA and most *poskim*, it is kosher on Pesaḥ (especially since the uncertainty relates to a rabbinic law), and according to Rema it is prohibited. 4) In 451:6, regarding the proper method for koshering utensils: according to SA, we determine the method based on the main use of the utensil, and according to Rema we determine the method based on the most severe usage. 5) In 451:11, regarding koshering a frying pan: according to SA, it may be koshered in boiling water (*hagala*), and according to Rema, it is koshered in fire (light *libun*). 6) In 451:16 and 17, regarding koshering *ḥametz* pounding and kneading utensils: according to SA, they are koshered via *hagala*, and according to Rema, they are koshered via light *libun*. 7) In 453:1, the well-known custom of *kitniyot*. 8) In 462:1, regarding egg matza: according to SA, it is kosher, and according to Rema, we are concerned that perhaps a drop of water mixed in with the fruit juice, causing it to become *ḥametz*. Rema states in 462:4 that we are only lenient in extreme cases, for sick people. 9) In 467:9, regarding whole, uncracked kernels of wheat or barley that are found in a cooked dish: according to SA, the dish is permissible, and according to Rema, it is prohibited. 10) In 467:10 and 447:1, regarding a cracked kernel of wheat that is found in a cooked dish: according to SA, one may sell the dish to a gentile, excluding the value of the wheat kernel, and according to Rema, he must burn the entire dish. 11) The custom of the Ḥasidim is to prohibit *gebrokts*.

In general, Sephardim follow *Shulḥan Arukh* and Ashkenazim follow Rema. However, some Sephardic *poskim* tend to be stringent, and their rulings are accepted in some Sephardic communities.[4]

4. PRINCIPLES OF KOSHER SUPERVISION ON PESAḤ

There is a fundamental question regarding the laws of *kashrut* on Pesaḥ: what is the status of foods that are not normally made with *ḥametz* all year round? Are they kosher for Pesaḥ as they are, without any special supervision, or must we consider the possibility that they were somehow mixed with *ḥametz* and should not be eaten on Pesaḥ?

According to *Shulḥan Arukh*, as long as there is no real concern that some *ḥametz* fell into this food or that it has absorbed the taste of *ḥametz* by being cooked in a pot in which *ḥametz* was cooked recently, there is no need to suspect that the food contains *ḥametz*.

However, Rema writes that Ashkenazic custom is preferably to avoid eating specific products without special supervision for Pesaḥ. This is because *ḥametz* is used throughout the year, and we are not generally cautious about it, so we suspect that some of it may have fallen unnoticed into these particular foods. We are also concerned that the foods may have been unwittingly cooked in *ḥametz* pots.

In practice, all *kashrut* organizations today tend to follow the stringent ruling of Rema and do not certify foods for Pesaḥ unless due caution to avoid *ḥametz* was exercised during the food's preparation. Perhaps this is the way one must act today even according to *Shulḥan Arukh*, because all industrially produced foods contain a variety of ingredients, and there is concern that one of them is not kosher for Pesaḥ. Therefore, during Pesaḥ, one must be careful not to eat any factory food products that are not certified kosher for Pesaḥ.

Where the facts of a case are not in doubt, there are still often practical differences between the rulings of *Shulḥan Arukh* and Rema.

---

4. Some Sephardic *poskim* are stringent like Rema, as *Kaf Ha-ḥayim* states in 447:86, 88, and 119. Also, *Zekhor Le-Avraham* states at the beginning of the laws of Pesaḥ that the Sephardim have the practice to be stringent like Rema "to the extent that when it comes to Pesaḥ, we are Ashkenazim." This is echoed by additional Sephardic *poskim*. On the other hand, in extenuating circumstances even Rema rules to be lenient in accordance with SA (in most cases).

Although fundamentally the law accords with *Shulḥan Arukh,* the tendency today is to be stringent so that food will be kosher for all communities. This is the appropriate practice when it is not overly difficult to be stringent. However, when stringency causes significant loss, there is room to support those who follow *Shulḥan Arukh.*[5]

5. MILK FROM AN ANIMAL THAT ATE *ḤAMETZ*

One issue that the foremost Aḥaronim dealt with is the status of milk which came from a cow that ate *ḥametz.* Clearly the milk itself does not contain *ḥametz,* for it was digested and completely transformed to the point that it is no longer considered *ḥametz* at all. However, the cow was able to produce milk by virtue of the *ḥametz,* and since it is forbidden to derive benefit from *ḥametz,* perhaps it is forbidden to benefit from milk produced by the virtue of *ḥametz.*

The *poskim* agree that milk obtained from a cow before the onset of the prohibition of *ḥametz* is kosher for Pesaḥ, because one is allowed to derive benefit from *ḥametz* before Pesaḥ. Just as it is permissible to

5. The issue of *ḥozer ve-ne'or* lies at the heart of this question. Those who are stringent are concerned that a crumb of *ḥametz* fell into a food before Pesaḥ, and that when Pesaḥ begins *ḥametz* "reawakens" and causes the entire mixture to become forbidden (Rema 447:4 based on several Ashkenazic Rishonim, and Radbaz 1:487). However, according to the opinion that *ḥametz* is not *ḥozer ve-ne'or,* even if a crumb had fallen into the mixture, it would have been *batel* before Pesaḥ and does not reawaken on Pesaḥ. Moreover, *Pri Ḥadash* states that even according to the opinion that *ḥametz* is *ḥozer ve-ne'or* there is room to be lenient in this case, since there is no reason to suspect that a crumb of *ḥametz* fell into the mixture. Furthermore, all agree that the prohibition of eating a food into which a drop of *ḥametz* fell is rabbinic, and according to *She'iltot,* even *ḥametz* is *batel be-shishim.*

There is another concern that one cooked the food in *ḥametz* utensils, and the food absorbed some of the *ḥametz* taste from the utensils. However, those who are lenient hold that there is no reason to suspect this, since it is assumed that most utensils have not been used within twenty-four hours and would then not influence the taste of the dish in a positive way (and would not make the dish prohibited). Furthermore, even if the utensils had been used within twenty-four hours of cooking the dish, *ḥametz* before Pesaḥ is permissible, thus the cooked dish is a "*nat bar nat*" (the pot absorbed the taste of the *ḥametz* and in turn, passed the taste on to the cooked dish) of permissible food, which is permitted; and see *Yeḥaveh Da'at* 1, 11 and in the notes. This fundamental dispute is dependent on other issues, including ones that involve sharp foods (*davar ḥarif*) and their interaction with absorbed tastes; and see MB 447:5.

sell *ḥametz* before Pesaḥ and use the money to buy food for Pesaḥ, so too it is permissible to feed a cow *ḥametz* before Pesaḥ in order to produce milk that will be consumed on Pesaḥ.

The disagreement concerns milk from a gentile's cow that ate *ḥametz* after the onset of the prohibition. Some *poskim* take a lenient stance, contending that since the *ḥametz* prohibition does not apply to the animal of a gentile, its milk is not considered produced in a forbidden manner. Furthermore, *ḥametz* alone does not cause milk to be produced. Rather, it must be combined with other foods and processed by the animal's body. Since the *ḥametz* is only one component, it is not prohibited. On the other hand, some *poskim* rule stringently that as long as *ḥametz* is a factor causing the production of the milk, the milk is forbidden. Others say that if twenty-four hours have passed since the cow ate *ḥametz*, the milk is kosher.

If the animal owned by a Jew was fed *ḥametz* in violation of *halakha*, one may not drink its milk, firstly because it is forbidden for the animal's owner to derive benefit from *ḥametz*, and secondly because one may not assist those who violate the Torah.[6] The same applies to eggs and meat.

---

6. A cow's milk is the product of two factors: the cow's body and the food it eats. If the cow ate *ḥametz*, the status of the milk is subject to the tannaitic dispute (AZ 48b) about something that is produced by multiple factors ("*zeh ve-zeh gorem*"). One disputant forbids and the other permits. SA YD 142:11 states that something that is produced by a combination of two factors is permissible. Accordingly, the milk of a cow that ate *ḥametz* is permissible.

   However, MA 445:5 (as well as *Taz*) states that since we are stringent about *ḥametz*, maintaining that even a drop renders a mixture forbidden, it follows that something produced by a combination of two factors is forbidden if one of them is *ḥametz*. Most *poskim*, including SA, *Shakh*, and Gra, maintain even in the case of *ḥametz* "*zeh ve-zeh gorem*" is permitted. SAH (445:10 and *Kuntrus Aḥaron*) concludes that the consensus of most *poskim* is to be lenient, and one may certainly rely on this consensus in a situation of significant loss or an extenuating circumstance. This is also the view recorded in BHL 445:2.

   Some, however, argue that regardless of one's position on *zeh ve-zeh gorem*, milk from a gentile's cow that ate *ḥametz* is permitted. As explained in *Beit Ephraim* OḤ §35 (cited in *Sha'arei Teshuva* at the end of §448), since *ḥametz* is permissible for a gentile on Pesaḥ, we do not view the milk from his cow as having been produced by something from which one is forbidden to benefit. *Nishmat Adam* §9 permits on

During Pesaḥ, Tnuva, a major Israeli dairy producer (and perhaps others) only accepts milk from dairy farms that have been made kosher for Pesaḥ and whose cows are not fed *ḥametz*. In this case, it is unnecessary to be scrupulous and buy milk products before Pesaḥ, because even dairy products manufactured on Pesaḥ are completely kosher for the duration of the holiday.[7]

---

different grounds: MA's stringency only applies when the *ḥametz* is intact, unlike in the case of the milk. *Responsa Mahari Aszod* §127 and *Responsa Maharam Schick* §§212 and 222 echo the same idea and state that the milk of the gentile's animal that ate *ḥametz* is kosher on Pesaḥ. *Igrot Moshe* OḤ 1:147 states at length that even if the gentile's cow ate only *ḥametz*, its milk is permissible even according to the strict opinions.

On the other hand, *Pri Megadim* (in *Eshel Avraham* on §448) is concerned about causing benefit that derives from *ḥametz*. Thus, there is still uncertainty if less than twenty-four hours passed between when the cow ate *ḥametz* and the milking (if more than twenty-four hours passed, the milk is permissible). *Yeshu'ot Yaakov* also states that one should preferably use milk that was extracted from the cow more than twenty-four hours after the cow ate *ḥametz*, but if less than twenty-four hours passed, the milk is still permissible as long as the cow ate permissible foods in addition to the *ḥametz* (because of *zeh ve-zeh gorem*; see MB 448:33). Some authorities ruled stringently: *Kitzur* SA 117:13 cites both opinions and concludes: "One who guards his soul should be strict, and especially in places where the prevalent custom is to be stringent, God forbid one should be lenient." *Arugat Ha-bosem* §138 states that even according to those who permit the milk, a righteous person ("*ba'al nefesh*") should refrain from drinking it, since it has negative spiritual effects. *Ben Ish Ḥai* (Year One, Tzav 42) states that one should not drink milk from a gentile's cow out of concern that the gentile fed it *ḥametz*. R. Ḥayim Palachi writes similarly in *Ru'aḥ Ḥayim* 448:1.

If the cow ate *ḥametz* before the *ḥametz* became prohibited and was milked after the *ḥametz* became prohibited, the vast majority of *poskim* maintain that the milk is kosher for Pesaḥ. *Sdei Ḥemed* mentions the opinion of *Rinun Yitzḥak* forbidding the milk of a cow that ate *ḥametz* before Pesaḥ and was milked after the *ḥametz* became forbidden, and states that this goes too far, since all other *poskim* say that this milk would be permissible. Nonetheless, because of this opinion some act stringently and only purchase dairy products before Pesaḥ. *Sdei Ḥemed* expands this topic in *Ma'arekhet Ḥametz U-matza* 2:4, and see *Kaf Ha-ḥayim* 448:113 as well.

7. According to *Nishmat Adam* and *Igrot Moshe* OḤ 1:147, if a Jew feeds his animal *ḥametz* on Pesaḥ, the animal's milk is kosher for Pesaḥ. Nonetheless, many others are stringent, not only because of *zeh ve-zeh gorem*, but because the Jew assists in the violation of a prohibition ("*mesayei'a*"). In fact, I heard from R. Weitman, the rabbi of Tnuva, that all dairy products produced on Pesaḥ are made from the milk of cows that did not eat *ḥametz*, so that the milk will be acceptable to everyone and can

6. MEAT AND EGGS

The status of beef and chicken in this regard is the same as that of milk. If the animal was slaughtered before Pesaḥ, there is no halakhic problem, even if it had eaten *ḥametz*. However, since the stomach may contain undigested leavened barley grains, its contents must be thrown out. If a gentile's animal was fed *ḥametz* and slaughtered during Pesaḥ, some *poskim* forbid consuming its meat, while others are lenient. It is proper to be stringent and not buy the meat of a Jew's animal that was fed *ḥametz* on Pesaḥ.

In actuality, most meat is sold in packages, which thus must be labeled kosher for Pesaḥ. Even if the animal was slaughtered before Pesaḥ, when there is no problem if it was fed *ḥametz*, supervision is nevertheless required to ensure that no *ḥametz* fell into the meat between the slaughtering and the packaging.

The same applies to eggs: as long as the eggs were bought before Pesaḥ, they are entirely kosher for Pesaḥ; that the hens were fed *ḥametz* makes no difference because it was not prohibited when eaten. The halakhic status of an egg that comes from a hen that ate *ḥametz* on Pesaḥ depends who the owner is. If the hen belongs to a gentile, the *poskim* disagree about the permissibility of the eggs. If the hen belongs to a Jew, even though some *poskim* are lenient, it is proper to be stringent and refrain from buying such eggs. In practice, there is no supervision on eggs laid during Pesaḥ, so it is best to buy eggs laid before Pesaḥ.[8]

---

be bought on Pesaḥ. Another potential problem was that straw and possibly some grain might stick to the cows' bodies as they wallow in mud, and these grains might accidentally get mixed into the milk. If the milk was produced before Pesaḥ, the taste of the grain is *batel be-shishim* even if it found its way into the milk, and since this is a liquid mixture even Rema (447:4) would agree that the taste of the *ḥametz* is not *ḥozer ve-ne'or*. If the grain fell into the milk on Pesaḥ, however, it is not *batel*. Although in the present case it is uncertain that any grain fell in, it would nevertheless be commendable to buy dairy products before Pesaḥ. However, I heard from R. Weitman that Tnuva recently introduced the practice of filtering all the milk very thoroughly right after the milking, so that no grain that falls in would have enough time to flavor the milk. Thus, one may purchase dairy products on Pesaḥ even according to the strictest opinions.

8. Nevertheless, those who are lenient and purchase eggs on Pesaḥ have committed no transgression, even if the eggs are not certified kosher for Pesaḥ. As noted, even

Another problem that has arisen pertains to the markings stamped on each egg. There was some concern that these markings contain *ḥametz* and that a drop of it might fall into Pesaḥ food. However, I heard from Tnuva's R. Zev Weitman that all eggs brought to market via Israel's Egg Production Council (which does not include the black market) are marked before Pesaḥ with a stamp that contains no *ḥametz* (the relevant mark is a series of stars).

7. MEDICINES ON PESAḤ

Medicines are the subject of some of the most common questions on Pesaḥ. There is concern that pills contain wheat-based starch. The purpose of the starch is to solidify and harden the pills. Had the starch been produced from potatoes or *kitniyot,* there would be no problem even for Ashkenazim, as for medicinal purposes one may swallow pills containing *kitniyot.* But what about starch extracted from a type of grain that can become *ḥametz*? It must be emphasized that a dangerously ill person whose treatment requires eating *ḥametz* has a mitzva to eat *ḥametz.* Saving a life overrides the prohibition against eating *ḥametz.* The question applies to an ill person whose life is not at risk.

The answer depends on the taste of the medicine: if it is flavored, like syrup, lozenges, or chewables, then one must ascertain that it is kosher for Pesaḥ. In case of doubt, its use is forbidden. However, if the medicine is bitter or tasteless to the point that it is not fit as food, it may be swallowed on Pesaḥ. Even if the starch was derived from wheat, since it has been mixed with various bitter substances it is inedible and has lost its status as *ḥametz.* As we have seen, *ḥametz* that was rendered unfit for a dog's consumption before Pesaḥ is no longer considered *ḥametz* and may be kept on Pesaḥ. The fact that one wants to swallow the medicine does not demonstrate that the *ḥametz* in the medicine is important to him, since the medicine, not the *ḥametz,* is significant for him, and the

though a Jew owns the chickens and fed them *ḥametz,* there are lenient authorities. Furthermore, most of the food chickens consume on Pesaḥ is not *ḥametz,* so even according to the stringent opinions it is unclear that these eggs are forbidden. Thus, there are two uncertainties ("*sfek sfeika*") about a rabbinic prohibition.

ḥametz itself is bitter and unfit for consumption. The *ḥametz* in it is thus *batel* and not prohibited (*Ḥazon Ish*, Mo'ed 116:8; *Igrot Moshe*, OḤ 2:92).

Some meticulously observant people try to avoid even bitter medicines that contain *ḥametz*. They show concern for the opinion of the few *poskim* who maintain that medicine is not considered unfit for animal consumption since we deem it significant, and it is thus rabbinically prohibited. Other *poskim* permit bitter medicines that contain *ḥametz* starch for one who is bedridden or whose entire body is in pain, but rule stringently for one suffering from mild aches and pains.

However, most *poskim* maintain that bitter medicines containing *ḥametz* may be taken by any ill person, even only to reduce mild pain, as a prophylactic, or to fortify the body.

Practically speaking, if one is uncertain whether certain bitter or tasteless medicines contain wheat starch, he may swallow them without ensuring that they are free of wheat starch. As we have seen, most *poskim* maintain that medicines rendered unfit for animal consumption before Pesaḥ may be consumed during Pesaḥ even if they are known to contain *ḥametz*. Even one who prefers to comply with the stringent opinion on this issue need not be strict if he is uncertain whether the medicine contains *ḥametz*. This is especially true nowadays, when we know that potato and corn starch are used more widely than wheat starch. Thus, in practice, one may consume bitter or tasteless medicines on Pesaḥ without ascertaining whether they contain *ḥametz*. When one knows for certain that a particular medicine contains *ḥametz* starch, he may choose to rely on the lenient opinion of most *poskim* or the stringent minority.[9]

9. *Ḥametz* that was rendered unfit for a dog's consumption prior to Pesaḥ is no longer considered *ḥametz*, and according to *Ha-ma'or*, Ran, and other Rishonim it may even be eaten on Pesaḥ. Conversely, Rosh, Rabbeinu Yeruḥam, and other Rishonim maintain that this type of *ḥametz* is rabbinically prohibited, since by eating it the person assigns importance ("*aḥshevei*") to it and shows that, for him, the food is still edible. Accordingly, SA 442:9 and MB 43 *ad loc.* rule that one may keep such an item over Pesaḥ since it is unfit for a dog's consumption and thus not considered *ḥametz*. However, he may not eat it, since by eating it he assigns significance to it. Thus, according to *Ha-ma'or* and Ran one would certainly be permitted to swallow bitter *ḥametz*-containing pills on Pesaḥ, and even according to Rosh and those who agree with him it may be permissible, since the Aḥaronim debate whether swallowing *ḥametz* that is unfit for a dog's consumption for medicinal purposes assigns

8. CITRIC ACID

Citric acid is used to flavor juices, jams, candies, and various food items. In the past it was produced from lemons and other fruit, but nowadays it is produced industrially from wheat flour.

Although during the production process the flour is initially mixed with water and may become *ḥametz,* at a later stage it loses its taste and appearance, is rendered unfit for a dog's consumption, and thus loses its status as *ḥametz.* Some *poskim* therefore permit eating products containing citric acid on Pesaḥ (*Yeḥaveh Da'at* 2:62).

However, many *poskim* are stringent in this case. In their opinion, *ḥametz* only loses its status if it becomes unfit for a dog's consumption due to spoilage. If it is intentionally rendered inedible so that it may be used to flavor foods, it is not nullified and is considered *ḥametz* for all purposes (*Minḥat Yitzḥak* 7:27; *Or Le-Tziyon* 1:34; *Shevet Ha-Levi* 4:47).

---

significance to the *ḥametz. Sha'agat Aryeh* §75 states this indeed assigns significance to the *ḥametz,* whereas *Ktav Sofer* OḤ §111 states that it does not impart significance. If the *ḥametz* is not the main ingredient in the pill, most Aḥaronim maintain that even Rosh would concede that swallowing a bitter pill does not impart significance to the *ḥametz.* See *Ḥavalim Ba-ne'imim* 5:4; *Ḥazon Ish,* Mo'ed 116:8; *Igrot Moshe* OḤ 2:92; *Yeḥaveh Da'at* 2:60; SSK 40:74; and many others.

However, it seems that SAH 442:22 derives from the case of *tiryaka,* an edible type of medicine, that Rosh would prohibit swallowing a pill as well. Most authorities, who are lenient, would differentiate between *tiryaka,* which is **eaten** by the ill, and medicines that are swallowed but not eaten. Moreover, even when the starch is from wheat flour, it generally did not have time to rise, and at worst would be classified as *ḥametz nuksheh,* which did not undergo a complete leavening and is only rabbinically prohibited. Since this *ḥametz nuksheh* is part of a mixture within a bitter pill, there is no reason to be stringent. Nevertheless, some incline toward stringency (*Arugat Ha-bosem* §99, and *Atzei Ha-Levanon* §19). As stated, some have written that these pills are permissible according to the letter of the law, but the holy people of Israel are customarily strict even about avoiding *ḥametz* mixed into a bitter pill (*Tzitz Eliezer* 10:25:20). On the other hand, *Nishmat Avraham* OḤ 1:466:1 states that most pills do not contain *ḥametz* at all. It is further stated there in the name of R. Ovadia Yosef that even though he writes in *Yeḥaveh Da'at* 2:60 that only a genuinely sick person may be lenient, if it is uncertain whether or not the pill contains *ḥametz,* there is no need to ascertain. As noted, the vast majority of *poskim* maintain that it is not at all prohibited to swallow a bitter pill, and even one with a minor ailment may take a pill that contains *ḥametz* rendered unfit for a dog before Pesaḥ started.

Rabbi She'ar Yashuv Cohen, the municipal rabbi of Haifa, investigated and found that there is no concern that citric acid is *ḥametz*. To begin with, the flour that starts the process does not become *ḥametz* since it sits in water for only six minutes – not enough time to become *ḥametz*. At this point, the starch is extracted from the mixture, and starch alone cannot become *ḥametz*. Moreover, citric acid is not produced from the wheat starch itself, but from molds that feed off a substance whose ingredients include a material extracted from the unleavened starch.[10]

---

10. This debate is very extensive, and the key questions are: is something that was *batel be-shishim* before Pesaḥ *ḥozer ve-ne'or* once Pesaḥ begins? Even if not, would a stabilizing agent ("*davar ha-ma'amid*") be any different? And what if it is not the sole agent? See *Yalkut Yosef*, Mo'adim p. 358 which responds to *Minḥat Yitzḥak*'s criticism of R. Ovadia Yosef. The Badatz and many other kosher-certification agencies are very strict about citric acid and similar products. Nevertheless, according to R. She'ar Yashuv Cohen's long essay in *Teḥumin* vol. 1, it seems clear that there is no reason for concern that citric acid contains *ḥametz*. More precisely: the starch is first separated from the gluten by spinning the wheat flour in water for six minutes. As we know, it takes eighteen minutes for flour and water to become *ḥametz*, so the flour could not have become *ḥametz* in those six minutes. By then the starch has already been separated from the gluten, and it is well known that the leavening process takes place in the gluten. Thus once the starch has been isolated from the gluten, it can no longer become *ḥametz*. The starch is then heated to 140° Celsius until it liquefies as dextrose (also known as glucose). This heating process destroys the existing molecules and changes their composition. To dispel any doubt, an attempt was made to leaven this substance, but it was unsuccessful.

R. Levi Yitzḥak Halperin writes that at worst this substance can be considered *ḥametz nuksheh*, which is rabbinically prohibited, becomes *batel* in any mixture prior to Pesaḥ, and would be *ḥozer ve-ne'or* on Pesaḥ. According to R. She'ar Yashuv Cohen, this substance is not even considered *ḥametz nuksheh*, which is dough whose leavening process was halted after it began; the substance in question never even began the leavening process.

The liquid dextrose is then mixed with sulfur to destroy the enzymes in the glucose and render it inert and unable to ferment. Since it never had the chance to become *ḥametz*, it certainly will not become *ḥametz* in the future. This is the first stage of the process, which shows that the extracted starch does not become *ḥametz*. The next step is to place the liquid into large vats, to feed the molds. It is left until the mold has finished digesting all of the dextrose and excreted another substance: citric acid. Thus, citric acid is not a product of the starch, but a product of the mold. Just as if one used organic fertilizer that contained remnants of bread to fertilize vegetables, the vegetables would undoubtedly be kosher for Pesaḥ, certainly citric acid excreted by molds that digested a liquid that never became *ḥametz* in the first place would

9. SOAPS AND COSMETICS

Poskim disagree whether body ointments that contain *ḥametz* may be used on Pesaḥ. While soaps, shampoos, and creams are not made from *ḥametz,* they sometimes contain grain alcohol or other *ḥametz* derivatives, leading to queries about their status on Pesaḥ.

Some say that applying an ointment is equivalent, by rabbinic enactment, to drinking. Consequently, even if the *ḥametz* in these products is not fit for a dog's consumption, it retains the status of *ḥametz* because it is suitable for anointing, and thus it is forbidden to use them on Pesaḥ. Accordingly, one must use soaps, shampoos, and creams that are kosher for Pesaḥ.

Others maintain that the Sages only equated the application of ointment to drinking with regard to Yom Kippur and anointing with oil consecrated as *teruma* (priestly gift). All other Torah prohibitions relate to eating alone, not anointing. Although it is forbidden to derive benefit from *ḥametz,* the *ḥametz* in these products was rendered unfit for a dog's consumption even before Pesaḥ began and thus lost the status of *ḥametz.* It is therefore permissible to derive benefit from them and apply them to the body during Pesaḥ.

Since this dispute relates to rabbinic law, the *halakha* accords with the lenient opinion, and meticulously observant individuals act stringently.[11]

---

be *kosher* for Pesaḥ. This conclusion has major implications for other industrial ingredients that use wheat starch that never became *ḥametz* and that undergoes fundamental alterations before being reintegrated into food.

11. The Rishonim disagree about the principle that equates anointing with drinking: some apply it only to Yom Kippur and *teruma* oil, while others hold that it applies to other prohibitions, though only on the rabbinic level. The question arises with regard to soap made of lard, and many Aḥaronim tend toward stringency if the item is for enjoyment and leniently if it is needed for health reasons (see *Yeḥaveh Da'at* 4:53). They incline toward leniency if the lard's taste has been befouled (AHS YD 117:29). Regarding Pesaḥ, there is a more stringent aspect, namely, that one is forbidden to derive any benefit from *ḥametz,* but there is also a more lenient aspect, namely, that the *ḥametz* lost its status when it became inedible before Pesaḥ, making it less strict than something that had been forbidden from the outset. In practice, *Responsa Sho'el U-meishiv* 3:2:146 states that one may keep soap that contains *ḥametz* over Pesaḥ since its taste has been befouled. It does not address whether or not the soap

Distinctions must be made between four gradations of products containing *ḥametz*, of which the middle two are subject to dispute:

1. Toothpastes must be certified kosher for Pesaḥ because they are flavored and thus like any other food product.

---

may be used on Pesaḥ. *Responsa Divrei Malkiel* 4:24:43 states that one may not use cosmetics that contain wheat-derived alcohol, since the alcohol helps spread their scent and is thus significant. The alcohol is not *batel* since it can be isolated from the rest of the mixture. *Responsa Divrei Naḥum* §46 states that the law follows the current situation, namely, that the taste of the *ḥametz* has been befouled, and the mixture is thus permissible. *Ḥazon Ish*, Demai 15:1, suggests that only something edible may not be used as an ointment. *Igrot Moshe* OḤ 3:62 rules leniently in the case of an ointment that contains *ḥametz* that is used for health purposes. *Bedikat Ḥametz U-vi'uro* 2:43 summarizes the topic and rules stringently unless it is uncertain whether a product contains *ḥametz*, in which case one may be lenient. It seems to me that even those who rule stringently should distinguish between fat-based soap and contemporary soaps: fat-based soaps are absorbed in the skin and may be considered ointments, whereas contemporary soaps merely clean and remove dirt from the body, but are not absorbed into it. I have thus distinguished between ointments and creams, which are absorbed into the body, and soaps and shampoos, which are not (though hair conditioner may be more akin to an ointment). In practice, I heard from R. Naḥum Rabinovitch that he rules leniently regarding all products unfit for a dog's consumption, as did his mentor, R. Pinḥas Hirschprung. This is the opinion of R. Dov Lior as well.

In reality, the vast majority of cosmetic products produced in Israel do not contain wheat-derived alcohol. Even the majority of products produced abroad do not contain wheat-derived alcohol, since it is more expensive than potato-derived alcohol. However, a few products in fact contain wheat-derived alcohol, and according to the stringent views one should not use them on Pesaḥ. Still, when one has a product and is not sure whether it contains wheat-derived alcohol, even if he is normally stringent he may be lenient, based on a combination of several uncertainties and doubts.

Another issue arises regarding the use of products that contain wheat germ oil, which is a source of Vitamin E, since it is unclear whether liquids exuded by wheat are considered *ḥametz*. According to Rav Kook (*Oraḥ Mishpat* p. 129), even if these liquids are forbidden, they were already *batel be-shishim* before Pesaḥ and are not *ḥozer ve-ne'or* on Pesaḥ. Moreover, many authorities maintain that even if this liquid was considered *ḥametz*, since it is not fit for consumption it loses its status as *ḥametz*. Another issue arises regarding lotions, although it is not certain that wheat starch-based lotions are considered *ḥametz*, and moreover they are inedible. Therefore, in practice, one may be lenient and use any cosmetic product not fit for consumption.

2. Creams that are absorbed into the skin, flavorless lipstick, and perfumes that contain alcohol need not be certified kosher for Pesaḥ, in keeping with the lenient opinion, since they are not fit for consumption and generally do not contain *ḥametz* ingredients. Nonetheless, many choose to be stringent and buy creams and perfumes that are certified kosher for Pesaḥ.
3. Soaps and shampoos warrant even more room for leniency because they are designed to clean, not to be absorbed into the skin. Nevertheless, some are stringent.
4. Detergents, shoe polish, and the like do not require any kosher certification. Even dishwashing detergents need no certification because their taste is foul. Even if these substances were mixed with *ḥametz,* its taste was befouled before Pesaḥ and it is no longer considered *ḥametz.*

Chapter Nine

Kitniyot

1. THE ORIGINS OF THE ASHKENAZIC CUSTOM

The *ḥametz* prohibited by the Torah is produced from one of the five types of grain: wheat, barley, spelt, oats, and rye. Other species such as rice and millet, even if they rise, do not undergo the same fermentation process as the five cereal grains, and they may be eaten on Pesaḥ. Although one Tanna, R. Yoḥanan b. Nuri, maintains that rice is also a cereal grain and forbidden by the Torah in its leavened state, the rest of the Sages maintain that even if rice rises, it may be eaten on Pesaḥ (*Pesaḥim* 35a). This was the practice of all the great Tanna'im and Amora'im. In fact, Rava ate rice at the Seder (*ibid.* 114b).

During the medieval era of the Rishonim (c. seven centuries ago), the Jews of Ashkenaz (Germany, especially the Rhineland) began to refrain from eating *kitniyot*[1] on Pesaḥ. Initially, only some communities observed this stringency, but within a few generations the custom had spread to all Ashkenazic communities.

---

1. Editor's note: We have refrained from translating the term "*kitniyot*" since there is no precise equivalent in English, and an imprecise translation would be misleading. In earlier contexts (such as the laws of *kilayim*, which prohibit cultivating dissimilar species in close proximity), *kitniyot* referred specifically to members of the legume family. As currently used, the category of *kitniyot* includes species that are not legumes, and not every member of the legume family is considered *kitniyot*.

Three principal reasons for this custom have been offered: A) Since *kitniyot* are cooked in the same manner as grains, in a pot, there is concern that if people cook rice on Pesaḥ they will end up mistakenly cooking forbidden types of grain. B) Since *kitniyot*, like cereal grains, are often made into flour, if the unlearned masses see pious Jews cooking and baking foods with *kitniyot* flour without concern for it becoming *ḥametz*, they are liable to do the same with grain flour as well. The rabbis of the Talmud were not concerned about this because, in their day, Jewish tradition was clear and established. However, the tribulations of the exile and the scattering of Jewish communities gave rise to a fear that some Jews would be cut off from tradition and come to forget what is forbidden and what is permitted. Eating *kitniyot* on Pesaḥ would cause them to err and eat forbidden cereal grains without taking care that they do not become *ḥametz*. C) Grain and *kitniyot* kernels are similar in appearance and are kept in the same storehouses for relatively long periods. It is therefore eminently possible that wheat or barley kernels would find their way into *kitniyot*, and when the *kitniyot* are cooked the grain will become *ḥametz*. This concern persists today, and indeed it is possible to find kernels of grain when checking *kitniyot*.

Another reason why kernels of *kitniyot* and cereal grain got mixed together was the common practice of crop rotation. Farmers often grow legumes for a year to replenish the soil of a field that had been used for growing grain for many years. However, kernels of the previous crop inevitably remain in the field. Thus, if a coriander or fenugreek crop is grown after a wheat crop, wheat will sprout among the coriander or fenugreek, and some kernels of wheat or barley will be found in the harvested crop of legumes. Experience shows that sometimes the quantity of cereal kernels in the *kitniyot* exceeds one sixtieth of the entire quantity. This problem applies to those species of *kitniyot* that physically resemble cereal grain.

2. THE SEPHARDIC CUSTOM

During the era of the Rishonim, all Sephardic communities ate *kitniyot* and rice during Pesaḥ, though they were careful to pick out forbidden grains. Indeed, R. Yosef Karo writes (*Beit Yosef* §453) that nobody worries about "such things except for Ashkenazim."

However, some leading Sephardic Aḥaronim have written that many pious Jews refrain from eating rice during Pesaḥ because of a case in which some wheat was discovered in rice even after it had been checked several times (*Pri Ḥadash*, Ḥida). The Jews of Izmir have a custom not to eat rice on Pesaḥ (*Lev Ḥayim* 2:94), and the Jews of Morocco refrain from eating rice and other types of dry *kitniyot* on Pesaḥ. *Ben Ish Ḥai* (Year One, Tzav 41) states that in Baghdad many laypeople do not eat rice on Pesaḥ, and those who do must first check it two or three times. Each person should perpetuate his ancestral custom. Where there is doubt or difficulty in doing so, it is best to consult a rabbinic authority.

Certain spices such as cumin, turmeric, and fenugreek often have grains mixed in and should not be eaten without a prior meticulous inspection.

Nowadays rice is stored in the same packing-houses as flours and semolina. Therefore, those who eat rice on Pesaḥ must buy packages that are certified kosher for Pesaḥ and then check the rice thoroughly three times (*Ama Devar* 1:62).

3. SPOUSES FROM DIFFERENT COMMUNITIES

The following question arises frequently nowadays: what should a married couple do when one spouse comes from a family that refrains from *kitniyot* and the other from a family that eats *kitniyot*? A similar matter was addressed by one of the great Rishonim, R. Shimon b. Tzemaḥ Duran (*Tashbetz* 3:179), who writes that they obviously cannot eat together at the same table while food permissible to one is forbidden to the other. Therefore, the wife must adopt her husband's customs, for "a man's wife is like his own body." If the husband dies, it depends: if she has a child from him, she keeps his custom; otherwise, she reverts to her family's custom.

R. Moshe Feinstein (*Igrot Moshe* OḤ 1:158) adds that the wife's status is similar to that of one who moves to a place where the accepted custom is different from his own. If he intends to settle there, he relinquishes his previous custom and accepts the custom of his new home (based on SA YD 214:2, OḤ 468:4, and MB 14 *ad loc.*). When a woman marries, it is as if she moves permanently into her husband's house, and she must therefore adopt his customs.

Accordingly, if an Ashkenazic woman marries a Sephardic man, she may eat *kitniyot* during Pesaḥ and need not perform *hatarat nedarim* (annulment of vows) because she is acting in accordance with the law that a woman adopts the customs of her husband. Nevertheless, some *poskim* recommend that she perform *hatarat nedarim.*[2]

---

2. *Igrot Moshe* OḤ 1:158 proves that this is a Torah law from the fact that the Torah exempts a married woman from the obligation to honor her parents, since this mitzva would require her to actively clothe and feed her parents if necessary, and her obligations to her household take priority (SA YD 240:17; obviously if there is no clash between the two obligations, she is commanded to honor her parents). Thus, according to the Torah, a woman's place is in her husband's home.

   Igrot Moshe also asserts that she need not perform *hatarat nedarim.* MB 468:14 states that one who moves from one locale to another must behave according to the custom of the new place. It is implied that since this is the *halakha,* there is no need for *hatarat nedarim.* This is also the opinion of *Kaf Ha-ḥayim* 468:43. Additionally, in extenuating circumstances even Ashkenazic communities did not accept the custom of refraining from *kitniyot* and can therefore be lenient in situations of famine or sickness (MB 453:7). Similarly, two different customs in one household would certainly cause tension, and thus she changes her custom without performing *hatarat nedarim. Sidur Pesaḥ Ke-hilkhato* 16:13 states that she must perform *hatarat nedarim,* and *Ḥazon Ovadia* (p. 56 and n. 10) states that it is better to perform *hatarat nedarim.*

   May Ashkenazim perform *hatarat nedarim* and eat *kitniyot*? *Kaf Ha-ḥayim* 453:15 states that according to Mahari Ben Lev (§38), one who refrained from eating *kitniyot* because he thought they are *ḥametz* may perform *hatarat nedarim,* but one who knew, or whose ancestors knew, that *kitniyot* is merely a stringent custom may not perform *hatarat nedarim.* Thus, Ashkenazim may not perform *hatarat nedarim* and eat *kitniyot.* According to *Pri Ḥadash* §468, one need not perform *hatarat nedarim* to annul a custom that originated in a mistake, so even one who knew that *kitniyot* is just a stringent custom may annul his vow and eat *kitniyot.* However, we need to examine whether he would apply this reasoning to a custom accepted by an entire community; perhaps even according to *Pri Ḥadash hatarat nedarim* would not be effective in such a case. *Ḥatam Sofer* OḤ §122 upholds the opinion of Mahari Ben Lev. This is in fact the customary practice: we find that Ashkenazim do not perform *hatarat nedarim* and eat *kitniyot* except in the case of a sick person. *Sidur Pesaḥ Ke-hilkhato* 16 n. 47 and in the addenda quotes some who believe that *kitniyot* originated as an enactment ("*gezeira*"). According to this, even an Ashkenazic woman who marries a Sephardic man would not be permitted to eat *kitniyot.* Nevertheless, we do not follow this opinion, and an Ashkenazic woman should follow her husband's customs.

4. PROHIBITED SPECIES

The familiar foods included in this custom are: rice, alfalfa, peas, millet, sorghum, chickpeas, fenugreek seeds, sunflower seeds, mustard, buckwheat (*kusemet,* not to be confused with *kusmin* – spelt – which is a forbidden cereal grain), cumin, vetch, black-eyed peas, arum, soy, mung beans, lentils, fava beans, lupin beans, poppy seeds, flaxseed, pulse, caraway, hemp seeds, common beans (*Phaseolus vulgaris*), sesame seeds, lupine seeds, corn, clover seed, and tamarind fruit. Products made from *kitniyot* – corn flakes, corn flour, and rice cakes, for example – are also included in the custom. Saffron was originally called "*karkom*" in Hebrew and is included in the prohibition. Turmeric, the Modern Hebrew *karkom,* is permitted. Mustard and flaxseed are not *kitniyot,* but the custom is to forbid them because they grow in pods like *kitniyot.*

Rema writes that it is permitted to eat dill and coriander because they are not *kitniyot.* Nonetheless, Aḥaronim write that they must be examined well because they often contain wheat (MA, MB 453:13).

There are differing customs regarding peanuts. In Jerusalem and many other places people refrain from eating them (*Mikra'ei Kodesh* 2:60), but in Greater Lithuania they were customarily eaten. One who does not know whether his family was stringent in this regard may eat them (*Igrot Moshe* OḤ 3:63).

Regarding quinoa, some are strict due to its similarity to some types of kitniyot. Some are lenient since the customary prohibition does not apply to quinoa, which entered our diets only recently. Moreover, its seeds are much smaller than those of cereal grains, making them easy to distinguish. Stringency is commendable, but those who practice leniently have authorities upon whom to rely, on condition that they thoroughly inspect the quinoa.

Potato flour is permitted on Pesaḥ. There is no contention that based on the customary prohibition of *kitniyot* anything from which flour can be made should be forbidden. Rather, the custom only includes what the great Ashkenazic Rishonim forbade. Since potatoes had not yet arrived in Europe then, they are not included in the prohibition (*ibid.*).

5. RULES GOVERNING THIS CUSTOM

People who adhere to the custom of not eating *kitniyot* may keep them in the house during Pesaḥ and derive benefit from them, for example, by lighting a lamp with *kitniyot* oil (Rema 453:1).

One who does not eat *kitniyot* on Pesaḥ may cook them for somebody who does, but it is recommended that he use some sort of reminder that he is not cooking for himself (*Kaf Ha-ḥayim* 453:17; *Sidur Pesaḥ Ke-hilkhato* 16:8). It is likewise permissible for a storeowner to sell *kitniyot* during Pesaḥ; however, if there could be wheat grains among the *kitniyot* that make up more than one sixtieth of the mixture, the storeowner may not sell the *kitniyot,* because this could cause customers to transgress the *ḥametz* prohibition. It would be better to sell such *kitniyot* along with the *ḥametz.*

If *kitniyot* fall into a cooked food, they should be removed, and whatever cannot be removed is *batel* in the majority of the dish. If, however, such a large amount of *kitniyot* falls in that they become the majority, the dish is considered a *kitniyot* dish and its consumption is forbidden (Rema 453:1; MB 8-9 *ad loc.*).

It is permissible for one who does not eat *kitniyot* on Pesaḥ to eat from and cook with utensils that belong to one who does eat *kitniyot,* provided that 24 hours have elapsed since *kitniyot* were last cooked in them. If food was cooked in such a utensil before 24 hours elapsed, the food remains kosher.[3]

---

3. *Kitniyot* in a mixture are *batel* in a simple majority (*batel be-rov*). Although the implication of *Terumat Ha-deshen* is that it is only *batel be-shishim,* the Aḥaronim rule that it is *batel be-rov* (SAH 453:5; *Ḥayei Adam* 127:1; *Ḥavot Ya'ir* §6; *Eliya Rabba* §4; and *Kaf Ha-ḥayim* 453:25, which also adds more sources). All of this only applies when one found that *kitniyot* had been mixed with permissible food, but it is forbidden to mix *kitniyot* with permissible food intentionally, contrary to the opinion of the *Pri Ḥadash* that one may intentionally add *kitniyot* to a mixture as long as they do not become the majority of the mixture. If one who does not eat *kitniyot* visits one who does eat *kitniyot* and there is nothing else for the guest to eat, he may, if absolutely necessary, eat the non-*kitniyot* food from a mixture containing *kitniyot.* For example, he may eat potatoes and zucchini from a dish containing *kitniyot,* even though the food he is eating absorbed some flavor from the *kitniyot.*

Even those who abstain from *kitniyot* are permitted to eat food cooked in a pot in which *kitniyot* had been cooked within the prior 24 hours, since the taste of the

6. *KITNIYOT* THAT NEVER TOUCHED WATER AND *KITNIYOT* OILS

We are not stricter with *kitniyot* than we are with the five cereal grains, so whatever is acceptable regarding these grains is kosher for *kitniyot*, too. Thus, *kitniyot* that have not come into contact with water, or that have come into contact with water but were not left for more than 18 minutes before being cooked (like matza), may be eaten. Some *poskim* are stringent in this respect, but most are lenient.[4]

The *poskim* disagree about oils and whiskeys made from *kitniyot*. Those who rule leniently contend that the *kitniyot* prohibition does not apply to oil extracted from them, while those who rule stringently

---

kitniyot is a very small minority. If 24 hours elapsed since the cooking of the *kitniyot*, one may cook food in the pot even *le-khatḥila*, since the taste of the *kitniyot* in the pot has already turned foul, and *kitniyot* are technically kosher for Pesaḥ anyway (*Pri Ḥadash* 496:24 and *Responsa Maharalbaḥ* §121). If one is in doubt whether or not 24 hours passed since the cooking of the *kitniyot*, he may still use the pot *le-khatḥila* because of the principle that most pots have not been used in the past 24 hours. See also *Kaf Ha-ḥayim* 453:27, which lists additional sources.

Some maintain that the prohibition of *kitniyot* begins at the onset of Pesaḥ (*Sidur Pesaḥ Ke-hilkhato* 16:10 n. 42), and in time of pressing need one can rely on this opinion. In practice, however, the mainstream opinion is that the custom of *kitniyot* corresponds to the prohibition of *ḥametz*. Thus, *kitniyot* are forbidden from the time that *ḥametz* is prohibited (*Ḥok Yaakov* 471:2; *Responsa Maharsham* 1:183; *Shevet Ha-Levi* 3:31).

4. Most authorities are not stricter about *kitniyot* than about the cereal grains (SAH 453:5; *Ḥayei Adam* 127:1; *Responsa Maharsham* 1:183; *Be'er Yitzḥak* §11; *Responsa Marḥeshet* §3; and Rav Kook's *Oraḥ Mishpat* §111). Some, however, are more stringent (*Sho'el U-meishiv* 1:1:175 and *Ma'amar Mordechai* §32). Their rationale is that no one would understand these distinctions since *kitniyot* do not become *ḥametz*. Additionally, they were concerned that making the *kitniyot* exactly like the cereal grains would mislead people to think they could use *kitniyot* to fulfill the mitzva of matza. As noted, though, most *poskim* are lenient, and in any dispute about a custom the *halakha* follows the lenient opinion.

The Rishonim also debate whether or not scalding works for *kitniyot*, since scalding any of the five cereal grains technically eliminates the possibility of its leavening, though the Ge'onim agree that no one knows how to scald the grains properly (SA 454:3). However, according to *Or Zaru'a* 2:256, since the prohibition of *kitniyot* is just a custom, scalding the *kitniyot* is effective and permits them. *Mordechai* rules stringently, and Rabbeinu Peretz's glosses to *Smak* §222 notes the lenient opinion but rules stringently.

maintain that *kitniyot* oil has the same status as the *kitniyot* themselves. There is a middle position that asserts that if the *kitniyot* had been rinsed in water (for example, as part of the malting process) they become forbidden, and the oil extracted from them is prohibited. However, if they are ground and made into oil without having been moistened, they do not have the status of *kitniyot*.[5]

---

5. **The controversy over *kitniyot* oils:** *Terumat Ha-deshen* §113 explains that oil extracted from *kitniyot* is prohibited because the *kitniyot* are first malted. This is also the opinion of Rema 453:1. The implication of *Terumat Ha-deshen* is that if the *kitniyot* were not malted, their oil would be permitted. R. Yitzḥak Elḥanan Spektor in *Responsa Be'er Yitzḥak* §11 rules even more leniently, explaining that if the *kitniyot* were checked to ensure that no grain seeds were mixed in, the oil extracted from them is permitted, since the act of checking proves that the person is familiar with the prohibition. Similarly, *Responsa Emek Halakha* §134 permits whiskey distilled from *kitniyot*, as the prohibition applies to *kitniyot* themselves, not the liquid extracted from them.

Conversely, other Aḥaronim maintain that oil extracted from *kitniyot* is prohibited even when the *kitniyot* are not malted (*Nishmat Adam* §33 and *Avnei Nezer* OḤ §373). However, *Terumat Ha-deshen* and Rema imply that such oil is permissible. This raises an apparent difficulty, since the oil will eventually be mixed with water, a process that would be forbidden to apply to grain. Thus, according to these authorities, the custom is to prohibit *kitniyot* in their seed and flour state, but not in their oil state. One need not be concerned that grain kernels got mixed in with the *kitniyot*, which would turn to *ḥametz* when the extracted oil is mixed with water, since any oil extracted from the grain is *batel be-shishim* and is not *ḥozer ve-ne'or* on Pesaḥ (SA 447:4). Additionally, it appears that even liquid that is exuded by grain does not become *ḥametz*, as explained in *Oraḥ Mishpat* §§111-112 and *Responsa Marḥeshet* §3. *Tzemaḥ Tzedek* permits this for poor people, provided that the *kitniyot* did not come into contact with water while in seed form.

Rav Kook has a well-known ruling (*Oraḥ Mishpat* 108-114) in which he broadly permitted sesame oil since not only are the seeds not malted, but the oil is also fried, which would prevent cereal grain from becoming *ḥametz* and is certainly enough to alleviate the problem of *kitniyot*. This idea is echoed by *Avnei Nezer* OḤ §533 with regard to rapeseed oil (this responsum appeared in 5458, 11 years before Rav Kook's responsum). The Ḥasidic-Ashkenazic rabbinical court in Jerusalem vociferously opposed Rav Kook without any regard for the honor of Torah or of all of the *poskim* who had previously ruled even more leniently than Rav Kook on this matter. Rav Kook responded to them sharply, with erudition, and with strong proofs. As part of his response, he wrote (p. 123): "In truth, the path of my righteous and ingenious mentors, may their merit protect us and all of Israel, whom I merited to serve, was not to incline toward stringency when it

Soybean, cottonseed, and canola (rapeseed) oils are not included in the prohibition. Many are stringent about soybean and canola oils, but whoever wishes to be lenient may be so. The widespread custom regarding cottonseed oil is to be lenient.[6]

---

was possible to be lenient, especially regarding issues without a strong basis in the words of the talmudic Sages. It is sufficient that we do not budge, God forbid, from the customs we accepted at the guidance of our rabbis, the *poskim*. But as for the details that can be argued one way or the other, certainly one who inclines toward a lenient ruling in an effort to be wise and benevolent is praiseworthy, as long as his words are based on the profundity of *halakha* and sound reasoning..." Furthermore, one who adds prohibitions to a prohibition that is not rooted in the law may violate a prohibition implied by a positive commandment ("*lav ha-ba mi-khlal aseh*") according to Rashi's comments in the first chapter of *Beitza*. As Rav Kook wrote (p. 126): "That which the Talmud often states, that we do not make decrees on top of other decrees, is derived from the following verse: 'You shall safeguard my observances' ['*u-shmartem et mishmarti*' – Vayikra 18:30]: make safeguards, i.e., enact decrees, for my observances, that is, for the Torah. But do not make safeguards for safeguards; do not make decrees upon decrees." Against the claim that we must be increasingly stringent nowadays, Rav Kook writes: "I know the character of our contemporaries well: it is precisely when they see that everything that can be permitted based on the profundity of *halakha* is permitted, they will understand that when we do not permit it is based on the truth of Torah law. Consequently, many people will adhere to the Torah and heed the words of the Sages, God willing. On the other hand, when they discover that there are things that can be permitted according to the letter of the law, but the rabbis were not sensitive to the travails and hardships of the Jewish people and leave these matters in their prohibited state, it will cause a terrible desecration of God's name, Heaven forbid. Ultimately, there will be an increase of outbursts saying about core elements of the Torah that if the rabbis want to permit it, they can; thus, the law will be perverted" (p. 126).

6. Soybean oil is produced without moistening the soybeans, so according to Rav Kook and most *poskim* it is not forbidden. Furthermore, it is questionable whether soybeans were even included in the prohibition of *kitniyot*, since they did not arrive in Europe until about 100 years ago. *Igrot Moshe* OḤ 3:63 writes that only what has customarily been accepted as prohibited is included in the custom. This is also the opinion of R. Dov Lior, the rabbi and head of the rabbinical court in Kiryat Arba.

   Regarding cottonseed oil, *Mikra'ei Kodesh* 2:60 is lenient, citing a ruling attributed to R. Ḥayim Soloveitchik of Brisk. *Sidur Pesaḥ Ke-hilkhato* (16:4) rules leniently in the name of R. Moshe Feinstein. However, *Minḥat Ḥinukh* 3:138 is stringent.

   Peanut Oil: We learned in section 4 above that in Greater Lithuania the custom was to eat peanuts, as per *Igrot Moshe* OḤ 3:63, since only items that are known not to have been eaten because of *kitniyot* are prohibited. Peanuts, which were discovered

Lecithin extracted from rapeseed and added to chocolate is not included in the *kitniyot* prohibition, though some are stringent.[7]

Chocolate and candy labeled "Kosher for Pesaḥ only for those who eat *kitniyot*" are technically permissible even for those who do not eat *kitniyot*, because the *kitniyot* in these products are added before Pesaḥ and are *batel be-rov*. In addition, these products generally contain *kitniyot* oils, which, according to several leading *poskim*, are not included in the custom to prohibit *kitniyot*. In practice, however, many people are stringent in this respect, and kosher certification agencies therefore label them as kosher for Pesaḥ only for those who eat *kitniyot*.[8]

---

later on, were not included in the original prohibition. On the other hand, *Mikra'ei Kodesh* 2:60 and *Ḥelkat Yaakov* §97 prohibit peanuts but permit peanut oil. This is also the opinion of *Melamed Le-ho'il* OḤ §88. *Seridei Esh* 2:37 also echoes this idea, and quotes that *Avnei Nezer* OḤ §383 prohibited peanut oil, as did *Minḥat Elazar*. Practically, if one is unaware of a family custom to be stringent, he may be lenient, since this is an unclear custom.

7. The Badatz is strict about lecithin derived from rapeseed. Halakhically there is nothing wrong with this substance; however, there are many uncertainties that mitigate toward leniency. Firstly, rapeseed is not a legume (the technical meaning of *kitniyot*), but a member of the *Brassicaceae* family of crucifers, whose fruit grips the stalk and whose seeds grow in pods, much like the mustard plant. Oil is extracted from these seeds. According to *Igrot Moshe* OḤ 3:63, we do not forbid anything that was not explicitly prohibited by custom. Additionally, it is debatable whether the status of *kitniyot* can be applied to the seeds of a plant when it is clear that the plant itself is not *kitniyot*. However, according to *Avnei Nezer* OḤ §373, rapeseed oil is considered *kitniyot*, just like mustard (although even according to *Avnei Nezer*, if one boiled the seeds they would be permissible, as explained in §533). Moreover, we already saw that there are opinions that permit oil produced from any type of *kitniyot*. According to *Maharsham* 1:183, rapeseed oil is kosher for Pesaḥ since the oil is extracted without malting the seeds, and we have seen that most *poskim* are lenient in these situations, akin to the case of sesame oil. Finally, the oil is *batel be-rov* before Pesaḥ. According to *Be'er Yitzḥak*, any oil that was added to a mixture before Pesaḥ is *batel*. Ultimately, when there are so many uncertainties regarding a custom, we rule leniently. This is the ruling of R. Mordechai Eliyahu, as cited in *Responsa Ama Devar* 1:62.
8. According to Rema 453:1 and MB 9 *ad loc.*, even if *kitniyot* were mixed in on Pesaḥ, they are *batel be-rov*, although clearly one may not do so *le-khatḥila*. In this case, the mixing took place before Pesaḥ, and not for the purpose of nullifying the prohibited ingredients in the majority of permissible ingredients, since they may be eaten according to Sephardic custom. Therefore, since they were *batel be-rov* before Pesaḥ,

7. EXTENUATING CIRCUMSTANCES, THE SICK, AND BABIES

Clearly, the Ashkenazic custom to refrain from *kitniyot* cannot be stricter than the prohibition against *ḥametz* itself. Therefore, in extenuating circumstances like drought or famine, leading halakhic authorities permitted eating *kitniyot*. In actuality, rabbis have often disagreed whether the need was pressing enough to permit eating *kitniyot*. Some rabbis were inclined to be lenient, others to be stringent, and still others to permit *kitniyot* to the poor alone, requiring the wealthy to buy other types of foods. On such matters, one must follow the ruling of the accepted local rabbinic authorities.

Some Aḥaronim write that when applying these leniencies to *kitniyot*, it is better first to permit *kitniyot* that do not resemble cereal grain, and only permit rice, millet, and buckwheat when there is no choice (*Nishmat Adam*). Additionally, some Aḥaronim state that when applying these leniencies, one should first scald the *kitniyot* in boiling water, since scalding prevents even cereal grains from becoming *ḥametz*. Even though in practice we do not permit scalding cereal grains on Pesaḥ, when it is necessary to be lenient with *kitniyot*, it is best to take precautions as much as possible (*Ḥatam Sofer* OḤ §122; MB 453:7).[9]

---

the mixture may be eaten on Pesaḥ. Additionally, R. Yitzḥak Elḥanan Spektor writes in *Be'er Yitzḥak* §11 (quoted in n. 4 above) that the prohibition of *kitniyot* does not apply to *kitniyot* oil that was checked before Pesaḥ. This is the opinion of R. Lior and R. Rabinovitch.

R. Lior also rules that string beans and fava beans in their pods are kosher for Pesaḥ, since in this state they are considered vegetables and not *kitniyot*. They were never included in the original prohibition since all of the concerns that were mentioned as the reason for the custom of *kitniyot* never applied to them.

9. *Ḥayei Adam* (127:1) permits eating *kitniyot* in truly extenuating circumstances, like if one has nothing else to eat. See also *Nishmat Adam* §20 and *Mor U-ketzi'a* (which assert that ideally the custom of *kitniyot* should be abolished altogether). *Ha-mo'adim Be-halakha*'s chapter on *kitniyot* states that *Teshuva Me-ahava, Ma'amar Mordechai,* and Mahariz Enzil maintain that one may not eat *kitniyot* even in an extreme situation. Conversely, Maharim Padua of Brisk (§48) permits *kitniyot* in extenuating circumstances. *Divrei Malkiel* 1:28 and *Sho'el U-meishiv* 2:4:158 rule leniently for poor people only. *Ḥatam Sofer* OḤ §122 does not oppose the lenient authorities but notes that they should require scalding the *kitniyot* before eating. *Nishmat Adam* §20 states that one should first permit *kitniyot* that do not resemble cereal grain, and only as

One who is ill and needs to eat *kitniyot* may do so, even if he is not dangerously ill. For example, one may swallow flaxseed with water as a laxative. One may likewise feed rice to children who need it (*Ḥayei Adam* 127:6), though special utensils should be set aside for this. Anytime one acts leniently, the *kitniyot* should be thoroughly inspected to ensure that they contain no cereal grains.

---

a last option permit those that resemble grain. MB states that one may certainly be lenient in extenuating circumstances and cites *Ḥatam Sofer* and *Ḥayei Adam* that scalding is required before eating. AHS 453:5 states: "They explicitly accepted that if there would be famine and the poor would be starving for food, all of the local sages, led by the chief rabbi, would permit *kitniyot* on that Pesaḥ."

Chapter Ten

The Principles of *Hagalat Kelim*

1. WHEN DOES TASTE ABSORBED INTO UTENSILS RENDER THEIR CONTENTS FORBIDDEN?

Though the walls of pots and other vessels appear solid and impervious, they actually absorb the taste of food cooked in them. Thus, if one cooks non-kosher meat in a pot, its flavor gets absorbed into the pot's walls, and kosher meat subsequently cooked in the same pot becomes forbidden, as the non-kosher taste absorbed in the walls is released and absorbed by the meat.[1]

---

1. It is impossible to measure how much taste the walls of a pot absorb and how much they release back into the food; some vessels absorb more than others do, and some tastes are more easily absorbed than others. Since this is a persistent uncertainty with no means of resolution, the Sages determined that one should consider the entire wall of the pot to be completely filled with the taste of whatever is cooked inside of it. Thus, if one cooked non-kosher meat in a pot and then cooked kosher meat in the same pot, we assume that the walls of the pot absorbed taste from the non-kosher meat and subsequently discharged the taste back into the kosher meat. And since our pots and utensils do not hold sixty times the amount that can be absorbed into the walls of the pot, anything that was cooked in a pot that had previously absorbed the taste of a prohibited food becomes prohibited. Even if one cooked another piece of kosher meat afterward, it too would become prohibited, since perhaps not all of the absorbed forbidden taste was released during the first usage and was released

However, there is a principle that anything which contributes foul taste (*"noten ta'am li-fgam"*) does not cause other foods to become forbidden. For example, if a bit of foul-tasting non-kosher meat falls into some kosher meat, the meat may be eaten since the non-kosher taste is foul. The same applies to tastes absorbed by vessels. Moreover, the rule is that any taste absorbed by a vessel becomes foul after twenty-four hours. Therefore, if non-kosher meat is cooked in a pot, and twenty-four hours later kosher food is cooked in the same pot, the latter dish remains kosher because the taste in the pot is foul, and foul taste does not render food forbidden (SA YD 103:5).

However, it is forbidden *le-khatḥila* to use a pot that has absorbed non-kosher taste, even after twenty-four hours have elapsed, because the Sages were concerned that one would forget and inadvertently cook in it **before** twenty-four hours have elapsed. They therefore ruled that since such a pot is forbidden to begin with, it may not be used until koshered (SA 122:2). *Be-di'avad,* if one forgot that the pot absorbed the taste of forbidden food and cooked another food in it, if twenty-four hours passed from the time the non-kosher food was cooked, the food in question remains kosher. But if one knows that a pot had absorbed a non-kosher taste, but cooks kosher food in it anyway, the Sages penalized him by prohibiting this dish for him and his family, even though the non-kosher taste in it had already turned foul.[2]

2. ḤAMETZ UTENSILS ON PESAḤ

Vessels used throughout the year with hot *ḥametz* foods cannot be used during Pesaḥ since heat causes vessels to absorb the taste of *ḥametz.* In order to use such utensils during Pesaḥ, one must first remove the taste of the *ḥametz* through *hagala* or *libun.*

---

during the second usage. In sum: in the case of a perpetual uncertainty where it is impossible to determine absolutely how much taste was absorbed and how much was released, we are stringent.

2. Most *poskim* maintain that if one intentionally cooked in a pot that required *hagala,* the Sages penalize him by forbidding the food for him and those for whom he cooked it (*Knesset Ha-gedola* YD 122; *Hagahot Ha-Tur* 26; *Darkhei Teshuva* YD 122:5; *Yabi'a Omer* YD 8:14; and *Hagalat Kelim Le-Pesaḥ,* second introduction, p. 17).

If one cooks in such a pot on Pesaḥ knowing that it had not been koshered, even if twenty-four hours have passed and the taste of the *ḥametz* has been befouled, the cooked food is forbidden. As we have learned, the Sages forbade such food in order to penalize people who deliberately cook in vessels that have absorbed *ḥametz* and have not been koshered.

What if one errs and cooks in a pot that was not koshered for Pesaḥ? According to *Shulḥan Arukh*, if twenty-four hours have elapsed since the *ḥametz* was cooked in the pot, the food may be eaten on Pesaḥ, because the taste of the released *ḥametz* is foul. According to Rema, the food is forbidden even though the *ḥametz* is foul because the prohibition of *ḥametz* is especially severe, for even a drop of *ḥametz* causes a food to be forbidden (SA 447:10; see above 7:5).

Ḥametz utensils that one does not wish to make kosher for Pesaḥ must be cleansed of any residual *ḥametz* and put away in a closed place so that nobody inadvertently uses them during Pesaḥ (SA 451:1; see also above 6:4, where we learned that such utensils should not be sold).

3. RELEASING THROUGH THE SAME METHOD AS ABSORPTION – *HAGALA* AND HEAVY *LIBUN*

The most basic principle of koshering cooking utensils is that forbidden taste is released from the vessel in the same manner that it was absorbed: "*ke-bole'o kakh polto.*" There are two principal media through which utensils absorb taste: boiling liquid and direct flame.

If a pot absorbs a forbidden food through a process of boiling – for example, if it was used to cook *ḥametz* food like pasta or porridge – the pot is made kosher for Pesaḥ by immersing it in boiling water, which causes the *ḥametz* taste to be released. The same applies to ladles and serving spoons: when used with *ḥametz* foods hotter than *yad soledet bo* (hot enough to cause the hand to recoil), they absorb the taste of the *ḥametz* and must be koshered through immersion in boiling water.

However, if a vessel absorbs *ḥametz* through direct heat of fire, without a liquid medium – such as in the case of a cake baked on a tray, dough baked on skewers, or jachnun or kugel baked in a pot – it is koshered by means of heavy *libun*, that is, heating the vessel by fire until it gives off sparks or becomes red hot.

Absorption through a liquid medium is relatively mild, so boiling hot water is sufficient to extract the taste of the *ḥametz* from the utensil. Absorption into a tray or skewer is more intense, as the heat of the fire causes the taste of the food to be absorbed deep into the very particles of the utensil. Boiling water is insufficient to remove all of the absorbed taste, and such utensils must be koshered by the same means that they absorbed – by fire. This is "heavy *libun*," in which the fire incinerates the taste that had been absorbed in the utensil.

To highlight the difference – *hagala* extracts the taste absorbed in the vessel, while *libun* incinerates it *in situ*.

Therefore, before undergoing *hagala*, a vessel must be cleaned of any residual food, because *hagala* releases the taste absorbed into a utensil but does not destroy the residual food stuck to it. There is no need, however, to clean a utensil before *libun*, because any food that remains will be completely incinerated in the *libun* process.

4. ABSORPTION THROUGH LIQUID AND ABSORPTION THROUGH FIRE – FRYING PANS

Even when a baking tray is coated with oil to prevent sticking, the absorption that occurs during the cooking process is considered to be by means of fire, thus requiring heavy *libun* to render it kosher. Only when the oil at the bottom of the vessel sizzles and bubbles is the absorption considered to be by means of a liquid.[3]

In light of this, most Rishonim maintain that a frying pan can be koshered through *hagala* (Rosh, Raavya). Even if the oil is used up and the food burns, *hagala* is sufficient since there was oil present at

3. This is according to *Pri Ḥadash* 451:1, quoted by SAH 451:36 as saying: "Since the dough is not sizzling with oil or fat, it means that fire alone causes the *ḥametz* to be absorbed." *Kaf Ha-ḥayim ad loc.* 139 cites them, and this is the ruling of *Yeḥaveh Da'at* 1:7 (although *Kaf Ha-ḥayim* 451:76 states that if there was enough liquid present in the pot to wet something that touched something that was in the pot ("*tofei'aḥ al menat le-hatfi'aḥ*"), the pot can be koshered by *hagala*; this requires further investigation). Accordingly, a utensil used to cook jachnun or kugel is considered to have absorbed by means of fire, since there is no sizzling liquid (see *Hagalat Kelim Le-Pesaḥ* 5:23 and the supplementary material *ad loc.*). If a pot is generally used to cook through a liquid medium but less frequently used to make jachnun or kugel, it may be koshered by *hagala* in extenuating circumstances, as will be explained below in section 9.

the beginning of the frying process, and the taste of the food absorbed into the pan was by means of the oil, i.e., the milder form of absorption. The same applies to a pot in which a non-kosher food was cooked: the pot can be koshered by *hagala* even if the food dries up and burns (MB 451:63; *Kaf Ha-ḥayim ad loc.* 137).

However, several leading Rishonim maintain that a frying pan has the status of a baking tray and must be koshered via heavy *libun,* because people often fry with small amounts of oil, and the oil is often used up, causing the taste of the food to be absorbed via fire (Rashba). Although there is agreement that a pot can be koshered through *hagala* even if the food dries up and burns, there is reason to be more stringent about frying pans because only a small amount of oil is used from the outset, and it often gets used up.

In practice, frying pans should ideally be koshered via light *libun* (as will be explained in the next section), although if twenty-four hours have passed since the frying of the forbidden food, *hagala* is sufficient *be-di'avad.*[4]

---

4. BHL 451:11 concludes that most *poskim* maintain that one may kosher a frying pan via *hagala,* and I have already mentioned the leading Rishonim on this topic. SA YD 121:4 rules that a frying pan generally requires *libun* to be koshered from forbidden foods, but for Pesaḥ *hagala* is sufficient. Many Aḥaronim (Gra and *Shakh ad loc.*) explain that regarding Pesaḥ R. Karo combines the opinion that *hagala* is sufficient with the view that *ḥametz* before Pesaḥ is considered permissible, and thus rules leniently that one may kosher a frying pan for Pesaḥ via *hagala.* Rema agrees in principle but states that light *libun* is the proper method *le-khatḥila.* Later Aḥaronim also disagree about this issue: *Pri Ḥadash* and R. Ḥayim ibn Attar require *libun* since *ḥametz* is considered a forbidden substance even before Pesaḥ, while SAH permits using *hagala* even *le-khatḥila.* See *Hagalat Kelim Le-Pesaḥ* 13:202.

   I have written that the preferable method for koshering a frying pan is light *libun,* and although apparently light *libun* is ineffective according to those who require heavy *libun,* there are in fact those who maintain that light *libun* is as effective as heavy *libun* (this may be the opinion of R. Avigdor, quoted in the *Hagahot Maimoniyot*). Additionally, some authorities explain that the principle of *ke-bole'o kakh polto* also applies to the temperature of the *libun,* as will be explained in the next section. Consequently, light *libun* is sufficient, since it takes place at least at the same temperature as the initial absorption. On the other hand, it is better to use light *libun* since sometimes there are small grooves or cracks in the pan which are difficult to clean, in which case even those who maintain that *hagala* is enough to kosher a frying pan would require *libun* to eradicate the residue in the cracks. However, one

A Teflon or "non-stick" frying pan, in which food is fried without oil, cannot be koshered for Pesaḥ. In theory it is possible to kosher it via heavy *libun* like a baking tray, but as a practical matter this will damage the pan (as will be explained below, section 7).

A frying pan used primarily for making malawach, which is baked and heated without sizzling oil, must be koshered by heavy *libun* since the absorption takes place via fire. But a pan generally used for other things and infrequently used for malawach may, in extenuating circumstances, be koshered via *hagala,* in accordance with its primary usage (as will be explained below, section 9).

5. HEAVY AND LIGHT *LIBUN* – DOES TEMPERATURE AFFECT ABSORPTION?

Heavy *libun* means heating a utensil by fire until any *ḥametz* taste in it is incinerated. One indication that *libun* has taken place is that the utensil undergoing *libun* becomes so hot that sparks fly from it when it is brought into contact with iron. Another indication is that its outer layer peels off, or that it becomes red hot.

Light *libun* means heating a utensil by fire to the point that a piece of straw or thread placed on the opposite side of the utensil becomes blackened from the heat. For example, to kosher a frying pan through light *libun* one must place the pan over fire and then put a piece of paper on the frying surface. When the paper starts to become scorched, the pan has been koshered.

Light *libun* is not effective where heavy *libun* is required, because the objective of *libun* is to incinerate any taste absorbed into the utensil, and this is only achieved through heavy *libun*. However, light *libun* is more effective than *hagala* because it is more capable than *hagala* at extracting the taste of *ḥametz* from the utensil, and apparently it can also incinerate some of the absorbed taste. Sometimes, when it is uncertain if *libun* is necessary, one may suffice with light *libun*. Light *libun* has another advantage as well: if a utensil has crevices that are difficult to

---

may rely, *be-di'avad,* on the majority of *poskim* who maintain that one may kosher a frying pan via *hagala,* especially since once twenty-four hours have elapsed since its last use, any uncertainty pertains to a rabbinic prohibition.

clean, *hagala* cannot kosher it, since *hagala* removes the taste absorbed into a utensil but cannot render kosher the residual food stuck in its grooves. However, if one performs light *libun* and aims the fire at the grooves, the residual food will be incinerated, and the utensil will be rendered kosher. Light *libun* can be performed by putting a utensil in an oven and heating it at the highest temperature for about half an hour.

It is worth noting, however, that some *poskim* rule leniently that a utensil that has absorbed *ḥametz* via fire does not necessarily require heavy *libun*. In their opinion, the principle of *ke-bole'o kakh polto* applies to the temperature at the time of absorption. Thus, if a utensil absorbed the taste of forbidden food at a temperature of 300°C, it can be koshered at the same temperature, and if the absorption occurred at 200°C, it can be koshered at 200°C, even though it does not become red hot or give off sparks at this temperature. According to these authorities, a cooking tray that absorbed a forbidden taste in an oven can be koshered in that oven at the same temperature as the absorption. The practical *halakha* follows the majority opinion, namely, that a vessel that absorbed taste via fire and reached a temperature beyond *yad soledet* must be koshered by heavy *libun*. However, in extenuating circumstances and when there are other reasons to be lenient, we take the lenient opinion into consideration.[5]

---

5. The laws of light and heavy *libun* are discussed in SA and Rema 451:4 and in MB *ad loc.* (see R. Pfeuffer's *Kitzur* SA, *Basar Be-ḥalav* vol. 2 ch. 12, and explanation 3 regarding the laws of light *libun*). However, it seems that according to R. Avigdor, cited in *Hagahot Maimoniyot* on MT, Laws of Forbidden Foods 17:5, light *libun* works just as well as heavy *libun*, but other *poskim* disagree. See *Hagalat Kelim Le-Pesaḥ* ch. 5 n. 3 that according to the accurate version of *Hagahot Maimoniyot*, even R. Avigdor agrees that light *libun* does not work like heavy *libun*.

SAH 451:16 and 19 states that in order to render the crevices in the frying pan kosher, one must aim the flame at them. See also *Taz* 451:8, which states that light *libun* causes the other side of the pan to reach the temperature of *yad soledet bo*, and see *Piskei Teshuvot* 451:18. The *halakha* does not follow this view; rather, light *libun* is when the pan reaches the temperature that would scorch a piece of straw on the other side of the pan, as Rema 451:4, MB 31 *ad loc.*, and other Aḥaronim explain.

According to most *poskim*, a utensil that absorbed taste by fire requires heavy *libun*, even if the utensil itself only reached *yad soledet bo*. However, there are authorities who are lenient, as noted above. See *Arugat Ha-bosem* §119 and *Minḥat Yitzḥak* 3:66. See also *Kitzur* SA *op. cit.* explanation 5 and *Piskei Teshuvot* 451:17.

It should be emphasized that absorption through fire can only happen while the food is being cooked by the fire on the flame. For example, if one cuts a baked good while it is on the burner, the knife absorbs the taste of the food through fire. However, if the baked goods were first taken off the fire and then cut, even if the baked goods are dry, the absorption is considered mild, and the knife may be koshered through *hagala.*

6. KOSHERING VESSELS THAT ABSORBED *ḤAMETZ* PRIOR TO THE ONSET OF THE PROHIBITION

We have learned that if a utensil absorbs a forbidden food by means of fire, it must be koshered by fire. It is important to note that this principle applies only when non-kosher food has been absorbed. For example, if one roasts non-kosher meat on a skewer, the skewer must be koshered through *libun,* because the non-kosher food was absorbed by means of fire. However, if at the time of absorption the meat was kosher, and only later became non-kosher, the utensil may be koshered through *hagala.* To use a classic example, if a *korban* (Temple offering) was roasted on a skewer, and the meat of the *korban* later becomes *notar* (the sacrificial meat left over when the time to eat the *korban* ends, which must be incinerated and not eaten), the taste absorbed by the skewer is also *notar* and thus forbidden. The skewer may not be used until it has been koshered, but it is not necessary to perform *libun. Hagala* is sufficient because the skewer absorbed the taste of the meat while it was still permitted for consumption.[6]

6. The basis for the distinction between utensils that absorbed permissible matter (*heteira bala*) and those that absorbed forbidden matter (*isura bala*) is explained in AZ 86a. The idea is that *hagala* releases most of the taste that is absorbed in the utensil. Thus, if the utensil absorbed forbidden taste, all of the taste must be eliminated from the utensil since the utensil became subject to a presumption (*ḥazaka*) of being forbidden. On the other hand, when the taste absorbed in the utensil was permitted at the time of absorption, there is no need to extract the weakened taste that remains after *hagala.* This distinction was subject to the discretion of the Sages since, after twenty-four hours, the taste absorbed in the walls of the utensil befouls the food instead of improving it and must only be extracted due to rabbinic injunction. Therefore, the Sages did not require this extraction when permissible taste was

Accordingly, if one mistakenly baked meat and then dairy (or vice versa) in the same tray, the status of the tray depends on whether twenty-four hours elapsed between the baking of meat and dairy. If less than twenty-four hours elapsed, the baked food is forbidden because the flavor of meat mixed with the dairy food. The tray also absorbed forbidden taste, and thus heavy *libun* is required to kosher it. But if twenty-four hours elapsed, the taste of the meat became foul, and thus the dairy food may be eaten. Moreover, although the Sages rule that the tray must be koshered, *hagala* is sufficient, because it did not absorb any forbidden taste. In practice, since people are accustomed to putting such trays in the oven, the best thing is to kosher it through light *libun*, i.e., by putting it in the oven at the highest temperature for half an hour, for we have already seen that light *libun* is more effective than *hagala*.[7]

The leading Rishonim disagree about whether the absorption of *ḥametz* during the year is considered the absorption of permissible matter, in which case baking trays can be koshered for Pesaḥ by means of *hagala*, or the absorption of forbidden matter. According to most *poskim* and SA 551:4, *ḥametz* has the status of forbidden food even though it is completely permissible throughout the year, since vis-à-vis Pesaḥ *ḥametz* is always considered forbidden and even before Pesaḥ it bears the name "*ḥametz*." According to this opinion, baking trays must be koshered via heavy *libun*. However, in extenuating circumstances and where there are

absorbed. According to this, we may only be lenient in a case of *heteira bala* once twenty-four hours have elapsed since the utensil absorbed the permitted taste. See also R. Pfeuffer's *Kitzur* SA, *Basar Be-ḥalav* vol. 2 explanation 9 for an examination of other explanations.

7. This law is explained very well in R. Pfeuffer's *Kitzur* SA, *Basar Be-ḥalav* vol. 2, ch. 2, based on *Responsa Rama Mi-Fano* §96 and *Ḥatam Sofer* YD §110. See also *Kaf Ha-ḥayim* 451:70, which lists the opinions and tended toward requiring light *libun* if it would not ruin the utensil, even though many authorities rule leniently that *hagala* is sufficient. See *Kitzur* SA (*op. cit.* ch. 12 nn. 7 and 10) for a discussion of the possibility of performing light *libun* in a pastry oven. It also seems that we can be lenient and allow light *libun* in an oven by factoring in the opinion that *ke-bole'o kakh polto* is a function of temperature, and the fact that the oven becomes an uncertainty about a rabbinic law after twenty-four hours. Thus, light *libun* koshers an oven even *le-khatḥila*.

other reasons to be lenient, the lenient position is occasionally relied upon (MB 451:28).[8]

7. UTENSILS LIKELY TO BE DAMAGED BY *LIBUN*; BAKING TRAYS

As we have learned, the objective of *libun* is to incinerate all taste absorbed into a utensil. To that end, the utensil must be heated to a very high temperature (more than 300°C). There are two ways to tell that a vessel has reached such a temperature. One is that the utensil undergoing *libun* becomes so hot that sparks fly from it when it is brought into contact with iron. The other indication is that its outer layer peels off, or that it reddens completely.

However, some utensils are likely to be damaged by this process. It is forbidden to kosher such utensils through *libun* because we are concerned that, in an attempt to protect his utensil from damage, the owner will not perform *libun* properly. For example, it is forbidden to kosher an earthenware vessel that has absorbed non-kosher food or *ḥametz*, because *libun* is liable to crack the vessel. Nor is *hagala* effective on earthenware vessels because their unique composition causes them to absorb taste but not sufficiently release it. The only way to kosher an earthenware vessel is to return it to the kiln, where it is impossible to protect it from the full force of the kiln's furnace. As a result, the vessel will either break and be lost or survive and be kosher (SA 451:1; MB *ad loc.* 13, 14).

Wonder Pots (an Israeli invention used for baking on stovetops) absorb taste though fire and therefore require heavy *libun*. However, since they are made of aluminum they cannot endure the *libun* process, and hence there is no way to kosher them for Pesaḥ (although if it was used to bake only simple cakes, one may be lenient and kosher it by means of *hagala*, as explained above in section 4).

Baking trays designed for domestic ovens become severely damaged by heavy *libun*. They lose their pleasant appearance and become

---

8. See *Hagalat Kelim*, 7th introduction, which lists the opinions of the Rishonim in detail. Among the stringent opinions are: Rif, Rosh, Ran, and Rashba. Among the lenient opinions: Rambam, Rabbeinu Tam, and *Or Zaru'a*.

warped to the extent that most people would no longer consider them usable. Therefore, they cannot be koshered through *libun*. There are, however, industrial baking trays that do not become seriously damaged by fire, and it is permissible to perform *libun* on such trays for Pesaḥ.

It is possible that one who knows that he will not care if his tray becomes warped and unattractive would be permitted, in time of need, to perform *libun* on such a tray. After all, every time *libun* is performed there is a risk of some damage, and the Sages only forbade *libun* where there is concern that the utensil will be completely ruined. When one will not be distraught if his baking tray is damaged, he may kosher it via *libun*. In practice, though, one should ask a competent authority what to do in this case.[9]

8. THE PRINCIPLES OF *HAGALA*

As we have learned, a pot absorbs the taste of the foods cooked in it. Cooking has the capacity to mix the tastes of different foods with one another, and just as cooking can cause the taste of meat to be absorbed by potatoes cooked with it, so too it can cause the taste of a food to be absorbed in the walls of the pot in which it is cooked.

There are, however, different levels of intensity in cooking, and the operative principle is *ke-bole'o kakh polto*. Thus, if the absorption is caused by intense cooking, the koshering process must be equally intense. However, if the cooked food never reaches the temperature of *yad soledet* (45°C according to the opinion that sets *yad soledet* at the

9. *Pri Megadim* explains (*Mishbetzot Zahav* §452) that one may perform *libun* on a utensil that might become partially damaged. *Sidur Pesaḥ Ke-hilkhato* 8:40 and *Hagalat Kelim Le-Pesaḥ* 5:6 and 13:315 state that one should not kosher baking trays using *libun*. Although it is possible to use baking trays that have undergone *libun*, most people nowadays prefer to throw them out. The question is whether the law is different for one who is unfazed by a warped baking tray (as per *Pri Megadim*). Perhaps someone whose baking tray became non-kosher – meaning that unless he koshers it he will have to throw it out anyway – may perform *libun* on it, for if he does not like the way it looks afterward he will simply throw it out. Some authorities rule leniently in this regard, but I am inclined to be stringent unless it is absolutely necessary. In extenuating circumstances, perhaps one may rely on *Arugat Ha-bosem*, cited in n. 5.

lowest temperature), there is no reason to be concerned about absorption, and it is not necessary to perform *hagala* to kosher the utensil.

The levels of koshering are as follows:

A *kli rishon* on the flame: The most intense form of cooking is that of a *kli rishon* (the vessel in which the food is cooked) on a flame, where the fire heats the mixture of food continuously, causing its different tastes to be absorbed into each other and by the walls of the pot. *Ke-bole'o kakh polto*: In order to kosher such a vessel, one must immerse it into the boiling water of a *kli rishon* on a flame. It must be emphasized that even if the water in the pot was not boiling when the non-kosher food or *ḥametz* was absorbed, it must boil during *hagala,* because the principle of *ke-bole'o kakh polto* relates only to the type of absorption – *kli rishon* or *kli sheni* – but whenever dealing with absorption in a *kli rishon* on the burner, the koshering must be carried out with boiling water.

A *kli rishon* removed from the flame: This refers to a vessel that was heated over a flame and then removed, or the flame was extinguished. Such a vessel still has the capacity to cook, and food placed in it will become slightly cooked from the lingering heat from the fire. Nevertheless, the heat continuously dissipates, as does its capacity to cook. Therefore, it need not be koshered in a pot of boiling water on a flame; it is sufficient to place it in a *kli rishon* that is no longer on a flame.

Liquid poured ("*irui*") from a *kli rishon*: This has the capacity to cook the surface layer ("*kedei klipa*") of a food item. For example, if *ḥametz* soup was poured into a bowl from a *kli rishon,* the taste of *ḥametz* will be absorbed by the surface layer of the bowl but will not penetrate its entire width. To kosher such a bowl, it is sufficient to pour boiling water over it from a *kli rishon.*

A *kli sheni*: This refers to hot food that was first cooked in a vessel over fire and then transferred to a different one. The *poskim*

> disagree about whether such a food can cause its taste to be absorbed into the surface layer of other foods or utensils. For example, if one places a spoon in a *kli sheni,* some *poskim* say it will not absorb the taste of the food in the vessel, and others say it will. Regarding all other forbidden foods, SA (YD 105:2) rules that although, according to the prevailing opinion, *hagala* is not required, it is nonetheless proper to do so *le-khatḥila*. Regarding Pesaḥ, however, SA (451:5) rules that *hagala* is required. Due to the severity of the *ḥametz* prohibition, the lenient position is not even mentioned (*Kaf Ha-ḥayim ad loc.* 20).

Some are even stringent regarding a *kli shlishi* and beyond, that is, utensils at least twice removed from the vessel in which the food was cooked, maintaining that as long as a food remains at the temperature of *yad soledet,* a vessel will absorb its taste and must be koshered – *ke-bole'o kakh polto*. However, most *poskim* are lenient in this respect. Nevertheless, because of the gravity of the *ḥametz* prohibition, it is customarily preferable to be strict about koshering any vessel that contained *ḥametz* at the temperature of *yad soledet.*[10]

---

10. A *kli rishon* on the flame must always be koshered in boiling water. Whether its temperature was just barely *yad soledet* or beyond the boiling point at the time of the absorption, all absorption in a utensil on the fire is treated uniformly and the utensil must always be koshered in boiling water. This principle is explained beautifully in R. Pfeuffer's *Kitzur* SA, *Basar Be-ḥalav* vol. 2. However, some authorities maintain that even a utensil sitting on the fire is subject to the standard principle of *ke-bole'o kakh polto,* meaning that if it absorbed taste at 80°C it releases the taste at the same temperature. See *Sidur Pesaḥ Ke-hilkhato* 1:4, SAH 451, and *Kaf Ha-ḥayim ad loc.* 82.

    Regarding a *kli rishon* not on the flame, most *poskim* agree that the koshering process must be done at a temperature of *yad soledet bo,* as stated in MA OḤ 451:7, *Pri Ḥadash* 452:3, and *Pri Megadim* 451 (*Mishbetzot Zahav* 9). However, *Sidur Pesaḥ Ke-hilkhato* 1:4 mentions opinions that the koshering temperature must be the same as the absorption temperature, so to avoid uncertainty it is best to kosher such a utensil in boiling water. The temperature of *yad soledet* is uncertain, somewhere between 45°C and 71°C (see *Peninei Halakha: Shabbat* 1:10:7), so to kosher a utensil, the water must be at least 71°C. On the other hand, if the utensil was used at a temperature of at least 45°C, there is concern that absorption took place and therefore one should be stringent.

9. WHAT DETERMINES THE TYPE OF *HAGALA* – MAIN USE OR MOST INTENSE ABSORPTION?

According to SA (451:6), if a utensil was sometimes used as a *kli rishon* and other times as *kli sheni* it is koshered based on majority usage. Thus, if it was used primarily as a *kli sheni,* it can be koshered like a *kli sheni.* Likewise, if it was sometimes used in fire, but primarily used as a *kli rishon,* it may be koshered in a *kli rishon.* And if it was sometimes used as a *kli rishon,* but primarily used cold, it can be koshered in cold water. According to Rema, on the other hand, the utensil must be koshered based upon its most intense usage, not according to its predominant use.

To illustrate, if a particular spoon is usually used to eat soup from a *kli sheni,* and occasionally used to stir food in a pot on the fire, *Shulḥan Arukh* maintains that it is koshered based on its primary usage, which in this case would mean *hagala* in a *kli sheni,* whereas according to Rema it must be koshered via *hagala* in a *kli rishon,* in keeping with its more intense form of absorption.

Rema's rationale is that once the utensil has absorbed the taste of foods in a more intense fashion, the only way to remove what has been absorbed is by koshering the utensil with the same intensity. *Shulḥan Arukh*'s opinion is based upon the presumption that the koshering of the utensil takes place more than twenty-four hours after its last use, at which point the absorbed taste is foul. According to the Torah, such a utensil does not require *hagala.* The Sages, however, required that any utensil that has absorbed the taste of forbidden food be koshered, out of

---

Most *poskim* maintain that a *kli sheini* does not absorb, but due to the stringent nature of the prohibition of *ḥametz,* they mandated *hagala. Be-di'avad,* if the utensil was not koshered and was later inserted into hot food, the food is not forbidden (MB 451:11). The vast majority of *poskim* maintain that a *kli shlishi* does not absorb at all. Even so, several authorities insist that every utensil, even ten times removed from the fire, must be koshered if its contents reached the temperature of *yad soledet* (*Pri Ḥadash*). See *Hagalat Kelim Le-Pesaḥ* 5:52. This is the *le-khatḥila* practice.

We should also note that the *poskim* disagree about the status of a solid food ("*davar gush*") at the temperature of *yad soledet*: According to Rabbeinu Yona, Me'iri, Maharshal, Shakh, and MA, even if it is in a *kli shlishi,* the food has the status of a *kli rishon* removed from the flame, since it retains its heat. Conversely, according to *Tosafot,* Ran, Rema, and Gra, the food assumes the status of the utensil that contains it. Regarding *hagala,* the custom is to kosher such utensils in boiling water on the fire.

concern that if they were to permit the use of such utensils after twenty-four hours had elapsed, people might misjudge the time and inadvertently treat leniently utensils that had been used in the past twenty-four hours. But the Sages required that such utensils be koshered according to their common use, and not their most intense use.

In practice, the custom *le-khatḥila* is to be stringent and to kosher every utensil according to its most intense usage. Furthermore, even if a utensil's most intense usage was *irui*, the custom today is to kosher all utensils in a *kli rishon* on a flame, in order to avoid a situation in which one has forgotten that a utensil was in fact used as a *kli rishon* on a flame. However, in extenuating circumstances, one may be lenient and kosher a utensil according to its primary use (MB 451:47; *Kaf Ha-ḥayim ad loc.* 100).

If a utensil was used primarily as a *kli rishon* and occasionally on the fire, even Rema allows koshering via light *libun* (MB *ad loc.* 48). If there is a concern that even light *libun* will damage the utensil, it is considered a *be-di'avad* situation, and one may kosher it in a *kli rishon*, in accordance with its primary use (*Kaf Ha-ḥayim ad loc.* 108).[11]

11. Among the authorities who rule leniently and allow one to kosher utensils based on main usage: Rif, Rambam, Ran, and Rashba. The authorities who require koshering based on the most intense usage are: *She'iltot*, Rashi, *Tosafot*, and Raavya. These groups disagree about *ḥametz* as well as other prohibitions. There is another reason to be stringent regarding *ḥametz* alone: According to Rema 447:10, even *ḥametz* that contributes foul taste (*noten ta'am li-fgam*) renders other foods forbidden; therefore, one must perform the most intense form of *hagala* on such a pot. On the other hand, regarding absorption that takes place due to fire, there is a reason to be lenient, namely, there is an opinion that a pot that absorbs *ḥametz* before Pesaḥ is considered to have absorbed permissible matter (*heteira bala*). We calculate majority and minority usage based on use with *ḥametz* that requires koshering; in other words, a utensil that is primarily used for cold permitted food and was used once for hot *ḥametz* must undergo *hagala* in boiling water. However, if most of the *ḥametz* usage was cold, as in the case of a table or countertop, it can be cleaned with cold water according to SA, even though it was occasionally used with hot *ḥametz* (*Ḥazon Ish* OḤ 119:15; and see *Hagalat Kelim Le-Pesaḥ* 4:8-17). Since we know that *Kaf Ha-ḥayim* (451:100 and 107) states that the preferable custom is to be stringent and kosher the utensil according to its minority usage, and Rema and MB also state that one may only rely on the lenient opinion *be-di'avad* (see SHT *ad loc.* 144 and *Hagalat Kelim* 4 n. 18, against the implication of SAH 451:28 and 33, that this leniency is only *be-di'avad*), I have written that preferably one should be stringent and follow the minority usage, but in extenuating circumstances one may be lenient. This is true according to all

10. CLEANING AND PREPARING UTENSILS FOR *HAGALA*

A utensil must be cleaned properly before undergoing *hagala*, for although boiling water extracts the taste absorbed in the utensil, it does not clean the utensil of residual food stuck to its walls. If *hagala* is performed without first removing food residue, it is completely ineffective; the utensil must be cleaned, and *hagala* must be redone.

If the utensil has crevices containing food particles that cannot be removed, the residue can be incinerated via light *libun*. It is best to do so before performing *hagala*, but the utensil becomes kosher even if it the *libun* is done afterward (MB 451:25; see *Kaf Ha-ḥayim* 160).

If it is impractical to incinerate the food particles in these areas because it will damage the utensil, one may soak the utensil in a mixture of water and bleach or soap for a short while (thus rendering the food foul and inedible), and then perform *hagala*.[12]

Pot and pan handles must also be koshered because when metal vessels are heated during cooking, the heat spreads to the handles, and if they reach the temperature of *yad soledet*, the taste might be transferred

---

customs. Regarding forks that are sometimes used in fire, there is an additional reason to be lenient and require only *hagala* – the fork that was used in the fire is *batel* in the majority of forks that were not.

12. Obviously, once the food residue in the crevices absorbs the taste of the soap, it is no longer edible and thus no longer forbidden (see also *Hagalat Kelim Le-Pesaḥ* 6:4). This seems problematic, though, as MA 451:5, *Taz*, and many other Aḥaronim state that knives comprised of two pieces cannot be koshered due to the food residue that is stuck in the groove between the pieces. They did not raise the option of simply befouling the taste of the food stuck in between. Perhaps a distinction can be drawn between the crevices that are near the food and grooves that are further away, like where the handle connects with the utensil (see SAH 451:21, which makes this distinction when *be-di'avad* one forgot to kosher the handle of a utensil). In truth, even the case of the knife needs further examination, since the reason for the rabbinic prohibition against using a utensil even twenty-four hours after absorbing prohibited matter is so that one will not mistakenly use a utensil within twenty-four hours of the absorption. However, the Sages did not include the food stuck in the grooves in this prohibition, and if this food is not fit for a dog's consumption, it is no longer considered *ḥametz*. Perhaps one need not take the words of the Aḥaronim literally; rather, they just meant to teach that when the utensil has nicks and grooves that may have trapped *ḥametz*, simply performing *hagala* is insufficient. This matter requires further examination.

to them. The handles of wooden pots must also be koshered, even though they do not become very hot, because hot food often spills over or splashes onto them, and they absorb the taste. Therefore, both the utensil and its handles must undergo *hagala* (SA 451:12; MB *ad loc.* 68). However, even if the pot itself absorbs at a heat of a *kli rishon* over fire, its handles can be koshered through *irui* from a *kli rishon,* because they do not absorb with the same intensity as a *kli rishon* over fire (Rema 451:12).

Many pots have handles that are attached with small screws, and food particles get stuck in their grooves. Therefore, before performing *hagala* the bolts must be taken off so that all of these particles can be removed. If this is difficult to do, one may soak this area of the pot in a mixture of water and bleach or some other harsh liquid cleanser in order to render the food particles completely befouled.[13]

11. THE REASON TO WAIT TWENTY-FOUR HOURS BEFORE *HAGALA*

It is customary not to perform *hagala* on a utensil until twenty-four hours have elapsed (and it is no longer "*ben yomo*") since the last time it absorbed a forbidden food. This is because the absorbed taste remains flavorful during these twenty-four hours, and if the boiling water is not sixty times the volume of the utensil, the water will absorb the forbidden taste and transfer it back into the walls of the utensil, rendering the *hagala* ineffective. But if twenty-four hours have elapsed, the taste in the utensil becomes foul, and the utensil can be koshered even if the water is not sixty times its volume. This is because the utensil releases a foul taste into the water, and such a taste will not render the utensil un-kosher, even

13. Regarding a pot in which one cooked prohibited food, if it is known that the pot did not boil over and its handles did not become hot, there is no need to kosher the handles. It is sufficient to boil water inside the pot, as will be explained below (section 13). Additionally, if the handles got hot but are attached to the pot with screws, they do not have to be koshered, since taste does not transfer from metal to metal. Similarly, if one accidentally put a dairy spoon into a meat pot, one must only kosher the section of the spoon that was submerged in the pot and the section that got hot, but not the rest. However, one must kosher the handles of a *ḥametz* pot, since there is a concern that perhaps during the year some *ḥametz* splattered onto the handles. Similarly, if one wants to kosher a *ḥametz* spoon, he must perform *hagala* on the entire thing; see MB 451:68.

if it is reabsorbed. The utensil is only rendered un-kosher if it absorbed positive flavor, in which case it remains un-kosher even once the flavor has become foul. However, if at the time of its absorption the taste was foul to begin with, the utensil is kosher.

Another reason for this twenty-four hour delay is our concern that meat and dairy utensils will undergo *hagala* in the same water. In such a case, the positive flavors of meat and milk will be released into the water, and if the water is not sixty times the volume of either the meat or the dairy, they will not be *batel.* Rather, these flavors mingle and then render all of the water forbidden. Consequently, any utensil that undergoes *hagala* in this water will absorb *basar be-ḥalav* (the forbidden mixture of milk and meat) and become forbidden. However, once the utensil is not *ben yomo,* the tastes of milk and of meat in the utensils is foul, and even if the tastes mingle within the water, they do not become forbidden, since *noten ta'am li-fgam* is permitted (SA 452:2; MB *ad loc.*). Accordingly, one must ensure that a large pot in which other utensils undergo *hagala* did not absorb the *ben yomo* taste of meat, milk, or *ḥametz.*

The common practice at public *hagala* stations is to presume that at least some of the utensils brought are not *ben yomo.* In order to avoid problems, a strong cleanser such as bleach or liquid soap is added to the water, thereby immediately rendering any taste released by the utensils foul. Consequently, there is no concern that meat and dairy flavors will mix or that the tastes released will be reabsorbed by the utensils, because once a taste has become foul, it cannot render utensils forbidden.[14]

14. These principles are explained in SA 453:1-2 and in MB 1 *ad loc.* One who wishes to perform *hagala* must ensure that one of two conditions is met: 1) the utensil is not *ben yomo,* rendering any absorbed taste foul and thus incapable of rendering the utensil forbidden, even if reabsorbed; 2) the boiling water is sixty times the volume of the utensil's walls, so that any taste released into the water is *batel be-shishim.* If many utensils are undergoing *hagala,* clearly the water will not have sixty times the volume of all the utensils collectively, so the custom is to kosher only utensils that are not *ben yomo,* lest the water have less than sixty times the volume of the utensils' walls (Rema 452:2 and MB 20 *ad loc.*). These rules pertain to any forbidden food absorbed into a utensil, except for *ḥametz.* Regarding *ḥametz,* SA 452:1 states that if one boils a *ḥametz* utensil before the *ḥametz* actually becomes forbidden, *hagala* is effective even if the utensil is *ben yomo,* and even if the quantity of boiled water is less than sixty times that of the utensil walls, since the *ḥametz* was permitted at the time of

12. *HAGALA* IN PRACTICE

The *hagala* water must actually be boiling, and this is a *sine qua non* with regard to utensils that have absorbed *ḥametz* as a *kli rishon* on the fire. As we have learned, the practice, *le-khatḥila,* is to perform *hagala* on all utensils in a *kli rishon* over fire.

---

its absorption. The only reason the utensil needs to be koshered is that it contains the taste of *ḥametz* in its walls, and taste that is released into boiling water and then reabsorbed into the utensil is not sufficient reason to require the utensil to undergo *hagala* again, as the reabsorbed taste is already twice removed from the original food (*noten ta'am bar noten ta'am,* or *nat bar nat*). One need only take care not to kosher *ben yomo* meat and dairy utensils together. Many questioned this ruling of SA, since in 451:4 it states that one must kosher utensils using *libun* if they absorbed *ḥametz* by fire, which means that SA follows those who maintain that *ḥametz* before Pesaḥ is considered "*isura bala.*" How, then, can it state in 452:4 that *ḥametz* before Pesaḥ is considered "*heteira bala*"? Indeed, *Olat Shabbat, Pri Ḥadash,* and *Bi'ur Ha-Gra* maintain that even when koshering a *ḥametz* utensil before the onset of the prohibition of *ḥametz,* one must ensure either that the utensil is not *ben yomo* or that there is enough water that anything absorbed in the walls of the utensil is *batel be-shishim.* This is the custom that is followed. (Perhaps, though, we can solve SA's apparent contradiction as follows: *Hagala* addresses a situation of *nat bar nat bar nat,* in which the taste is thrice removed from its origins. Thus, SA felt it was appropriate to rely on the lenient opinion. But in the *libun* case, the taste is only once removed from its origins, so SA ruled stringently.)

Regarding whether one may perform *hagala* on Pesaḥ: According to SA, it is permissible as long as the utensil is not *ben yomo*; merely having enough water is insufficient, since on Pesaḥ *ḥametz* is not *batel be-shishim.* According to Rema (447:10), even a drop of foul-tasting *ḥametz* renders forbidden whatever absorbs it on Pesaḥ. Thus, there is no permissible method of *hagala* on Pesaḥ. Only *libun,* which incinerates the taste absorbed in the utensil, is permitted on Pesaḥ.

Le-khatḥila, no other substance is mixed with the water used for *hagala,* as explained in Rema 452:5. *Be-di'avad, hagala* is effective in any liquid. MB *ad loc.* 26 states in the name of *Pri Megadim* that if Pesaḥ had not yet begun, one should re-kosher the utensil in boiling water alone. Nevertheless, in communal *hagala* it is difficult to ensure that everyone's utensils are not *ben yomo,* and since we want to avoid any problems that could arise from mixing meat and dairy utensils, the custom is to add soap or bleach to the boiling water. See *Sidur Pesaḥ Ke-hilkhato* 7:20, which states that the validity of the *hagala* only comes into question if the water becomes thickened from the added substances. In n. 7 *ad loc.* it states in the name of Ḥazon Ish that it is preferable to use cleaning fluids to avoid the potential problem of mixing milk and meat and to avoid relying on the opinion that *ḥametz* before Pesaḥ is considered "*isura bala.*"

The entire utensil must be submerged in the water for a few seconds.[15] Sometimes the immersion of utensils cools the water to the point that it stops boiling. In this case, the utensils should be left in the water until it returns to a boil.

If a utensil cannot be immersed in its entirety into the water, it can be immersed one half at a time (SA 451:11).

Furthermore, when immersing two utensils into the boiling water at one time, one should shake the utensils to ensure that the boiling water circulates between them (based on SA 452:3-4).

Common practice, *le-khatḥila,* is to rinse the utensils with cold water after *hagala,* so that the hot water does not remain on them and cause them to reabsorb the taste released during *hagala*. This is not essential, however, since *hagala* is normally performed when the utensil is not *ben yomo* or in water that has a foul taste, so that even if the utensil reabsorbs the taste of the water, it will not be rendered un-kosher (SA 452:7; MB *ad loc.* 34). Therefore, one should not rinse utensils with cold water if this is liable to damage them. Likewise, if for some reason it is difficult to rinse a utensil with cold water, one need not make an effort to do so.

Though some people have reservations about performing *hagala* on their utensils, the procedure is actually quite simple. In brief: First, one cleans the utensil and waits twenty-four hours after it absorbed forbidden food. Next, one immerses the utensil in boiling water. If it is possible to take it out and rinse it immediately in cold water, this should

15. See SA 452:1 and MB *ad loc.* 4, which state that one should not leave the utensils in the water for too long, so that they do not reabsorb what they released. On the other hand, too short a time in the water will not give the utensils enough time to release. MB states that it is difficult to ascertain the precise amount of time that is neither too quick nor too long. However, it states: "If one performs *hagala* before the time that [*ḥametz*] becomes forbidden, there is no need to be so precise, and one may leave [the utensils] in the water longer," since at that point *noten ta'am li-fgam* is permitted and the *ḥametz* is *batel be-shishim*. See *Kaf Ha-ḥayim* 452:2 which states that some Rishonim maintain that one should leave the utensils in the water until they have released what they absorbed, while other Rishonim maintain that one should insert the utensils in the water and then remove them immediately. Common practice follows the latter opinion, and *Pri Ḥadash* states, regarding this practice, that Jewish custom has attained the status of law (see *Sidur Pesaḥ Ke-hilkhato* 7:17 and n. 67). The prevalent custom is to leave the utensils in the boiling water for about three seconds.

be done, but if it is difficult, one may extinguish the fire under the pot of boiling water, wait for the pot to cool down somewhat, and then pour out the hot water, and rinse the utensil a bit in cold water. One may use any pot in the kitchen for *hagala,* provided that it has not been used for cooking in the previous twenty-four hours.[16]

13. KOSHERING POTS VIA *HAGALA*

We have seen that in order to kosher a pot used to cook *ḥametz* (barley soup, for instance), it must be immersed in boiling water. When the boiling water inundates the vessel on all sides, it extracts the taste of the *ḥametz* from it. Based on the principle of *ke-bole'o kakh polto,* it ought to be possible to kosher such a pot by simply boiling water in it, and the pot will expel the taste just as it absorbed it. However, during the course of the year some cooked foods certainly boiled over the sides of the pot, causing the absorption of taste along the pot's rim. The taste would not be released by water boiled inside the pot. Thus, in order to kosher such a pot for Pesaḥ, it must be completely immersed in a large vat of boiling water.

If one cannot find a vat large enough for immersing the pot one wishes to kosher, the *poskim* suggest the following: fill the pot you wish to kosher with water and bring it to a boil. At the same time, heat a stone so that it becomes scorching hot. When the water boils, insert the scorching hot stone into the pot. This will cause a lot of water to spill over the sides of the pot, koshering its rim and its outer walls.

This method is effective where a vessel has absorbed *ḥametz* through overflow, but if a pot was inserted into another pot and absorbed

---

16. The custom of Ashkenazic communities and some Sephardic communities is to avoid using *hagala* to switch utensils from meat to dairy and vice versa, so that one does not forget which utensils are meat and which are dairy. However, if a utensil became non-kosher and one koshered it through *hagala,* he may use it for whatever he wants (if it was meat before, he may use it for dairy and vice versa). Similarly, *Ḥatam Sofer* §101 states that following the *hagala* for Pesaḥ, one may change the status of his utensils. One who receives a utensil as a gift may change its status through *hagala* (*Darkhei Teshuva* YD 121:59). One may also sell the utensil to a friend, reacquire it, and then change its status through *hagala.* (*Pri Megadim* [*Eshel Avraham*] 452:13, states that in extenuating circumstances one may change the status of his utensils through *hagala.*)

taste, it has absorbed in a *kli rishon*, and *hagala* by the overflow method is not effective. Instead, it must be koshered through complete immersion in boiling water (SA 452:6; MB *ad loc.* 31).

It is difficult, however, to heat stones in this manner in domestic kitchens. Therefore, a possible alternative is to boil water in a small vessel, and when the water in the large vessel begins to boil, insert the small vessel into the center of the larger vessel. This will cause the water in the larger vessel to overflow and kosher its rim and outer walls.

If the pots have removable handles, it is proper to remove them and perform *hagala* on them. However, if the handles were not removed, and one cleaned around them with plenty of soap and then performed *hagala* on them, the pot is kosher.

Another problem is that many pots have a lip along the rim and on the edges of the cover where food sometimes gets stuck. The preferred practice is to heat these areas with a blowtorch in order to incinerate the residue found there. However, one need not be meticulous about this, because the pot goes through enough rinsing and cleaning with detergents to render the taste of any residual food foul and unfit for a dog's consumption, so that it does not even have the status of *ḥametz*. Therefore, if a blowtorch is used, its flame should not be directed at one place for too long, because doing so might damage the pot's nice appearance. When necessary, one who cannot perform light *libun* on this lip may suffice with *hagala*.[17]

---

17. We once examined the lip of a pot, and the substance contained in it was black, ugly, and extremely foul-tasting. Therefore, even without *libun* it is not forbidden. Similarly, whatever builds up around the pot handles is exceedingly foul, so even if one did not remove the handles, the *hagala* is valid. Nevertheless, to be on the safe side, one should rinse that area with a lot of soap. Regarding *hagala* on a large pot that does not fit inside an even larger pot, I have seen it suggested that one cause the water to overflow by pouring boiling water into it from an electric kettle that is still connected to a power source. My solution is better, though, since with the pouring method, the water cools down slightly, whereas in my method, the whole pot boils and becomes a *kli rishon* without cooling down at all.

Regarding milk and meat: Sometimes some liquid from a boiling dairy pot splashes onto a cold meat pot, and we consider the outer layer of the meat pot to have absorbed some dairy taste at the spot that was hit by the liquid. The way to kosher the meat pot is by pouring boiling water on it, and since we are dealing with a very

14. ABSORPTION THROUGH PICKLING

Utensils into which cold *ḥametz* has been placed do not require *hagala* in boiling water; a thorough washing is sufficient to kosher them for Pesaḥ. For example, beer mugs become kosher for Pesaḥ by means of a thorough washing, even though beer is *ḥametz gamur*, because as long as the *ḥametz* in a utensil has not reached the temperature of *yad soledet*, the utensil does not absorb the taste of its contents. Certainly, then, a cake plate used for *ḥametz* can be koshered for Pesaḥ with a thorough washing, because in addition to the fact that cookies never reach *yad soledet*, they are dry, and taste does not transfer to a utensil without a liquid medium.

But if beer is left in a mug for more than twenty-four hours, *kvisha* ("pickling," or the absorption of taste through prolonged soaking) occurs, and the taste of the *ḥametz* gets absorbed into the glass based on the Sages' rule: "*kavush ke-mevushal*" (pickling is akin to cooking). Therefore, it is forbidden to use such a utensil on Pesaḥ unless it has been koshered.

Utensils that have absorbed taste via *kvisha* can certainly be koshered through *hagala* in boiling water; if *hagala* is effective on utensils that absorbed via cooking, it certainly works on utensils that absorbed via *kvisha*. Moreover, since *kvisha* is a milder form of absorption, one may kosher such a utensil by soaking it in water for three twenty-four hour periods: First, one places the utensil in water and leaves it there for twenty-four hours. Second, the water is changed and the utensil is left there for another twenty-four hours. Then the water is changed once again, and the utensil soaks for a final twenty-four-hour period. Nevertheless, this method of koshering is generally not helpful because it is

---

small absorption, one need not even wait twenty-four hours, since it is possible to pour sixty times the amount absorbed on the spot. If one is concerned that there is not sixty times the absorbed amount, he may mix soap into the boiling water, which will befoul the absorbed taste. On the other hand, if the meat pot contained hot food when it was splashed by the dairy liquid, the pot needs to be koshered in boiling water. One should consult with a halakhic authority about the status of the food in the meat pot, since sometimes it is sufficient to have sixty times the amount of dairy liquid, while other times there needs to be 3,600 (sixty times sixty) times the amount of splashed liquid.

faster and easier to perform *hagala* with boiling water. But when dealing with utensils that are liable to be damaged by boiling water, soaking in water for three twenty-four-hour periods can be a very useful solution.

It is also worth mentioning that when it comes to alcoholic beverages such as whiskey, some *poskim* are of the opinion that the taste of the *ḥametz* is absorbed by the glass in a mere eighteen minutes. Thus, if one wishes to use such a glass on Pesaḥ, it must first be koshered using one of the aforementioned methods.[18]

---

18. See *Kaf Ha-ḥayim* YD 105:1 on the dispute among the *poskim* regarding the degree to which, vis-à-vis prohibitions other than *ḥametz*, utensils absorb taste via the pickling process. Some *poskim* maintain that utensils absorb taste via pickling to the same degree that they do via cooking, while others maintain that pickling causes utensils to absorb taste only in their outermost layers. *Kaf Ha-ḥayim* concludes that one may rely on the lenient opinions to prevent a significant financial loss. For example, if one cooked in a pot that had previously contained prohibited liquids for a period of twenty-four hours, one may rely on the lenient opinions that permit the food, since the amount absorbed in the outermost layer of the pot is not sufficient to prohibit the food. On the other hand, when not dealing with a significant loss, one should be stringent, following the many authorities that consider the food forbidden. It is clear that one preferably should not use utensils that have had prohibited liquid in them for more than twenty-four hours. Regarding the pickling time for a sharp food, *Darkhei Teshuva* 105:42 states that there is a dispute: some say it takes ten minutes (*Yad Yehuda*) and others say eighteen minutes (*Tiferet Yisrael*). It is also uncertain whether these times apply to absorption into a utensil as well. *Nishmat Adam* 57:10 and *Binat Adam* §59 state that, according to *Shakh*, even the taste of a sharp food is only absorbed into a utensil after twenty-four hours, while according to MA the taste of sharp foods is absorbed more quickly. Preferably, one should be stringent. See *Sidur Pesaḥ Ke-hilkhato* 6:5.

Even though an earthenware utensil that absorbed *ḥametz* during the cooking process cannot be koshered through *hagala*, if such a utensil absorbed the taste through the pickling process, it can be koshered through *hagala* or through soaking for three days, as per SA 451:21. See also MB *ad loc.* 118 and *Kaf Ha-ḥayim* 242, which state in the name of *Shakh* YD 135:33 that the leniency of permitting one to kosher an earthenware vessel that absorbed forbidden taste via pickling applies only to *ḥametz* and not to other forbidden foods.

Chapter Eleven

Koshering the Kitchen

1. COUNTERTOPS

Kitchen countertops are generally cold, but sometimes hot *ḥametz* foods or boiling pots from the stove are placed on them, and if some sauce spills on the countertop, it is absorbed at the level of a "*kli rishon* removed from the flame" (see 10:8 above).

In order to kosher a countertop, one must first clean it well, paying special attention to crevices and making sure that no food remains stuck in them.

Marble countertops should ideally be koshered by pouring boiling water over them while placing a scalding hot stone or piece of metal on them. By doing so, the water is brought to a boil and reaches a koshering level of a *kli rishon* removed from the flame. However, it is difficult to bring metal to such a heat in private homes, and doing so could damage the countertop. Therefore, the general practice is to suffice with pouring boiling water on the countertop. In this case, one should make sure not to use the countertop for Pesaḥ foods until twenty-four hours have elapsed since the last time hot *ḥametz* foods were on the countertops. Instead of pouring hot water, one may also cover the countertops entirely with oilcloth or thick foil in order to separate between the countertops and the Pesaḥ utensils.

Those who are stringent do both – they pour boiling water on the countertop and then cover it with linoleum or thick foil.

Fragile countertops, on which boiling pots are never placed, can be koshered by merely cleaning and pouring boiling water on them.

Some think that it is possible to kosher marble countertops by burning alcohol on them, but the koshering strength of alcoholic spirits is less than that of boiling water, and therefore boiling water should be poured on the countertop. Cleaning countertops with a steam cleaner is as effective as pouring boiling water on them, but where *hagala* in a *kli rishon* is required, it is ineffective.[1]

2. THE SINK

In general, the status of a sink is similar to that of a countertop, though in one respect it is less strict because it usually contains soap, which befouls the tastes of foods, and in another respect, it is more strict (if made of porcelain), because many *poskim* say that porcelain has the status of earthenware, which does not release tastes through *hagala*.

---

1. SA 451:20 states that one can kosher the tables on which pots are placed by pouring boiling water on them (and does not rule leniently based on the principle that koshering method is determined by main usage, which in this case is with cold food). MB 114 *ad loc.* cites Rabbeinu Yeruḥam that one must kosher such a table according to its most intense usage, i.e., a *kli rishon* removed from the flame. Therefore, one must pour boiling water over a scorching stone on the table, effectively koshering it on the level of a *kli rishon* removed from the flame. However, as we saw in 10:9 above, in extenuating circumstances one may kosher a utensil based on its main usage; in this case merely washing the table would suffice.

   Practically, even one relying on the lenient opinions should at least pour boiling water on the countertop or cover it with an oilcloth. Those who act stringently both pour boiling water and cover the table, preferring not to rely solely on a covering that may slide around. It is worth mentioning the concern raised by some that cheaper countertops made of compressed stone have the status of earthenware, on which *hagala* is ineffective. However, even earthenware can be koshered by merely washing it, as long as the majority of its usage is with cold items. Additionally, it seems more likely that compressed stone countertops do not have the same status as earthenware vessels; see *Hagalat Kelim Le-Pesaḥ* 13:1. Nevertheless, there are better grounds for covering this type of countertop. See also *Sidur Pesaḥ Ke-hilkhato* 8:2 and *Piskei Teshuvot* 451:44.

   See *Hagalat Kelim Le-Pesaḥ* 13:433 regarding koshering a countertop with alcohol. We do not condemn one who uses this method, as long as he cleaned the countertop well, since *be-di'avad* cleaning a countertop, whose primary usage is cold, with cold water is effective. Cleaning with the alcohol alone, however, is ineffective.

There are two accepted practices for koshering sinks. Those who are lenient clean the sink well and then pour boiling water all over it. Before pouring boiling water on a sink or countertop, it must be dried well, so that the boiling water touches it directly and is not cooled by any cold water on its surface. For this reason, one must first pour the boiling water on the sink and then on the countertop, starting with the areas closest to the sink and moving further away.

Those who are stringent, in addition to pouring boiling water on the sink, put a plastic insert in it or line it with thick aluminum foil in order to separate between the sink, which has absorbed *ḥametz,* and the Pesaḥ utensils. These people are also careful not to use boiling water in the sink during Pesaḥ.[2]

3. GRATES, BURNERS, AND STOVETOPS

Throughout the year, people usually use the same stovetop grates for both meat and milk, because even if some meat or dairy food spills onto

2. Its most intense form of absorption is as a *kli rishon* removed from the flame, since sometimes one places pots of boiling-hot *ḥametz* in it. One who wants to kosher it based on its most serious usage must place a scalding stone in boiling water and pour the water onto the sink. However, according to many *poskim,* a porcelain sink has the status of earthenware and cannot be koshered via *hagala.* In such a case, one must cover the walls of the sink with a plastic insert or aluminum foil. They are also careful not to fill the sink with boiling water, lest the taste absorbed in the walls of the sink become absorbed in the Pesaḥ utensils. Even if the sink is not *ben yomo* and tastes absorbed in it are thus foul, according to Rema 447:10 even this is forbidden on Pesaḥ.

Those who are lenient rely on SA 451:6 that we follow the main usage, which in the case of a sink is with cold foods. This method is thus effective even if the sink is made of earthenware. Additionally, according to *Knesset Ha-gedola,* porcelain is akin to glass, which does not absorb at all, and not earthenware. Moreover, since there is usually residual dish soap in the sink, any *ḥametz* taste absorbed into the sink would have been foul from the outset, so the sink would not need to be koshered. And even if we assume that the sink absorbed flavorful *ḥametz,* it would turn foul once twenty-four hours had elapsed. Even though according to Rema foul-tasting *ḥametz* is forbidden on Pesaḥ, the present case involved absorption that is, at worst, third degree (*nat bar nat bar nat*), and, as we have seen, MB 447:98 states that one may be lenient about foul tastes where there is no existing custom, and there is no existing custom about *nat bar nat bar nat. Sidur Pesaḥ Ke-hilkhato* 8:1 and *Hagalat Kelim Le-Pesaḥ* 124-127 write more about koshering sinks.

them, the flame incinerates and befouls whatever has spilled. However, people customarily perform light *libun* on such grates for Pesaḥ, because of the seriousness of the *ḥametz* prohibition (Rema 451:4; MB *ad loc.* 34). Alternatively, one may wrap thick aluminum foil around the bars on which pots sit, so that there is a barrier between the Pesaḥ pots and the parts of the grates that came into contact with *ḥametz*. *Be-di'avad,* the food remains kosher even if cooked on grates that did not undergo *libun*.

The areas of the grates that do not come into contact with the pots, the enamel cook top beneath the grates, and the burners must be cleaned well of all residual food. Since none of these parts come into contact with the pots, they need not undergo *libun* or be covered with foil. Generally, people turn on all the flames for half an hour.[3]

It is also important to know that throughout the year one should be stringent and refrain from eating food that has fallen onto the enamel cook top under the grates, because meat and dairy foods spill there, and the enamel becomes not kosher. If one knows that the enamel has been cleaned thoroughly and that no meat and dairy foods have spilled on it in the past twenty-four hours, one may eat what falls there. But when these two conditions have not been met, one should be stringent and refrain from eating whatever comes into contact with this enamel, because it might have absorbed the taste of meat and milk. If a thick piece of food

3. Throughout the year, we cook both meat and dairy pots atop the grate because taste is not transferred through dry metal. For example, if a hot meat pot touched a hot dairy pot, as long as both pots were dry in the spot that they touched, both pots are kosher. Similarly, even if the grate absorbed the taste of meat, once it dries the taste does not transfer to a dairy pot. Even if a drop of dairy spilled onto the grate in the same spot that meat liquid had previously spilled, the pot remains kosher, since the flame is constantly heating the grate, and whatever liquid had previously spilled on it has already been incinerated. Due to the stringent nature of the *ḥametz* prohibition, light *libun* is required but not heavy *libun,* since technically the grates need not be koshered at all. *Kaf Ha-ḥayim* 451:82 (citing *Ma'amar Mordechai*) concurs that *le-khatḥila* grates should undergo *libun*, but *be-di'avad* they are not prohibited. *Ḥazon Ovadia* p. 75 states that *hagala* is sufficient to kosher grates, but SAH maintains that light *libun* is necessary. I believe that covering the grates with aluminum foil is as effective as light *libun* and perhaps even heavy *libun,* since it completely separates the grate from the pots, so that even if some liquid spills, it would not connect the grate and the pot.

falls there, one may cut off the side that has come into contact with the enamel and eat the rest.

Electric ranges: Clean thoroughly and run on the highest setting for half an hour.

Ceramic burners: These look like smooth and unbroken glass surfaces on which pots are placed directly. They are koshered by cleaning and then heating on the highest setting for half an hour, based on the principle of *ke-bole'o kakh polto*.

4. OVENS

To kosher an oven, clean it thoroughly and run it at its highest setting for half an hour.

It is difficult to kosher baking trays. Because they absorb through fire, they require heavy *libun*, but since heavy *libun* will cause them serious damage, they may not be koshered (see above 9:7). One must therefore buy special baking trays for Pesaḥ, while the *ḥametz* trays must be cleaned and put away like all other *ḥametz* utensils. If one does not have Pesaḥ trays, he may use disposable trays. However, he must also kosher the racks along with the oven and cover them with aluminum foil, and only then he may place the disposable trays on the racks.

Ovens that self-clean at a temperature of 500°C need not be cleaned before koshering because such intense heat is considered heavy *libun* and is sufficient to kosher the oven for Pesaḥ.[4]

---

4. Some are stringent and insist that ovens cannot be koshered for Pesaḥ, due to a concern (present in older ovens) that crumbs would fall into the door of the oven before Pesaḥ and mix into the Pesaḥ food. The solution to this problem is to clean the door of the oven with a lot of soap, thereby befouling the taste of any crumbs stuck there and rendering them unfit for a dog's consumption. Others are stringent out of concern that perhaps food touched the walls of the oven, which would mean the oven would need to be koshered with heavy *libun* – impossible without damaging the oven. But most *poskim* rule that ovens can be koshered since the oven itself rarely comes into contact with food and only absorbs steam from the food. Light *libun* at the oven's highest temperature would certainly kosher it. Even if some *ḥametz* spilled and its taste was absorbed in the walls of the oven, we have seen that SA (451:6) permits koshering utensils (and ovens) based on the main usage. Even MB (451:48)

5. WARMING TRAYS (SHABBAT "*PLATA*"S)

Sauce from *ḥametz* food occasionally spills from pots onto the warming tray ("*plata*"), and since the *plata* is a heat source, the *ḥametz* is absorbed with the intensity of a *kli rishon* on the flame. On other occasions, dry *ḥametz* dishes (such as porridges, kugels, and quiches) fall onto the *plata*, which constitutes absorption through fire and must be koshered through *libun*.

A *blekh* (a metal sheet that is placed atop a gas range on Shabbat) can be koshered through *libun* if there is no alternative, even though it will warp and become damaged. But when it comes to an electric warming tray, *libun* is liable to melt the electrical wires and ruin it. Therefore, one must clean it, heat it for an hour, and then cover it with aluminum foil to separate the *plata* from the Pesaḥ pots.[5]

---

is lenient in such a case, provided that one performs light *libun*. We can also add the opinion that the absorption of *ḥametz* before Pesaḥ is considered *heteira bala*, for which light *libun* is effective even *le-khatḥila* (see above 10:6). Finally, we may factor in the opinion that *ke-bole'o kakh polto* applies to the temperature of the *libun* (see above 10:5), so heating the oven at its highest setting is effective.

With regard to baking trays, however, we are stringent and require heavy *libun*. However, if one conducts light *libun* on a tray, he may place a disposable tray inside of the multi-use tray, and certainly atop the racks. It is best to cover the racks with aluminum foil, so that if something spills onto them it will not connect the Pesaḥ tray to the insufficiently koshered racks. One need not wait twenty-four hours before koshering them, since light *libun* releases and incinerates the taste absorbed in the utensil. See *Sidur Pesaḥ Ke-hilkhato* 8:3, which treats this issue at length and explains the entire process of koshering an oven.

For ovens that self-clean at 500°C and incinerate all dirt, since they heat to a temperature that certainly would cause obsolete alloys to spark or redden (see above 10:5), this self-cleaning qualifies as heavy *libun* and koshers the oven. Baking trays may also be koshered at this heat, but manufacturers' instructions caution that leaving trays in such heat can ruin them. Consequently, they cannot be koshered by this method (see above 10:7).

5. *Sidur Pesaḥ Ke-hilkhato* 8:5 states that one should heat up the *plata* for an hour and then pour boiling water on it, since it has the status of a *kli rishon* on the flame. It is also good to cover it with aluminum foil. *Hagalat Kelim Le-Pesaḥ* 13:381 states that one may heat it up or cover it with aluminum foil. I believe that the primary solution is to cover the *plata* with aluminum foil, since it absorbs like a *kli rishon* on a flame and possibly even like a direct flame, whereas it is doubtful that the standard heat of a *plata* would reach the boiling point. R. Mordechai Eliyahu also writes that a *plata* must be covered with aluminum foil.

6. MICROWAVE OVENS

The common practice is to kosher a microwave oven in four steps: 1) cleaning it thoroughly of any residual food resulting from spillage or vaporization; 2) waiting twenty-four hours so that the absorbed taste becomes foul; 3) heating a container of water in it for three minutes (since microwave ovens absorb *ḥametz* via vapor that rises from food as it is heated); 4) placing something as a barrier between the turntable and the food that will be heated in the microwave, because *ḥametz* may have spilled onto the turntable.[6]

7. DISHWASHERS

The filter, where residual food often gets stuck, must be cleaned thoroughly. Then the dishwasher should be run at its hottest setting, so that any absorbed *ḥametz* is released, *ke-bole'o kakh polto*. Regarding the racks, *le-khatḥila* they should undergo *hagala* or *irui* with boiling water or be replaced. If it is difficult to kosher them through *hagala* or to replace them, one may perform *hagala* by running them through the dishwasher's longest and hottest setting.

In any event, one must wait twenty-four hours after the last load of *ḥametz* utensils before using the machine with Pesaḥ utensils.

Some take a stringent approach to dishwashers and consider them to have the status of a *kli rishon* on a flame. This means that to kosher a dishwasher one must put a white-hot piece of metal in it in order to

---

6. I have written in accordance with the currently accepted ruling. R. Mordechai Eliyahu rules that one must also take care to cover any food that he heats up on Pesaḥ. Conversely, R. Naḥum Rabinovitch writes that it is sufficient to simply clean the microwave and place a barrier between the turntable and the food. R. Henkin also agreed with R. Rabinovitch.

(The accepted practice for switching between meat and dairy use is as written above. Alternatively, one may hermetically seal all food, or at least one of the types [meat or dairy]. One may also use perforated covers, one designated for meat and one for dairy, every time he heats food in the microwave, which allows steam to escape but prevents it from going into the food. In either of these last two options, one must place a barrier between the food and the turntable. According to R. Rabinovitch, simply cleaning the microwave suffices, even if one did not cover the food.)

boil the water. However, those who follow the lenient approach have authorities on whom to rely.[7]

7. The highest temperature of the water in the dishwasher is c. 80°C. A dishwasher absorbs at the level of *irui* from a *kli rishon* (see above 10:8), since the water is heated by an element (the *kli rishon*) and then sprayed at the dishes. Thus, *ke-bole'o kakh polto* applies. Nevertheless, the custom is to kosher all utensils in a *kli rishon* on a flame; thus, *Igrot Moshe* OḤ 3:58 states that one should place a scorching hot stone in the dishwasher. When this is difficult, one may perform *hagala* using the mechanism of absorption, because most *poskim* maintain that one must perform *hagala* using boiling water only when koshering a *kli rishon* used on the flame; when koshering a utensil that absorbed via *irui* from a *kli rishon*, the *hagala* water only needs to reach *yad soledet* (see above ch. 10, n. 10). This is certainly the case vis-à-vis the dishwasher, which is koshered at least at the same temperature at which it absorbed. Technically, the racks may be koshered in this manner, but since they actually came into contact with food, some authorities ruled that they must be koshered via *hagala* in boiling water, or at least via pouring boiling water on them (*Igrot Moshe*). Additionally, some authorities consider the dishwasher to be akin to a *kli rishon* on the flame; according to these authorities, one must kosher the dishwasher at the intensity of a *kli rishon* on the flame. According to these authorities, one may only be lenient vis-à-vis the walls of the dishwasher, which do not usually come into contact with food, but not vis-à-vis the racks (R. Pfeuffer's *Kitzur* SA, *Basar Be-ḥalav* vol. 2, explanations 6 and 7). Notwithstanding this stringent view, the mainstream opinion is that the absorption was at the level of *irui*; therefore, when alternatives are difficult, one may kosher the racks inside the dishwasher. This is the opinion in *Hagalat Kelim Le-Pesaḥ* 13:225-228. Additionally, several authorities maintain that the principle of *ke-bole'o kakh polto* applies to the temperature of the absorption in a *kli rishon*, so certainly the dishwasher's highest setting is sufficient to kosher the trays (see SAH 451:25 and *Sidur Pesaḥ Ke-hilkhato* 1:4).

   Igrot Moshe maintains that if the body of the dishwasher is made of porcelain, it cannot be koshered (this is very uncommon; see also below n. 11 that there are those who are lenient, especially since the food does not touch the walls and it is likely that the dishwashing detergent ruined any taste even before it was absorbed. Thus, there is room to be lenient, as with a sink). See also *Sidur Pesaḥ Ke-hilkhato* 8:32, which rules stringently and requires one to use a white-hot stone to kosher a dishwasher. *Piskei Teshuvot* 451:25 states that there is concern about koshering plastic, as some *poskim* maintain that it is impossible to kosher plastic (*ibid.* 53). However, the mainstream opinion and the view of most *poskim* is that plastic can be koshered via *hagala*, plus this is a situation of uncertainty regarding a rabbinic prohibition, as twenty-four hours have elapsed since the dishwasher's last use. *Hagalat Kelim Le-Pesaḥ* 13:91 concludes that *poskim* maintain that plastic utensils can be koshered. R. Dov Lior is lenient regarding all types, as I have written.

8. THE DINING TABLE

In the past, people would kosher their tables by pouring boiling water over them, and some took the stringent approach of pouring boiling water onto a white-hot stone on the table, so that the koshering would be at the level of *kli rishon*. However, today's tables are more delicate and fragile, and would be damaged, warped, or defaced by boiling hot water.

Therefore, the mainstream approach is to clean the table well and affix nylon or paper to it, creating a set barrier between the table and Pesaḥ utensils and foods. In addition, a tablecloth should be spread over the nylon or paper, and it is a good idea to avoid placing boiling hot pots directly on the table.

One may kosher a tablecloth used for *ḥametz* by laundering it in a washing machine.

Those who wish to knead dough for Pesaḥ must prepare a different surface, because it is difficult to kosher tables for kneading dough.

A table on which no hot *ḥametz* foods were placed throughout the year must be cleaned well, but there is no need to cover it.[8]

---

8. SA 451:20 states that the custom is to pour boiling water on the tables, since *ḥametz* soup would sometimes spill onto the table. MB 114 adds in the name of *Responsa Mahari Weil* §193 that since sometimes hot quiches are placed on the table, it absorbs taste on the level of *kli rishon*, so one would need to kosher it with a white-hot stone. Additionally, it states in par. 17 that one must perform *hagala* on kneading tablets since dough is routinely left on the tables until it turns into *ḥametz*, making them comparable to a container for storing sourdough ("*beit se'or*"). Rema states that the custom is to avoid Pesaḥ use of tables that were used for kneading *ḥametz*, since they would need to be koshered via light *libun*. Rema also states in par. 16 that the custom is to kosher a *beit se'or* via light *libun*.

   It is clear that there is a difference between their tables, made of thick, strong wood that could withstand a koshering process involving boiling water and white-hot stones, and our tables, made of fiber board or plywood covered in Formica, wood veneer, or an alternative. Technically, when necessary one may follow the main use of the table, which is with cold items; therefore, SA states, "the **general practice** is to pour boiling water on the tables," implying that this is not an absolute requirement. Even according to Rema, who says that the koshering method follows the most severe usage, if the table is separated from the Pesaḥ food by a nylon or paper covering, there is no concern that the food absorbed in the table will pass through the barrier, especially if one is careful not to place boiling hot pots directly on the table, only atop a plate or trivet. Moreover, since our tables are more fragile, people rarely place boiling hot

9. THE REFRIGERATOR AND KITCHEN CABINETS

Because they are used with cold food, the only concern is that some *ḥametz* crumbs might remain there. Therefore, cleaning them is what koshers them. In hard to reach places where *ḥametz* crumbs may have gotten stuck, one must pour soapy water or some other substance that will befoul the crumbs and render them unfit for animal consumption.

When kitchen cupboards were made of natural wood, they often had cracks that were difficult to clean completely from *ḥametz* that got stuck there. Aḥaronim therefore ruled that the shelves should be covered with paper or cloth (MB 451:115). However, there is no concern that *ḥametz* remained in smooth shelves like those used today. Therefore, once they have been cleaned properly, they need not be covered with paper or cloth.

10. POTS, SKILLETS, SILVERWARE, AND NON-EARTHENWARE BOWLS

We detailed the laws relating to *hagala* of pots in the previous chapter. The principle is that intensity of koshering must match the intensity of absorption (see above 10:8), but the custom, *le-khatḥila,* is to kosher everything through *hagala* in a *kli rishon* (*ibid.* 9). Before koshering a pot one must clean it (*ibid.* 10). We have already learned how to perform *hagala* in practice (*ibid.* 12), and how to kosher a large pot that cannot be inserted into another pot (*ibid.* 13).

According to *Shulḥan Arukh,* skillets are koshered for Pesaḥ through *hagala,* and during the rest of the year they are koshered through *libun.* According to Rema, they are koshered through light *libun* for Pesaḥ as well (*ibid.* 4). Non-stick or Teflon frying pans cannot be koshered, since people fry in them without using oil that has been brought to a sizzle, which means that such pans require heavy *libun.* Since this procedure ruins them, they cannot be koshered.

Though eating utensils absorb principally as a *kli sheni,* the custom is to kosher them through *hagala* in a *kli rishon* on the flame. This is because the custom, *le-khatḥila,* is to kosher all utensils in a *kli rishon* on a flame. Even if one sometimes uses a fork in a pot on the flame, it

---

pots directly on the table, so the concern that the table will absorb *ḥametz* on the level of a *kli rishon* is more implausible.

may be koshered through *hagala* because it will be damaged by *libun* and is *batel be-rov* (as explained above 10:9 n. 11).

11. BLENDERS AND MIXERS

Electrical appliances such as blenders and mixers are occasionally used to mince and mix hot and sometimes sharp foods.

Regarding such appliances, one must follow the established principles and always relate to two problems: 1) *ḥametz* may have gotten stuck in crevices and holes; 2) the taste of *ḥametz* may have been absorbed into the walls of the appliance.

If such an appliance was used with cold, non-sharp foods only, there is no problem of absorption, but there is still concern that food particles got stuck in its crevices. It must therefore be cleaned thoroughly. If there are grooves in which food particles remain, the appliance may not be koshered; alternatively, it may be soaked in soapy water or in some other agent that renders the residual food unfit for canine consumption.

Mixers have holes designed to provide ventilation for the motor, so that it does not overheat. Flour and pieces of dough splatter into these holes, and there is concern that, when used with Pesaḥ foods, pieces of *ḥametz* will fall into the food. In order to kosher a mixer, one must open the motor compartment and clean it thoroughly, or plug up the holes completely. This rule applies to any appliance about which there are similar concerns.

If such an appliance was used with hot foods, and one was not cautious about *ḥametz* throughout the year, there is concern that it has absorbed the taste of *ḥametz*. Therefore, one must perform *hagala* on all parts that came into contact with hot food.

And if such an appliance was used with sharp foods, and one was not cautious about *ḥametz* throughout the year, even if the foods were always cold, there is concern that contact with the strong sharpness caused the taste of *ḥametz* to be absorbed by the appliance. One must therefore perform *hagala* on all parts that came into contact with food (see SA YD 96:1; *Kaf Ha-ḥayim ad loc.* 1).

If the appliance was used for kneading dough, according to the Sephardic custom *hagala* is necessary, and according to Ashkenazic custom light *libun* is needed (based on SA 451:17).

12. OTHER UTENSILS

Silver goblets: It is proper, *le-khatḥila,* to perform *hagala* on silver goblets used for *kiddush* wine and other hard drinks, because crumbs sometimes fall into the goblet along with these strong drinks, which, according to some *poskim,* causes their taste to be absorbed into the goblet after eighteen minutes (as explained above 10:14).

Plastic baby bottles: It is better to replace them because they absorb tastes at a level of *irui* from a *kli rishon*. When necessary, one may clean them and perform *hagala.*

Electric water heaters, urns, samovars, and hot water kettles must undergo *hagala,* because *ḥametz* crumbs may have fallen into them, causing their taste to be absorbed. *Hagala* in this case means filling the device to the top with water, boiling it, and then pouring it out through the opening generally used to dispense the water. Before *hagala,* it is good to clean out the stone deposits that accumulated inside. If one puts challah loaves on the lid of the urn to warm them before the *Shabbat* meal, *hagala* should be performed on the kettle and its lid.[9]

Thermos: After cleaning it properly, *hagala* should be performed on it. If this is difficult, pouring boiling water into it and around its opening is sufficient.

---

9. This matter is unclear. Since there is no liquid present and the challah reached the temperature of *yad soledet,* perhaps it should be considered to have absorbed the taste of challah as though by means of direct fire, meaning that the lid would need heavy *libun* – a process that it certainly will not be able to withstand. On the other hand, since there is no liquid present the taste of the challah may not become absorbed into the lid at all, just as taste does not pass between two dry pieces of metal. The custom is to be lenient, especially once factoring in the opinion that *ḥametz* throughout the year has the status of "*heteira,*" and thus *hagala* is effective where normally *libun* would be (see above 10:6) and that once twenty-four hours passed since its use, it becomes a doubt relating to a rabbinic law. However, since there was definitely *ḥametz* on the urn, the lid should undergo *hagala* in boiling water.

Toaster: This requires heavy *libun,* and since it is liable to be damaged in the process, it should not be koshered.

Kneading Utensils: Rema maintains that such utensils *le-khatḥila* require light *libun,* but since they are likely to be damaged, they should not be koshered (451:16, 17). According to *Shulḥan Arukh,* it is possible to kosher them via *hagala. Le-khatḥila,* the custom is to be stringent, in keeping with Rema's ruling (*Kaf Ha-ḥayim* 451:196, 263).

False Teeth: These should be cleaned thoroughly before the onset of the *ḥametz* prohibition. They need not undergo *hagala,* because people do not normally put boiling foods or liquids in their mouths; just as they are used for both meat and dairy when cleaned in between, so can they be used on Pesaḥ. Some believe that due to the gravity of the *ḥametz* prohibition, they must be koshered in a *kli rishon* or *kli sheni.*[10]

13. EARTHENWARE AND PORCELAIN UTENSILS

If earthenware absorbs *ḥametz* hot, even via a *kli sheni, hagala* is not effective. Although *libun* would effectively burn the taste absorbed in the utensil, the Sages forbid koshering earthenware utensils through *libun* because there is concern that they will crack (see above 10:7). If used cold, however, one may kosher them by washing them thoroughly. If a *ḥametz* beverage was allowed to sit in such a vessel for twenty-four hours, one may kosher it by soaking it in water for three consecutive days (*ibid.* 14).

China, clay, and ceramic utensils are considered earthenware.

Regarding porcelain which, though made like earthenware, has a smooth surface like glass, most *poskim* maintain that it has the status of

10. Among the lenient opinions are: *Responsa Beit Yitzḥak* YD 1:43:12, *Melamed Le-ho'il* OḤ 93, R. Zvi Pesaḥ Frank, and *Yabi'a Omer* 3:24. *Responsa Maharsham* 1:192 is lenient regarding meat and dairy but is stringent vis-à-vis Pesaḥ, insisting that they be koshered by *irui* of boiling water. *Tzitz Eliezer* 9:25 states that technically one need only scrub them well, but there are stringent opinions that insist on performing *hagala* in either a *kli rishon* or *kli sheini.*

earthenware, and there is no way to kosher it. This is the *halakha* (MB 451:163; *Kaf Ha-ḥayim ibid.* 305). However, some *poskim* believe that since the surface of porcelain is smooth like glass, it does not absorb at all. When there are additional doubts, their lenient opinion is taken into account.[11]

14. GLASSWARE

Leading Rishonim take diametrically opposed positions regarding the status of glass utensils.

According to Rabbeinu Tam, Rosh, Rashba, Ran, and many others, glass is smooth and hard, and even if it had been used to hold boiling

11. *Shiyarei Knesset Ha-gedola* OḤ 451, *Hagahot Beit Yosef* 30 states that the universal custom is to use porcelain on Pesaḥ even if it was used for *ḥametz* throughout the year, since porcelain is like glass which does not absorb. He was stringent for himself, as per the opinion of Radbaz, but did not rule stringently for others. *She'elat Yaavetz* 1:67 also permits it. *Pri Ḥadash* states that one may only be lenient if he has authentic porcelain, but nowadays, since there is much counterfeit porcelain, all agree that one must be stringent. This is also the opinion of *Maḥzik Berakha* 451:10, as quoted in *Kaf Ha-ḥayim* 451:305, and *Kol Mevasser* 1:80. This is the accepted custom. However, one may be lenient if there are other doubts, as explained by the Aḥaronim cited in *Hagalat Kelim Le-Pesaḥ* 13:368 and *Yabi'a Omer* YD 1:6 and 7:10.

When porcelain breaks, one can see that its inner texture is coarse, like earthenware, and its outer texture is smooth. There are also porcelain utensils that are smooth on the inside and coarse on the outside. It seems that if a utensil like this absorbed in its coarse area, everyone would agree that it has the status of earthenware. Nowadays, most dishes are made of tempered glass, which is sand-based and has a hard texture like glass, even though it is not always smooth as glass. I am often asked whether such dishes can be koshered via *hagala* if they were used for non-kosher or for milk and meat. In my humble opinion, these dishes should be considered like glass, since when they break one can see that they are made of dense material – like glass, not like porcelain. They thus have the status of quality glass utensils that can withstand the *hagala* process, as will be explained in the next section. Even the Ashkenazic custom is to be lenient when necessary to kosher such a utensil from forbidden taste it absorbed. To dispel all doubt, one should kosher the utensil with *hagala* three times (it is not necessary to use three separate refills of water), since according to *Itur* this would even work for earthenware. It seems that even according to the custom of SA glassware does not need to be koshered, since today's dishes are not so smooth that they should undergo triple *hagala*. (I have not mentioned any particular brand names since companies constantly change the composition of their products; I have referred specifically to utensils whose hard texture is similar to that of glass.)

hot foods, it does not absorb their tastes. Therefore, even if glass utensils were used with boiling-hot *ḥametz* throughout the year, they may be rinsed thoroughly and used on Pesaḥ. This is the position adopted in SA 451:26. Similarly, glass utensils may be used alternately for hot meat and hot dairy foods, as long as they are cleaned well in between.

According to *Smag, Smak, Mordechai, Agur,* and *Terumat Hadeshen,* glass, because it is made of sand, has the status of earthenware, which is also made of sand and which absorbs tastes but does not release them. Therefore, if one uses glass utensils with hot *ḥametz* foods, there is no way to kosher them for Pesaḥ. This is the position adopted by Rema.

There is also a third position, which maintains that glass utensils have the same status as metal utensils, which can absorb and release when boiling hot. However, since glass utensils are fragile and liable to break during *hagala,* there is no way to kosher them for Pesaḥ (*Or Zaru'a, Shibolei Ha-leket*).

In practice, many Sephardim follow *Shulḥan Arukh*'s opinion that glass utensils do not absorb and thus may be rinsed thoroughly and used on Pesaḥ. However, there are important Sephardic authorities who are stringent in this regard, Ben Ish Ḥai among them (Year One, Tzav 14).

In Ashkenazic communities, some follow Rema's stringent ruling while others adopt the middle opinion, allowing glass to be koshered via *hagala* on the grounds that today's glass is stronger than in the past and capable of enduring *hagala*. There is even more of a tendency to be lenient with tempered glass cookware (like Pyrex), which is fire resistant. Some rule that *hagala* should be performed three times on glassware.

In practice, Ashkenazic Jews do not kosher glass utensils for Pesaḥ through *hagala,* in keeping with Rema, and only under pressing circumstances rely upon the lenient position. With regard to prohibitions other than *ḥametz,* the tendency is to rely upon the lenient *poskim,* waiting twenty-four hours from when the utensil last contained hot food and performing *hagala* three times.[12]

12. Among Ashkenazic *poskim* who permit *hagala* on glassware if there is no concern that it will break are: R. Shlomo Kluger in *Responsa Tuv Ta'am Va-da'at,* third edition 2:25 and *Responsa Maharam Schick* YD 141. *Tzitz Eliezer* 9:26 leans toward permitting one to kosher glassware via *hagala* and quotes R. Zvi Pesaḥ Frank that one may kosher

15. ENAMEL UTENSILS

Enamel utensils are made of metal and coated with a thin layer of enamel for aesthetic reasons. The inside of the pot is usually colored white, while the outside is decorated with different colors. Enamel is made of sand like glassware, but it is processed differently. Great uncertainty arose regarding such utensils. At first, *poskim* were uncertain because the craftsmen kept enamel's composition secret. Then, when it became known that enamel is made of sand, uncertainly arose again as to whether such utensils have the status of earthenware.

In practice, the *poskim* rule that one may perform *hagala* on enamel utensils like all other metal utensils, and some recommend performing *hagala* three times. Yet regarding Pesaḥ, some instruct not to perform *hagala* on enamel utensils in light of the severity of the *ḥametz* prohibition.[13]

16. PLASTIC UTENSILS

Plastic utensils that have absorbed the taste of boiling hot food are koshered via *hagala* with boiling water, like all other utensils. This is true

---

tempered glass cookware for Pesaḥ, but should do so via triple *hagala,* since according to *Itur* triple *hagala* works even for earthenware vessels if twenty-four hours have elapsed since their last use. According to these *poskim,* even those who adopt SA's lenient ruling vis-à-vis glassware would agree that any glassware strong enough to withstand the heat of a *kli rishon* must be koshered via *hagala,* out of concern that these utensils may have absorbed taste at such high temperatures. This is the opinion of *Responsa Yaskil Avdi* 4:14. See also *Hagalat Kelim Le-Pesaḥ* 13:59 for a detailed list of the opinions regarding glassware and 13:375 for the opinions about tempered glass cookware.

13. *Responsa Ḥatam Sofer* YD 113 states that enamel is koshered via light *libun*. R. Shlomo Kluger rules stringently that one may not kosher enamel even via *libun,* since it might get damaged in the process (*Tuv Ta'am Va-da'at,* first edition §183). *Ktav Sofer* YD 78 permits koshering enamel via triple *hagala*. SHT 451:191 quotes *Ḥatam Sofer* and then states that many great authorities were more stringent in this matter when it came to Pesaḥ. This is also the view of *Maharsham* 1:53. Aderet rules that one may kosher such utensils via *hagala,* but out of respect for *Ḥatam Sofer* states that one should use triple *hagala* (which according to *Itur* works even for earthenware vessels once twenty-four hours have elapsed since they were last used). This is also the opinion of AHS YD 121:27. R. Mordechai Eliyahu states that one may kosher these utensils for Pesaḥ via *hagala,* and preferably triple *hagala*.

of all types of metal, such as silver, copper, iron, aluminum, etc., as well as utensils of leather, wood, and bone. It is earthenware alone that the *poskim* say cannot be koshered, because, due to its unique composition, it is very absorbent, but does not release all that it absorbs. And some *poskim* say that glassware has the same status as earthenware.

However, *Igrot Moshe* (OḤ 1:92) states that one should not perform *hagala* on utensils made of plastic or other synthetic materials not mentioned by the Rishonim, since such materials might be like earthenware, which does not release what it has absorbed. Nonetheless, the overwhelming majority of Aḥaronim agree that *hagala* is effective on plastic utensils, and this is the *halakha*. Utensils made of hard plastic are koshered through *hagala* in a *kli rishon* on the flame, whereas plastic utensils that are liable to be damaged in a *kli rishon* on the burner can be koshered at the same level they absorbed the *ḥametz*.[14]

14. Those who ruled leniently are: *Responsa Ḥelkat Yaakov* 2:163, *Seridei Esh* 2:160, *Tzitz Eliezer* 4:6, and many others. This is also what *Hagalat Kelim Le-Pesaḥ* states in 13:91. *Sidur Pesaḥ Ke-hilkhato* 9:25 assigns greater weight to the stringent opinions, and states that triple *hagala* seemingly works according to everyone (based on the opinion of *Itur* that triple *hagala* is effective even on earthenware vessels once twenty-four hours have elapsed since their last use, although it seems that one needs to change the water between each stage of *hagala*; see *Sidur Pesaḥ Ke-hilkhato* 9:25 n. 10). It seems proper to wait twenty-four hours, ensuring that any absorbed taste is foul, in which case *hagala* is only rabbinically required, and one may be lenient in a case of uncertainty about a rabbinic law.

Chapter Twelve

The Laws of Matza

1. THE MITZVA OF EATING MATZA

It is a Torah commandment to eat matza on the night of the fifteenth of the month of Nisan, as it says, "In the evening, you shall eat *matzot*" (Shemot 12:18). Even though the Torah also says, "you shall eat *matzot* for seven days" (Shemot 12:15), the Sages inferred, based on the rules for interpreting the Torah, that the Torah does not mean to command us to eat *matzot* all seven days, but rather that matza is the staple food that we eat on Pesaḥ instead of bread. However, one who wants to live off of fruits, vegetables, meat, and dairy products may do so.

The simple meaning of this is that one who eats *matzot* all seven days of Pesaḥ does not thereby fulfill a mitzva. This is what the Sages meant when they said (*Pesaḥim* 120a) that eating matza during the seven days is "voluntary" ("*reshut*"). Yet many leading halakhic authorities have written that although eating matza is obligatory only at the Seder, and indeed that is why the Sages instituted the special blessing over the eating of matza at the Seder only, nevertheless one who eats matza on the other days of Pesaḥ still fulfills a mitzva, even if it is not obligatory. In this view, the Sages referred to eating matza on the remaining days of Pesaḥ as a "*reshut*" only by way of contrast with the obligation to eat matza on the night of the fifteenth. According to this view, the verse "you shall eat *matzot* for seven days" retains its simple meaning. This is how Ibn Ezra and Ḥizkuni explained the verse, this is implied by a statement by Rosh, and this was the practice of the Vilna Gaon. However, even they maintained that the mitzva consists of eating a *kezayit* (olive's bulk) of matza at each meal, and that eating more does not add to the mitzva.[1]

2. *SHMURA* MATZA

The Torah states, "And you shall observe (*u-shemartem*) the *matzot*" (Shemot 12:17). The Sages interpreted this to mean that the matza must be guarded from becoming *ḥametz*. This refers specifically to the *matzot* eaten on the Seder night in fulfillment of the mitzva, for the very next verse states, "in the evening you shall eat *matzot*." The other *matzot* one eats on Pesaḥ are like any other food: they may be eaten as long as there is no concern that they may have become *ḥametz*. However, we have been commanded to guard carefully the matza used for the mitzva on Seder night from becoming *ḥametz*. Such matza is called "*shmura*" matza.

Ideally, the wheat that will be used for the *matzot* should be guarded from when it is harvested. It is customary to harvest the wheat while it is still a bit moist, for if it were to dry out completely and then get drenched by rain, it would become *ḥametz*. Similarly, later on the grains must be stored where they will not come into contact with water.

---

1. *Pesaḥim* 120a explains this based on one of the rules for interpreting the Torah, namely, that any item singled out from a class of items did not leave the class to teach a new idea only about itself, but to apply the new teaching to the entire class. In this case, the "class" is "you shall eat matza for seven days." However, the Torah says later on, "for six days you shall eat matza, and the seventh day will be a festival for the Lord, your God" (Devarim 16:8). Clearly, the "seventh day" was excluded from the general class in that there is no mitzva to eat matza on that day. This in turn teaches about the entire class – all seven days – that there is no mitzva to eat matza. Only on the night of the fifteenth, the Seder night, is there such a mitzva, based on the verse "in the evening you shall eat matzot" (Shemot 12:18).

   Most Rishonim and Aḥaronim do not mention any mitzva associated with eating matza during the seven days of Pesaḥ, implying that there is in fact no such mitzva. However, many Rishonim and Aḥaronim do actually mention such a mitzva, including: Ibn Ezra on Shemot 23:15, Ḥizkuni on Shemot 12:15, and *Responsa Rosh* 3:23 citing the Ge'onim that one does not wear *tefillin* on *Ḥol Ha-mo'ed* Pesaḥ, since there is already a "sign" on Pesaḥ, namely, eating matza. So states MB 475:45 in the name of Gra (*Ma'aseh Rav* §185). See *Ha-Seder He-arukh* I:78:7-14.

One may also fulfill the mitzva of eating *shmura* matza with *matzot* that were guarded from the time the wheat was ground into flour. As long as the wheat kernels showed no signs of becoming *ḥametz* and nothing has happened that would undermine the presumption that they are not *ḥametz*, one need not be concerned that they had become wet and became *ḥametz*. However, this is not the best kind of *shmura* matza since it was guarded only from the time of grinding.

In extenuating circumstances, when flour that has been guarded from the time of grinding is also not available, one may buy regular flour and fulfill the mitzva by guarding the dough from the time of kneading (SA 453:4). Even where it is customary to rinse grains of wheat lightly before grinding them, it is still permissible in extenuating circumstances to buy regular flour in the market, since a brief rinse is presumed not to be enough to cause the grains to become *ḥametz*. However, where it is customary to briefly soak the grains in water, one may not buy flour for matza in the market, since it is presumed to be *ḥametz* (MB 451:24). Therefore, in practice, one should not buy flour that is not certified kosher for Pesaḥ since the wheat is often soaked in water and may have become *ḥametz*.[2]

2. According to Rif, Rambam, and other Rishonim, the wheat needs to be guarded from the time it is harvested; according to Rosh, from the time that it is ground, since the mitzva only begins when the wheat encounters water, and the wheat was usually ground in water mills. The implication of Rosh's opinion is that as long as one grinds the wheat without using water, the mitzva of guarding the wheat begins at the time of kneading (MA 453:7). However, several Rishonim write that the wheat needs supervision from the time of grinding regardless of whether a water mill is used; among them are Rashi, *Shibolei Ha-leket*, and *Smak*.

According to geonic responsa cited by many Rishonim, if one neglected to guard the wheat from the time of the grinding, he may purchase flour from the market *be-di'avad*. According to *Berur Halakha* 40a, one may certainly recite the *berakha* over matza if it was guarded from the time of grinding (BHL 453:4), because according to Ran and many other Rishonim, the position of Rif and those who agree with him is that guarding matza from the time of harvesting is merely the best way to fulfill the mitzva. According to *Kaf Ha-ḥayim* 482:1, in an extreme situation one may even use matza that was only supervised from the time of kneading and recite a *berakha* on it. It seems that most *poskim* concur that *be-di'avad* one may use matza that was guarded only from the time of kneading.

In practice, today's custom is to be scrupulous about *shmura* matza; *matzot* that have been guarded from the time of harvest are used to fulfill the mitzva of eating matza on the Seder night. This practice has taken root so thoroughly that people have come to call matza that has been guarded only from the time of grinding "non-*shmura* matza," even though it is considered *shmura* halakhically, and one may use it to fulfill the mitzva of eating matza.

3. DOES THE GUARDING HAVE TO BE WITH THE INTENT TO FULFILL A MITZVA?

Guarding the *matzot* to be used for fulfilling the mitzva of eating matza on the Seder night has two implications: being extra vigilant to prevent it from becoming *ḥametz* and having the intention that the matza is to be used for the mitzva ("*le-shem matzat mitzva*"). It is therefore necessary that the matza be kneaded and baked by Jews who are halakhic adults, who can be relied upon both to guard against fermentation and to keep in mind that their actions are for the sake of *matzat mitzva*. One may not employ gentiles, minors, or mentally unfit workers to knead or bake matza, since they cannot be relied upon to have the proper intent (*She'iltot*, Rashba).

Some dispute the second implication above. In their opinion, the mitzva of guarding the matza requires extra vigilance to prevent the *matzat mitzva* from becoming *ḥametz*, but requires no special intent while doing it. Thus, gentiles and minors are fit to bake *matzat mitzva*, as long as an adult Jew supervises their work, ensuring that they work with alacrity and that the dough does not become *ḥametz* (Ra'ah).

Tur and *Beit Yosef* state that according to Rif, Rabbeinu Yeruḥam, Ran, and *Magid Mishneh*, the need to guard the matza pertains only to the matza used to fulfill the mitzva on the first night of Pesaḥ. All other matza eaten on Pesaḥ need not be guarded (MB 453:21). (Others maintain that one must use *shmura* matza for the entire holiday, either out of concern that non-*shmura* matza will become *ḥametz* or because they believe that there is a mitzva to eat *shmura* matza all Pesaḥ; see below, section 5.) According to *Baḥ* and those who agree with him, the need to guard the matza is rabbinic in origin, and the rabbis merely supported their enactment using a verse from the Torah. However, according to most *poskim*, this mitzva is from the Torah (BHL 460:1 s.v. "ein", citing Rashba, *Pri Ḥadash*, and other Rishonim and Aḥaronim).

In practice, at the time of kneading one should take care to fulfill both meanings of "guarding." Thus, one must insist that Jews knead and bake the *matzat mitzva,* taking care that the dough does not become *ḥametz* and intending that the matza be for the sake of the mitzva. However, at the time of harvesting and grinding, the first meaning is sufficient. Thus, the wheat may be harvested and ground by gentiles as long as a Jew stands nearby and supervises their work, ensuring that it does not become *ḥametz* (SA 460:1; MB and SHT 4 *ad loc.*).[3]

Le-khatḥila, one should say out loud, when starting to work on *matzot,* that all the work is being done for the sake of producing *matzat mitzva; be-di'avad,* it is sufficient that he thought it (BHL 460:1, based

3. According to most *poskim,* there are two implications of guarding the wheat: ensuring that it does not become *ḥametz* and intending that it is for *matzat mitzva.* According to Ra'ah, there is only one purpose: ensuring that it does not become *ḥametz.* According to R. Hai Gaon and others, it is indeed necessary to intend to use the wheat for the mitzva, but if a Jew supervises a gentile or child and instructs him to knead the dough specifically *le-shem matzat mitzva,* we may rely on this for proper intent. SA 460:1 follows the view of most *poskim* that the mitzva of guarding the wheat requires both aspects. Therefore, one may not use matza that was kneaded or baked by a gentile (MB 460:3, SHT *ad loc.*).

According to *Baḥ* and *Eliya Rabba,* those who believe that the guarding must begin at the time of the harvest (see the previous section) also require a Jew to harvest and grind the wheat *le-shem matzat mitzva.* Some are meticulous about this in practice. (According to those who maintain that turning on a machine does not constitute proper intent – see the next section – the harvesting and grinding must be done by hand, not with agricultural machinery; very few people insist on this.)

Taz explains that the harvesting and grinding need not be done with the intention to use the wheat for a mitzva; therefore, one may have a gentile harvest and grind the wheat, provided that a Jew supervises and ensures that the wheat does not become *ḥametz.* Intentions to use the wheat for the mitzva are only necessary from the time of kneading; therefore, a Jew must be the one to knead and bake the matza (according to most *poskim*). Consequently, SA 460:1 rules that gentiles may not perform the kneading or baking of the matza. BHL 460:1 s.v. "ein" states that the universal custom is to be lenient in accordance with *Taz* to allow gentiles to harvest and grind the wheat under the supervision of a Jew. This is also the opinion of *Ḥok Yaakov* and SAH 453:16. Matza that is made this way is called "*shmura mi-she'at ketzira*" – supervised from the time of the harvest. See *Hilkhot Ḥag Be-ḥag* 16 n. 19, which beautifully explains *Taz* to mean that there are two types of guarding.

on *Pri Megadim*). He should also have in mind that it is for the *matzat mitzva* that one eats on Seder night, but if he had in mind that it is for matza for Pesaḥ, he has fulfilled the obligation (SAH 453:14).

4. HANDMADE VERSUS MACHINE-MADE MATZA AT THE SEDER

A great dispute has raged among *poskim* ever since the invention of matza-baking machines. The dispute centers on two principal questions: 1) Is there indeed no concern that machine-made *matzot* may become *ḥametz*? 2) Can one use them to fulfill the mitzva of eating matza on the Seder night?

Concerning the question of *ḥametz*, it is agreed that everything depends on the nature of the machine and on its supervision. As long as there are *kashrut* supervisors who ensure that there is no risk of *ḥametz*, the *matzot* are kosher for Pesaḥ. Thus even the most pious and God-fearing Jews eat machine-made *matzot* on Pesaḥ.

The second question, however, is still debated. Some say that the mitzva of guarding the matza requires that the entire process of kneading and baking be done with explicit intent that they are *le-shem matzat mitzva*, and since a machine cannot have intentions, one would not fulfill the mitzva of eating matza on the Seder night with machine-made matza.

Most *poskim* maintain that one can fulfill the mitzva by eating machine-made *matzot*, for several reasons. Firstly, some explain that the mitzva of guarding the matza only requires one to ensure that it does not become *ḥametz*, and it is irrelevant whether this is done while making the matza by hand or by supervising the activity of a machine. Furthermore, a human being operates the machine, and if he operates it with the intent of making *matzat mitzva*, then automatically all of the machine's operations are considered to have been done for the sake of the mitzva.

In practice, machine-made matza may be used to fulfill the mitzva of eating matza on the Seder night. Many are scrupulous about fulfilling the mitzva with handmade *matzot* that were baked under proper supervision, although even they concede that it is not necessary to eat handmade *matzot* throughout the Seder meal. Rather, they beautify the mitzva by eating handmade matza for those *kezayit* quantities that constitute the mitzva (see below 16:22-25).[4]

4. See R. Harari's *Mikra'ei Kodesh* pp. 326-335 for a summary of the opinions. Originally, the machines were operated with more human input, which caused concerns of *ḥametz* and of breaking from tradition. After the machines were enhanced and improved, these concerns abated, but the concern that operating the machine does not constitute intent remained and was even magnified. Among those who prohibit machine matza are: R. Shlomo Kluger, R. Ḥayim Halberstam (the Sanzer Rebbe, author of *Divrei Ḥayim*), R. Yitzḥak Meir Alter (the Gerrer Rebbe, author of *Ḥidushei Ha-Rim*), R. Avraham Bornstein of Sochatchov (author of *Avnei Nezer*), and most of the great Ḥasidic leaders. Even today, most Ḥasidic *poskim* tend to dismiss machine-made matza. Among those who permit are: the authors of *Sho'el U-meishiv, Tiferet Yisrael, Ktav Sofer,* and *Arukh Le-ner*. Some *poskim* even prefer machine matza to handmade matza, since there is less of a chance of the machine matza becoming *ḥametz*. This is the opinion of R. Meir Simḥa of Dvinsk (author of *Or Same'aḥ*) and R. Shmuel Salant, the head of the Jerusalem rabbinical court, who personally ate machine matza as did the Lithuanian community in old Jerusalem. The main reason for preferring machine matza is that the most important dimension of guarding the matza is to ensure that it does not become *ḥametz*, and based on what they saw, machine matza was less likely to become *ḥametz*. R. Zvi Pesaḥ Frank, cited in *Mikra'ei Kodesh* 2:3, states that since gentiles and children are intelligent, a supervising Jew cannot supply proper intent on their behalf while they knead. A machine, on the other hand, has no intelligence, so the intent of the Jew operating the machine is effective. Thus, my teacher R. Zvi Yehuda Kook would eat machine-made matza at the Seder. R. Min-Hahar and R. Messas also preferred machine-made matza. R. Shaul Yisraeli stated that there is no preference for handmade matza over machine-made matza. According to R. Mordechai Eliyahu, even though one may recite the *berakha* over machine-made matza, handmade matza is preferable. (*Responsa Oneg Yom Tov* OḤ 42 explains that even though the mitzva to guard the matza is from the Torah, if for some reason one does not have matza that was guarded for the sake of the mitzva, he still has a Torah obligation to eat matza on the Seder night, presumably with a *berakha*, even though he has not fulfilled the mitzva of guarding the matza.)

I have written that using handmade matza enhances the mitzva based on my father's reasoning. He explained that many things changed over the past few decades: the machines are more automated than ever, and it is thus questionable whether there is proper intent. Perhaps in the past, when more human input was necessary to operate the machinery, this problem was less of a concern, but today the machines operate at the touch of a button. Moreover, when all of the matza was handmade, there was a concern that the pressure to supply matza to the entire nation meant that matza bakers would not be sufficiently meticulous in their efforts to keep the matza from becoming *ḥametz*. The machines were a great solution to that issue. Nowadays, on the other hand, most handmade matza factories are extraordinarily scrupulous, to

5. IS THERE VALUE IN EATING HANDMADE *MATZOT* ALL PESAḤ?

The mitzva of guarding the *matzot* was stated about the *matzat mitzva* we are commanded to eat on the night of the fifteenth of Nisan. The idea is to honor the mitzva by guarding them especially carefully. In other words, *matzot* that were not guarded but about which there is no concern that they may have become *ḥametz* may be eaten on Pesaḥ. They are just not fit for use as *matzot mitzva* since they were not guarded specifically for that purpose.

Thus, throughout Pesaḥ, it is permissible to eat matza that is kosher for Pesaḥ, even if it is not *shmura*.

Nevertheless, some are meticulous about eating *shmura* matza throughout Pesaḥ. There are two reasons for this: one is that some *poskim* maintain that while there is no duty to eat *matzot* throughout Pesaḥ, one who does so fulfills a mitzva; therefore, one should eat *shmura* matza. According to this, it is sufficient to eat a *kezayit* of *shmura* matza at every meal. Similarly, it is sufficient to use our regular *matzot* (not labeled as *shmura*), which have been guarded from the time of grinding, because, as we have learned, one can fulfill the requirement for *matzat mitzva* with matza that has been guarded from the time of grinding.

The second reason for eating *shmura* matza is concern about *ḥametz*. Out of all the foods we eat on Pesaḥ, matza is the likeliest to become *ḥametz*. Therefore, if the wheat grains are not guarded from harvest time, there is concern that they may have become *ḥametz*. Thus, there is good reason to be stringent and to eat only matza that has been guarded from harvest time.

Today, the advantage of *matzot* that have been guarded from harvest time is not only in their having been protected from contact with water since the grain was harvested. In general, much more care is taken

---

the point that the situation may have been reversed, and handmade matza is actually less likely to become *ḥametz* than is machine-made matza. Even though there is a consensus that the intent of the machine operator or the *kashrut* supervisor is sufficient, having the proper intent throughout the process (as is the case with handmade matza) enhances the mitzva. This is especially true if one bakes his own matza, since it is always better for one to fulfill a mitzva on his own rather than through an agent (this is indeed my father's custom – to bake his own *matzot mitzva*).

throughout their entire manufacturing process. For example, the baking machines are stopped every eighteen minutes for a thorough cleaning. Thus these *matzot* benefit from a whole series of enhancements.

In sum, regular *matzot*, which have been guarded from the time of the grinding, are kosher for all of Pesaḥ, *le-khatḥila*. Even those who maintain that there is a mitzva to eat matza throughout the seven days of Pesaḥ agree that one fulfills the mitzva with such *matzot*. Those who are more scrupulous eat *matzot* that have been guarded from harvest time, primarily because these *matzot* are more carefully guarded against becoming *ḥametz*.[5]

---

5. The custom of the Vilna Gaon was to eat *shmura* matza the entire Pesaḥ for two reasons. Firstly, he maintained that there is a mitzva to eat *shmura* matza all seven days, but in this regard he reasoned that it only needs to be supervised from the time of kneading. Secondly, he was concerned about *ḥametz*, and, accordingly, supervision would be necessary from the time of harvesting. This is quoted in BHL 453:4. AHS 453:20-23 states that according to Rif and Rambam, there is a rabbinic mitzva to guard the matza from the time of harvesting to prevent it from becoming *ḥametz*; accordingly, this applies to all matza that one eats over Pesaḥ. However, according to most *poskim* one need not eat matza that was supervised from the time of harvesting, and this is the implication of SA 453:4 and MB *ad loc.*

It thus emerges that the primary enhancement of the mitzva is to guard the wheat against becoming *ḥametz* from the time of harvesting. Thus, the kernels are harvested before they dry out to prevent any concerns of rainwater potentially making them *ḥametz*. The kernels are then stored in a dry place, preventing any kernels from puffing up or splitting, which would indicate that they have started to become *ḥametz*. On the other hand, wheat imported from abroad, from which all other matza is made, sometimes contains kernels that have already become *ḥametz*. Even though matza bakers are careful to purchase clean shipments, there is still a concern that some *ḥametz* kernels mixed in. And even though these kernels are *batel be-shishim* (because the matza is baked before Pesaḥ, the *ḥametz* is not *ḥozer ve-ne'or* on Pesaḥ according to most *poskim*; see above 7:3-4), this matza is as ideal as that which is supervised from the time of harvesting. Since matza that was guarded from the time of harvesting is the best and most special, bakers are careful to perform all of the other steps in the most meticulous way possible: during baking, they stop the machines every eighteen minutes and clean them thoroughly; they constantly declare that they are working *le-shem matzat mitzva*; and they are more careful to supervise the entire process. Conversely, the trend with regard to non-*shmura* matza is to produce and sell it as cheaply as possible, so that the general public will be able to afford it. Therefore, only the mixers used for kneading are changed every eighteen minutes, but the rollers are cleaned while they are running. Although they are cleaned in a way that ensures that

6. WATER THAT HAS STAYED OVERNIGHT

The Sages prohibited kneading the dough for Pesaḥ *matzot* with lukewarm water. Warmth accelerates the leavening process, increasing the risk of the dough becoming *ḥametz* if the workers are not especially quick in kneading and baking it. The Sages forbade kneading the dough even with regular cold water found in cisterns and in springs, lest the surrounding ground, which had absorbed the heat of the sun, in turn warmed the water. Therefore, they required that the water be drawn before nightfall and kept overnight in a cool place. Such water is called *mayim she-lanu*. This water is used to prepare *matzot* for Pesaḥ (SA 495:1 and 3).[6]

However, a problem arose in countries with warm climates. No matter where the water was kept overnight, it would warm up a bit. On the contrary, had the water been left in the springs, it would have stayed cooler! Nevertheless, the *halakha* is that the water must be left out, as the Sages enacted. If, as a result, the water warms up a bit, it must be refrigerated (*Mikra'ei Kodesh* 2:7).

Some maintain that one should leave tap water overnight for baking the *matzot*, since the water might be from an open reservoir and may have been warmed by the sun. Furthermore, there is concern that the chlorine mixed into the water will accelerate the leavening process (*She'arim Metzuyanim Be-halakha* 109:3). In practice, this possibility is

---

every part is cleaned every eighteen minutes, since the cleaning is done while the machines are running, it is more difficult to clean the machines thoroughly.

Yet *shmura* matza is far more expensive than the regular matza (even if it is only guarded from the time of grinding the wheat, and can thus be used to fulfill the mitzva of eating matza according to those who maintain that there is a mitzva for the entire holiday). Some say that it is preferable to give charity to the poor or to support Torah study than to buy *shmura* matza. On the other hand, why shouldn't one who spends lavishly on furniture, clothing, and other luxuries spend extra money to fulfill *mitzvot* in the best possible way? Ultimately, in practice, regular matza is kosher, and one may rely on the fact that the *kashrut* supervisors do their jobs properly. When it comes to fulfilling higher standards of *mitzvot*, one must decide if and how he wishes to go beyond the letter of the law.

6. One who did not prepare *mayim she-lanu* should not bake matza using regular water. Rather, he should suffice with fruits, vegetables, and other foods for the rest of the holiday. However, if he otherwise will not have a *kezayit* of matza with which to fulfill the Torah commandment on the Seder night, he may bake matza using regular cold water, so that he does not neglect this mitzva (MB 455:36).

of no concern, and only a few meticulous people who make handmade *matzot* are scrupulous about drawing the water from wells or springs. In machine-matza factories, they take regular tap water from the municipal system, filter it thoroughly, and leave it in a cool place all night (R. Zvi Yehuda Kook similarly would prepare *mayim she-lanu* from tap water).

7. PREVENTING LEAVENING DURING KNEADING

The flour for *matzot* is ground at least one day before it is kneaded into dough, since the grinding heats the flour slightly, increasing the risk that the dough will become *ḥametz* (SA 453:9).

No salt or pepper is added to the dough, since they might warm the dough, increasing the risk that it will become *ḥametz* (SA 455:5-6).

Le-khatḥila, one should not make matza dough with more than c. 1.5kg (c. 3.3 lbs.) of flour (the *shi'ur* for having to separate *ḥalla* from the dough with a *berakha*). It is hard for one person to knead such a large piece of dough thoroughly and quickly, and there is concern that parts of the dough may become *ḥametz. Be-di'avad,* if one kneaded a larger quantity, the matza is kosher as long as the dough did not rest for eighteen minutes and no signs of leavening appeared (SA 456:1-2).

When there are several people engaged in kneading, flattening, and rolling out the dough, some *poskim* maintain that it is permissible to knead larger quantities, and indeed many do so. Even so, initially it is proper to be stringent and not to knead more than the measure that the Sages fixed (MB 456:7).

When the kneading is done by machine, it is customary, even *le-khatḥila,* to permit kneading large volumes of dough.

One may not knead the dough in a hot place, since heat accelerates the leavening process. Therefore, one should not knead in a sunny place. Sometimes it is hot even on a cloudy day, so even if the sun is not shining, one should not knead the dough outside, nor inside next to windows, lest the heat radiate through them. Obviously one should not knead in a place warmed by an oven (SA 459:1). One authority put a number on this: one should not knead where the temperature is 30°C or higher (*Sefer Matzot Mitzva,* ch. 7, n. 29). *Be-di'avad,* if one kneaded dough in a hot place but did not see any signs of leavening in the dough or the matza, the matza is kosher for Pesaḥ (SA 459:5).

Le-khatḥila, one may not stop working the dough for even a moment (SA 459:2). If the hands of the person kneading the dough heat up, he should cool them in cold water. Some are scrupulous to cool their hands in water occasionally while they are kneading (MB 459:27).

8. MORE LAWS ABOUT MATZA

The oven should be heated thoroughly, so that the dough begins to bake immediately. If the heat is low, the dough might begin to become *ḥametz* before it bakes. Clearly one may not bake matza in the heat of the sun, and if he did so, then even if the heat was very strong and it is obvious that the dough did not leaven, one does not fulfill the mitzva of eating matza with it, as the Torah calls matza the "bread of affliction," and something sun-baked is not properly called bread (SAH 461:6).

It is not necessary, however, to bake the bread specifically in the flames of the fire. Rather, even if the flames burn under a metal or earthenware plate, as long as the plate is burning hot, one may bake on it (SA 461:2).

Similarly, one may bake in an electric oven whose heating elements glow hot, for that is considered like fire. Matza baked in a microwave oven is disqualified from being used in the mitzva of eating matza, since it was not baked by fire. Some say it is kosher, for no early source indicates that the *matzot* must be baked specifically with fire (see *Mikra'ei Kodesh* p. 335 – R. Shlomo Zalman Auerbach disqualified such *matzot*, and R. Shaul Yisraeli held them to be kosher).

One may not decorate matza with pictures, as it may become *ḥametz* during the delay caused by drawing. One may not make a thick matza (thicker than 7.6 cm) on Pesaḥ, out of concern that the fire will not reach the center and it will become *ḥametz* (SA 460:4-5). However, one may bake a matza that is a bit thinner than a *tefaḥ*.

The Ashkenazic custom is to make the *matzot* thin and hard, so that the heat goes through them thoroughly and there is hardly any concern that the matza will become *ḥametz* (Rema 460:4). Some Sephardim bake matza that is about as thick as a finger, while others make them thin like wafers, as Ashkenazim do, since they usually bake them before Pesaḥ, and if they were not wafer-like, they would not last long (*Kaf Ha-ḥayim* 460:44).

One does not fulfill his obligation with a stolen matza (SA 454:4). Sometimes a purchaser takes the *matzot* into his possession without paying immediately. If the seller indicates that he wants to receive payment immediately, the purchaser must be careful to pay as the seller requested. If the seller seeks the buyer out, demanding payment for the *matzot*, and the purchaser dismisses him by saying "come back later," then the purchaser does not fulfill his obligation with those *matzot*, because they do not belong to him (MB 454:15).

Chapter Thirteen

The Laws and Customs of Erev Pesaḥ

1. THE PROHIBITION AGAINST WORK ON EREV PESAḤ

When the Temple stood, one who offered a sacrifice was prohibited from performing *melakha* (doing productive work) that day, as it was like a holiday for him, and it is inappropriate to perform *melakha* while one's sacrifice is being offered up on the altar. The same applies to Erev Pesaḥ, a day on which Israel is obligated to offer the *korban Pesaḥ* (Paschal sacrifice), and which is consequently like a holiday for everyone. But since the time for offering the *korban Pesaḥ* does not begin until midday, the prohibition against *melakha* also does not begin until midday. In some places, people adopted the stringent practice of refraining from *melakha* from the morning of the fourteenth of Nisan, and in such places this custom was binding. Even now, after the destruction of the Temple, this prohibition remains in effect, and it is forbidden do perform significant *melakha* after midday on the fourteenth of Nisan. This custom also prevents one from becoming preoccupied with work and forgetting to destroy his *ḥametz* and prepare matza, wine, and other necessities for the Seder night.

Indeed, the Sages instituted a ban on significant *melakha* every Erev Shabbat so that people would be free to prepare for Shabbat. However, the prohibition on Erev Pesaḥ is more severe, for while the Sages taught that whoever performs *melakha* on Erev Shabbat will see no sign of blessing from it, those who performed *melakha* on Erev Pesaḥ were actually excommunicated.

In practice, the *halakha* is that *melakha* is forbidden on Erev Shabbat from the time of *minḥa ketana* (two and a half seasonal hours before sunset), while the prohibition on Erev Pesaḥ begins at midday.[1]

---

1. The "*korban*" reason is explained in *y. Pesaḥim* 4:1 and is the opinion of *Tosafot,* Rambam, and most *poskim*. *Tosafot* implies that this is a Torah prohibition, but according to Rambam and many other *poskim,* the prohibition is rabbinic. All agree that after the destruction of the Temple the prohibition is only rabbinic. The first reason is the primary one; therefore, if the first night of Pesaḥ coincides with *Motza'ei* Shabbat, one may work until *minḥa ketana* on Friday just like on a regular week, even though he burns the *ḥametz* and takes care of other Pesaḥ preparations on Friday (BHL 468:1; see also *Ḥazon Ovadia* vol. 2 p. 82 and *Hilkhot Ḥag Be-ḥag* 14:8). The prohibition against work on Friday afternoon is explained in *Pesaḥim* 50b, and the Rishonim are divided as to whether the prohibition refers to *minḥa gedola* (5.5 seasonal hours before sunset) or *minḥa ketana* (2.5 seasonal hours before sunset). Because this constitutes a doubt about a rabbinic law, *halakha* follows the lenient opinion (see SA 251:1 and MB *ad loc.*; *Peninei Halakha: Shabbat* 2:8).

   See MB 468:12 and *Kaf Ha-ḥayim* 32 *ad loc.* regarding the modern day custom regarding Erev Pesaḥ before midday. The fact that they wonder about the custom in Jerusalem makes it clear that there is no fixed custom to prohibit work, since where work is prohibited, it is also prohibited for guests, and certainly for the residents of the community. There are no communities nowadays that prohibit work on Erev Pesaḥ before midday.

   However, according to SA 468:5 in the name of Rambam, even where there is no custom to prohibit work, only three types of craftsmen are permitted to begin working before midday: tailors, barbers, and launderers, since their work is done expressly for the holiday. For everyone else, if one began a task before the morning of the fourteenth and the work is necessary for Pesaḥ, he may work until midday, but if he did not begin before the morning of the fourteenth, he may not start. According to Rema, based on the opinion of most Rishonim, including Rashi, Raavad, Rosh, Ran, and others, the aforementioned distinction only applies where the custom is to refrain from work (like in Rema's community), but where the custom is to permit work until midday (like in our communities), everything is permissible. This is the custom of the Ashkenazic communities. Even some Sephardic communities follow Rema; see *Kaf Ha-ḥayim ad loc.* 32. In any event, we follow the lenient view when there is uncertainty regarding a rabbinic law.

2. WHICH *MELAKHOT* ARE FORBIDDEN?

The ban on *melakha* after midday on Erev Pesaḥ applies to full-fledged work that people typically do for a living, such as sewing, building furniture, and gardening. However, one may cook, clean the house, or travel before the holiday. As a rule, the ban on *melakha* on Erev Pesaḥ is similar to the ban on *melakha* during *Ḥol Ha-mo'ed,* and in certain cases is even slightly more lenient. Therefore, everything the Sages permit on *Ḥol Ha-mo'ed* is also permitted on Erev Pesaḥ.

There are three types of *melakha*: *melakha gemura* (full-fledged work), professional repair work, and the simple work of a non-professional. *Melakha gemura* like sewing garments, building furniture, and cutting hair, is always forbidden, even if it is done for free. However, mending clothes, even if it demands professional expertise, is not considered *melakha gemura*. Therefore, if the mender receives payment, it is forbidden, but if he works for free and the mending is needed for the festival, it is permitted. Simple work like sewing a button, if needed for the festival, is permitted even for pay on a temporary basis. It is likewise permissible for one to summarize his ideas in writing as he studies, but if he earns a living from typing or copying, it is a *melakha gemura* and thus forbidden (SA 468:1, 2).[2]

Though it is forbidden to have one's hair cut after midday on Erev Pesaḥ, it is permitted to shave with one's own shaver, because this is non-professional work. It is likewise permitted to iron clothes, shine shoes, and cut fingernails after midday in preparation for the festival. However, some are stringent to shave and cut fingernails before midday.[3]

---

2. SHT 468:10 and *Kaf Ha-ḥayim ad loc.* 24 explain that a non-professional may accept temporary work and even receive payment for it. In this regard, Erev Pesaḥ is less strict than *Ḥol Ha-mo'ed,* since according to SHT 541:21 this type of work is prohibited on *Ḥol Ha-mo'ed* but permitted on Erev Pesaḥ as it is on Friday after *minḥa ketana.* However, SAH rules stringently on this matter vis-à-vis Erev Pesaḥ as well.

   I did not mention laundering even though it is listed as a *melakha gemura* in SA, since nowadays laundry is done by machine and might be considered non-professional work done for the sake of the holiday, as stated in SSK ch. 42 n. 139. Laundering is permitted on Friday after *minḥa.*

3. MB 468:5 states that preferably one should cut his nails before midday, although many permit one to cut his nails even on *Ḥol Ha-mo'ed* (SA §532 and *Ḥazon Ovadia* vol. 2 pp. 89-91). *She'arim Metzuyanim Be-halakha* 113:6 also permits polishing shoes.

As noted, all *melakhot* permitted by the Sages on *Ḥol Ha-mo'ed* are also permitted after midday on Erev Pesaḥ. This, in short, includes five types of *melakhot*: 1) *melakha* to prepare food for the festival; 2) non-professional work for pay and impromptu skilled labor for free; 3) *melakha* to prevent substantial loss; 4) *melakha* done for public benefit or for the sake of a mitzva; 5) *melakha* performed by a poor person who lacks the money to buy festival necessities.

3. *TA'ANIT BEKHOROT* – THE FAST OF THE FIRSTBORNS

Firstborn males have a custom to fast on Erev Pesaḥ to commemorate the miracle performed for them: all Egyptian firstborn males died while firstborn Israelites were saved.

In order to give some sense of the significance of *Makat Bekhorot* (the Plague of the Firstborn), we must first note that besides being the eldest male child, the firstborn embodies something primal, for with his birth the new life of the next generation begins to unfold. The firstborn thus bears great responsibility. If he chooses the path of virtue, he will express that primal root – faith in the Creator of the universe – and the rest of the children in the family will follow in his path. But if he chooses the path of evil, denying God and viewing himself as great and significant, he will always be striving to enhance his own glory and satisfy his appetites. This was the sin of the Egyptians, who considered themselves the lords of the earth and denied God's existence. When they were commanded to send Israel away to worship God, they stubbornly refused to let them go. Pharaoh, himself a firstborn, led them in their pride and heresy.

The first day of Pesaḥ is itself a kind of "firstborn": it is the first day on which God began to reveal Himself in the world. Until this time, individual miracles were performed for special people, but not on a national level, via an entire people, the people of Israel. When the great

---

According to R. Mordechai Eliyahu (*Kitzur* SA 113:5), one may shave even after midday, although it is better to shave before midday.

If one forgot to get a haircut before midday and his appearance is not appropriate for the holiday, he may get his hair cut by a gentile, since the ban on work applies only to Jews. Even though the Jew getting his hair cut helps the gentile do his job, it is permissible so that he will have his hair cut for the festival.

day arrived, the day designated for the revelation of the root of faith in the world, a severe accusation against the firstborns of Egypt, who denied God's existence, was aroused. Upon God's revelation at midnight, they were all broken and slain. In contrast, the *bekhorim* of Israel, who expressed their faith in God by obeying His commandment, on the eve of the Exodus, to slaughter a lamb, which was an Egyptian god, risking their lives by smearing its blood on the doorposts, were saved and sanctified.

Each year, we relive the special time of Seder night, when the source of our faith was revealed. However, as this holy night approaches, the accusation against the *bekhorim* is reawakened: are they as committed to the Torah and the *mitzvot* as they should be? Are they expressing God's name in the world as they should? Firstborns therefore have a custom to fast and repent on Erev Pesaḥ.

This fast is less strict than other fasts. All of the other fasts were instituted by the Sages, but *Ta'anit Bekhorot,* a custom adopted by many *bekhorim,* was never instituted as a binding obligation by the Sages. It is therefore customary to be lenient. For example, if one suffers from a headache, or from a pain in his eye, he is exempt from *Ta'anit Bekhorot,* even though he is not considered sick and would not be exempt from other fasts. Likewise, if one thinks that by fasting he will not be able to fulfill the mitzva of eating matza and recount the story of the Exodus, it is better that he not fast. Furthermore, the custom is that whoever participates in a *se'udat mitzva* is exempt from *Ta'anit Bekhorot* (*Birkei Yosef* §470; MB 470:2, 10).[4]

4. *Y. Pesaḥim* 10:1 has two versions of this. According to one version, the custom of the firstborns is to fast on Erev Pesaḥ; this also appears in *Sofrim* 21:3 (compiled at the end of the savoraic period in Eretz Yisrael). This is also the version quoted by Ramban and Ran. According to the second version of the Yerushalmi, they did not have the custom to fast; this is the version quoted by Raavya and is also the opinion of the Vilna Gaon. Me'iri states that the custom in Germany and France was to fast, although the fast was not mandatory, and *Birkei Yosef* quotes Rishonim who echo this idea. Therefore, one may be lenient about this fast and rely on a *siyum* in order to eat. *Mordechai* states in the name of Rabbeinu Yeḥiel that the custom of the firstborns is only to refrain from eating bread and other baked goods, but meat, fish, fruits, vegetables, and the like are permissible. Practically, SA 470:1 states that the custom is to fast. However, MB 2, SHT 6 *ad loc.* state that when necessary, such as if the firstborn has great difficulty fasting, one may rely on Rabbeinu Yeḥiel. The book

4. WHO IS INCLUDED IN THE CUSTOM TO FAST?

There are two types of *bekhorim*, and both are included in this custom, because both types of *bekhorim* died in Egypt. The first type is a *bekhor* to one's father, the *bekhor* who inherits a double portion of his father's estate. Even if his mother bore children from a previous husband, or had an earlier miscarriage (and he is therefore not considered his mother's firstborn and need not be redeemed by *pidyon ha-ben*), the custom of fasting applies to him, because he is a *bekhor* to his father with regard to the law of inheritance.

The second type is a *bekhor* to one's mother, the *bekhor* to whom *pidyon ha-ben* applies. Customarily, he too observes *Ta'anit Bekhorot*, even if his father already had children with another woman and he will not inherit the double portion. He has the status of "*petter reḥem*" (the first to emerge from his mother's womb). The firstborn to a mother who was born via Caesarean section lacks the status of *bekhor* both with regard to inheritance and with regard to *pidyon ha-ben*, and therefore need not fast on Erev Pesaḥ (*Kaf Ha-ḥayim* 470:3; however, some are scrupulous about participating in a *siyum*).

Firstborn Kohanim and Levi'im also observe the custom of fasting. Although the Torah exempts them from *pidyon ha-ben*, they are nonetheless *bekhorim* (MB 470:2).

A firstborn female need not fast. While it is true that some authorities maintain that female *bekhorot* also died in Egypt, the prevailing custom is that they do not fast (Rema, Ḥida, *Baḥ*, and *Kaf Ha-ḥayim* 470:17).

Customarily the father of a *bekhor*, even if he himself is not a *bekhor*, fasts instead of his son until the boy grows up (Rema 470:2). If the father is also a *bekhor*, his own fast counts for his son, and if he participates in a *se'udat mitzva*, he is exempt from fasting for his son as well. This is the custom according to many *poskim*, but Rema takes a more stringent position.

When Pesaḥ falls on Shabbat, the custom is to move *Ta'anit Bekhorot* up two days, to Thursday.

Ta'anit Bekhorot discusses all of the opinions and laws in this matter; see *Yabi'a Omer* 1:25 for a shorter summary.

5. THE CUSTOM TO RELY ON A *SIYUM MASEKHET*

Bekhorim customarily participate in a *siyum masekhet* (a festive ceremonial meal occasioned by the completion of a tractate of the Talmud) on Erev Pesaḥ after *Shaḥarit*. Afterward, refreshments are served to everyone in attendance, and the *bekhorim* present are permitted to partake, sharing in the joy of a *se'udat mitzva* and celebrating the mitzva of Torah study and the completion of the tractate. Having already broken their fast with the *se'udat mitzva*, *bekhorim* are no longer obligated to fast.

However, *poskim* of past generations were divided over this custom. Some took a stringent position, ruling that only a *bekhor* who himself completed a tractate may partake of the *se'udat mitzva*, while other firstborns, who are not so connected to the joy of the *siyum*, may not break the fast by partaking in someone else's *se'uda*. This is especially true when those completing the tractate do not hold a *se'udat mitzva* on such occasions during the course of the year, and the *bekhorim* as well do not generally attend their friends' *siyumim*. By arranging a *siyum* for firstborns once a year on Erev Pesaḥ, it appears as though they are coming not to celebrate the mitzva, but to exempt themselves from the fast. Moreover, often the person making the *siyum* completed the tractate a week or two earlier and postponed the *siyum* until Erev Pesaḥ in order to exempt himself from fasting. According to the stringent opinion, it is improper to act in this manner, because the real joy is felt when one completes his study, not when he recites the last few lines so that he can make a *siyum* on Erev Pesaḥ (*Teshuva Me-ahava* vol. 2 p. 261; *Noda Bi-Yehuda*).

Nevertheless, the custom nowadays is to rely on the lenient *poskim* who rule that anyone who participates in the *se'udat mitzva* is exempt from fasting, even if he does not usually make or attend *siyumim* during the course of the year, and even if the *siyum* was delayed until Erev Pesaḥ. The simple reason for this is that when a *masekhet* is completed, it is fitting to celebrate, and this is therefore a *se'udat mitzva*. Moreover, *Ta'anit Bekhorot* is predicated entirely on custom, not on a binding enactment, and is not mentioned at all in the Bavli or by Rambam. Furthermore, some leading Rishonim were of the opinion that *bekhorim* are not obligated to fast on Erev Pesaḥ. This being the case, whenever there is a halakhic disagreement, the lenient *poskim* have the upper hand. What is more, in recent generations we no longer fast often, and if the *bekhorim* fast, their preparations for Pesaḥ will most likely suffer from the weakness it induces; they will even want to rush through the Hagada in order to get to the meal. Therefore, many leading rabbis would exempt themselves from the fast via a *siyum*. Only one who knows that the fast will not impair his preparations for Pesaḥ or his fulfillment of the *mitzvot* of Seder night may act stringently and fast on Erev Pesaḥ. Indeed, Rav Kook and his son R. Zvi Yehuda, both of whom were firstborns, customarily fasted on Erev Pesaḥ.

The type of *siyum* that exempts its participants from fasting is one that marks the completion of a tractate of the Bavli or Yerushalmi, or an entire *seder* of Mishna. The study must involve understanding and not mere rote reading.[5]

6. THE PROHIBITION ON EATING MATZA ON EREV PESAḤ

The Sages forbade eating matza on Erev Pesaḥ, in order to increase our desire to eat it during the Seder and in order to distinguish between

---

5. As mentioned in the previous note, this custom is universally accepted. Even according to the opinions that this is a binding custom, it is still of rabbinic origin, so one may be lenient. This is especially true since there are authorities, Gra among them, who maintain that this custom is not binding at all. There is certainly room to be lenient when observing this custom conflicts with fulfilling the *mitzvot* of the Seder, as is the case nowadays when most people are not accustomed to fasting (*Responsa Olat Shmuel* §58). Therefore, our custom is to rely on a *siyum*, which in turn reminds firstborns that they are inherently holy and have great responsibilities. *Arugat Habosem* has a similar opinion in §139.

A *siyum* on a book of Nevi'im is a *se'udat mitzva* (*Igrot Moshe* OḤ 1:157). It seems that anyone who finishes one of the four sections of *Shulḥan Arukh* or an important book can also make a *se'udat mitzva*, since making a *siyum* was never essentially limited just to a tractate of the Bavli; see *Ḥavot Ya'ir* §70. Someone who completes one tractate of Mishna with commentaries can make a *siyum* for himself, but it would not exempt others (*Yabi'a Omer* OḤ 26; see also *Piskei Teshuvot* 470:9).

In sum, a *siyum* on a significant work exempts all participants from fasting. When the *siyum* is on a work that is significant to the one who studied it but not so significant in the eyes of the public, the one who makes the *siyum* can make a *se'udat mitzva* and exempt himself from fasting. Thus, one who is just beginning to study Torah and has difficulty learning a tractate of Mishna in depth may make a *siyum* on completing a superficial study of a tractate of Mishna or a book from Tanakh, but others are not exempted from fasting by his *siyum* and *se'uda*.

matza eaten before Pesaḥ and the matza eaten as a mitzva during the Seder. This prohibition applies even to children who understand the idea that the matza commemorates the Exodus from Egypt. It is permissible to feed matza on Erev Pesaḥ to small children who do not understand this.

The prohibition begins at dawn on the fourteenth of Nisan, though some choose to be stringent and refrain from eating matza from the beginning of Nisan. Others refrain from eating matza thirty days before Pesaḥ. However, the letter of the law only requires one to refrain from eating matza on the fourteenth of Nisan (MB 471:12).[6]

Israeli hospitals and army bases ordinarily destroy *ḥametz* several days before Pesaḥ, because otherwise there is concern that *ḥametz* will remain in the kitchens and camps during Pesaḥ. Matza is served so that the soldiers and patients have what to eat, so they should refrain from eating such *matzot* on Erev Pesaḥ.

The prohibition against eating matza on Erev Pesaḥ includes even small pieces of matza that have been kneaded with wine or oil. Even if such a mixture is baked, as long as the pieces are identifiable as matza, the blessing before eating them is "*ha-motzi*" and it is forbidden to eat them on Erev Pesaḥ. However, if after being kneaded and baked the pieces are no longer identifiable as matza, their *berakha* is "*mezonot*" and they may be eaten on Erev Pesaḥ (implied in Rema 461:2 and MB *ad loc.* 19-20). Some *poskim* are more stringent, maintaining that even if the matza is crumbled like matza meal, kneaded with oil or wine, and baked into cake or cookies so that they are no longer identifiable as matza, it is forbidden to eat them. This is because one who eats enough of them to constitute a meal ("*kevi'at se'uda*") still must recite the *berakha* of "*ha-motzi.*" Thus, it is apparent that they have not yet lost the status

6. Let us briefly summarize the opinions: According to Rosh and *Ha-ma'or,* the prohibition begins at midday. According to Maharam Halawa, *Tashbetz,* and Rambam in *Magid Mishneh's* reading, the prohibition begins at dawn. According to *Orḥot Ḥayim,* the prohibition begins at from the time of *bedikat ḥametz* on the night of the fourteenth. Rema rules that the prohibition begins at dawn, and this is the opinion of most Aḥaronim. However, *Ben Ish Ḥai* (Tzav 26) states that the prohibition begins on the night of the fourteenth (see *Berur Halakha* 99b).

of matza, and consequently the prohibition applies to pastries made of matza meal (Gra, Rav Kook, and Ḥazon Ish).[7]

However, all *poskim* agree that it is permissible to eat matza balls on Erev Pesaḥ, because after being cooked they no longer carry the status of matza. Even if one eats enough of them to constitute a meal, their *berakha* is "*mezonot*," because they are a cooked food, not a baked good (MB *ad loc.* 20). Moreover, even if one cooks a whole piece of matza the size of a *kezayit* or more, most *poskim* maintain that although its *berakha* is "*ha-motzi*," one may eat it on Erev Pesaḥ (as explained below 14:1).

7. SUMMARY – WHAT CAN BE EATEN ON EREV PESAḤ

As we have learned, the Torah prohibits eating *ḥametz* after midday on the fourteenth of Nisan, and the Sages extended the prohibition by two hours as a safeguard. Hence, one may eat *ḥametz* on Erev Pesaḥ until the

7. Some authorities maintain that any matza that is not fit for the mitzva is permissible on Erev Pesaḥ; this is the opinion of Me'iri, R. Yeshaya di Trani (Rid), and Rivash. Others maintain that anything that has the taste of matza is forbidden on Erev Pesaḥ, even if it is unfit for the mitzva. This position can be imputed to several Rishonim who permitted only egg matza (Rabbeinu Tam in *Tosafot* on *Pesaḥim* 99b, Rosh, *Mordechai, Tashbetz,* and Maharsha). In practice, however, the custom is to follow Rema and refrain from eating *matza ashira.* If one crumbles the matza and kneads it with oil or something sweet, whether he bakes it or not, there are some who maintain that as long as the *berakha* is "*ha-motzi*," the mixture is forbidden, but if the *berakha* becomes "*mezonot*" it is permissible (SA 168:10). According to the stringent opinions, including *Olat Re'iyah* (vol. 2 p. 243 §22), any baked matza meal is forbidden on Erev Pesaḥ, since any products made from matza meal would still require the *berakha* of *ha-motzi* if eaten in the requisite quantities (they have the status of "*pat ha-ba'ah be-kisnin*"). If one cooked the matza meal, even if the cooked dish still requires *berakha* of *ha-motzi* if eaten in the requisite quantities, he may eat in on Erev Pesaḥ since its taste has changed. This is the opinion of MB 471:20 and SHT 19 *ad loc.* Some authorities are stringent; see below 14:1 and *Yeḥaveh Da'at* 1:91, n. 10. Nonetheless, all agree that one may eat less than a *kezayit* of cooked matza, as I wrote above. See *Yeḥaveh Da'at* 3:26, which allows hospitals to serve non-*shmura* matza on Erev Pesaḥ in extenuating circumstances, since in these types of situations we can rely on the Rishonim who maintain that only matza that is fit for the mitzva is forbidden on Erev Pesaḥ. Practically, however, this does not apply, since all *matzot* nowadays are guarded at least from the time of grinding, are made for the purpose of fulfilling the mitzva, and are thus acceptable to fulfill the mitzva (SA 453:4).

end of the fourth seasonal hour (i.e., the first third of the day). There are, as is evident from Jewish calendars, two approaches to calculating these hours. According to *Magen Avraham,* we begin calculating them from dawn; according to the Vilna Gaon, from sunrise. Ideally, one should be stringent and calculate the onset of the prohibition according to *Magen Avraham*. However, when necessary, since the prohibition against eating *ḥametz* after the fourth hour is rabbinic, one may be lenient and finish one's *ḥametz* meal by the end of the fourth hour according to Gra's calculation (see above 3:6).[8]

After four hours, a problem arises for those who customarily refrain from eating *kitniyot* on Pesaḥ: what can one eat to satisfy his hunger? *Ḥametz* and *kitniyot* are forbidden, and even matza is rabbinically forbidden on the fourteenth of Nisan. We have seen that even matza meal-based cakes and cookies are subject to dispute among *poskim*. In practice, since this disagreement pertains to a rabbinic prohibition, one may be lenient, though stringency is commendable. According to all opinions, one may eat matza balls.

Egg matza (or *matza ashira,* which includes matza kneaded with oil, wine, or any other fruit juice) may be eaten on Erev Pesaḥ and Pesaḥ according to *Shulḥan Arukh,* but according to the custom of Rema it is forbidden (SA 461:1-4). Nowadays, serious concerns have arisen about the way *matza ashira* is produced, and according to most *poskim,* even Sephardic Jews must refrain from *matza ashira,* even on Erev Pesaḥ after midday (see above 8:1).

Even those whose custom is to eat *matza ashira* (when produced in a completely halakhic way) may eat it only until the end of the ninth seasonal hour of the day. With the onset of the tenth hour, three hours before the beginning of the holiday, the Sages forbid eating any sort of baked goods, so that one's appetite is whet for the matza and festive meal of the Seder. If one is hungry during these hours, he may eat fruit, vegetables, meat, or fish, as long as he is careful to eat a small amount so that he will be hungry in the evening. If one is so sensitive that if he eats meat or some other food in the afternoon he will not be hungry at

8. The end of the fourth hour according to MA's calculation is c. twenty-four minutes before that of Gra. Many people make mistakes in this area.

night, he must plan his meals on Erev Pesaḥ so that he has an appetite when he eats the matza that evening (SA 471:1-2).

8. BAKING MATZA AND RECITING *SEDER KORBAN PESAḤ*

Some practice the enhancement of baking the *matzot* to be used for the Seder night mitzva after midday on the fourteenth of Nisan, at the time of day when the Paschal sacrifice would be offered (SA 458:1). Many do not do so because it is labor intensive and this is the time when people are usually busy preparing the house for the Seder. Some *poskim* say that the possibility of the dough becoming *ḥametz* also makes it preferable to bake the matza beforehand, because some authorities are of the opinion that, at this time of day, even a drop of *ḥametz* renders everything forbidden, whereas if a drop of dough becomes *ḥametz* before midday, it is *batel be-shishim* and it will not "reawaken" later with the onset of Pesaḥ (MB 458:3; see above ch. 7 n. 1). Indeed, Rav Kook's custom was not to bake matza on Erev Pesaḥ after midday (*Mo'adei Ha-Re'aya* p. 284).

After the *minḥa* prayer on Erev Pesaḥ, people customarily recite the *seder korban Pesaḥ*, a description of the procedure of offering the Paschal sacrifice, including relevant biblical verses. The Sages teach (*Megilla* 31b) that after the destruction of the Temple, reciting and studying the sacrificial procedures are considered a substitute for the *korban* itself.

Maharal of Prague (*Gevurot Hashem* chs. 36, 37) explains that the significance of the Paschal sacrifice lies in the expression it gives to the unity of the Creator, and consequently the unity of Israel, whose purpose it is to reveal His name in the world. It is therefore eaten in groups, whose membership is predetermined, so that the *korban* is offered by a group of people who have united for this purpose. It is also forbidden to go from one group to another during the Seder, because this would disrupt the unity of the group. The offering is eaten with matza and *maror* in order to express the inner unity of all of the values alluded to by Paschal sacrifice, matza, and *maror*. We are commanded to roast the Paschal sacrifice because roasting solidifies and unifies the meat. It is forbidden to break any of its bones, because breaking is an expression of division.

When the Paschal sacrifice cannot be offered, the unity of the Creator is not revealed in the world, and the people of Israel are scattered and divided. May it be God's will that the Temple be rebuilt speedily in our days, and that we merit to offer the Paschal sacrifice together, as in the days of yore.

O Purest One, Who dwells on high
Raise up the uncountable assembly of Your community
Soon guide the saplings You planted
Redeemed, to Zion in joy!

Chapter Fourteen

When Erev Pesaḥ Falls on Shabbat

1. *BI'UR ḤAMETZ* AND SHABBAT MEALS

When the fourteenth of Nisan coincides with Shabbat, *bedikat ḥametz* is performed with a *berakha* on the night of the thirteenth, Thursday night, because it is impossible to seek and eliminate *ḥametz* on Shabbat. After the search, the *ḥametz* is nullified like in any other year, and on the following day, Friday, it is burned. It is best to burn it by the sixth seasonal hour of the day, like in any other year (SA 444:1-2). *Ḥametz* that will be eaten during the first two Shabbat meals is carefully set aside.

If it were permissible, we would certainly eat matza with the Shabbat meals in order to avoid the problem of *ḥametz*. However, it is forbidden to eat matza on Erev Pesaḥ so that it is appetizing to us at the Seder (see above 13:6). Therefore, we must save *ḥametz* for the first two Shabbat meals. In order to avoid problems with *ḥametz* foods, many people cook kosher-for-Pesaḥ foods for that Shabbat. They make *kiddush* and eat bread with spreads or salads in a room where people will not eat during Pesaḥ. After eating bread, they clean their hands and brush off their clothes, then eat the rest of the meal in the kosher-for-Pesaḥ dining room.

The second Shabbat meal must be completed by the end of the fourth seasonal hour of the day, at which time *ḥametz* becomes forbidden. Shabbat morning prayers must begin and end early so that the meal can be completed in time (see above 3:6).

After the morning meal, all remaining *ḥametz* must be gathered from the plates and tablecloth. Since it may not be burned on Shabbat, it is a good idea to flush it down the toilet and thus completely destroy it. People generally plan their Shabbat meals wisely, so that it will be easy to gather up the leftover *ḥametz* and dispose of it. After this, the *ḥametz* must be nullified; the *bitul* must be recited by the end of the fifth hour of the day.

Those who customarily perform *hagala* on their false teeth should do so on Friday and not eat any hot *ḥametz* food with them on Shabbat. Those who suffice with brushing their teeth should brush them thoroughly after the second meal (see above 11:12).

Se'uda shlishit, the third Shabbat meal, presents a problem: it is forbidden to eat *ḥametz* after the fourth hour of the day, and matza is forbidden the entire day. As a result, the obligation to eat a third meal is met by eating meat and fish or various fruits (SA 444:1). One may also eat matza balls, and according to many authorities, one may eat matza that has been thoroughly cooked, though some have a custom not to eat *gebrokts* on Pesaḥ (see above 8:2). One must avoid eating excessively during the third meal so that the matza of Seder night remains appetizing. Those who wish to destroy all of their *ḥametz* before Shabbat have options, explained in the notes.[1]

---

1. **Egg matza** or *matza ashira* is made out of flour that was kneaded with fruit juice, which does not become *ḥametz*. The Sephardic custom is to permit eating it on Pesaḥ, while the Ashkenazic custom is to forbid (see above 8:1). According to all customs, *matza ashira* can be used for the first two Shabbat meals, but in such a case one must be *kovei'a se'uda* ("establish a meal") by eating four egg-volumes (*ke-beitzim*) of egg matza and by eating a fully satisfying meal. This will change the *berakhot* on egg matza from "*mezonot*" and "*Al Ha-miḥya*" to "*ha-motzi*" and "*Birkat Ha-mazon*" (see *Peninei Halakha: Berakhot* 6:4). If *matza ashira* was baked with a reliable process (see above 13:7), Sephardim may use it for *se'uda shlishit*, but it should be eaten before *plag ha-minḥa* (c. three seasonal hours before sunset). According to Ashkenazic custom, *matza ashira* may not be eaten after the fourth hour of the day (SHT and *Igrot Moshe*, in contrast to AHS, which permits eating it on Erev Pesaḥ, until the beginning of the holiday).

2. ADDITIONAL LAWS

Ta'anit Bekhorot is moved forward to Thursday, the twelfth of Nisan (SA and Rema 470:2). As mentioned, the custom nowadays is to arrange a *siyum* instead of fasting (see above 13:5). One should prepare the needs of the Seder – such as cooking the meal, preparing the *ḥaroset, maror*, and shank bone, and then freezing or refrigerating them – on Friday. They should not be taken out of the refrigerator until after Shabbat, as it is forbidden to prepare on Shabbat for Yom Tov. If preparations were not made before Shabbat, they must be prepared after Shabbat. However, this is less than ideal, as it may delay the Seder. Similarly, one may not set the Seder table on Shabbat. Rather, it should be set immediately upon the conclusion of Shabbat.

Two sets of candles should be set up before Shabbat: one for Shabbat and one for Yom Tov, as it is forbidden to stick candles on candlesticks with melted wax on Yom Tov. If one did not prepare them in advance, he may wedge them into the candlesticks without melting them in place.

Cooked matza: Another option is to cook a whole matza. According to most opinions, one may eat cooked matza on Erev Pesaḥ, since it has been fundamentally altered and one would not fulfill the mitzva of eating matza on Seder night with such matza. Because it constitutes at least a *kezayit*, its *berakhot* are still "*ha-motzi*" and "*Birkat Ha-mazon*" and consequently one may use it to fulfill the obligation to eat three Shabbat meals. This is the ruling of MB 471:20 and SHT 19 *ad loc.*, AHS 444:5, and *Yeḥaveh Da'at* 1:91 n. 10. SHT 471:20 mentions in the name of SAH and *Ḥayei Adam* that frying is the same as cooking, and that *Pri Megadim* equivocates. On the other hand, MA 444:2 asserts, citing Maharil, never having seen anyone adopt the practice of eating cooked matza at *se'uda shlishit*, and Gra implies that it may not be eaten on Erev Pesaḥ. Those who wish to follow the majority ruling and fulfill their obligation with cooked matza may do so (see SHT 444:1 and above 13:7). MB 444:8 raises the idea of splitting the second meal into two, but this is not ideal, as *se'uda shlishit* should be eaten after midday.

Chapter Fifteen

The Hagada

1. "TELL YOUR CHILD"

There is a positive mitzva to tell the story of the Exodus from Egypt on the night of the fifteenth of Nisan. The more one embellishes the telling, elucidates the great kindness God showed us by saving us from the Egyptians and avenging us upon them, interprets the signs and wonders that God performed at that time and place for our sake, delves into the laws of Pesaḥ, and gives expansive gratitude to God – the more commendable it is. The essence of the mitzva is to tell the children, as it is stated: "Tell your child on that day: 'It is because of this that God did for me when I left Egypt'" (Shemot 13:8). Even one who is childless is commanded by the Torah to recall the Exodus on Pesaḥ night, as it states: "Remember this day on which you came out of Egypt, of the house of bondage; how, with a mighty hand, God took you out of there" (*ibid.* 3).

Note that two *mitzvot* require us to educate our children: the first is to teach them the written and oral Torah, so they understand the world properly and may live their lives according to divine guidance. Part of this mitzva is to habituate and familiarize children with the observance of *mitzvot*; it is impossible to teach about Shabbat or *kashrut* without training for their observance. The second mitzva is to tell our children about the Exodus from Egypt on the Seder night.

At first glance, this is puzzling. Is narrating the Exodus not part of the general mitzva of teaching Torah? In that case, what is different about the Seder night? The purpose of the stories told to the children on Seder night is to convey the fundamentals of faith that logically precede Torah study: they must know how the nation of Israel was formed, that God chose Israel to be His special nation, and that He gave them a special duty to receive the Torah and rectify the world. Parents, of course, do not live forever. The next generation will have to bear the torch of tradition, the great and awesome task that God intended for Israel, until the world has been fully repaired. This is the lesson of the Seder night. All of its *mitzvot* lead to that end.

Note that the obligation to study Torah is derived from the verse: "Teach them to your children, to speak of them" (Devarim 11:19). The Sages explain that one who must teach his son Torah must himself study Torah (*Kiddushin* 29b). The fundamental goal of the Torah is to positively influence others and add life to the world, not just to elevate the individual Jew. Therefore, the Torah emphasizes in this commandment the obligation to teach the children, for the essential goal of the Torah is to influence the entire people of Israel in every generation. Clearly, then, every individual is likewise commanded to study Torah as much as he is able. What is more, when one studies in order to teach others, his study is more thorough and profound. Similarly, the primary emphasis of the mitzva to tell the story of the Exodus is to pass the tradition on to the children, but it follows that the parents should also attempt to understand it more profoundly, so that they are worthy of Israel's great destiny.

2. THE MITZVA TO TELL THE EXODUS STORY ON PESAḤ NIGHT

The Torah commands us to tell the story of the Exodus from Egypt on the very night we left Egypt for freedom. Actually, we are commanded to remember the Exodus every day of the year, as it states: "So that you remember the day you left Egypt every day of your life" (Devarim 16:3). Ben Zoma infers from an apparent superfluity in this verse ("*kol yemei*" instead of "*yemei*") that we must invoke the Exodus not only every day, but also even every night (*Berakhot* 12b). To fulfill the obligation to invoke the Exodus every day and night, we recite the third paragraph of *Shema* each morning and evening, as this paragraph states: "I am the

Lord your God Who has taken you out of Egypt to be your God: I am the Lord your God" (Bamidbar 15:41).

Yet there are several differences between the daily mitzva and the mitzva on the night of the fifteenth of Nisan. Firstly, in order to fulfill the daily mitzva, it is sufficient to mention the Exodus, whereas the mitzva on Pesaḥ night is to narrate broadly the events of the Exodus from Egypt. In addition, the mitzva on Pesaḥ night is to relate the story while the matza and *maror* are set out in front of us. Another difference is that on Pesaḥ night we tell the story by way of questions and answers. Women are exempt from the daily mitzva to commemorate the Exodus, but are obligated to tell the story of the Exodus from Egypt on the night of the fifteenth of Nisan.[1]

The Exodus from Egypt is the basis of Jewish faith, for it was the first time that God's providence was revealed in the world to an entire nation with great signs and wonders. With the Exodus, it became clear that God had chosen Israel to be His nation and to reveal His word in the world. For this reason, every Shabbat and Yom Tov commemorates the Exodus from Egypt, especially in prayers and *kiddush*. By virtue of the unique mitzva to tell the story of the Exodus in depth on the Seder night, our faith becomes more firmly established, and added meaning is given to all the brief remembrances of the Exodus throughout the year.

3. THE MITZVA TO BEGIN THE SEDER WITH A QUESTION

There is a mitzva to tell the story of the Exodus by way of question and answer, as it is stated: "When in the future your child asks you… say to your child, 'We were slaves to Pharaoh in Egypt…'" (Devarim 6:20-22).

1. SA 472:14. The *poskim* disagree whether women are obligated in the mitzva of telling the story on a Torah level or a rabbinic level. *Sefer Ha-ḥinukh* §21 infers from the fact that women are obligated in matza and the Paschal offering on the Torah level that they are obligated by the Torah to tell the Exodus story, which is linked to the matza, *maror*, and Paschal offering, as well. Other *poskim* maintain that since the mitzva of telling the story is a time-bound positive mitzva, women are exempt according to the Torah, but the Sages obligated them in the *mitzvot* of the Seder night, since women also experienced the miracles of the Exodus. This is the view implied by *Tosafot* on *Pesaḥim* 108b.

It is likewise stated: "When your children ask you, 'What is this service to you?' say, 'It is a Paschal sacrifice to God'" (Shemot 12:26-27). And: "When in the future your child asks: 'What is this?' Say to him, 'With a mighty hand God took us out of Egypt'" (*ibid.* 13:14).

Questions open the heart and mind to accept answers. The message we need to convey on the Seder night is so important and fundamental that we are commanded to do it in the most effective way – by way of question and answer.

This is the main reason for the unique *mitzvot* of the Seder night: eating matza, the Paschal sacrifice, and *maror*. They cause the children to ask "*Ma nishtana*?" "Why is this night different?" and helps them understand that this is a special night whose essence must be understood. As a result, the Sages instituted several unusual practices in order to inspire children to wonder and enquire further. We begin by giving the children nuts and roasted grain, through which they realize that this is a special, festive night. The Sages instituted washing hands and eating *karpas* dipped in a liquid after *kiddush*, something we never do throughout the year. Furthermore, instead of starting the meal at this point, we pour the second cup of wine and remove the Seder plate and the *matzot* from the table, all to cause the children to realize that this is a very special night. They will thus truly be interested in its meaning, and they will sincerely ask: "Why is this night different?"

It can be said that this question, "*Ma nishtana*?" embodies a bigger and deeper question about the Jewish people: Why are we different from all other nations – in our faith, in our *mitzvot*, in our suffering, in our spiritual achievements, in our exile, and in our redemption? There is no complete answer to this question. Only by contemplating the Exodus from Egypt and the election of Israel can we understand that this is a divine matter; we are capable of understanding part of it, but we will never understand it all. This same question spurs us on, toward infinitely deeper and more sublime understanding. Perhaps this is why the Torah instructs us to tell the story of the Exodus and of Israel's singularity using questions and answers: the ideological basis of Jewish peoplehood lies in a question that opens us to an endless profusion of ideas. If we do not impart the Torah and the story of the Exodus to the children, no new questions would be asked and we would be unable to continue rising higher.

4. THE TEXT OF "*MA NISHTANA*"

In order to give this seminal question a structured framework, the Sages formulated the "*Ma nishtana*" text, through which the children express their surprise at how different this night is, paving the way for the telling of the Exodus story. The text contains questions about all of the Seder night *mitzvot* related to eating: matza, *maror*, the Paschal sacrifice, and the two dippings. After the destruction of the Temple, we no longer ask about the Paschal sacrifice and instead ask about reclining at the Seder.

If there are no children present to ask "*Ma nishtana*?" the youngest participant asks. Even if all the participants are Torah scholars well versed in the story of the Exodus, one of them must ask "*Ma nishtana*?" Even an individual performing the Seder alone must begin with "*Ma nishtana*?" This is how the Seder is arranged; we begin with a question because it makes the explanation more complete. Once a child or someone else has asked "*Ma nishtana*?" the other participants need not repeat the question and may proceed immediately to "*Avadim Hayinu*" (SA and Rema 473:7).[2]

2. According to several Rishonim, including *Rokei'aḥ* and Maharil, if a child asks any question about the Seder, the obligation to ask questions has been fulfilled, and there is no need to recite the "*Ma nishtana*" formula specifically. However, according to most Rishonim, including *Tosafot* and Rambam, even if a child autonomously asks a question relating to the Seder, the entire "*Ma nishtana*" formula must be recited. The *halakha* follows this opinion. See *Berur Halakha* on *Pesaḥim* 115b (p. 134) for a summary of opinions. This ruling notwithstanding, one should encourage his children to ask their own questions, to fulfill the verse "when your child asks…"

One authority writes that the mitzva *de-Oraita* to tell the Exodus story only applies when a child actually asks a question, but if the child does not inquire, the biblical mitzva is only to commemorate the Exodus from Egypt, though one is still rabbinically required to tell the story. This is the implication of *Responsa Rosh* 24:2, but the majority of *poskim* maintain that anyone who has a child is obligated by the Torah to tell him the story, as the Torah states regarding the son who does not know how to ask, "Tell your child on this day: 'It is because of this that God did for me when I left Egypt'" (Shemot 13:8). So states SAH 473:42. (R. Yeruḥam Fishel Perla, in his commentary on R. Saadia Gaon's *Sefer Ha-mitzvot* §32, states that according to Ramban and other Rishonim, one who does not have matza is exempt from the mitzva

5. THE TORAH SPEAKS OF FOUR CHILDREN

On four occasions the Torah states that one must tell his child about the Exodus from Egypt, and each time it uses a different formulation. This teaches us that one must tailor his storytelling to the abilities and personality of each child.

In one place it states: "When in the future your child asks you, 'What are these testimonies, laws, and principles that the Lord our God commanded you?'" (Devarim 6:20). The fact that he asks in a detailed manner – "What are these testimonies, laws, and principles" – implies that we are dealing with a wise child, and the verses that follow teach us that the answer we give must be detailed. We must clarify at length the whole matter of the Exodus from Egypt, the *mitzvot* of Pesaḥ, and the destiny of the Jewish people. Therefore, the answer for the wise child is the longest and most detailed (as shown in the next section).

Elsewhere it states: "When your children ask you, 'What is this service to you?,' say, 'It is a Paschal sacrifice to God, Who passed over ('*pasaḥ*') the houses of the Israelites in Egypt, when He smote Egypt and spared our homes'" (Shemot 12:26-27). Since the child calls the *mitzvot* "service" ("*avoda*"), which connotes "work," and since he excludes himself from the *mitzvot*, saying, "What is this service to **you**?," it is clear that he does not feel like a participant in the *mitzvot*. Nevertheless, the Torah commands us to address him and explain to him Israel's uniqueness, as expressed in the Paschal sacrifice.

It also states: "When in the future your child asks: 'What is this?,' say to him, 'With a mighty hand God took us out of Egypt, out of the

---

of telling the story of the Exodus, based on the phrase "because of this" ["*ba-avur zeh*" – the Hebrew uses the demonstrative pronoun "*zeh*" instead of the expected indefinite relative pronoun, indicating that it refers to an object that is present, i.e., the matza]. Additionally, see *Sidur Pesaḥ Ke-hilkhato* ch. 6 n. 2 which mentions a distinction between a child who asks his father a question, which obligates his father to tell the story in detail, and a child who does not ask, which only obligates the father to tell the story briefly. We can explain that if the son asks, the father must embellish his response based on the question, but if the child does not ask, the father need only tell the story briefly. Embellishment depends on the child's desire to listen and obtain answers.) In any event, it is clear that at least on the rabbinic level one must recite the entire Hagada as formulated. Even if he is alone, he asks himself the questions (*Pesaḥim* 116a) and thus extends to himself the obligation to answer.

house of bondage. When Pharaoh refused to free us, God killed every firstborn in Egypt, human and beast alike'" (Shemot 13:14-15). The question "What is this?" indicates that the asker is simple and does not know how to sharpen his question. The Torah commands us to explain to him, according to his abilities, the impressive events that took place during the Exodus from Egypt, the mighty plagues that struck the Egyptians, and the hardening of Pharaoh's heart, which was finally softened by the Plague of the Firstborn. These are things the simple child absorbs and finds most impressive.

Even if the child is not moved to ask at all, one must tell him about the Exodus, as it states: "*Matzot* are to be eaten... Tell your child on that day: 'It is because of this that God did for me when I left Egypt'" (Shemot 13:7-8). Since he does not ask any questions, his interest must be aroused with tangible objects. We therefore say to him, "It is because of this" – by virtue of the *matzot, maror,* and Paschal sacrifice God performed miracles for us and took us out of Egypt. Thus, we put the Seder plate on the table so that each food on it can illustrate one of the ideas that find expression at the Seder.[3]

---

3. It is interesting to note that the answer given to the wicked child is taken from Shemot 12, in the context of the mitzva of the *Pesaḥ* sacrifice both in Egypt and for future generations. Sacrificing an animal and sprinkling its blood raise the biggest questions for him. Nevertheless, the answer to his question is not evasive. It addresses the uniqueness of the Jewish people, a topic whose roots are beyond human comprehension and whose branches appear throughout the course of history. The response to the child who does not know how to ask comes from Shemot 13:8 following the commandment to eat the *Pesaḥ* sacrifice. While partaking in actual eating of the matza, one can try to connect him to the memory of the Exodus until he develops greater understanding (the child who does not know how to ask is not stupid, merely uninterested). The response to the simple son is written in the context of the sanctity of firstborns. Because he is not very intelligent, his father must teach him fear of heaven and respect for sanctity. This is accomplished by contemplating God's power and the Plague of the Firstborn. As a result, this child will accept the *mitzvot,* whose goal is to sanctify us and distinguish us from all other nations. The question of the wise son is not mentioned specifically in the context of Pesaḥ; rather, it is mentioned in Devarim 6 regarding the foundations of belief and the destiny of the Jewish people. Since everything stems from the Exodus, the Sages understood that the wise child's question is related to the *mitzvot* of Pesaḥ. Through that we explain to the wise son all the basic principles of faith.

6. THE MAIN MESSAGE OF THE HAGADA

In order to understand fully the goal of the Hagada and the story of the Exodus from Egypt, we must consider the question of the wise child and the answer he receives, for he is the preferred child, and we pray that all our children develop and succeed in becoming wise.

The wise child poses a detailed question, as it is stated: "When in the future your child asks you, 'What are these testimonies, laws, and principles that the Lord our God commanded you?'" (Devarim 6:20). The answer initially addresses the Exodus from Egypt but then broadens to include the overall purpose of the Jewish people: to come to Eretz Yisrael, to adhere to God, to fulfill all of His *mitzvot*, and to earn His benevolence:

> Say to your child, "We were slaves to Pharaoh in Egypt, but God took us out of Egypt with a mighty hand. God brought great and terrible miracles and demonstrations upon Egypt, Pharaoh, and his entire household before our very eyes. He brought us out of there in order to bring us to, and give us, the land He promised to our forebears. God commanded us to keep all of these laws, to fear the Lord our God, for the sake of our everlasting benefit, so that He might sustains us as we are today. And it shall be considered our virtue to observe and perform all these commandments before the Lord our God, as He commanded us. (*ibid.* 6:21-25)

We see, then, that the aim of the Seder is to impart to our children, by telling the story of the Exodus, the desire to belong to the people of Israel, to inherit the Promised Land, to adhere to God, and to perform all of His *mitzvot*.

To enable us to tell the story of the Exodus to the wise child without leaving out any of its essential components, the Men of the Great Assembly, who lived at the beginning of the Second Temple period, composed the text of the Hagada. Over time, the leading Tanna'im, Amora'im, and Ge'onim added passages containing important elements related to the *mitzvot* of the Hagada. Finally, about 800 years ago, a consensus version was accepted by all Jewish communities, based on the text of R. Amram Gaon.

The text of the Hagada is thus the complete story, and whoever recites it covers all aspects of the Exodus from Egypt. Nonetheless, the more one explains the Hagada and expands upon it with illuminating ideas, stories, and laws related to Pesaḥ and the Exodus, the more commendable it is.[4]

7. FROM INDIGNITY TO PRAISE

The Sages state that one must begin the story of the Exodus with indignity ("*genut*") and end it with praise ("*shevaḥ*"). To what sort of "indignity" does this refer, physical or spiritual? According to one talmudic sage (Shmuel), it refers to physical indignity – the fact that we were slaves to Pharaoh in Egypt, that the Egyptians embittered our lives with all manner of hard labor, until God redeemed us from their

4. In this sense, the entire text of the Hagada is the complete answer to the wise child. However, in the Hagada itself the wise child is answered simply: "After the Paschal sacrifice, we do not conclude with dessert (*afikoman*)." The Hagada means to say that we teach the wise son all of the laws of Pesaḥ until the very last one, namely, that we do not eat anything after the consumption of the *afikoman*. (Originally, the sacrifice was the last thing eaten at the Seder; we now eat matza – the *afikoman* – instead.) This law highlights how beloved the Seder is: we do not want to eat anything after the *afikoman*, so that the taste of the mitzva remains in our mouths. It also seems that the wise child has a tendency to discuss and attend to peripheral issues. On the Seder night, the goal is to understand the larger principles in all their profound simplicity. Thus, we say to him: "Do not go for dessert after eating the Paschal sacrifice. Focus on the main thing, without going off on tangents."

Some had the custom of reciting the *berakha* "*al sipur yetzi'at Mitzrayim*" ("regarding the telling of the Exodus from Egypt") before reciting the Hagada. This is not our practice, for several possible reasons: According to Me'iri, the *berakha* of "*emet ve-emuna*," recited following the recitation of the nighttime *Shema*, counts as the *berakha* on the Hagada. According to Rabbeinu Yeruḥam, *kiddush* at the beginning of the Seder counts as the *berakha* on the Hagada. According to *Responsa Rosh* 24:2, it is not necessary to recite a *berakha* on the Hagada, since the main aspect of the mitzva is to eat the matza and *maror* while also telling the story. *Berakhot* are in fact recited on the matza and *maror*. According to Maharal (*Gevurot Hashem* 5:62), the key aspect of the mitzva is to understand, and we do not recite *berakhot* on thoughts. According to *Shibolei Ha-leket*, the *berakha* recited at the end, "*asher ga'alanu*" ("Who has redeemed us"), is a *berakha* on the Hagada. *Ma'aseh Nisim* adds that since we recite "*asher ga'alanu*" as part of the Hagada, we should not recite a *berakha* beforehand just as one does not recite a *berakha* on the mitzva of reciting *Birkat Ha-mazon*. See *Ha-Seder He-arukh* ch. 59 for more explanations.

oppression. Another sage (Rav) maintains that this refers to spiritual indignity – the fact that our distant ancestors, Teraḥ and Lavan, were pagans, and through a long process of refinement we became an entire nation of monotheists. In practice, we follow both approaches, recounting in the Hagada the process of our emergence from enslavement to freedom as well as the process that took us from idolatry to the point when God revealed Himself to us, and we achieved complete faith (*Pesaḥim* 116a).

At first glance, it might seem preferable to tell only the pleasant and agreeable stories. A deeper second glance, however, makes it clear that the more we contemplate the hardships of the enslavement and the ignominy of the paganism practiced by our forefathers, the better we can grasp the enormity of our redemption. Light is more discernible in the midst of darkness.

In addition, discussing our undignified beginnings allows us to better understand that Israel's uniqueness is not contingent upon our success or good deeds, but is rooted in divine election that lies beyond all human comprehension. Though we lacked all dignity as contemptible slaves, God chose us from all other nations and took us out of Egypt with signs and demonstrations. Despite the fact that our forefathers were idolaters, God chose to reveal Himself to us and give us the Torah. Thus, Israel's special status is not contingent on anything of this world, but on divine fiat.

This can also teach us about Israel's unique ability to bring redemption to the world, to turn darkness into light and evil into good. We start the story by emphasizing our former indignity, to show that from the ignorance of paganism and servitude we rose up and achieved great things. This is an encouraging and comforting message: as then, so too now – our redemption will emerge from the suffering and travails of recent generations.

Additionally, discussing the fact that we were ignoble slaves awakens our sensitivity and consideration for strangers and for the unfortunate who suffer and need help, as it is stated: "Do not oppress the stranger, for you know how it feels to be a stranger, since you were strangers in the land of Egypt" (Shemot 23:9).

8. THE MEANING OF THE TEN PLAGUES

The Torah describes the ten plagues at length and in great detail, without omitting a single plague. There are many things we can learn from this. The most obvious is that there is a Judge and there is justice, and the wicked eventually will be punished. Those who are especially wicked, like the Egyptians, who enslaved an entire nation, imposed backbreaking labor, and drowned their male children in the Nile, deserved to receive their full punishment, so that all generations might learn this lesson.

There is also a profound allusion here. As we know, the world was created with ten divine utterances (RH 32a). *Kabbala* interprets these as ten *sefirot*, or "emanations," with which God created the world and continues to maintain and sustain it. However, until the nation of Israel emerged, these *sefirot* were concealed and hidden. Just as these ten spiritual elements were hidden, so too the Israelites, before they matured enough to emerge as a nation, were enslaved in Egypt.

When Israel finally reached maturity, numbering 600,000 (see above 1:4), the time had come for them to go free. It was then that God commanded Moshe to go to Pharaoh and order him to "free My people so they may make a pilgrimage to Me in the wilderness." Moshe did so, but Pharaoh refused to free them, saying, "Who is God that I should heed His call to free Israel. I do not know God and I will not free Israel" (Shemot 5:1-2). Pharaoh stubbornly refused God's command many times. But God's will prevails and no man can stand up to God's word, not even the leader of the strongest empire in the world. Using the same elements He used to create the world, God rocked the Egyptian empire with plague after plague, so that the ten utterances of Creation took the form of ten plagues, until the Egyptians were completely broken, and Israel went free.

When we arrived at Mount Sinai, God revealed the meaning of those same ten utterances in the Ten Commandments, the Torah's foundation.

9. *PESAḤ*, MATZA, AND *MAROR*

The Mishna teaches: "Rabban Gamliel would say: 'Whoever does not say these three things on Pesaḥ has not fulfilled his obligation, and they are: *Pesaḥ*, matza, and *maror*'" (*Pesaḥim* 126a).

This means that even one who cannot recite the entire Hagada must at least delve into the three food-related *mitzvot* of the Seder night. The Torah thus states regarding the mitzva to teach the child who does not know how to ask: "Tell your child on that day: 'It is because of this that God did for me when I left Egypt'" (Shemot 13:8), and the Sages teach: "'Because of this' means when matza and *maror* are before you on your table" (*Mekhilta Bo* 17). This teaches that one must at least reflect upon the reasons for the three foods we have been commanded to eat on the Seder night. Even though we are unable to offer the Paschal sacrifice nowadays, we are nonetheless commanded to recall its meaning.[5]

Because, as we have seen, the Seder is conducted in question and answer form, we recite: "The *Pesaḥ* [sacrifice] that our ancestors would eat when the Temple still stood, what is it for?"; "This matza that we eat, what is it for?"; and "This *maror* that we eat, what is it for?"

The Paschal offering expresses Israel's special relationship with God, matza expresses freedom, and *maror* expresses the significance of the enslavement.

The Paschal offering expresses Israel's special relationship with God because it recalls God's miraculous differentiation between Israel and other nations, slaying the Egyptian firstborn while "passing over"

5. According to Ran and Ramban, one who recites the entire Hagada except for the sections about *Pesaḥ*, matza, and *maror* fulfills his obligation, albeit not in the optimal fashion. Some explain that according to Rambam (MT Laws of *Ḥametz* and Matza 8:4) and *Tosafot*, if one neglects to invoke *Pesaḥ*, matza, and *maror* he does not fulfill his obligation to tell the story of the Exodus; see *Hilkhot Ḥag Be-ḥag* 16. However, a literal reading of their words is not compelling, for it is possible they referred to one who did not tell the story of the Exodus at all. If such a person mentions *Pesaḥ*, matza, and *maror* he fulfills his obligation, and if not, he does not. See *Berur Halakha* on *Pesaḥim* 116b which explains that the *poskim* debate the reason for mentioning *Pesaḥ*, matza, and *maror*. Some maintain that invoking them is necessary for the proper fulfillment of eating *Pesaḥ*, matza, and *maror*. Without explaining their meanings, one does not properly fulfill the *mitzvot* of eating them. Others maintain that invoking *Pesaḥ*, matza, and *maror* is needed to properly perform the telling of the Exodus. *Binyan Tziyon* §30 suggests that *Pesaḥ Sheini*, the make-up date for those who were unable to offer the Paschal sacrifice at its proper time, constitutes a practical difference between these two approaches: if invoking these elements is connected to the eating, one would still need to invoke them, but if it is connected to the telling of the story, one need not invoke them.

the homes of the Israelites. One might say that Israel's special status is not obvious to all as long as the Temple lies in ruins, and so we cannot offer the Paschal sacrifice nowadays.

The matza, though, which expresses our redemption from Egypt, is a perpetual mitzva, as we have never lost the freedom we obtained when we left Egypt and became wholly attached to God. This is true freedom, because only one who occupies himself with Torah is truly free. Even when we are enslaved among the nations, our spirit remains free, for the Torah allows us to transcend material enslavement.

Maror is a mitzva of rabbinic origin during periods when the Temple is in ruins and the Paschal sacrifice cannot be offered. Perhaps this is because *maror* alludes to the pain and bitterness of the enslavement, and we cannot yet fully grasp the meaning of our suffering. Only when we are able to offer the Paschal sacrifice will we grasp the full meaning of our suffering; only when we can see how it refines and purifies us and understand how our salvation sprouted from within all the difficult times does the mitzva to eat *maror* become *de-Oraita*. Until then, we have faith that everything is for the best.

Chapter Sixteen

Seder Night

1. INTRODUCTION

Before detailing the laws of the Seder, let us briefly survey the *mitzvot* we fulfill on the Seder night.

Two elements constitute the foci of the Seder: The first is commemoration of our Exodus from Egypt and emancipation from slavery and reflection on the significance of Israel's freedom. The second is to transmit our tradition to the next generation. Both of these are included in the Torah's commandment to tell the story of the Exodus on the night of the fifteenth of Nisan.

In order to make this commemoration tangible, the Torah commands us to eat the *korban Pesaḥ* (Paschal sacrifice), matza, and *maror* on this night. The Paschal sacrifice recalls God's miraculous slaying of the Egyptian firstborn while "passing over" the houses of the Israelites, sparing their firstborns. The matza recalls the *matzot* our forefathers ate when they left Egypt for freedom. And the *maror* recalls the hard labor and bitter enslavement our forefathers experienced at the hands of the Egyptians.

Because the Temple is now in ruins, we are unable to offer the Paschal sacrifice; we eat the *afikoman* in its stead. On the Torah level, the mitzva to eat *maror* is contingent on eating the Paschal sacrifice; when the *Pesaḥ* sacrifice is not offered, there is no mitzva to eat *maror*. However, the Sages instituted eating *maror* even after the destruction of the Temple.

No change has taken place regarding the mitzva to eat matza. Thus, even after the destruction of the Temple there is a Torah commandment to eat an olive's bulk (*kezayit*) of matza.

The Sages also instituted the integration of four cups of wine into the recitation of the Hagada, which we drink as an expression of joy and freedom.

They also instituted that we eat *matzot* and drink wine while reclining, as a demonstration of freedom.

2. PREPARING FOR THE SEDER

As noted, one of the two key objectives of the Seder is to transmit the tradition of the Exodus to our children. In order to keep younger children alert, we do many unusual things at the Seder: we dip vegetables in liquid twice, wash our hands twice, and give the appearance of beginning the meal before suddenly starting to recite the Hagada. In addition, the *mitzvot* of eating matza, drinking four cups of wine, and reclining also prompt the children to ask: "Why is this night different from all other nights?"

The Sages also instruct one to give nuts and candy to small children at the beginning of the Seder, so they see yet another change and ask: "Why is this night different?" (SA 472:16). It is good to give them small candies throughout the Seder, keeping them alert and happy.

An effort is made to buy new clothes for the children and the entire household before Pesaḥ, in order to make everybody happy. Indeed, the mitzva to be joyful applies to each of the three pilgrimage festivals (Pesaḥ, Shavu'ot, and Sukkot), and it is therefore a mitzva to buy clothes and jewelry for the women and girls, give young children candy and nuts, and serve meat and wine to men at each festival (SA 528:2-3). However, we are even more careful about buying new clothes for Pesaḥ, because wearing them for the Seder evokes a special sense of excitement for this exalted night.

It is proper to set the table and arrange the Seder plate before evening, so that *kiddush* can be recited as soon as possible after the *Ma'ariv* prayer. In this way, there is no wasting of the precious time when the children are still alert and can still participate in reciting the Hagada, eating the matza, and drinking the wine. However, *kiddush* should not be recited before *tzeit ha-kokhavim* (the appearance of three distinct stars), because *kiddush* must be recited at a time when matza can be eaten, i.e., the night of the fifteenth of Nisan. Moreover, the *kiddush* wine is the first of the four cups, and one must drink all four cups at night (*ibid.* 472:1; MB *ad loc.* 4).

When setting the table, one should put out comfortable chairs so that participants will be able to recline. Ideally, the table should be set with the finest silverware and dishes. During the course of the year, we refrain from setting the table with overly attractive utensils, in remembrance of the Temple's destruction, but on Shabbat and holidays we do everything we can to enhance the table's beauty (SA 560:2; MB *ad loc.* 5). On the Seder night, it is a mitzva to beautify the table with the absolute best utensils, as it expresses freedom and joy (SA 472:2; MB *ad loc.* 6).

3. THE SEDER PLATE

Before the Seder, one must prepare the Seder plate, on which all of the special Seder foods are arranged. Setting the Seder plate is not merely to keep the foods close by and at the ready, but also because each food commemorates and emphasizes a particular idea, and we must keep all the foods in front of us to express the uniqueness of the Seder. These foods are placed on the Seder plate:

> **Three *matzot*** with which we fulfill the Torah's commandment to eat matza. We place them on the Seder plate so we can recite the Hagada in the presence of matza and *maror*, fulfilling the verse: "Tell your child on that day: 'It is because of **this** that God did for me when I left Egypt'" (Shemot 13:8), which the Sages interpret: "'Because of this' means when matza and *maror* are before you" (*Mekhilta Bo* 17). Additionally, matza is called "*leḥem oni*" – "poor man's bread" (Devarim 16:3), which the Sages interpret to mean "bread over which we '*onim*' – answer or say – many things." The matza must therefore be uncovered while we recite the Hagada. However, out of respect for the matza, which is the most important food on the table and over which we recite the "*ha-motzi*" blessing, we do not recite *kiddush* while the matza is uncovered. Therefore, we cover the *matzot* during *kiddush* and

> when we lift our wine glasses, but otherwise they remain exposed while we recite the Hagada. Some have a custom to separate the three *matzot* with cloth (based on the writings of Arizal), and others have a custom not to separate the *matzot* (*Ḥayei Adam*).
>
> ***Maror*** is lettuce or horseradish. When the Temple stood, there was a Torah commandment to eat *maror* with the *korban Pesaḥ*, but since the destruction of the Temple, the mitzva to eat *maror* is rabbinic.

In Temple times, the meat of the *korban Pesaḥ* was also put on the Seder table, but with the Temple's destruction, the Sages enacted that two cooked foods be placed on the table: one to commemorate Paschal sacrifice, and the other to commemorate the *korban ḥagiga* (pilgrimage sacrifice), offered on every pilgrimage festival (*Pesaḥim* 114a-b). Customarily, the Paschal sacrifice is commemorated with a ***zero'a***, alluding to the fact that God redeemed us with an "outstretched arm" ("*zero'a netuya*"). We roast the *zero'a*, just as the Paschal sacrifice was roasted. Sephardic Jews customarily use the foreleg of a lamb or goat, whereas Ashkenazim use the wing of a fowl. The *korban ḥagiga* is customarily commemorated with a roasted or boiled **egg**. Eggs are customarily served to mourners, as their round shape consolingly reminds them of life's cyclical nature. At the Seder, the egg similarly reminds us that the Temple will be speedily rebuilt and we will again be able to offer the Paschal and *ḥagiga* sacrifices. Additionally, the Aramaic word for egg, "*bei'a*," can also refer to prayerful petition – alluding to our petitioning God to redeem us once again (SA 473:4). The custom in most communities is not to eat the *zero'a* on the Seder night (see below section 32).

We also place ***karpas*** and either vinegar or salt water on the Seder plate. *Karpas* is the vegetable that we eat before reciting the Hagada. It is dipped in vinegar or salt water both to make it tastier and to create the need for an additional hand-washing, which causes the children to ask more questions.

We place ***ḥaroset*** on the Seder plate as well. *Ḥaroset* alludes to the clay mortar our forefathers made when they were enslaved in Egypt. Before eating the *maror*, we dip it in the *ḥaroset*.

Wine is not placed on the Seder plate because it is a drink, not a food.

4. ARRANGING THE SEDER PLATE

The Talmud does not mention the Seder plate, but it does say that "matza, lettuce, *ḥaroset,* and two cooked foods" are served to the person leading the Seder (*Pesaḥim* 114a). The Rishonim and SA (473:4) state that all of these foods should be placed on a plate. However, this is not obligatory. The main thing is that these foods be placed before the Seder leader. It is not necessary to place a Seder plate before each participant or even before each married participant. Rather, it is enough to place the plate before the Seder leader (MB 473:17). Nevertheless, some have a custom to place *matzot* before the head of every household, while the complete Seder plate is placed in front of the Seder leader only.

Since a number of foods must be placed on the plate, the question arises: what is the best way to arrange them? There are several opinions on this matter.

According to Rema, the principle is that the earlier a food appears in the Seder, the closer to the Seder leader it should be placed. This is done in order to avoid "passing over the *mitzvot.*" For example, if the *matzot* were closer to the leader than the *karpas,* he would have to pass over the *matzot* when reaching for the *karpas,* and this would be somewhat disrespectful to the *matzot.* Therefore, according to Rema, one should place the *karpas* and salt water closest to the leader, because these are eaten at the beginning, even before reciting the Hagada. Next come the *matzot,* which are eaten at the start of the meal. Then come the *maror* and the *ḥaroset,* because after eating matza we eat *maror* dipped in the *ḥaroset.* Furthest away on the plate are the *zero'a* and egg, which commemorate the Paschal and *ḥagiga* offerings.

Some say that there is no need to be particular about arranging the Seder plate in a manner that will prevent "passing over *mitzvot,*" because such behavior is only improper when one is presented with the simultaneous opportunity to perform two *mitzvot.* However, on the Seder night, each mitzva has a specific time of its own, and there is no problem in passing over a mitzva whose time for fulfillment has not yet arrived, in order to get to a food that must be eaten now.

The Seder plate arrangement based on Arizal's teaching alludes to the ten kabbalistic *sefirot*.[1] This arrangement is practiced today by most Sephardic, Ḥasidic, and even some non-Ḥasidic Ashkenazim. Other Ashkenazim follow Rema, while still others follow the Vilna Gaon. Many *Hagadot* contain diagrams of the Seder plate arrangement, and each of these varying customs has a place in Jewish law.

5. *KADESH*

The Seder begins with *kiddush*, which expresses the sanctity of the Jewish people and of the Pesaḥ holiday. The *kiddush* of Shabbat and other holidays contains the phrase "in commemoration of the Exodus from Egypt," for the source of Israel's sanctity began to reveal itself with the Exodus from Egypt, when it was made known that God chose Israel to be His special nation. At the Seder, on the night we left Egypt and are commanded to tell the Exodus story, the importance of *kiddush* is thus compounded. It is therefore fitting to begin the Seder with it.[2]

Thus, unlike other *kiddushim* where only one person recites *kiddush* and drinks the majority of a cup of wine, on the Seder night each

---

1. Arizal's arrangement is as follows: The three *matzot* are on top, corresponding to the *sefirot* of *ḥokhma, bina,* and *da'at*. Under the *matzot* on the right is the *zero'a*, corresponding to the *sefira* of *ḥesed*, and the egg on the left corresponding to *gevura*. Underneath them in the middle is the *maror*, which corresponds to *tiferet*. Below the *maror* on the right is the *ḥaroset*, corresponding to *netzaḥ*, and on the left is the *karpas*, corresponding to *hod*. Underneath them in the center is the *maror* used for the *korekh* sandwich, corresponding to the *sefira* of *yesod*. The plate itself corresponds to the *sefira* of *malkhut* (*Kaf Ha-ḥayim* 473:58).
2. *Kiddush* on Shabbat is clearly a Torah precept, as it states: "Remember the Sabbath day to sanctify it." According to Rambam and the majority of *poskim*, one fulfills his Torah obligation to remember Shabbat by reciting the Friday night prayers. The Sages, however, instituted that *kiddush* be recited over wine. According to some Rishonim, the biblical mitzva is to sanctify the Shabbat over a cup of wine.

   With regard to *kiddush* on Yom Tov, the *poskim* disagree whether it is from the Torah or of rabbinic origin. *Magid Mishneh* on MT Laws of Shabbat 29:18 states that *kiddush* on Yom Tov is rabbinic, and this is also the opinion of MA 271:1 and most Aḥaronim. Conversely, many Rishonim – *She'iltot, Behag,* Raavya, and Maharam of Rothenburg – maintain that *kiddush* on Yom Tov is from the Torah, as it states: "These are the festivals of God, that you shall call holy." See *Responsa Ḥazon Ovadia* §2 for a summary.

participant is poured a cup of wine, and after *kiddush* everyone reclines and drinks most of the wine in his cup. This is the first of the four cups of wine.

The rabbinic enactment to recite *kiddush* over wine expresses an important principle in Judaism. People tend to think that sanctity manifests itself in the spiritual realm alone, through prayer and Torah study, assuming that the more one denies the body, the more sanctity he attains. Yet, the fact that the Sages instituted *kiddush* over wine teaches us that sanctity can infuse and find expression even through physical food. This is true not only of the staple foods necessary for human sustenance, but even of wine, which brings people joy. Israel's sanctity can be revealed in its totality specifically through the fullness of life, which combines the truth of Torah and faith with happiness and joy. We therefore recite *kiddush* over wine.

On every Yom Tov, we recite the *berakha* of "*she-heḥeyanu*," blessing God "Who has given us life, sustained us, and guided us to reach this season," because Yom Tov is a mitzva that is celebrated anew during a specific season. The Sages inserted *she-heḥeyanu* at the end of *kiddush*; after declaring the day's sanctity, it is only fitting to bless and thank God for having guided us to this sacred time. If one neglects to recite the *she-heḥeyanu* after *kiddush*, he must recite it whenever he remembers, as long as Pesaḥ has not ended.

Many people say a preliminary statement of intention ("*hineni mukhan*" or "*le-shem yiḥud*") before each of the four cups of wine. One should not do so between the *berakha* and drinking, as this constitutes an interruption. Rather, the formula should be recited before *kiddush*, and in the case of the other three cups, before the *berakha* on the wine (MB 473:1).

If the first day of Pesaḥ coincides with Shabbat, we invoke Shabbat in the *kiddush*. If it begins on Saturday night, two *berakhot* are added: on the creation of fire ("*borei me'orei ha-esh*") and on the separation of different forms of sanctity ("*Ha-mavdil bein kodesh le-kodesh*") (SA 473:2).

6. THE FOUR CUPS

The Sages instituted drinking four cups of wine on the Seder night in order to increase the joy of redemption and give expression to our freedom. On every Yom Tov there is a mitzva to rejoice by drinking wine, but for Pesaḥ the Sages further integrated four cups of wine into the Seder, so that our joy finds expression in each of its phases. *Kiddush* is recited over the first cup, and thus everyone's cup is filled prior to *kiddush*. The story of the Exodus and the first part of *Hallel* are recited over the second cup, which is therefore filled just before the telling of the story is begun. *Birkat Ha-mazon* is recited over the third cup; we refill our glasses prior to its recitation and drink the wine right after. Finally, we pour the fourth cup, recite the second part of *Hallel* and "the Great *Hallel*" (see below section 35) over it, and then drink the cup. Thus, every recitation at the Seder is over wine.

If one drinks four cups of wine one after another, it is as if he drank only one cup (SA 472:8). Even if one waited between cups, if he did not recite any of the Hagada during these pauses, he has not fulfilled this obligation according to several *poskim* (Rashbam, Ran, *Pri Ḥadash*). This is because one must drink while discussing the Exodus. According to *Beit Yosef*, however, if one pauses between cups he fulfills his obligation *be-di'avad* (BHL *ad loc.* s.v. "she-lo").

The Sages explain the four cups as alluding to several things: the four expressions of redemption used in the Torah's account of the Exodus; the four kingdoms that subjugated Israel after it became a nation (Babylon, Persia, Greece, and Rome), and from which the Almighty saved us; the four cups of calamity that God will serve to the wicked among the nations of the world; and the corresponding four cups of consolation that God will pour out to Israel (*y. Pesaḥim* 10:1).

As a rule, the number four represents completeness, for everything in the world has four sides, corresponding to the four points of the compass. Since the Exodus brought about a complete upheaval in the world, the Torah uses four expressions of redemption in relation to it:

> Therefore, say to the Israelites: "I am the Lord. **I will rescue you** from beneath the burden of Egypt; **I will save you** from their enslavement; **I will redeem you** with an outstretched arm and great acts of judgment; and **I will take you** for Myself as a people and be your God. Thus you will know that I am the Lord your

> God, Who is taking you out from beneath the burden of Egypt." (Shemot 6:6-7)

Israel's bondage in Egypt was more than just the enslavement of those 600,000 Jews. It manifested the subjugation of the spirit to the material, because the possibility of expressing spirituality in the world depends on the people of Israel, who were enslaved by the most materialistic of kingdoms, Egypt. In order to free Israel so that they could receive the Torah and illuminate and rectify the world, it was necessary to break all barriers of oppression, from each direction. The four expressions of redemption correspond to these.

In fact, a fifth expression of redemption appears in the very next verse: "**I will bring you** to the land that I swore to give to Avraham, Yitzḥak, and Yaakov. I will give it to you as an inheritance; I am the Lord" (*ibid.* 8). Since this verse does not address the Exodus itself, the Sages did not institute a corresponding fifth cup. Nonetheless, it is customary to pour a fifth cup, known as Eliyahu's Cup ("*Kos shel Eliyahu*"), which alludes to the complete redemption that begins with entry into the Promised Land (see section 35 below).

7. THE WINE

The Sages stated (*Pesaḥim* 108b) that in order to fulfill the mitzva of the four cups properly, one must dilute the wine with water, because otherwise it will be too strong and cause intoxication. Though the alcohol in such wine gives one pleasure, the mitzva is to drink the wine in the manner of free people, that is, like wealthy people who have control of their own time and permit themselves to drink the best wine, making sure it is diluted properly so that one can enjoy it without getting drunk. Today's wine is not as strong, and there is no need to dilute it. Even when it *is* necessary to dilute it, this is done at the winery. Therefore, there is no mitzva today to dilute the wine (MB 472:29), though some do so to enhance the mitzva.

Instead, nowadays we enhance the expression of our freedom by purchasing the finest wine that is strong enough to intoxicate, because such wine causes a sense of joy, liberation, and freedom. However, one must be careful not to use a wine so strong that it disrupts one's ability to concentrate on the Hagada and to fulfill the *mitzvot* of the Seder night.

One must therefore drink four cups of wine in a manner that brings joy and does not cause drowsiness or intoxication. If one fears that by drinking a full cup of regular wine he will be unable to concentrate properly while reading the Hagada, he should mix his wine with grape juice. This will allow him to drink wine that intoxicates, while properly fulfilling all the *mitzvot* of the Seder night. One who finds it difficult to drink wine that contains even just a small amount of alcohol may fulfill the mitzva by drinking grape juice (*Mikra'ei Kodesh* 2:35).

When the Sages instituted the four cups, they did not imagine that one would fulfill this mitzva with grape juice, as in their day there was no way to preserve the juice without it turning into vinegar. They wanted us to recite the Hagada and tell the Exodus story while drinking wine that enhances enjoyment. One who uses grape juice does not fulfill the mitzva in the way the Sages intended it. Even one who does not enjoy the taste of wine or who gets headaches from it must drink the four cups. In fact, the Gemara recounts that R. Yehuda b. Ilai had to wrap his head in a kerchief from Pesaḥ until Shavu'ot due to a headache caused by drinking four cups of wine (*Nedarim* 49b; SA 472:10; MB *ad loc.* 35). However, if wine will cause one to be ill and lie down he is exempt from this mitzva. Now that grape juice is available, even one who merely suffers from the effects of wine – for example, it gives him headaches – may discharge his obligation using grape juice.

Women are also commanded to drink four cups of wine, just as they are commanded to fulfill all of the *mitzvot* of the Seder night (SA 472:14). *Le-khatḥila,* they too should drink wine that maximizes enjoyment. However, if a woman fears becoming intoxicated, she may use grape juice to dilute or even completely replace the wine if she prefers.[3]

3. In the past, it was only possible to obtain grape juice during the grape harvest. Since last season's wine would have already been used up and it would take another forty days to prepare wine from the new crop, the Sages permitted making *kiddush* on grape juice (BB 97b; SA 272:2). This is *be-di'avad,* especially when it comes to the Seder, where reciting the Hagada joyfully is an integral part of the institution. This argument is also advanced in *Mikra'ei Kodesh* 2:35, although in the notes on p. 130 the author advocates that women may fulfill the mitzva using grape juice. He argues that the reason for using intoxicating wine is to fulfill the mitzva of rejoicing on Yom Tov. *Pesaḥim* 109a states: "Every person must rejoice during the festival… men with what

The Sages also stated that there is a mitzva to seek out fine red wine (*y. Pesaḥim* 10:1). However, *be-di'avad,* any wine is adequate, even cheap white wine (SA 472:11).

8. THE AMOUNT OF WINE AND CUP SIZE

In order to fulfill the mitzva of the four cups, or any other mitzva that involves drinking wine (such as *kiddush, havdala, Birkat Ha-mazon,* and wedding ceremonies), there must be a significant amount of wine in the cup. The Sages determined that the cup must contain at least a quarter of a *log* (a "*revi'it*") of wine. Less than this is not a significant amount of wine and does not suffice to fulfill the obligation (*Pesaḥim* 108b).

A *revi'it* is equal in volume to an egg and a half. R. Ḥayim Naeh calculated, based on writings of Rambam and other Rishonim, that this is 86 milliliters. However, more precise measurements showed that it is c. 75 ml (see *Peninei Halakha: Berakhot* 10:11). This amount, however, is not agreed upon by everyone. The exile gave rise to uncertainties regarding the size of olives and eggs, and some later Ashkenazic *poskim* (*Noda Bi-Yehuda, Ḥazon Ish*) rule that today's eggs are only about half the size of eggs in the time of the Sages. Therefore, a *revi'it* is closer to the volume of three of today's eggs, c. 150 ml. This stringent measure is known today as a "Ḥazon Ish *shi'ur.*"

In practice, the lenient opinion is the standard, and this is the practice of Sephardim. However, MB 271:68 and 486:1 states regarding the practice of Ashkenazim that it is best to take the stringent opinion into account with regard to *mitzvot* of Torah origin like *kiddush* and *havdala.* However, when it comes to rabbinic *mitzvot* like the four cups at the Seder or the minimum amount that must be drunk in order to recite a *berakha aḥarona* (a blessing recited after eating or drinking), we use

---

is appropriate for them – with wine, and women ... in Babylonia with dyed clothing and in Eretz Yisrael with pressed linen clothing." SA 529:2 and BHL *ad loc.* rule that, indeed, the joy of wine relates primarily to men.

Nevertheless, the most straightforward understanding of this mitzva requires women to drink the four cups of wine just like men, as "they too participated in that miracle" (*Pesaḥim* 108b). Until recent generations, this was the common practice of women. Nevertheless, intoxication is more disgraceful for women than for men (*Ketubot* 65a), so women concerned about intoxication may mix more grape juice into their wine.

the smaller measure, in keeping with the majority opinion. Those who wish to be stringent, and who enjoy drinking wine, are commendable.

One must also take care to meet the Sages' requirements for a *kos shel berakha* (a cup of wine linked to the performance of a mitzva). A broken cup must not be used, and the cup, however large, must be filled with wine in honor of the mitzva.

The cup must be clean, thoroughly rinsed inside and out, before the first cup. However, as long as it has not become dirtied, it is unnecessary to wash it again for subsequent cups, since all four cups are considered one continuum (MB 473:68). Nonetheless, some take care to wash the cup before drinking each time (*Kaf Ha-ḥayim* 473:1).[4]

9. HOW MUCH WINE?

Optimally, one should drink all of the wine in the cup, which means at least a *revi'it*. If one uses a large cup that contains more than a *revi'it*, he should, *le-khatḥila*, drink all of the wine in the cup. If he does not want to, he should at least try to drink most of it. At the very least, one must drink most of a *revi'it* and a "*melo lugmav*." In other words, there are two conditions: first, he must drink most of the wine that is required to be in the cup, i.e., most of a *revi'it* (38 ml or 76 ml in Ḥazon Ish *shi'ur*). Secondly, this amount must fill *melo lugmav* – enough wine to fill the drinker's mouth with one cheek inflated. This is the amount of wine that settles one's mind. For someone with a normal size mouth, *melo lugmav* a bit more than most of a *revi'it*. For one with a large mouth, *melo lugmav* is closer to a *revi'it*. A thirteen-year-old, whose mouth is small and whose *melo lugmav* is less than half a *revi'it* must drink most of a *revi'it* in order to fulfill the first condition (SA 472:9; MB *ad loc.* 30; BHL *ad loc.* s.v. "ve-yishteh").[5]

---

4. *Kaf Ha-ḥayim* 472:1 states, based on *Zohar*, that one should rinse the cup again before *Birkat Ha-mazon*. Some had the custom of preparing a basin of water and immersing the cups in it between each drinking. Nowadays, this practice is not as nice, since the water in the bowl becomes dirty; we would not consider such cups clean. One who wants to be strict should rinse his glass in the sink. Most *poskim* maintain that one need not rinse out the cups in the middle of the Seder.

5. According to Ramban, cited as an alternative opinion in SA 472:9, one must drink the majority of the cup, no matter how large. However, most *poskim* maintain that

Children who have reached the age of mitzva education are given four cups of wine (SA 472:15). The age of education is when the child understands the meaning of the things that are said while the cups are filled – *kiddush,* the Hagada, *Birkat Ha-mazon,* and *Hallel* (SAH 472:25) – generally around age five or six. There is no need for them to drink most of a *revi'it; melo lugmav* suffices (MB 472:47).

One must drink most of the wine in the cup "at once." It is obvious that if one drinks half of the necessary amount, and then, after a long pause, drinks the second half, he did not drink the necessary amount "at once" and thus did not fulfill drinking one of the four cups. However, leading Rishonim and Aḥaronim are divided over precisely how quickly one must drink the requisite amount of wine in order for it to be considered "at once." According to Rambam, since people are accustomed to drink continuously, albeit with short breaks to breathe or swallow, one is only considered to have drunk "at once" if he drank continuously, as one would normally drink a *revi'it.* In other words, the amount of time one takes to drink most of a *revi'it* must be no longer than the amount of time it normally takes to drink an entire *revi'it.* If it takes one longer to drink most of a *revi'it* than it normally takes people to drink a *revi'it,* he has not fulfilled the mitzva according to Rambam. Raavad, on the other hand, maintains that as long as it does not take longer than the time it takes to eat a half a loaf of bread ("*shi'ur akhilat pras*"), i.e., within several minutes, it is still considered "at once."

---

although it is preferable to follow Ramban, one fulfills the obligation without meeting that condition (MB *ad loc.* 33). Although the accepted opinion is the primary one, in this context I stressed that following the Ḥazon Ish *shi'ur* enhances the mitzva, since more wine adds to the mitzva of rejoicing and those who want to enhance the mitzva always drank more than the minimum *revi'it.*

Thus, to satisfy unquestionably all opinions one should preferably use a cup that contains 150 ml and drink most of it. This satisfies the higher *melo lugmav* requirement as well as Ramban's condition. However, if it is difficult for him to drink an entire 150 ml "Ḥazon Ish *shi'ur*" cup, he ends up losing the enhancement of drinking an entire cup. Although we have stated that one may fulfill his obligation *le-khatḥila* by using the standard *shi'ur,* one who wishes to enhance the mitzva should first satisfy all opinions, including the Ḥazon Ish *shi'ur,* and only then undertake to drink an entire cup. If he enjoys drinking wine, the greatest enhancement is to drink a full 150 ml cup; if he is worried that he might become intoxicated, he may mix grape juice into the wine.

To summarize, one should preferably follow the stringent ruling of Rambam and drink most of the cup continuously, taking short breaks to breathe and swallow. *Be-di'avad,* if one drinks most of the wine in the cup within a *shi'ur akhilat pras* (6-7 minutes), he fulfills his obligation and need not drink the cup again, since the law of four cups is of rabbinic origin, and the *halakha* therefore follows the lenient position. Nonetheless, some practice stringency.[6]

---

6. More broadly, "*shi'ur akhilat pras*" is a unit of time within which all eating is treated as a single act. There is a dispute as to whether or not this time period applies to drinking as well. According to Rambam, since one drinks faster than he eats, the measurement of time for drinking is different than that of eating, and only uninterrupted drinking is considered as one unit. According to Raavad, the measurement of time for drinking is the same as for eating, and as long as one drank within a "*shi'ur akhilat pras,*" it is considered a single act. See section 25 below for a more precise definition of a "*pras.*"

Optimally, one must drink uninterruptedly, as per Rambam, and if he drank the minimum amount within the time of *akhilat pras,* he has not fulfilled his obligation according to Rambam, only Raavad. But since we rule leniently when there is uncertainty pertaining to rabbinic law, one would not have to drink again. This is what AHS 472:13 and *Ḥazon Ovadia* §12 state. Moreover, according to *Knesset Ha-gedola,* SAH, and *Ḥatam Sofer,* Rambam only stated his opinion with regard to a forbidden drink, where one incurs lashes if he drinks continuously. But regarding *berakhot* over consumption of food or drink, Rambam would concur that *shi'ur akhilat pras* is the relevant time frame, since the determining factor of *berakhot* is enjoyment, and he certainly derives pleasure even if he only completes his drink during a *shi'ur akhilat pras.* Accordingly, perhaps Rambam would concur that one who drinks a cup of wine within a *shi'ur akhilat pras* would fulfill his obligation. Nevertheless, some *poskim* say that where it is easy to fulfill one's obligation according to all opinions, one should be stringent even with regard to a disputed rabbinic law. Therefore, MA and SAH 472:20 and MB 472:34 state that if one drank the second cup only within the time of *akhilat pras,* he should drink it again. If it was the third or fourth cup, though, he should not drink again, since it would look like he was adding to the four cups. Rather, in this case he should rely on the opinion of Raavad that he has fulfilled his obligation (see MB 472:21 regarding the first cup). According to those who follow SA that one may drink after the third and fourth cups, one should re-drink any of the four cups in question, as *Ben Ish Ḥai* (Tzav 29) states. This is why I wrote that some are stringent in this matter, despite the fact that this is a double uncertainty about a rabbinic law: according to Raavad, the obligation has certainly been fulfilled, and possibly even according to Rambam as well.

See section 25 below and the notes *ad loc.* for the differing opinions regarding the length of *shi'ur akhilat pras.* The average time is around six to seven minutes, but *le-khatḥila* it is four minutes, and *be-di'avad* it is nine minutes.

10. THE MITZVA OF RECLINING

The Sages ordained that one recline while eating matza and drinking wine at the Seder, because in every generation one must give the appearance of having just been freed from Egyptian bondage, as it is stated: "He rescued us from there" (Devarim 6:23). This reclining is called "*hasava*," and it was instituted so that a sense of liberation would be apparent in one's behavior (MT, Laws of *Ḥametz* and Matza 7:6-7).

One who is burdened with a task usually sits upright so that he will be able to rise at once when the time comes for him to carry out his work. Even though sitting upright requires some effort on the part of the back muscles and creates a state of constant tension, the need to be ready for action requires this state of alertness. However, one who has no burdens can lean back and lie on his side restfully, allowing all of his back muscles to relax. This is how we eat on the Seder night, in the manner of the liberated.

In the past, people would sit on pillows and cushions, which meant that sitting erect indeed required effort. In such circumstances, *hasava* – the position between sitting and lying down, where the entire body reclines on a couch or on pillows and cushions – was very comfortable and demonstrated a sense of freedom. But today, people sit on chairs and are not accustomed to reclining on couches or eating while reclining to the side. In fact, if one were to eat while reclining on a couch these days, it would be more burdensome than comfortable. Therefore, according to Raavya and Raavan, two leading Rishonim, there is no mitzva to practice *hasava* nowadays. However, most Rishonim maintain that since the Sages mandated reclining at the Seder, their ordinance stands firm, and there continues to be a mitzva to eat matza and drink the four cups of wine while reclining (Rambam, Rosh, *Tur*, SA 472:2). Today we recline by leaning against the back left of our chairs.

The requirement of *hasava* applies when eating a *kezayit* of matza, a *kezayit* of *korekh*, a *kezayit* of *afikoman*, and while drinking the four cups of wine. It is commendable to recline during the rest of the meal as well, but if one finds this uncomfortable, there is no obligation (MT, Laws of *Ḥametz* and Matza 7:8). One need not recline while eating the *maror* (MB 475:14, based on *Beit Yosef*). One should not recline while reciting *Birkat Ha-mazon*, which must be recited with awe and reverence

(SA 183:9). Likewise, it is customary to refrain from *hasava* while reading the Hagada, so that it is recited with full concentration and seriousness (MB 473:81, based on *Shlah*).

11. HOW TO RECLINE

Nowadays, people are not used to reclining on couches while eating, and it is therefore necessary to explain how to perform *hasava* in a chair on the Seder night. Instead of sitting erect with one's back against the seat back, one slides his bottom forward to the middle of the seat so that he may lean back against the chair back, and tilts to the left. If possible, one should use an upholstered chair with armrests, or try to use a pillow to make sitting more comfortable. Regardless, anyone who uses a chair with a backrest fulfills his obligation by reclining against the back of the chair and tilting to the left, for this too is an expression of freedom. After all, an office worker, for example, must sit erect in his chair in order to carry out his work, but one who has no burdens can stretch out, lean back, and rest in liberated manner.

The reason for reclining to the left is that it is easier to eat this way; with the left hand and back reclining against the chair, the right hand, which we generally use, remains free to hold the matza or wine. Additionally, some say that one who reclines to the right runs the risk of choking on his food and suffocating. Because of this risk, it was ruled that even a left-handed person must recline to the left and use his right hand on the Seder night. *Be-di'avad*, a right-handed person who mistakenly reclines to his right does not fulfill his obligation, but a left-handed person who reclines to the right does (SA 472:3, MB *ad loc.* 10-11).

If one is sitting in the company of his rabbi or a leading Torah sage, he must ask his permission before reclining, because *hasava* contains an expression of disrespect and irreverence toward the rabbi, and the mitzva to honor the Torah takes precedence over the mitzva of *hasava*. But if one receives permission from his rabbi, then *hasava* no longer constitutes a display of disrespect (SA 472: 5).

12. IF ONE FORGETS TO RECLINE

If one eats a *kezayit* of matza without reclining, he does not fulfill his obligation, as he has not performed the mitzva as the Sages ordained it, and he must eat another *kezayit* while reclining. Even if one has already recited *Birkat Ha-mazon,* he must wash his hands again, recite *ha-motzi,* and eat a second *kezayit* while reclining. In this case, however, one does not recite the "*al akhilat matza*" blessing a second time, because, according to Raavya and Raavan, he already fulfilled the mitzva of eating matza with the *kezayit* he ate without *hasava* (SA 472:7, MB *ad loc.* 22).

If one forgets to recline for *korekh,* he need not eat it a second time, since some *poskim* rule that *korekh* does not require *hasava* because it contains *maror. Le-khatḥila,* we customarily recline for *korekh,* but if one forgets to do so, he may rely upon those who maintain that *hasava* is not necessary. If one eats the *afikoman* without reclining and he can easily eat another *kezayit* of *afikoman* while reclining, he should do so; but if eating another *kezayit* will be difficult for him, he may rely on Raavya and Raavan, who maintain that *hasava* is not necessary nowadays.[7]

---

7. The principle is that when in doubt about a Torah commandment one must be stringent, but when in doubt about a rabbinic enactment one may be lenient. Eating a *kezayit* of matza is a Torah obligation, and although reclining while eating is a rabbinic obligation, since it pertains to a Torah obligation we are stringent, and if one ate without reclining he must eat again and recline. Conversely, eating *korekh* and *afikoman* are rabbinic injunctions, and since according to Raavya and Raavan reclining while eating them is unnecessary, if one ate them without reclining, he would not have to eat again. However, since according to the overwhelming majority of *poskim* reclining is necessary when eating *korekh* and *afikoman* (and this is the *halakha*), and since it is an easy mitzva to redo, one should redo the mitzva.

Regarding *korekh, Rokei'aḥ* and *Shibolei Ha-leket* maintain that one need not recline while eating *korekh* since it contains *maror. Manhig,* though, says one should recline during *korekh,* and this is the view of most Rishonim as well as SA 475:1. However, if one ate *korekh* without reclining he still fulfills his obligation (*Kaf Ha-ḥayim* 475:36 in the name of *Pri Ḥadash* and SAH).

Regarding the *afikoman,* SA 477:1 states that one must recline while eating the *afikoman. Pri Ḥadash,* on the other hand, notes that Rambam and the Yerushalmi seem to imply that reclining while eating the *afikoman* is unnecessary. Based on this, MB 477:4 states that if one forgot to recline and eating another *kezayit* of *afikoman* would be difficult for him, he need not eat another *afikoman.* This is also the opinion of *Kaf Ha-ḥayim* 472:45 and 477:7. According to *Ḥayei Adam* 130:13, though, even if one was able to eat another *afikoman,* it is forbidden to eat the *afikoman* twice. MB 472:22 quotes this, which seemingly contradicts what he states in 477:4. Perhaps this can be reconciled: if one remembered immediately that he neglected to recline, he should continue eating another *kezayit* while reclining, but if he already finished

If one drinks one of the four cups without reclining, the *poskim* are divided over whether or not he must go back and drink it a second time. According to *Shulḥan Arukh,* he must indeed drink the cup again, this time reclining. According to Rema, though, this creates a problem, because by drinking again one appears to be adding to the number of cups ordained by the Sages. Therefore, if one drinks the second of the four cups without reclining, he must drink it again with *hasava,* because the second cup precedes the meal, and since it is permissible to drink wine during the meal, one who drinks at this point does not appear to be adding to the required four cups. But if one forgot to recline while drinking the first, third, or fourth cup, he may not go back and drink it a second time, because by doing so he would appear to be adding to the mitzva. He may rely on Raavya and Raavan who maintain that nowadays, when even important people are not accustomed to reclining, one need not perform *hasava* on the Seder night (SA 472:7, MB 21 *ad loc.*).

Shulḥan Arukh's ruling that one must drink any of the four cups again with *hasava,* and Rema's similar ruling about only the second cup, are *le-khatḥila.* If drinking again is difficult, one may rely on what he drank without *hasava* and need not drink again.[8]

---

eating, he should not go back and eat more, since this would be considered eating the *afikoman* twice. So states *Hilkhot Ḥag Be-ḥag* 22:5.

8. *Pesaḥim* 108a expresses uncertainty about which of the four cups require reclining – the first two or the last two – and concludes that one must recline while drinking all four cups. Some Rishonim ask why the Gemara rules stringently, to recline during all cups, if the mitzva to drink the four cups is only rabbinic in origin, which should indicate a lenient ruling. Maharam Halawa, *Tashbetz,* and others answer that indeed the Gemara should have been lenient, but since there is no difficulty involved in reclining, it is best to recline while drinking all four cups. According to this answer, if one drank the cups without reclining, he need not drink again, since, in principle, the Gemara would have ruled leniently were this not such an easy mitzva. In contrast, Rosh says that if one drank any of the cups without reclining, he must drink again. This leads us to the conclusion that the reason we recline during all four cups is not because we are in doubt, but because the Sages in fact decreed that this should be so. This is the opinion of SA 742:7. In practice, since Raavya and Raavan maintain that there is no need to recline nowadays, and we are uncertain about whether or not one is required to drink again, one may be lenient. This is the opinion of *Birkei Yosef* 472:8 and *Kaf Ha-ḥayim* 472:42. *Ḥazon Ovadia* (§13), however, rules in accordance with SA that the leniency to not have to drink again only applies to someone who

Women should preferably recline while eating matza and drinking the four cups of wine, but if they forgot, they need not eat or drink again. Important women who accidentally eat matza without reclining should eat it again while reclining.[9]

13. MAY ONE DRINK AFTER THE FIRST CUP?

Technically, one who wishes to drink after the first of the four cups may do so, but one should preferably not drink between the first and second cups so that he does not become intoxicated to the point of being unable to read the Hagada with proper concentration. However, it is permissible to drink non-alcoholic beverages such as grape juice or any other juice (SA 473:3, MB 16 *ad loc.*).

If, while reciting the blessing over the wine, one had in mind to drink other beverages, he need not recite a *berakha* over them, because the *berakha* over wine covers all beverages. Even if he did not intend to drink other beverages, but they were on the table and there was a chance that he might want to drink them, he need not recite a *berakha*

---

has difficulty doing so. In sum, Sephardim preferably follow SA that if one drank any of the cups without reclining, he has to drink again, and Ashkenazim follow Rema and only re-drink the second cup. However, if someone, whether Sephardic or Ashkenazic, wishes to be lenient, he may do so, since this is an uncertainty – and possibly a double uncertainty (*sfek sfeika*) regarding a rabbinic law.

9. *Pesaḥim* 108a states that a woman need not recline if she is in her husband's presence, with the exception of an important woman ("*isha ḥashuva*"). SA 472:4 rules accordingly. (The rationale is that if reclining in the manner of free people does not reflect an inner sense of freedom, it has no purpose. This is similar to the logic behind a disciple not reclining in the presence of his rabbi.) There are different opinions about what defines an *isha ḥashuva* – that she is not subservient to her husband, that she is wealthy, that she is pedigreed, or that her husband does not mind if she reclines. Rema states that all women nowadays are considered *ḥashuvot*, but the custom is nevertheless that they do not recline, as per Raavya, who says that there is no longer a mitzva to recline. In practice, all women from all communities should try to recline, as *Knesset Ha-gedola* and *Kaf Ha-ḥayim* (*ad loc.* 28) state. Many Ashkenazic women in fact do so. But if a woman forgot to recline, she need not eat or drink again, since the mitzva of reclining is rabbinic, and there are several *poskim* who maintain that women are exempt, either because they are not *ḥashuvot* or because the view of Raavya is correct. Nonetheless, it seems that women who see themselves as important should recline while eating the Torah-mandated *kezayit* of matza and refrain from relying on the opinion of Raavya.

before drinking them, because the blessing over wine covers these too (see SHT 473:18).[10]

A firstborn who fasted on Erev Pesaḥ, or someone so hungry that he finds it difficult to concentrate on reciting the Hagada, may eat foods such as eggs, fruits, potatoes, and *kitniyot* (for those who eat *kitniyot* on Pesaḥ) after *kiddush*. However, he should not eat too much, so that he saves his appetite for the matza. Furthermore, this is only permitted when there is great need. If one can restrain himself, it is best not to eat anything before the meal, because when one eats after *kiddush*, he runs into the problem of whether he has to recite a *berakha aḥarona* (and if one eats, he must recite a *berakha aḥarona*).[11]

10. According to SAH 473:13 and MB 479:5, if one wants to drink "*ḥamar medina*" (the alcoholic non-wine beverage locally considered significant), if it requires a new *berakha*, the beverage is prohibited, since *be-di'avad* one can fulfill the mitzva by drinking *ḥamar medina* for all four cups. This is the proper custom. (*Ḥemed Moshe* forbids even other drinks if one must make a *berakha* on them. See *Kaf Ha-ḥayim* 473:40. It remains unclear whether this stringency applies to the Sephardic custom, according to which a *berakha* is not recited before every cup.)

11. One would presumably need to recite a *berakha aḥarona*. Since the food one eats before a meal is not considered part of the meal, he must recite a *berakha* after finishing the food before beginning the meal. This is the opinion of *Ben Ish Ḥai* (Naso 4), *Kaf Ha-ḥayim* 177:7, and *Or Le-Tziyon* 12:7. In principle, MB 176:2 also rules this way, but states that according to several *poskim*, if the food is of a type that is not covered by the *berakha* of *ha-motzi*, such as fruit, and the person intends to continue eating fruit during the meal, he should not make a *berakha aḥarona*, since the *berakha* that he made on the fruit will include the fruit he eats during the meal. Also, since *Birkat Ha-mazon* covers the fruit that he ate during the meal, it will also cover the fruit he ate before the meal. Consequently, an uncertain situation arises, since according to Rashbam the *berakha* on the *karpas* is also supposed to cover the *maror*. Therefore, SA states that one should specifically eat less than a *kezayit* of *karpas* so that he will not have to recite a *berakha aḥarona*. If one recited a *berakha aḥarona* over the food he ate after *kiddush*, that *berakha* would cover the *karpas*, and he would be required to make a new *berakha* on the *maror*. Perhaps he can have in mind to cover everything except the *karpas* with his *berakha aḥarona*, but this demands further investigation. Perhaps we may say that since he is eating after *kiddush*, the food is considered part of the meal and is covered by *Birkat Ha-mazon*. The only problem is that according to many *poskim*, including *Ben Ish Ḥai* and *Kaf Ha-ḥayim* cited above, *Birkat Ha-mazon* does not cover anything eaten before the meal. Moreover, even those who generally maintain that *Birkat Ha-mazon* covers food eaten before the meal, at the Seder there is a large break between the food

This eating and drinking is only permissible before one pours the second cup and begins reciting the Hagada. However, after beginning the Hagada, it is forbidden to interrupt by eating or drinking, for reciting the Hagada is like prayer, which cannot be interrupted (BHL 473:3, based on Ramban and Ran; however, it notes that *Ha-ma'or* and *Tosafot* permit).

14. *RAḤATZ*

After *kiddush* we eat the *karpas,* a vegetable. The Sages ordained eating *karpas* to create a change that will cause the children to ask why it is that tonight, unlike all other nights, we are eating a vegetable before the meal (Rashi and Rashbam on *Pesaḥim* 114a). Another reason given for this is that free people generally begin their meals with a vegetable appetizer, and so we do the same at the beginning of the Seder (Maharil).

The Sages ordained dipping the vegetable in a liquid, because this necessitates washing the hands before eating it, which is also a departure from the usual order of things. Ordinarily, the hands are washed only once at the beginning of the meal before eating bread. Thereafter, a variety of other foods are eaten. However, even if we dip these other foods in liquids, it is not necessary to wash our hands a second time, because hand-washing for bread covers the whole meal. At the Seder, though, we wash once before eating the *karpas* and a second time after reciting the Hagada, before eating the matza. The children therefore ask: "Why is this night different that, unlike all other nights, on this night we wash our hands twice?" (*Tur* and *Beit Yosef* 473:6). In addition, dipping the vegetable in liquid gives expression to our freedom, because this is the best way to eat it: not only does it serve as an appetizer, we even pamper

---

eaten after *kiddush* and the meal, so it would seem that everyone would agree that in this case *Birkat Ha-mazon* does not cover anything eaten before the meal (*Yeḥaveh Da'at* 1:2). Indeed, *Birkat Ha-mazon* covers the wine that one drinks for the first cup, but this wine is different, because it is certainly connected to the meal, since the recitation of *kiddush* over this wine specifically allows one to partake in the meal. On the other hand, food that is eaten after *kiddush* might not be connected to the meal. In practice, one who eats after *kiddush* must recite a *berakha aḥarona* ("*borei nefashot*"), but should not recite a *borei pri ha-adama* on the *maror*. See R. Harari's *Mikra'ei Kodesh* ch. 4, nn. 141 and 142.

ourselves by dipping it in salt water or vinegar, which enhances flavor and stimulates the appetite.

A full explanation of this law lies beyond the scope of this book, but suffice it to say that liquids conduct impurity ("*tum'a*") more effectively than solid foods. The Sages therefore ordained the washing of hands before eating a food that has been dipped in liquid. According to most Rishonim, this hand washing has the same status as hand washing before eating bread: both were instituted to avoid *tum'a*. Even though nowadays we do not observe the laws of ritual purity and impurity, the institution remains in force. Thus, just as one must recite the *berakha* of "*al netilat yadayim*" over the hand washing before bread, so must one recite this blessing before eating a food dipped in liquid. This is the opinion of Rambam and Rosh. However, according to R. Meir of Rothenburg (Maharam), *Itur*, and *Tosafot* (*Pesaḥim* 115a), there is a difference between these two types of hand washing: *netilat yadayim* before bread was instituted for purposes of sanctity and cleanliness, and thus even today hands should be washed for cleanliness before a meal. Consequently, this hand washing requires a *berakha*. However, *netilat yadayim* before eating a food dipped in liquid is only due to *tum'a*, and since these laws are not practiced nowadays, there is no need to wash hands before eating a food dipped in liquid.[12]

12. The laws of year-round foods dipped in liquid are discussed in SA 158:4, which rules that one must wash his hands without a *berakha* before eating them. However, MA cites *Leḥem Ḥamudot* that many do not wash their hands before eating foods dipped in liquid, and that they may rely on the minority of Rishonim who maintain that this law does not apply nowadays. SAH 158:3 states that we do not reprimand people who act this way, though it is better to wash one's hands. MB 158:20 states that many Aḥaronim are stringent in this matter, though in practice many people are lenient, including many Torah scholars. They presumably base this lenient practice on the principle that when there is an uncertainty regarding a rabbinic law, we are lenient, since washing hands before eating is a rabbinic injunction (*Peninei Halakha: Berakhot* 2:5). If so, however, why do we deviate from the standard practice on Pesaḥ night and wash our hands before eating *karpas*? See *Taz* 473:6, which uses this question to prove that we should be careful to wash our hands all year round. Netziv states in his Hagada, *Imrei Shefer*, that this is not a valid question, since during the Seder we do many things that used to be done during Temple times, including this hand washing.

In practice, we wash our hands before eating *karpas,* but do not recite a blessing, in order to fulfill all opinions: on the one hand, we wash our hands in accordance with the *poskim* who require it, but on the other hand, we do not recite a *berakha* because there are those who maintain that nowadays there is no need to wash hands before eating food dipped in liquid (SA 473:6).

If one mistakenly recites a blessing over this hand washing, he is not guilty of a *berakha le-vatala* (a blessing in vain), since he has acted in accordance with the majority of *poskim,* including *Levush* and Gra, who require a *berakha* when washing hands for a food dipped in liquid. However, the *le-khatḥila* ruling is not to recite a *berakha,* because we rule leniently in cases of uncertainty about *berakhot.*[13]

Furthermore, if one mistakenly recites a *berakha* over the first hand washing, this does not exempt him from the second hand washing, and he must recite a blessing over it as well. This is because people are not meticulous about keeping their hands clean between the two washings. In addition, the time spent reciting the Hagada constitutes an interruption between the two hand washings, and therefore the Sages ordained washing hands twice at the Seder (see *Kaf Ha-ḥayim* 473:107; BHL 475:1; *Mikra'ei Kodesh* ch. 7 n. 8).

15. *KARPAS*

As noted, the Sages ordained eating a vegetable dipped in liquid between *kiddush* and the recitation of the Hagada in order to change routine; all year long, we eat vegetables during the meal, after washing hands over bread, but at the Seder we eat a bit of vegetable before reciting the Hagada and before washing hands for the meal. Two things are unusual about this: first, we eat a vegetable before the meal, and second, we wash our hands twice instead of once (Rashi and Rashbam on *Pesaḥim* 114a; *Tur* §473). In addition, because we eat a vegetable before reciting the Hagada, our Seder meal is imbued with added importance, because the finest banquets generally begin with appetizers and hors d'oeuvres,

---

13. If he recited a *berakha* accidentally, he should eat an egg's bulk (*kebeitza*) of the vegetable, since one is only required to wash with a *berakha* on a piece of food this size (SA 158:2, *Kaf Ha-ḥayim* 158:20, and the opinion of Rashbatz quoted there).

followed by a pause for a different part of the program, after which the main meal begins (based on *Baḥ*).

The word "*karpas*" appears neither in the Mishna nor in the Talmud; we are only told that a vegetable is eaten before the Hagada is recited (*Pesaḥim* 114-115). But a few Rishonim (Maharil, Raavan) write that *karpas* should be used, because its Hebrew name alludes to the 600,000 men put to hard labor in Egypt (the Hebrew letters of the word *karpas* can be rearranged to spell "*samekh parekh*"; the letter *samekh* has a numerical value of sixty or 600,000, and *parekh* means hard labor). Though not mandatory, the Aḥaronim say that it is good to use *karpas* (SA 473:6, MB 19 and *Kaf Ha-ḥayim* 49 *ad loc.*). However, there are differing opinions about what *karpas* is. Some say it is celery, and this is the widespread custom among Sephardim. Others say it is parsley, which is the custom of some Ashkenazim. Most Ashkenazim, however, use neither celery nor parsley, because there is uncertainty about what blessing to recite over them in the Ashkenazic custom. They instead use boiled potatoes. Each family should continue its own tradition.[14]

We dip the *karpas* in salt water or vinegar and recite the *berakha* of "*borei pri ha-adama*" (Who creates the food of the soil) with the intention that it also apply to the *maror* that will be eaten later in the meal. It is not necessary to recline while eating *karpas* because some *poskim* say

14. See *Mikra'ei Kodesh* pp. 184-187 and *Sidur Pesaḥ Ke-hilkhato* 2:5:3 regarding the opinions about and customs of eating *karpas*. In general, the advantage of eating celery or parsley, in addition to the fact that they are actually *karpas*, is that they are eaten raw and stimulate the appetite. Moreover, they are usually eaten in small amounts, which makes it easier to eat less than a *kezayit*, as will be explained below. On the other hand, in Ashkenazic communities they were not generally eaten raw, and consequently one who eats them raw should recite the *berakha* of "*she-hakol.*" But the *berakha* on *karpas* must be "*ha-adama.*" Therefore, the custom in Ashkenazic communities is to eat cooked potatoes for *karpas*, on which the *berakha* is undoubtedly "*ha-adama.*" In Middle Eastern and North African communities, where celery and parsley were eaten raw, one recites "*ha-adama*" over them.

It is worth adding that one should not use any food for *karpas* that is normally eaten outside the context of a meal – bananas and pineapples, for example – since it is not clear that they are being used as appetizers; rather, they look like separate foods that are eaten by themselves, do not seem different, and do not provoke questions. Vegetables, however, are usually eaten in the middle of the meal, so eating them before the meal is a change.

it alludes to the suffering of enslavement in Egypt, and therefore need not be eaten as a demonstration of freedom.

One must eat less than a *kezayit* of *karpas*. Though some Rishonim (Rambam) say that more than a *kezayit* of *karpas* should be eaten, it is best to avoid this. Eating more than a *kezayit* invites uncertainty about making a *berakha aḥarona,* since according to Ri, a *berakha aḥarona* is necessary, but according to Rashbam, one should not recite a *berakha aḥarona,* because the blessing over the *karpas* covers the *maror* we eat during the meal. Therefore, as said, it is best not to eat a *kezayit* of *karpas.* If one eats more than a *kezayit* of *karpas,* he should not recite a *berakha aḥarona,* because we rule leniently whenever there is uncertainty about reciting a *berakha* (Maharil; SA 473:6).[15]

15. This dispute hinges on whether one must recite a *berakha* on the *maror*. According to Rashbam, a *berakha* is necessary, since the *berakha* of "*ha-motzi*" over the matza covers everything that will be eaten during the meal, meaning anything that is eaten with matza to provide satisfaction. But *maror* is not eaten for this purpose, so it is not covered by the *berakha* of *ha-motzi*. Therefore, one must have in mind when making the *berakha* on the *karpas* to cover the *maror* as well. By doing this, he exempts himself from making a separate *berakha* on the *maror*. However, according to Ri, one need not make a *berakha* on *maror* at all, since it is considered a food that is eaten in the context of the meal and hence is covered by the *berakha* on the matza. Accordingly, if one eats more than a *kezayit* of *karpas,* he must recite a *berakha aḥarona*. He should not wait until *Birkat Ha-mazon,* since it only covers food that was eaten during the meal, not before it. So if one eats a *kezayit* of *karpas* and does not recite a *berakha aḥarona* right away, he misses his opportunity to make the *berakha*.

Nevertheless, *be-di'avad,* if one ate more than a *kezayit* of *karpas,* he should not recite a *berakha aḥarona*. This is because we are lenient in laws of *berakhot* in cases of uncertainty. On the one hand, perhaps Rashbam is correct that the *berakha* on the *karpas* covers the *maror,* and since *Birkat Ha-mazon* covers the *maror,* it also covers the *karpas,* which is connected to the *maror*. (See BHL 473:6, which cites Gra that one must make a *berakha* and concludes that the matter must be explored further. Nevertheless, practically speaking, one should not recite a *berakha* about which there is doubt.) On the other hand, if one ate a *kezayit* and recited a *berakha aḥarona* afterward, he should not recite a *berakha* on the *maror,* since perhaps Ri is correct that the *berakha* on the matza covers the *maror*.

If it is true that one must eat less than a *kezayit* of *karpas,* why is one required to wash his hands? We know (SA 158:3; *Peninei Halakha: Berakhot* 2:6) that one only needs to wash hands for a piece of bread larger than a *kezayit* – *kal va-ḥomer* that one need not wash for a food dipped in liquid. Indeed, according to Rambam (MT Laws of *Ḥametz* and Matza 8:2) and many other Rishonim, one should specifically eat a

16. YAḤATZ

Three *matzot* are arranged on the Seder plate. After eating *karpas,* before reciting the Hagada, the Seder leader (and whoever else has three *matzot* in front of him), breaks the middle matza in half. One piece is saved for the *afikoman,* and the other is left between the two whole *matzot* (SA 463:6).

The reason for this is that the matza alludes to our poverty and enslavement in Egypt, and is hence called "*leḥem oni*" – "poor man's bread" (Devarim 16:3). Paupers often eat partial loaves of bread because they are unable to buy whole loaves. So, in order to give expression to the poverty, we break the matza in half. We do this before beginning the Hagada since the Hagada should be recited in the presence of the matza. This is because the term "*leḥem oni*" also means "bread over which we '*onim*' – answer or say – many things," and this means that the Hagada must be recited while the matza, in the form it will be eaten, is before us. This is why it must be broken in half before we begin the Hagada.

Nevertheless, on the Seder night, just like on every Shabbat and Yom Tov, there is a mitzva to recite *ha-motzi* over two whole loaves of bread/matza ("*leḥem mishneh*"). Therefore, we set the table with three *matzot*: the middle one is broken in half to give expression to *leḥem oni,* while the top and bottom *matzot* remain whole and serve as *leḥem mishneh.* (Later, when reciting "*ha-motzi,*" one should hold all three *matzot* so that there is *leḥem mishneh,* and before reciting the *berakha* of "*al*

---

kezayit of *karpas* (in a responsum he instructed his correspondent to recite a *berakha aḥarona* afterward). This was in fact the practice of the Vilna Gaon and several other Aḥaronim (although it is unknown whether they recited a *berakha aḥarona* afterward). BHL 473:6 leaves this issue unresolved. Perhaps according to Netziv (cited above in n. 12), who says that we wash our hands before *karpas* to remember what used to be done in the Temple, we can suggest that in the times of the Temple people would eat pieces larger than a *kezayit,* and they knew whether or not to recite a *berakha aḥarona.* Nowadays, however, since we do not know whether to recite a *berakha aḥarona,* we eat less than a *kezayit* to avoid uncertainty, and although technically we need not wash our hands to eat less than a *kezayit,* we do so anyway to commemorate what was done in the Temple. See also *Kaf Ha-ḥayim* 158:20, which states that there are some who learned from the status of *karpas* that the law of washing for vegetables is different than the law of washing for bread: for bread one only washes for a *kezayit,* but for vegetables one washes even for less than a *kezayit.*

akhilat matza," we put down the bottom matza and recite the blessing over the top and middle *matzot,* in order to highlight the broken matza to a greater degree.)[16]

The larger piece of the broken matza is designated as the *afikoman,* and the custom is to wrap it in a napkin, in recollection of the verse, "The people took their dough before it was leavened; their kneading leftover dough was wrapped in their robes" (Shemot 12:34). Some people have a custom to place the *afikoman* on their shoulder for a moment, in remembrance of the Exodus, when people carried *matzot* on their shoulders (MB 473:59).

Afterward, we hide the *afikoman* and save it until the end of the Seder, when it is eaten in commemoration of the Paschal sacrifice (see sections 33 and 34 below).

In many homes, the children customarily "steal" the *afikoman* and keep it until the end of the meal, when they give it back in return for a gift. This helps them stay awake for the entire Seder. In my family, we give gifts to all children who remain awake until after the *afikoman* is eaten.

17. *MAGID*

After breaking the middle matza, we uncover the *matzot,* and the Seder leader lifts the entire Seder plate, or at least the *matzot,* for all of the participants to see. While doing so, he recites the paragraph "*Ha Laḥma Anya*" and explains the meaning of the words to the participants. Upon completing *Ha Laḥma Anya,* the Seder leader places the Seder plate or *matzot* back on the table (SA 473:6).

At this point, the Seder plate is removed, making it appear as if the Seder is over. This is done so that the children become surprised and ask why the *matzot* and Seder plate are being taken away before we have even begun eating. Consequently, they ask "*Ma nishtana*?" (SA 473:6).

After removing the Seder plate, and even before reciting "*Ma nishtana,*" we pour the second cup. This also surprises the children,

---

16. According to Rambam, one sets the table with only two *matzot* and breaks the bottom one. There is no need for two whole *matzot,* because at the Seder one is supposed to eat *leḥem oni,* and so one matza is broken This is the custom of the Yemenite community, who follow Rambam.

because we do not usually pour two cups of wine before a meal. Another reason we do this is that we want the whole Hagada, including the questions that precede it, to be said over a cup of wine.

It is best not to pour wine into the cups of the young children at this point, because they will have a hard time making it through the long Hagada without spilling the cup, and wine spilled on the table can cause aggravation and demonstrates disrespect for Yom Tov, which should be honored with a clean tablecloth and a beautifully set table. Therefore, it is best to pour wine for the children near the end of the Hagada, shortly before drinking the second cup.

After the second cup has been poured, the children ask "*Ma nishtana*?" Following this, the Seder plate is returned so that the Hagada can be recited in the presence of matza and *maror,* and we begin answering the children with the story of the Exodus. We have already seen (ch. 15) that the purpose of the Seder night is to fulfill the mitzva of narrating the Exodus, and that the essence of this mitzva is to tell this story to the children. We also saw that there is a Torah commandment to tell the story of the Exodus even when no children are present (above 15:1) and that there is a mitzva to begin the story with a question (*ibid.* 3-4). We also learned that the story must be tailored to the ability and understanding of each child (*ibid.* 5), and that when telling the story, one must begin with indignity and end with praise (*ibid.* 7). We also saw that the purpose of the Seder is that the children learn, by means of the Exodus story, about the mission of the Jewish people in this world: to adhere to God, uphold His *mitzvot,* live in the land that He swore to give to our ancestors and to us, to enumerate His praises among the nations, and to earn divine blessing and goodness (*ibid.* 6).

The Sages introduced a fixed text for the Hagada so people would relate the story of the Exodus with precision and without omitting any important elements. Additionally, it is commendable to continue telling the story after the Seder ends. However, during the recitation of the Hagada one must take care not to make things too tiresome and long-winded for the children and other participants. Reciting the text is sufficient to fulfill the mitzva in the optimal manner.

18. LAWS OF RECITING THE HAGADA

One who merely contemplates the Hagada does not fulfill the obligation to tell the Exodus story, as it is stated, "Tell your child" (Shemot 13:8), i.e., express the story verbally. However, it is not necessary for all participants to recite the Hagada; the main thing is that the Seder leader or someone else recites it aloud, and the others hear it. Indeed, it was customary for the oldest participant to read and explain the Hagada while everyone else listened. This is, in fact, the way stories are usually told (see *Pesaḥim* 116b).

Nowadays, in order to include everyone in the recitation of the Hagada, it is customary for the Seder leader to read it aloud while everyone else quietly reads along with him. Others have participants take turns reading paragraphs from the Hagada, but it is important to note that only a reader who has reached halakhic adulthood (i.e., is a bar or bat mitzva) can fulfill this obligation on another's behalf.

When several sets of parents and children have the Seder together, it is not necessary for each father to tell the story to his child separately; it is sufficient for the Seder leader or another participant to read the Hagada out loud, because as long as the father makes sure that his child hears the story of the Exodus, he has fulfilled the mitzva to "tell your child." One who wishes to enhance the mitzva can further explain the Exodus to his child.

In order to fulfill the mitzva of telling the Exodus story, one must at the very least explain or hear an explanation of the Paschal sacrifice, matza, and *maror.* This makes clear that we were slaves in Egypt and that God redeemed us. Therefore, if parents see that their children are tired and are unable to complete the Hagada, they must tell them about the *korban Pesaḥ*, matza, and *maror*, and explain their meaning. The same principle applies to a participant who is unable to complete the Hagada due to illness or military duty (see above 15:9).

19. CUSTOMS REGARDING THE RECITATION OF THE HAGADA

As stated, the custom is to refrain from reclining while reciting the Hagada, because it must be recited with seriousness and reverence (MB 473:71, based on *Shlah*). However, this seriousness incorporates joy and elation at the fact that God chose us from among all the nations and gave us the Torah (see *Kaf Ha-ḥayim* 473:152).

We have already seen that the matza must be kept uncovered while we recite the Hagada, in keeping with the words of the Sages: "'*leḥem oni*' – bread over which we '*onim*' – answer or say – many things" (*Pesaḥim* 115b). Giving concrete expression to the Exodus story is the foundation of the mitzva to eat matza on the Seder night.

However, when we raise the wine glasses to recite the paragraphs of "*Ve-hi she-amdah*" ("And this [promise] has stood") and "*Lefikhakh anaḥnu ḥayavim*" ("Therefore it is our duty"), as well as when reciting the long *berakha* on redemption ("*Birkat Ha-ge'ula*") just before drinking the second cup, the matza should be covered. The matza is more significant than the wine, and therefore, whenever we hold up the cup of wine and show it preference, the matza must be covered (SA 473:7, MB *ad loc.* 73). It is for the same reason that we cover the bread when reciting *kiddush* every Shabbat and Yom Tov.

When reciting the paragraph "*Matza zo she-anu okhlim*" ("This matza that we eat"), the Seder leader holds up the matza for all of the participants to see, in order to endear the mitzva to them. And when "*Maror zeh...*" ("This *maror...*") is said, the *maror* is held up. However, when "*Pesaḥ zeh...*" is said, the *zero'a* is not held up, because it is not the actual meat of the *korban Pesaḥ*, but merely a commemoration of it. Thus, one who holds it up is like one who offers sacrifices outside the Temple precincts (*Pesaḥim* 116b; SA 473:7).

It is customary to spill out a bit of wine from the cup when enumerating "*dam, va-esh, ve-timrot ashan*" ("blood, fire, and pillars of smoke" – Yoel 3:3), while reciting "*detzaḥ, adash,* and *be'aḥav*" (R. Yehuda's mnemonic device for remembering the Ten Plagues), and while enumerating the Ten Plagues. This comes to sixteen times. Some have a custom to drip the wine with the index finger, and others have a custom to pour out a little bit into a broken vessel (Rema 473:7; SHT 81 and *Kaf Ha-ḥayim* 163-4 *ad loc.*). Rav Kook rules that one should not spill out *Shemitta* wine (produced from grapes grown on the Torah's Sabbatical year; some *poskim* say that there is a mitzva to drink *Shemitta* wine, and therefore one should not refrain from using it for the four cups).

20. THE MITZVA TO RECITE *HALLEL* ON THE SEDER NIGHT

When the Temple stood, people would recite *Hallel* while offering the *korban Pesaḥ,* and again while eating it (*Pesaḥim* 95a). The main reason for reciting *Hallel* on the first night of Pesaḥ is to sing God's praises; every Jew must see himself, on Pesaḥ night, as though he left Egypt personally, and it is only natural to sing praises to God for redeeming us. In fact, this recitation of *Hallel* is unique: on all other holidays we recite *Hallel* as an expression of praise and thanksgiving to God, but on the night of Pesaḥ we proclaim it as a song (*ibid.* 95b).

The Sages ordained reciting half of *Hallel* before the meal and half of it after the meal, so that it encompasses the eating of the *korban Pesaḥ.* Although we no longer have the privilege of eating the *korban Pesaḥ* nowadays, we eat matza instead (Maharal, *Gevurot Hashem,* end of ch. 62). In addition, the first half of *Hallel* contains Psalm 114, "When Israel left Egypt" ("*Be-tzeit Yisrael Mi-Mitzrayim*"), which is a continuation of the Hagada's story. This is why, at its conclusion, we recite the blessing over the redemption from Egypt ("*Birkat Ha-ge'ula*"). The second half of *Hallel,* recited after the meal, is a more general song of thanks for all redemptions, past and future (*Levush*).

Another reason for dividing *Hallel* is that this enables us to drink all four cups over song. We drink the first cup over *kiddush,* the second over the first half of *Hallel,* the third over *Birkat Ha-mazon,* and the fourth over the second half of *Hallel* (*Manhig* §90).[17]

The Rishonim are divided over whether or not a *berakha* should be recited over *Hallel* on Pesaḥ night. Some say two *berakhot* should be recited, one over each half of *Hallel.* Others say one *berakha* should be recited. There are differing opinions over the wording of the *berakha* as well: some say it should be "*likro et ha-Hallel*" ("to recite *Hallel*") and others say "*ligmor et ha-Hallel*" ("to complete the *Hallel*"). Another group

17. The practice of saying half of *Hallel* before the meal is cited in a *mishna* in *Pesaḥim* 116b. *Ibid.* 117a explains the mitzva of saying *Hallel* to commemorate miracles. See the introduction to *Hagada Torah Sheleima* ch. 27, which summarizes both sides of the dispute about whether or not one should recite a *berakha* over this *Hallel.* See also *Kaf Ha-ḥayim* 473:160-161 and *Ha-Seder He-arukh.*

of authorities maintains that no blessing at all should be pronounced over *Hallel* on the Seder night, either because it is divided into two parts (Rosh), because a *berakha* was already pronounced over the *Hallel* that was recited in the synagogue during the *Ma'ariv* prayer (Rashba), or because this *Hallel* is like a song and therefore requires no *berakha* (R. Hai Gaon). Some maintain that *Birkat Ha-ge'ula* covers *Hallel* as well. In practice, the custom is to refrain from making a *berakha* over the *Hallel* we recite at the Seder.

During the rest of the year, we stand while reciting *Hallel*, because it is like attesting to God's greatness, and testimony must be given while standing. But the Sages did not wish to burden us on the Seder night, because all of our actions on this night must demonstrate freedom (*Beit Yosef* OḤ 422:7). Nevertheless, as we have learned, the Hagada should not be read while reclining, but with an air of solemnity (*Shlah*).

Hallel is customarily read aloud and with sweet singing (*Kaf Ha-ḥayim* 480:3).

21. THE LAWS OF THE SECOND AND FOURTH CUPS

The only significant practical difference between communal customs regarding the laws of the Seder pertains to the *berakha* over the second and fourth cups.

Many Rishonim maintain that "*borei pri ha-gefen*" must be recited over each of the four cups, even though our attention is not diverted from one cup to the next, because each cup is a mitzva in its own right. This is the opinion of R. Natronai Gaon, R. Amram Gaon, Rif, Rambam, Maharitz, and Rema, and it is the practice of Ashkenazim and of Yemeni Jews who follow Rambam.

However, Rosh maintains that "*ha-gefen*" must only be recited before the first and third cups. The *berakha* over the first cup covers the second cup because there is nothing between them to divert our attention. We recite a *berakha* over the third cup because it follows *Birkat Ha-mazon* and a *berakha* is always recited over wine we drink after *Birkat Ha-mazon*, even if "*ha-gefen*" was recited earlier in the meal, because *Birkat Ha-mazon* serves as a *berakha aḥarona* for the wine one drinks during the meal. The *berakha* over the third cup covers the fourth cup as well. R. Yona and Rashba also maintain that "*ha-gefen*" is recited over the first and third cups only. SA rules accordingly, and this is the Sephardic custom.

There are also differing opinions among Rishonim regarding the *berakha aḥarona* over the wine. In practice, however, there is a consensus not to recite a *berakha aḥarona* after each cup of wine. Rather, *Birkat Ha-mazon* covers the first two cups, and the *berakha aḥarona* ("*al ha-gefen*") recited after the fourth cup covers both the third and fourth cups.[18]

18. It is worth adding here that many families customarily prolong the recitation of the Hagada beyond seventy-two minutes, which is the time it takes to digest and is generally considered the amount of time that constitutes an interruption, after which one may not recite a *berakha aḥarona*. It would seem, then, that an extended recitation of the Hagada would mean that *Birkat Ha-mazon* does not cover the first cup of wine, in which case one will not have recited a *berakha aḥarona* over the first cup of wine. Moreover, according to MA 184:9, if one waited for this amount of time between the first and second cups, he must recite a new *berakha*, which contradicts the ruling of SA that one need not recite a new *berakha* over the second cup (since the *berakha* on the first cup covers it). Additionally, how does this issue fit with Rashbam's ruling that the *berakha* recited on the *karpas* also covers the *maror*? How can this work if more than seventy-two minutes have elapsed? This question is also raised in SA 473:6, which takes the view of Rashbam into consideration. Furthermore, the first cup is also *kiddush*, which must be part of a meal. When there is such a long break, perhaps *kiddush* must be recited again, so that it is part of the meal. Because of all of these problems, some *poskim* maintain that one should be careful to recite the Hagada in less than seventy-two minutes (see *Sidur Pesaḥ Ke-hilkhato* 3:9). Notwithstanding these concerns, many people still prolong the recitation of the Hagada for more than seventy-two minutes (see *Mikra'ei Kodesh* 2:30, *Hilkhot Ḥag Be-ḥag* 20:5, and *Responsa Ḥazon Ovadia* §11, which justify this practice based on various rationales, such as explaining that the *berakha aḥarona* on the fourth cup also covers the first cup). In my humble opinion, the entire issue of a significant interruption ("*hefsek*") in a meal only applies when one engages in unrelated activities (even if he does not take his mind off the meal). In this case, though, he is not dealing with unrelated issues; rather, he is involved in the Seder and the Hagada. Therefore, since the second cup is poured right at the beginning of the recitation of the Hagada, and since the entire recitation of the Hagada is connected to the second cup, the time between the first and second cups is not considered a *hefsek*. Consequently, there is no *hefsek* between *kiddush* and the meal; the recitation of the Hagada is considered part of the Seder, since telling the story of the Exodus is an integral part of the mitzva of eating matza. Similarly, telling the Exodus story is also inherently connected to the mitzva of eating *maror*, so the recitation of the Hagada does not constitute a *hefsek* between the eating of *karpas* and the eating of *maror* (and the *berakha* on *karpas* covers the *maror* as well).

22. THE MITZVA TO EAT MATZA AND *MAROR*

There is a Torah commandment to eat matza on the night of the fifteenth of Nisan, as it states: "In the evening, you shall eat *matzot*" (Shemot 12:18). This matza must have been guarded (*shmura*), as it states: "And you shall observe (*u-shemartem*) the *matzot*" (*ibid.* 17), and some *poskim* say it must be made by hand, with the specific intention of fulfilling this mitzva (see above 12:4). One who eats stolen matza does not fulfill his obligation (SA 454:4). Therefore, it is good to pay for the matza before Pesaḥ, or at least obtain the explicit consent of the storeowner to grant the buyer ownership of the matza even if it has not yet been paid for, because if the storeowner does not agree to give the matza on credit, one cannot fulfill his obligation with it (MB 454:15).[19] As soon as one eats a *kezayit* of *shmura* matza he has fulfilled the Torah commandment, because all eating-related commandments in the Torah require the consumption of at least a *kezayit.*

Beyond the Torah obligation, the Sages ordained three more *kezeytim* of matza to be eaten at the Seder, making a total of four. After reciting the *berakhot* of "*ha-motzi*" and "*al akhilat matza,*" we eat, *le-khatḥila,* two *kezeytim*: one from the top matza, for "*ha-motzi,*" and one from the broken middle matza for "*al akhilat matza.*" Later, we eat another *kezayit* with *maror,* for *korekh,* and at the end of the meal we eat one more *kezayit* as the *afikoman* (some say it is preferable to eat two *kezeytim* for the *afikoman*).

Before getting into the specifics of the size of a *kezayit,* let us clarify the practical *halakha*: there is a consensus that a *kezayit* is about a third of a piece of machine-made matza, and about the same-sized piece of a handmade matza. Thus, right after reciting "*ha-motzi*" and "*al akhilat matza,*" two-thirds of a machine matza must be eaten. Another third should be eaten for *korekh* and one more for the *afikoman* (for those who are stringent about eating two *kezeytim* for the *afikoman,* one half of a matza suffices for this purpose).

---

19. Some stringently insist that the head of the household purchases the matza specifically for his guests and adult children, so that they eat matza that belongs to them. See *Sidur Pesaḥ Ke-hilkhato* 2:8:3. Nevertheless, one who eats matza owned by the head of the household fulfills his obligation, even if he performed no act of acquisition, since one can fulfill his obligation with borrowed matza (MB 454:15).

The *kezayit* of matza must be eaten continuously. If one pauses while eating, and as a result takes longer than a *shi'ur akhilat pras* to eat a *kezayit*, he does not fulfill the mitzva. We shall soon discuss exactly how much time a *shi'ur akhilat pras* is, but for now, it is enough to say that whoever eats a *kezayit* of matza continuously fulfills the mitzva without question and need not look at the clock, because the only way it is possible to take longer than *akhilat pras* is if one stops eating for a few minutes.

23. CALCULATING THE SIZE OF A *KEZAYIT* FOR TORAH COMMANDMENTS

The long exile gave rise to uncertainty regarding the size of a *kezayit*. According to Rambam, a *kezayit* is slightly less than a third of the volume of an egg; according to *Tosafot*, it is about the volume of half an egg. In practice, due to this uncertainty, the custom is to follow the stricter ruling of *Tosafot*. The equivalent of half an egg was calculated as being a third of a piece of machine matza and as a similar-sized piece of hard handmade matza, whose thickness is similar to that of a machine matza.

This is the consensus of all Sephardic and most Ashkenazic authorities. However, one of the most prominent Ashkenazic Aḥaronim, R. Yeḥezkel Landau (also known as "Noda Bi-Yehuda"), reached the conclusion, based on his own calculations, that our eggs are half the volume of the eggs that existed at the time of the Sages. It follows that a *kezayit* is not half the size of one of our eggs, but is the size of a whole contemporary egg. R. Avraham Yeshaya Karelitz ("Ḥazon Ish") concurred with Noda Bi-Yehuda's calculations. Thus, in order to fulfill the Torah commandment using the "Ḥazon Ish *shi'ur*," one must eat an egg's bulk of matza. Although the *halakha* usually follows the standard *shi'ur* and does not take Ḥazon Ish's *shi'ur* into consideration, when it comes to the Torah commandment of eating matza, it is proper *le-khatḥila* to satisfy all opinions. Ideally, then, one should eat a Ḥazon Ish *kezayit* of matza, or approximately two-thirds of a matza.

This, however, is not really much of a stringency, since anyway our custom is to eat two *kezeytim* initially – one for "*ha-motzi*" and another for "*al akhilat matza*" (SA 475:1). Since these two *kezeytim* contain a single Ḥazon Ish *kezayit*, we fulfill the Torah commandment according to all opinions.

One who finds it difficult to eat two-thirds of a piece of machine matza can eat one third, because according to the standard calculation, a third of a matza contains a *kezayit*. One even recites the "*al akhilat matza*" blessing before eating this amount, for the standard measure is so well founded that it is not considered the sort of uncertainty that causes the *berakha* to be canceled.[20]

---

20. The size of a *kezayit* is a very long topic, and is explained in *Peninei Halakha: Berakhot* 10:5-6 and in the notes there. I will summarize it here.

SA 486:1 rules that regarding the requirement to eat matza, we follow *Tosafot* that a *kezayit* is the size of half an egg's bulk. SAH (486:1) states that for Torah commandments, one must be stringent and follow *Tosafot*, but for rabbinic *mitzvot*, such as *eiruvin*, one may follow the lenient opinion of Rambam, who maintains that a *kezayit* is slightly less than a third of an egg's bulk. MB 486:1 states that when it comes to reciting a *berakha aḥarona*, which is only required if one eats a *kezayit*, one must follow *Tosafot*, since we are lenient whenever there is uncertainty in the laws of *berakhot*. Thus, one is only required to recite a *berakha aḥarona* if he eats at least half an egg's bulk, not less. *Le-khatḥila* one should not invite an ambiguous situation, and should eat either less than one third of an egg's bulk, in which case he would be exempt from a *berakha aḥarona* according to everyone, or more than half an egg's bulk, in which case he would be required to recite a *berakha aḥarona* according to everyone. Regarding matza, one must be stringent and follow the opinion of *Tosafot*. Similarly, one must follow the opinion of *Tosafot* vis-à-vis *maror*, since we recite a *berakha* on it. On the other hand, when it comes to the requirement to eat a *kezayit* of *korekh* and the requirement to eat a *kezayit* of *afikoman*, one may be lenient and follow Rambam.

BHL on 271 explains the opinion of *Noda Bi-Yehuda*. MB (486:1) quotes *Sha'arei Teshuva* that regarding Torah commandments, including *mitzvot* like *kiddush* with a Torah basis, one should be stringent and follow *Noda Bi-Yehuda*. On the other hand, vis-à-vis rabbinic *mitzvot* like the four cups of wine, one need not follow *Noda Bi-Yehuda*. MB (*ibid.*) also states that regarding *berakha aḥarona* one need not follow *Noda Bi-Yehuda*; rather, he should recite a *berakha aḥarona* after eating the amount of half an egg, as per *Tosafot*. Sephardim do not show any concern for *Noda Bi-Yehuda*'s measurements, since the tradition regarding halakhic measurements was passed down, uninterrupted, in the regions near Eretz Yisrael, and every time the sizes were recalculated, the same results were found.

It should also be noted that there are two opinions within the view of *Noda Bi-Yehuda* that the *kezayit* of *Tosafot* is the size of a modern-day egg: according to MB this means an egg with its shell, and according to *Ḥazon Ish* this means an egg without its shell; the difference between these two opinions is about ten percent.

MB 486:3 states that one must realize that all of these measurements are based on volume, and only when there are large air pockets is one required to compress

24. THE SEPHARDIC CUSTOM REGARDING A *KEZAYIT*

Sephardic Jews customarily do not give any consideration to the Noda Bi-Yehuda/Ḥazon Ish position, because their own tradition about these measurements was handed down in an orderly manner from generation to generation, without change. Even with regard to Torah commandments, they are not concerned about the Ḥazon Ish *shi'ur*. It follows that the volume of a *kezayit* does not exceed one third of a piece of machine matza (based on the position of *Tosafot* that a *kezayit* is about half an egg).

---

the food. The food's natural texture does not need to be compressed. Therefore, the weight of a *kezayit* often varies, depending on the density of the food.

After measuring, it emerges that a *kezayit* according to *Tosafot*, which is the size of half a modern-day egg, is at most a third of a machine-made matza. If we multiply this *shi'ur* based on MB's stringent explanation of *Noda Bi-Yehuda*, namely, that a *kezayit* is the size of a whole egg with its shell, a *kezayit* is approximately two-thirds of a machine-made matza. According to *Ḥazon Ish*'s understanding of *Noda Bi-Yehuda*, roughly half of a machine-made matza is sufficient, or, according to some, slightly more than half. In any case, one who eats two-thirds of a machine-made matza fulfills his obligation according to even the most stringent opinions (the weight of a machine-made matza is approximately 33 grams). See *Sidur Pesaḥ Ke-hilkhato* 2:8:4, which explains the calculations practically.

After reciting the *berakha*, one must eat two *kezeytim* (SA 475:1 citing Rosh and *Mordechai*). One *kezayit* is taken from the top, whole matza for the *berakha* of "*ha-motzi*," and one *kezayit* is taken from the middle, broken matza for the *berakha* of "*al akhilat matza*." BHL questions this ruling, since it does not seem that any other Rishonim require eating two *kezayit*-sized pieces. Nevertheless, the custom is to follow SA. However, one certainly does not need to be stringent in measuring the two pieces; therefore, if he ate a *kezayit* according to the measurement of *Noda Bi-Yehuda*, he has already fulfilled the obligation to eat two *kezayit*-sized pieces according to the accepted measurement (that of *Tosafot*) and has eaten more than three *kezayit* sizes according to the measurement of Rambam.

One who has difficulty eating two-thirds of a machine-made matza may eat one third and may recite the *berakha* of "*al akhilat matza*," since, as we already mentioned, technically the *halakha* follows the accepted measurement (*Tosafot*), and even regarding *berakha aḥarona* one need not follow *Ḥazon Ish* (with the exception of his students and followers). Regarding the practice to eat two *kezeytim*, we have already mentioned that not all Rishonim agree that this is a requirement; moreover, one third of a machine-made matza likely contains two *kezayit* sizes according to Rambam. Therefore, one who eats one third altogether should eat a small piece from the whole matza and a small piece from the broken matza.

The above applies when one measures according to volume; however, most Sephardim actually have a custom to base the *shi'ur* on weight, as it is difficult to calculate the volume of each food independently to determine whether one must recite a *berakha aḥarona* after eating it. After all, foods come in all sorts of shapes and sizes: long and thin, round and square, etc. Some foods contain hollow spaces that are not factored into the volume. Thus, in order to make it easier to calculate *shi'urim*, the practice of measuring by water weight was adopted. It was thus determined that a *kezayit*, or half an egg, is equal to 29 grams (a more recent adjustment puts it at 25 grams). In order to eat this amount of matza, one must eat nearly a whole piece of machine matza. In other words, if we calculate a *kezayit* of matza by weight, it comes out almost three times more than if measured by volume.

This means that one must eat four machine *matzot* on the Seder night: two after the initial *berakhot*, one for *korekh*, and one more for the *afikoman* (and for those who are stringent – two more for the *afikoman*).

Yet is it clear that in principle all measurements are by volume, not weight, as several leading Sephardic *poskim* – R. Ben-Zion Abba Shaul and R. Shalom Messas – have ruled. Since the stringency of measuring matza by weight raises justifiable difficulties and consternation among many participants, we may instruct all Jews, Sephardic and Ashkenazic alike, that a *kezayit* is a third of a machine matza.[21]

21. The vast majority of Rishonim maintain that *shi'urim* are calculated by volume. This is the ruling of *Yeḥaveh Da'at* 4:55 regarding the minimum *shi'ur* for the tithing of *ḥalla*. See the addendum "*Shi'ur Kezayit*" at the back of R. Harari's *Mikra'ei Kodesh* part 4 and 6:3. See also *Peninei Halakha: Berakhot* 10:6, 7 and the expanded notes *ad loc.* Nevertheless, Sephardic Aḥaronim customarily calculate a *kezayit* by weight, as Ḥida writes in *Maḥzik Berakha* 168:6; see also *Kaf Ha-ḥayim* (168:45-46 and 486:1, 3) which cites more sources. This is also the ruling of R. Ovadia Yosef and R. Mordechai Eliyahu. Some *poskim* raise the possibility that *shi'urim* should be calculated by weight even in principle, since perhaps volume must be calculated after the food has been compressed, and a *kezayit* of fully compressed food will have the same weight as water. However, it is clear that the real justification for measuring by weight is that it is easier. Therefore, even a Sephardic Jew who normally measures by weight may rely on a volume-based measurement for matza. Indeed, R. Ben-Zion Abba Shaul and R. Shalom Messas maintain that one should calculate by volume *le-khatḥila*.

25. HOW MUCH IS A *SHI'UR AKHILAT PRAS*?

We have now seen that in order to fulfill the mitzva of eating matza, as well as any other Torah commandment governing eating, one must eat at least a *kezayit*. One condition must now be added: it is only considered a single act of eating if it is completed within the amount of time it takes to eat half a loaf of bread, or a *shi'ur akhilat pras*. If one eats half a *kezayit*, waits ten minutes, and then eats another half a *kezayit*, it is as if he has only eaten half a *kezayit*, and hence he has not fulfilled the mitzva (SA 475:6).

In the past, people would bake loaves of bread that would feed one person for a day – half a loaf (a *pras*) at each of the two main meals.

Once again, our long exile has caused disagreement among *poskim* over the precise size of a *pras*: according to Rambam, it is the volume of three eggs, and according to Rashi, four eggs. Several leading Aḥaronim tried to measure how long it takes to eat a *pras*, and many opinions have been offered: nine minutes (*Ḥatam Sofer*), seven and a half minutes (*Arukh La-ner*), seven minutes, six minutes, five minutes, and four minutes (R. Ḥayim Naeh and *Kaf Ha-ḥayim*).

However, all these opinions relate only to a *be-di'avad* situation, because *le-khatḥila* one should eat the matza continuously, and whoever does so certainly fulfills his obligation. In addition, there is no need to look at the clock while eating the matza, because any ordinary person who eats casually but without interruption will certainly finish eating in

---

Additionally, since our custom is to eat two *kezayit*-sized pieces initially, one must eat two-thirds of a machine-made matza. Even according to the weight-based measurement, two-thirds of a machine-made matza constitutes a *kezayit* according to Rambam.

It should also be noted that according to the latest calculations of Rambam's opinion, it emerges that the weight of half an egg is c. 25 grams, not 27, 28, or 29 grams as calculated by those who follow R. Ḥayim Naeh. See *Peninei Halakha: Berakhot* 10:6, 11. Nevertheless, the key point is that we calculate by volume, and by eating one third of a machine-made matza, one removes all doubt. See *Sidur Pesaḥ Ke-hilkhato* 2:8:4. Sephardim who eat thick, soft matza may also calculate by volume, since this is the primary halakhic method. However, it is easier to eat a weight-based (25 gm) *kezayit* of this matza. After the initial *berakhot*, when we eat two *kezeytim*, one may use Rambam's *kezayit*, which is less than a third of an egg, and c. 30 gm of matza would suffice in this instance.

time. Even a slow eater, if he does not stop to do other things, will assuredly finish eating a *kezayit* within a *shi'ur akhilat pras*, because a *pras* is eight or nine times the size of a *kezayit*, and it is inconceivable that one who eats a *kezayit* without stopping will not finish in the time it takes to eat eight or nine times that amount.[22]

---

22. As we have seen, according to Rashi, a *pras* is the size of four eggs, and according to *Tosafot*, a *kezayit* is half an egg. Thus, a *pras* is eight *kezeytim*. According to Rambam, a *pras* is the size of three eggs, and each egg is a bit more than three *kezeytim*. Thus, a *pras* is just over nine *kezeytim*. (If we combine Rashi's *pras* with Rambam's *kezayit*, a *pras* would come out to be twelve *kezeytim*. If we combine Rambam's *pras* with the *kezayit* of *Tosafot*, a *pras* would be six *kezeytim*.)

Although some individuals measured and discovered that they could not eat a *kezayit* of matza within a *shi'ur akhilat pras*, they only reached this conclusion because they used conflicting measurements. On the one hand, they measured a *kezayit* according to the most stringent opinion possible – a Ḥazon Ish *shi'ur* calculated by weight – and on the other hand, they calculated a *shi'ur akhilat pras* based on the smallest possible measure – Rambam's *shi'ur* of three eggs, calculated by volume. These two measurements are contradictory: a Ḥazon Ish *kezayit* by weight is c. 50 grams, while the three eggs' volume of matza is c. 54 grams. Since matza is difficult to chew, and a *shi'ur akhilat pras* is calculated based on the time it takes to eat bread that is easy to chew and swallow, these individuals discovered that they could not finish that "*kezayit*" in time. According to this, the Sephardic custom to eat two weight-based *kezayit*-sized pieces, or c. 58 grams of matza, in the time it takes to eat three eggs, or c. 54 grams, is certainly impossible under normal circumstances. Rather, one must calculate the size of a *kezayit* and the *shi'ur akhilat pras* using the same standard: if one is stringent regarding the size of a *kezayit* (and measures it by weight), he must allow himself more time to eat it by calculating the size of an egg based on weight as well, meaning that a *shi'ur akhilat pras* would be fifteen minutes or more.

Therefore, anyone who eats casually, provided that he does not pause or excessively procrastinate in his eating, will certainly be able to finish the *kezayit* within a *shi'ur akhilat pras*; thus, there is no need to glance at one's watch while eating.

Nevertheless, if one paused while eating and did not finish one third of a matza within four minutes, he should act stringently and eat another piece in that time. Logic dictates that since the determination of *shi'ur akhilat pras* is based on the average person, and since there are so many measurements offered, we should calculate it based on the median of the opinions of the Aḥaronim (6-7 minutes). However, since the mitzva of eating matza is from the Torah, one should follow the strictest opinions. See *Peninei Halakha: Berakhot* 10:7, 8.

Additionally, according to *Minḥat Ḥinukh* and *Responsa Torat Ḥessed* OḤ 32, the *shi'ur akhilat pras* is determined separately for every food, based on the ease or

26. HOW THE MATZA IS EATEN

Hands are now washed with a *berakha,* and the Seder leader holds up the three *matzot* and recites the *berakha* of "Who brings forth bread from the earth" ("*ha-motzi leḥem min ha-aretz*"). The top and bottom *matzot,* which are whole, constitute *leḥem mishneh.* After this *berakha,* he puts down the bottom matza so that he is left with the whole top matza and the broken middle matza (which represents "*leḥem oni*" – the "bread of poverty") and recites the *berakha* "Who sanctified us with His *mitzvot* and commanded us concerning eating matza" ("*asher kideshanu be-mitzvotav ve-tzivanu al akhilat matza*"). Then he takes a *kezayit* from the upper, whole matza, and a *kezayit* from the middle matza, and eats them together.

If there are many participants, it makes sense to add more *matzot* to the bottom matza, so that portions can be given to everybody. Once the Seder leader has finished distributing from the middle, broken matza, he no longer needs to give two *kezeytim* to the remaining participants, only one. Only when one distributes portions from the middle matza is it necessary to give a *kezayit* from the broken matza and a *kezayit* from the whole matza, but when the broken matza is finished, one gives only a *kezayit* to each person. However, as we have seen, in order to satisfy the opinion that today's eggs are smaller than those of the Sages' time, it is better to give each participant the equivalent of two-thirds of a machine-made matza. It makes no difference whether this is given from one matza or from parts of two *matzot.*

The Seder leader should taste a little bit of the matza before distributing portions, in order to avoid an interruption between the *berakha* and the eating. After distributing matza to everybody, he reclines and eats two *kezeytim* with the intention of fulfilling the mitzva.

According to Sephardic custom, the Seder leader dips the matza in salt before distributing it to the participants, just as he does throughout the year. The custom of Ashkenazic Jews, on the other hand, is not

---

difficulty of eating it. Accordingly, the *shi'ur akhilat pras* for matza would be longer than usual, since matza is difficult to chew and swallow. Nevertheless, most *poskim* who determined a *shi'ur akhilat pras* understood that it is a fixed standard based on the eating of regular bread.

to dip the matza in salt, because without salt it appears much more like *leḥem oni* (SA 475:1).

Some people have a custom of giving each participant three *matzot*, so that everyone can have a *kezayit* from a whole matza and a *kezayit* of a broken matza, and neither the leader nor the participants have to wait to receive matza after the *berakha*. But the widespread custom is that the Seder leader distributes matza to everybody, and the fact that everyone eats together and that the Seder leader recited the *berakhot* on everyone's behalf enhances the mitzva. Others have a custom to put out three *matzot* before the head of each household, who distributes portions to his family members. Even though each of these practices is fine, it is best for the head of each household to distribute matza to his family members.

The matza is eaten while reclining. One should have in mind to fulfill the Torah commandment, remembering that it is eaten in commemoration of the *matzot* our forefathers ate when they left Egypt for freedom.

27. THE MITZVA TO EAT *MAROR*

The Torah commandment to eat *maror* on the night of the fifteenth of Nisan is contingent upon the eating of the Paschal sacrifice, as it states: "They shall eat it with *matzot* and *merorim* [plural of *maror*]" (Bamidbar 9:11). Since we are unable to offer the Paschal sacrifice today, the mitzva to eat *maror* is now rabbinic (*Pesaḥim* 120a). We dip the *maror* in *ḥaroset* in order to counteract its bitterness, and then we shake off all the *ḥaroset* that sticks to it, because *ḥaroset* should not be eaten with the *maror* (SA 475:1, MB 13 and *Kaf Ha-ḥayim* 23 *ad loc.*). After this we recite the *berakha* "Who sanctified us with His *mitzvot* and commanded us concerning eating *maror*" ("*asher kideshanu be-mitzvotav ve-tzivanu al akhilat maror*"), and eat a *kezayit* of *maror*.

The Sages enumerate five types of *maror*: *ḥazeret, tamḥa, ḥarḥavina, ulshin,* and *maror*. Today we are only familiar with two of these: *ḥazeret*, which is lettuce, and *tamḥa*, which is horseradish. The Sages stated that the choicest type of *maror* is lettuce, and its Hebrew name ("*ḥasa*") even alludes to the fact that God has mercy ("*ḥas*") upon us. They also tell us that the Egyptian enslavement was like *maror*: just as *maror* begins soft and ends hard – the stalk starts off soft and later hardens – so too the enslavement began "softly" and became harder and bitterer with time (*Pesaḥim* 39a).

Several Aḥaronim questioned whether we fulfill the obligation of *maror* with today's lettuce, which is not bitter at all. Indeed, according to Ḥazon Ish, one may fulfill one's obligation only with lettuce that has become somewhat bitter. In practice, though, the *poskim* concur that one may fulfill one's obligation with lettuce even if it is not bitter, because this was the nature of the bondage: initially the Egyptians enslaved us with gentle words and paid us for our labor, while gradually intensifying the work until it was bitter as gall. The Yerushalmi (*Pesaḥim* 2:5) likewise tells us that lettuce starts out sweet and then becomes bitter. Thus, it is the custom of all Jews to optimize this mitzva by using lettuce for *maror*, because *maror* need not be bitter when it is eaten; rather, it must be of a species that eventually becomes bitter. Some people add a bit of horseradish to their lettuce so that they taste some bitterness.[23]

23. See *Ḥazon Ish* OḤ 124, commenting on *Pesaḥim* 39a. Ridbaz states that lettuce might not be *maror* at all. Nevertheless, most *poskim*, including Maharam Ḥalawa and *Tashbetz*, believe that lettuce is the best type of *maror*, because the Gemara finds allusions in its name and because it alludes to the enslavement by its very nature – starting off soft and sweet. This is the ruling in SA 473:5, *Pri Ḥadash* 472:5, and SAH 472:30. Additionally, according to Raavya and *Hagahot Maimoniyot* (quoted by *Tur* and SA), whatever is mentioned first in the Mishna is the preferable choice for *maror*, and lettuce (which the Mishna calls "*ḥazeret*" even though "*ḥazeret*" in modern Hebrew is horseradish) is in fact mentioned first. *Responsa Ḥazon Ovadia* §35 expands on this topic.

We should also add that another opinion appears in a *beraita* in *Pesaḥim* 39a: any bitter vegetable that exudes latex and has a blanched complexion (i.e., it is whitish-green) is *maror*. The Rishonim debated this: according to Ri'az, Maharam Halawa, and others, any vegetable that has these characteristics is indeed *maror*. According to *Smak*, on the other hand, these characteristics are just features common to the five types of vegetables mentioned in the Mishna, but no vegetable outside what is listed in the Mishna is acceptable for *maror*. Rif and Rambam do not mention these characteristics, either because they maintain that only the five vegetables listed in the Mishna are acceptable, and these characteristics consequently are meaningless, or because they maintain that we are not experts in identifying these characteristics, so we have no ability to determine what other vegetables are fit for *maror*. Practically, one who does not have lettuce or horseradish should use another vegetable that has these characteristics, but should not recite a *berakha* over it, in case we are not adept at identifying these characteristics or it is not one of the five acceptable species. This is the ruling in MB 473:46 and BHL *ad loc.*

Since lettuce often contains bugs, it should be cleaned and checked thoroughly on Erev Pesaḥ. Nowadays there are ways to grow bug-free lettuce, and it is best to use such lettuce in order to avoid potentially violating the prohibition against eating bugs.

One must eat a *kezayit* (half an egg's volume) of *maror*, and one may estimate this size by sight. As we have learned, some customarily calculate a *kezayit* by weight, which is about 29 grams. However, with lettuce there is very little difference between a weight- and volume-based *kezayit*.

28. *KOREKH*

After eating the *maror*, we make a sandwich from a *kezayit* of *maror* in a *kezayit* of matza and dip it in *ḥaroset*. Some people also shake off any *ḥaroset* that sticks to the *maror*, as with the eating of *maror* (MB 475:19). Others do not remove the *ḥaroset* from the *maror* in the case of *korekh* (*Kaf Ha-ḥayim* 457:32). We then say "*zekher le-Mikdash ke-Hillel*" ("in commemoration of the Temple, according to Hillel"), and eat the *korekh* while reclining (SA 475:1). As we learned, a *kezayit* is about a third of a machine matza.

According to Hillel the Elder, in Temple times the mitzva was fulfilled by eating matza and *maror* together, as it is stated: "They shall eat it with *matzot* and *merorim*" (Bamidbar 9:11). According to the other Sages, people would eat the matza and *maror* separately. Since no final decision was reached regarding this matter, we follow both practices.

However, even Hillel would concur that today it is impossible to fulfill one's obligation by eating matza with *maror*. This is because without the Paschal sacrifice the mitzva to eat matza remains Torah-based, while eating *maror* is of rabbinic origin. If they are eaten together, the *maror*, which is rabbinic, will detract from the matza, which is from the Torah. Therefore, one must first eat a *kezayit* of matza. After this, one eats a *kezayit* of *maror* without matza, because the matza obligation has already been fulfilled, and if one eats matza with *maror* at this point, the taste of the matza, which is no longer a mitzva, will overshadow the taste of the *maror*, which is a rabbinic mitzva. After fulfilling both *mitzvot* separately, we put matza and *maror* together like a sandwich and eat them in commemoration of Hillel's practice (*Pesaḥim* 115a and *Tosafot* s.v. "ella"; MB 475:16). And some say that while it is clear that today, according to Hillel, the matza must be eaten separately, nonetheless, in order to fulfill the rabbinic mitzva to eat *maror,* it must be eaten with matza. According to this opinion, when we eat the *korekh,* we are fulfilling the mitzva to eat *maror* (*Pri Ḥadash*).

In any event, according to all opinions one should be careful not to talk until he has finished eating *korekh.* Indeed, it is customary to refrain from talking between the blessing over the matza and that of the *maror,* until we have finished eating the *korekh.* It is only permissible to talk about matters related to fulfilling the mitzva.[24]

29. THOSE WHO HAVE DIFFICULTY EATING MATZA

As we have learned, a *kezayit* of matza is about a third of a machine matza, and on the Seder night we must eat four or five pieces of this size. After the *berakhot* of "*ha-motzi*" and "*al akhilat matza,*" we eat two *kezeytim*: one for "*ha-motzi*" and one for "*akhilat matza,*" and in order to fulfill the stringent opinion (*Ḥazon Ish*), which maintains that a *kezayit* is twice the accepted size. We eat another *kezayit* for *korekh,* and one more for the *afikoman,* though some practice the stringency of eating two *kezeytim* for the *afikoman*: one in memory of the Paschal sacrifice itself, and one in commemoration of the matza that would be eaten with it.

If one finds it difficult to eat a matza and a third (or two-thirds), he should do his best to eat the initial two-thirds of a matza as *matzat mitzva,* in order to fulfill the mitzva in accordance with all of the different opinions. After this, it is sufficient to eat a fifth of a matza for *korekh* and another fifth for the *afikoman.* If even this is difficult, one can eat a third of a matza – a *kezayit* according to the standard measure – to fulfill the mitzva of eating matza, and recite a *berakha* over it. In other words,

24. See *Hilkhot Ḥag Be-ḥag* 16:4 and *Ha-Seder He-arukh* ch. 92, which summarize that according to Hillel, if one ate each ingredient separately, he does not fulfill his obligation according to Rashbam and Ramban, while according to *Tosafot* and *Ha-ma'or,* he fulfills his obligation *be-di'avad.* As for the Sages' position, if one ate them together he does not fulfill his obligation according to Rashbam (citing R. Yoḥanan) and *Ha-ma'or,* but according to Ramban and Rashbam (citing R. Ashi), he fulfills his obligation *le-khatḥila.*

during the entire Seder, he would eat one third of a matza followed by an additional two-fifths.[25]

If one has difficulty chewing the matza – for example, one who has no teeth – he may crumble it up and eat the crumbs (BHL 461:4). If even this is too difficult, he may soak the matza in water before eating it. However, if one boils the matza or soaks it until it dissolves, he does not fulfill the mitzva with it, because it no longer has the taste of matza (SA 461:4, MB 19, 20).

It is forbidden, however, to soak the matza in wine, soup, or any other beverage that has a taste, because some believe that this weakens the taste of the matza. Some maintain that even dipping the matza in such liquids is improper. Nevertheless, a sick or elderly person who cannot eat the matza even if it were soaked in water may soak it in another liquid if it would help, recite a *berakha* over it, and eat it. But if a normal healthy person eats matza that has been soaked in a liquid, he must eat another *kezayit* of matza (MB 461:18, SHT 32 and *Kaf Ha-ḥayim* 47-48 *ad loc.*).[26]

30. THOSE EXEMPT FROM MATZA AND *MAROR*

One who is incapable of eating a *kezayit* of matza (one third of a matza) should at least try to eat a portion of matza equivalent to a modern-day olive, because some *poskim* maintain that this is the true size of a *kezayit.*

25. I explained the basics of this issue in n. 20 above. We learned there that according to Rambam, a *kezayit* is slightly less than one third of an egg, while according to *Tosafot* it is c. half an egg. Since we are stringent and follow *Tosafot* vis-à-vis Torah commandments, one should eat one third of a matza for every *kezayit*. However, regarding *korekh* and *afikoman*, which are rabbinic *mitzvot*, if one has difficulty following *Tosafot*, he may follow Rambam and eat approximately one fifth of a matza, which is about one third of an egg. Even those who wish to eat two *kezayit*-sized pieces for *afikoman* may suffice with a fifth of a matza, which contains two *kezeytim* according to many Ge'onim and Rishonim (see *Peninei Halakha: Berakhot* 10:6) who maintain that a *kezayit* is the size of an average contemporary olive. Regarding the stringency of eating two *kezeytim* for the *afikoman*, one need not adopt the larger measurement of a *kezayit*.

26. See R. Harari's *Mikra'ei Kodesh* 7:40 n. 103 regarding the ruling that one should recite a *berakha* even if he can only eat matza soaked in water; this is the conclusion even according to the strictest opinions.

However, one may not recite the *berakha* of "*al akhilat matza*" over this amount of matza, because most *poskim* maintain that it is insufficient for fulfilling the mitzva to eat matza. If one cannot eat even the volume of a modern-day olive, it is still good to eat as much matza as possible, even a small amount.[27]

Regarding one who knows that eating matza will cause him to become ill or intensify an existing illness but will certainly not threaten his life, the *poskim* disagree over whether he is obligated to eat matza: according to R. Shlomo of Vilna, such a person is exempt from eating matza on Pesaḥ (*Binyan Shlomo* §47), whereas according to Maharam Schick, a sick person is only exempt from eating matza where there is mortal danger (OḤ §260). The custom is to rule in accordance with the lenient opinion. (Regarding *maror* and the four cups of wine, which are rabbinic *mitzvot,* there is a consensus that one who will be consigned to bed if he eats them is exempt, as explained in section 7.)

According to this, most people who suffer from celiac disease must eat a *kezayit* of matza on the Seder night, because a *kezayit* of matza will not cause them to become sick. Even if it will cause one to suffer somewhat, this is not considered sickness. However, people who suffer from severe celiac disease, and who know that they are liable to have a strong reaction to matza, are exempt from the mitzva of eating matza. Nowadays one can find *matzot* made from oatmeal and spelt flour, which are better than wheat matza for people with celiac disease.[28]

---

27. It is implied by many Ge'onim and Rishonim that a *kezayit* is the size of today's common olive, of c. 7.5 cubic centimeters. It is further attested that R. Ḥayim Volozhiner and the author of *Avnei Nezer* ruled according to this opinion. See *Peninei Halakha: Berakhot* 10:5-6 and in the expanded notes, and in the addendum to *Mikra'ei Kodesh* 5. Nevertheless, the standard ruling is to be stringent and follow the opinion of *Tosafot* that a *kezayit* is half an egg, as explained in n. 20. Even if one cannot eat the requisite amount of matza according to any opinion, he should at least taste some matza, as per *Maḥzik Berakha* §475 and AHS 477:3. MB 473:43 states the same idea regarding *maror.*
28. For the definition of one who is exempt due to illness, see R. Frank's *Mikra'ei Kodesh* 2:32, which cites two opinions. *Ḥazon Ovadia* 1:33 and *Tzitz Eliezer* 14:27 are lenient. This is also what R. Harari writes in *Mikra'ei Kodesh* ch. 7 n. 110, in the name of Rav Mordechai Eliyahu.

31. THE TIME FOR EATING THE MATZA, *MAROR*, AND *AFIKOMAN*

The matza and *maror* must be eaten by midnight (the midpoint of the night, regardless of the time on the clock), but if one was unable to eat them before midnight, he should eat them after midnight without a *berakha*. *Le-khatḥila*, even the *afikoman* should be eaten before midnight.

The basis for this law lies in a dispute between two Sages of the Mishna, R. Elazar b. Azarya and R. Akiva. According to R. Elazar b. Azarya, the Paschal sacrifice could be eaten only until midnight, and no later, because it was at midnight that the firstborns of Egypt were struck down, and the Egyptians began frantically trying to send the Israelites out of Egypt. According to R. Akiva, the matza may be eaten all night, until dawn, because it was at this time that the Israelites hurried to leave Egypt (*Pesaḥim* 120b).

From a spiritual perspective, we must explain that the offering and eating of the Paschal sacrifice revealed the unique quality of Israel, and this therefore constituted a preparation for the redemption. Accordingly, the meat of the *korban Pesaḥ* is eaten each year until the time of the redemption's onset. The question is: which phase of redemption determines the time to stop eating the Paschal sacrifice? According to R. Elazar b. Azarya, the redemption started at midnight, when the firstborns of Egypt were struck down, for it was then that Egyptians' power was broken and they could no longer enslave us. Therefore, the Paschal sacrifice is eaten until midnight. However, according to R. Akiva, the complete redemption did not arrive until morning, when we went forth to freedom. Therefore, the entire night is a preparation for redemption, and it follows that one may eat the meat of the *korban Pesaḥ* all night.

Let us now return to the *halakha*. The time for eating the Paschal sacrifice also determines the time for eating matza and *maror*, because matza and *maror* were eaten together with the Paschal sacrifice, as it is stated, "They shall eat it with *matzot* and *merorim*" (Bamidbar 9:11). It follows that the time for eating matza is the same as the time for eating the Paschal sacrifice. The *afikoman*, which is eaten in commemoration of the *korban Pesaḥ*, must also be eaten at a time that is appropriate for eating the Paschal sacrifice.

Leading Rishonim disagree about which opinion to follow in practice. According to Rambam and *Itur*, the *halakha* follows R. Akiva, because, as a rule, we follow R. Akiva whenever he takes issue with one of his contemporaries. Thus, the *korban Pesaḥ* may be eaten throughout the entire night, and by extension so can matza, *maror*, and the *afikoman*. On the other hand, Rabbeinu Ḥananel and Rosh maintain that because the Mishna, in several places, states without dissent that the time for eating the *korban Pesaḥ* is until midnight, we may conclude that R. Yehuda Ha-Nasi, who compiled the Mishna, rules that on this issue the *halakha* follows R. Elazar b. Azarya.

Since this issue is subject to dispute, a *kezayit* of matza must be eaten before midnight, because according to those who maintain that the Paschal sacrifice may be eaten until midnight, eating it after midnight fails to fulfill the Torah commandment. Since the destruction of the Temple, *maror* has been a rabbinic enactment, and although we generally follow the lenient opinion with regard to rabbinic laws, *maror* must nevertheless be eaten before midnight since we recite a *berakha* over it. If circumstances prevented one from eating the matza and *maror* before midnight, he should eat them after midnight, in order to fulfill the mitzva according to R. Akiva's opinion. However, he should not recite the *berakhot* of "*al akhilat matza*" and "*al akhilat maror*," so as to avoid reciting a *berakha* in vain ("*le-vatala*") according to the opinion of R. Elazar b. Azarya (MB 477:6; *Kaf Ha-ḥayim* 10 *ad loc.*).

Regarding the *afikoman*, SA rules (477:1) that one must, *le-khatḥila*, eat it before midnight, in order to fulfill the mitzva according to all *poskim*. Similarly, *Hallel* should also be completed before midnight *le-khatḥila*, because it is connected to the telling of the Exodus story, which must be told at a time appropriate for eating matza.

There were Torah scholars who, *le-khatḥila*, ate the *afikoman* after midnight, reasoning that the *afikoman* is a rabbinic enactment and we may thus rely upon the lenient opinion that it may be eaten after midnight. However, with regard to the initial *kezayit* of matza, which is a Torah commandment, and the *maror*, over which we recite a *berakha*, one may not adopt the lenient position and eat them before midnight.[29]

---

29. A detailed explanation: On three occasions, the Mishna quotes the opinion of R. Elazar b. Azarya anonymously and without dissent – *Berakhot* 2a, *Pesaḥim* 120b, and *Zevaḥim* 56b – and R. Akiva's opinion anonymously and without dissent only

32. MEAL CUSTOMS – ROASTED FOODS, EGGS

During the time of the Mishna, some communities had a custom to refrain from eating roast meat on Pesaḥ night, since it would look like they were eating the meat of the Paschal sacrifice – which must be

---

once, in *Megilla* 20b. Rosh (*Pesaḥim* 10:38) wonders how that single *mishna* in *Megilla* could outweigh the three *mishnayot* that follow the opinion of R. Elazar b. Azarya. Consequently, Rosh says that although R. Akiva maintains that on the Torah level, the mitzva of eating the *korban Pesaḥ* applies all night, he concurs that, on the rabbinic level, one must finish eating it before midnight. Therefore, Rosh states that one must eat the *afikoman* before midnight, and this is the ruling of SA 477:1. However, it is said that Ḥatam Sofer, Netziv, and other great scholars did not insist on finishing the *afikoman* before midnight. Since this is a dispute about a matter of rabbinic law, one may be lenient. Even SA might mean that one finishes the *afikoman* before midnight *le-khatḥila,* but it is not an absolute requirement. *Responsa Avnei Nezer* §381 recommends that one who is in the middle of his meal and sees that midnight is approaching should eat a *kezayit* of matza while reclining and make the following stipulation: If the *halakha* follows the opinion of R. Elazar b. Azarya, this *kezayit* should be the *afikoman,* but if the *halakha* follows R. Akiva, the *kezayit* that will be eaten after the meal (at its normal place in the meal) should be the *afikoman.* This stipulation is based on a novel interpretation: the requirement that the taste of the matza remains in one's mouth only applies during the time of the mitzva, which according to R. Elazar b. Azarya ends at midnight. Thus, according to R. Elazar b. Azarya, one would be able to continue eating after midnight, when the time for the mitzva of *afikoman* ends.

However, one certainly must ensure that he eats a *kezayit* of matza before midnight, since eating a *kezayit* of matza is a Torah commandment, and hence one must be stringent. One must even be stringent vis-à-vis the mitzva of *maror,* since he cannot recite the *berakha* on it after midnight, as explained in MB 477:6 and BHL *ad loc. Responsa Mishkenot Yaakov* §139 and other Aḥaronim attempt to prove that the *halakha* follows Rambam. Nonetheless, the law still remains unclear, so one should not recite the *berakhot* on matza or *maror* after midnight and must likewise take care to fulfill the Torah obligation of matza before midnight. MB further states that if one begins late and does not have time to complete the recitation of the Hagada before midnight, he should eat the matza and *maror,* with *berakhot,* right after *kiddush,* and then recite the Hagada. *Kaf Ha-ḥayim* 477:10 echoes this idea, but rules that one may not recite the *Birkat Ha-ge'ula* (just before the second cup) after midnight, since we are lenient in a case of uncertainty regarding *berakhot.* See *Ḥazon Ovadia* vol. 2 p. 166, which agrees with MB and rules that one may recite *Birkat Ha-ge'ula* after midnight. Regarding the concluding *berakha* of *Hallel,* MB 477:7 and SHT 6 *ad loc.* cite *Ḥok Yaakov* that one may recite it after midnight. R. Harari's *Mikra'ei Kodesh,* ch. 6 n. 70 demonstrates that *be-di'avad* one may recite *Birkat Ha-ge'ula* and the concluding *berakha* of *Hallel* after midnight.

roasted – outside the precincts of Jerusalem. Elsewhere, people did eat roast meat on Pesaḥ but did not roast a whole lamb, which would really look like offering the *korban Pesaḥ* outside the Temple. The Sages stated that each custom is valid: where the custom is to refrain from roasted meat, one should not eat it, and where the custom is to eat it, one may (*Pesaḥim* 53a). In practice, Yemeni Jews customarily eat roasted meat on Pesaḥ night, but all Ashkenazim and most Sephardim customarily prohibit roasted meat on Pesaḥ night (*Ben Ish Ḥai,* Year One, Tzav 30; *Ḥazon Ovadia* p. 175). We shall now specify the details of this prohibition:

The prohibition against roasted meat applies to all types of meat, even from species that could not be used as the *korban Pesaḥ,* such as beef and fowl. However, one may roast foods that do not require ritual slaughtering, such as fish and eggs (SA 476:2). Though the meat of the Paschal sacrifice was roasted over the fire and not in a pot, pot roast is nevertheless forbidden, because it looks like meat roasted over fire. It is likewise forbidden to eat meat that was first cooked and then roasted, because it looks roasted. However, meat that was first roasted may be cooked and eaten on the Seder night, because it looks cooked (MB 476:1; *Kaf Ha-ḥayim* 4 *ad loc.*).[30]

Some have a custom to eat eggs during the Seder meal in order to recall the destruction of the Temple, as eggs are a sign of mourning, and because the first day of Pesaḥ always falls on the same day of the week as Tisha Be-Av (Rema 476:2). The Vilna Gaon explains that eggs commemorate the pilgrimage sacrifice (*korban ḥagiga*) that was eaten on the Seder night before the *korban Pesaḥ*. Therefore, the custom is to eat the egg from the Seder plate during the meal, as it is placed there to commemorate the *korban ḥagiga* (MB 476:11; *Kaf Ha-ḥayim* 25-26 *ad loc.*). Some people refrain from eating the egg from the Seder plate in order to keep the plate intact; they eat it on the following day (*Ma'amar Mordechai* 473:1). However, the widespread custom is to eat the egg from the Seder plate at the Seder.

30. Grilled and smoked meats are considered roasted and are prohibited. R. Harari states in *Mikra'ei Kodesh* p. 488 that there are opinions that consider baked meat to be roasted. According to most *poskim,* frying is not like roasting. See AHS 486:4.

As on any other Yom Tov, a distinguished feast should be prepared for the Seder night, with fine utensils and festive delicacies. One may drink wine during the meal; this is not considered adding to the four cups. However, one must be careful not to eat and drink too much, because the *afikoman* must be eaten with an appetite at the end of the meal (see below, section 33), and because one must be able to continue reciting the *Hallel* and the concluding songs without becoming too tired.

33. *TZAFUN*

After the Seder meal, we eat a *kezayit* (about a third of a machine matza) of the broken matza that was set aside at the beginning of the Seder. This matza is called the *afikoman*. After eating the *afikoman*, we do not eat anything else until we go to sleep, so that the taste of the matza lingers in our mouths (SA 477:1, 478:1). If the *afikoman* set aside at the beginning is not big enough to give each participant a *kezayit*, the Seder leader gives each participant a small piece of the *afikoman* together with additional *shmura* matza to constitute a *kezayit*. If there is not enough *afikoman* to give even a small piece to each participant, the leader may give out *shmura* matza to be eaten as the *afikoman*. Likewise, if the *afikoman* was lost, one may use a different piece of *shmura* matza instead (Rema 477:2).

One may drink water after eating the *afikoman*. After all, eating after the *afikoman* is prohibited only so its taste stays in our mouths, and water has no taste (SA 478:1, MB 2 *ad loc.*).

The word "*afikoman*" originally meant "dessert." On the night of the fifteenth of Nisan, the last thing one eats must be the meat of the Paschal sacrifice, so that its taste lingers with us, as the Mishna states: "After the Paschal sacrifice, we do not conclude with dessert (*afikoman*)" (*Pesaḥim* 119b).

Since we can no longer offer the *korban Pesaḥ*, the Sages ordained eating matza at the end of the Seder to commemorate the *korban Pesaḥ*. So that the taste of this matza remains in our mouths, nothing may be eaten after it. Since this matza is the final course of the Seder, it is in essence dessert. Therefore we call it "*afikoman*."

SA 477:1 explains that the *afikoman* commemorates the *korban Pesaḥ*, and just as the Paschal sacrifice was eaten "while satisfied" ("*al ha-sova*"), so too the *afikoman* must be eaten while satisfied. "*Al ha-sova*" means that one is already satiated but still wants to eat more. However, if one is so full that his appetite is gone, he does not fulfill the mitzva in the ideal manner, since he would prefer not to eat any more. If one is so stuffed that food is repugnant to him, but he nonetheless forces himself to eat the *afikoman*, this is called *akhila gasa* (gross overconsumption), which is not considered eating at all. One who does so does not fulfill the mitzva of eating the *afikoman* (MB 476:6, *Kaf Ha-ḥayim* 17 *ad loc.*).

The *afikoman* must be eaten in one place, because it commemorates the Paschal sacrifice, which had to be eaten in one place, as it is stated (Shemot 12:46): "It should be eaten in one house" (Rema 478:1, MB 4 *ad loc.*).

34. THE *AFIKOMAN* – TWO REASONS, TWO *KEZEYTIM*

As we have seen, according to most authorities the *afikoman* commemorates the Paschal sacrifice, which was eaten at the end of the meal (*Ha-ma'or*, Ramban, *Or Zaru'a*, Rosh, etc.). However, according to several major Rishonim (Rashi, Rashbam), the *afikoman* is actually the fulfillment of the fundamental mitzva of eating matza, which, they explain, must be eaten at the end of the meal along with the *korban Pesaḥ*. Since the Paschal sacrifice had to be eaten while satisfied, so must the matza. And even though we recite the *berakha* over the matza at the beginning of the meal, in their opinion the basic intention to fulfill the mitzva to eat matza must be at the end of the meal, when the *afikoman* is eaten.

Le-khatḥila, it is good to have both of these reasons – to commemorate the *korban Pesaḥ* and to fulfill the mitzva of eating matza – in mind while eating the *afikoman*. According to both opinions, the *afikoman* must be eaten while reclining to the left. However, if one forgets to recline, there is a difference between them: according to the opinion that the *afikoman* commemorates the *korban Pesaḥ*, one need not eat another *afikoman* while reclining. According to the opinion that the *afikoman* fulfills the mitzva of eating matza, reclining is a *sine qua non*. Therefore, if one forgot to recline while eating the *afikoman*, he should preferably eat a second one while reclining. However, if one is full and will have a hard time eating another *kezayit* of matza, he need not eat the *afikoman* a second time; he may rely on the mainstream opinion that the *afikoman* commemorates the *korban Pesaḥ*. Moreover, even according to

Rashbam, since one intended to fulfill the mitzva of eating matza at the beginning of the meal, he has fulfilled his obligation even though, for Rashbam, that was not the proper time to have such intention. Therefore, failing to recline while eating the *afikoman* no longer prevents the fulfillment of the mitzva.

Some have a custom to eat two *kezeytim* of the *afikoman*, either because they want to show how desirable the matza is and thus eat a sizable portion to become fully satiated (Maharil), or because they want to allude to both reasons for eating the *afikoman*: one *kezayit* commemorates the *korban Pesaḥ* and another fulfills the mitzva to eat matza (*Baḥ*). However, this is not obligatory, and if one does not want to eat two *kezeytim*, he may eat just one and still keep both reasons in mind.

We have seen that, simply stated, a *kezayit* is about a third of a machine-made matza, and two *kezeytim* are about two-thirds. This is based on *Tosafot*'s stringent opinion about the size of a *kezayit*. In light of the fact that the *afikoman* is a rabbinic mitzva and that consumption of two *kezeytim* is subject to disagreement, one may certainly fulfill the mitzva of *afikoman* with a single *kezayit* of one third of a matza and, if necessary, with one fifth of a matza (based on Rambam's smaller *kezayit*). And we have already learned that whoever eats the matza without interruption will certainly finish it within a *shi'ur akhilat pras*.[31]

---

31. SA states that one must eat a *kezayit* of matza for *afikoman*. *Darkhei Moshe* quotes Maharil that one must eat two *kezeytim* for *afikoman*, and similarly, MB states in 477:1 "*le-khatḥila*, one should take two *kezeytim*." This is also the opinion of *Kaf Ha-ḥayim* 477:1. *Sefer Ha-ḥinukh* §21 implies that one can fulfill his obligation with less than a *kezayit*, and AHS 477:3 states that in an extreme situation one may use less than a *kezayit*, since the *afikoman* is only intended to commemorate the *korban Pesaḥ*. *Responsa Ḥazon Ovadia* §44 expands on this topic and presents other opinions, concluding that the mitzva is to eat one *kezayit*, although one who wishes to be stringent should follow MB. Several Aḥaronim write that the one may have in mind to fulfill both intentions with just one *kezayit*.

Regarding the size of a *kezayit*, see above section 23 and nn. 20 and 25, where we wrote that in unclear situations regarding Torah commandments or *mitzvot* that require *berakhot* we follow the stringent view of *Tosafot* – that a *kezayit* is the volume of half an egg. On the other hand, in unclear situations vis-à-vis rabbinic *mitzvot* with no *berakhot* we may follow the lenient view of Rambam – that a *kezayit* is less than one third of an egg, or c. one fifth of a machine matza. Therefore, regarding the rabbinic mitzva of eating the *afikoman*, for which only a minority of *poskim* maintain

35. *HALLEL*, THE GREAT *HALLEL*, AND THE CONCLUDING *BERAKHA*

After *Birkat Ha-mazon*, we drink the third cup of wine and then pour the fourth cup, over which we recite *Hallel* and "the Great" *Hallel* ("*Hallel Ha-gadol*"). Before *Hallel* we recite the paragraph "*Shefokh Ḥamatkha*" ("Pour Your Wrath"). Some customarily open the door at this point to demonstrate that, on this night, we are protected against destructive forces and not afraid of our enemies. By virtue of this faith, the *Mashi'aḥ* (Messiah) will come and pour out his wrath upon the wicked enemies of Israel (Rema 480:1). Some have a custom to stand while reciting *Shefokh Ḥamatkha* (AHS *ad loc.*, and this was the practice of Rav Kook). After reciting *Shefokh Ḥamatkha*, we close the door.

We then continue with the second part of *Hallel* (see above, section 20). There is a mitzva to recite verses 1-4 and 24-25 of Tehilim 118 responsively, led by the eldest member of the household. There is a mitzva to ensure that three adults are present in order to recite the verses in this manner, with one leader and multiple respondents (Rema 479:1). This is all *le-khatḥila*; of course, an individual fulfills the mitzva even by reciting *Hallel* alone. If only two people are present, they should recite the verses together (MB 479:10-11).

After this, we recite the Great *Hallel* (chapter 136 of Tehilim) followed by *Nishmat Kol Ḥai* ("The Soul of All Life") and the concluding *berakha*. There are different opinions regarding the formula of the concluding *berakha*: Sephardim close with the paragraph "*Yehallelukha*," which concludes the normal recitation of *Hallel*. Ashkenazim close with "*Yishtabaḥ*," which concludes the psalms of praise recited at *Shaḥarit*

---

that one must eat two *kezeytim*, one may certainly fulfill the stringent opinion that eating two *kezeytim* of *afikoman* can be fulfilled by eating one fifth of a matza, since according to many Ge'onim and Rishonim a *kezayit* is the size of a common olive. One fifth of a matza thus constitutes several *kezeytim* by this standard. Regarding *shi'ur akhilat pras*, see above section 25 and n. 22.

See section 25 for a discussion of the measurement of *akhilat pras*; in general, the most stringent opinion is that the time of *akhilat pras* is four minutes, and the median opinion is that it is between six and seven minutes. Since *afikoman* is a rabbinical decree and no *berakha* is recited on it, one can eat the *afikoman* in 6-7 minutes, and even if he ate it in nine minutes, he fulfills his obligation, since we follow the lenient view in an unclear situation vis-à-vis rabbinic *mitzvot* with no *berakhot*.

(see section 31 above, where we learned that it is better to complete this *berakha* by midnight). Following this, we sing various songs composed in the period of the Rishonim.

Logic dictates that the fourth cup should be drunk right after the concluding *berakha* of *Hallel,* which also concludes the Seder that was instituted by the Sages in the times of the Mishna. The songs and poems that follow are merely a custom. Nevertheless, some drink the fourth cup after singing a few of these additional songs, so that they too are sung over a cup of wine and are thus included in the Seder (see MB 480:6). Each family should continue its own tradition.

The Sephardic custom is not to recite "*ha-gefen*" before the fourth cup, whereas the Ashkenazic custom is to recite it (see section 21 above). After the fourth cup, the *berakha aḥarona* of "*Al Ha-gefen*" is said.

36. THE FIFTH CUP – ELIYAHU'S CUP

A significant halakhic uncertainty arose concerning the fifth cup. Some say that there is an extra special mitzva to drink a fifth cup; the fourth cup should be drunk at the end of the *Hallel* and the fifth cup after the concluding *berakha.* Others say that the fifth cup is merely the Sages' recommendation for one who wishes to continue drinking after the fourth cup. Still others say it is forbidden to drink a fifth cup.[32]

---

32. The issue in brief: According to the text of the Bavli used by Rashi and Rashbam, the Gemara does not mention a fifth cup at all, meaning that it would certainly be forbidden to add to the mitzva of drinking four cups by adding a fifth cup. However, according to the text of Rabbeinu Ḥananel, Rif, and Rambam, a *beraita* in *Pesaḥim* 118a states: "One recites *Hallel Ha-gadol* over the fifth [cup] – these are the words of R. Tarfon." According to *Ha-ma'or,* R. Tarfon disagrees with the *mishna* (*Pesaḥim* 99b) that obligates giving paupers enough money to buy four cups of wine, implying that there is no fifth cup; the *halakha* would follow the *mishna,* as it is anonymous and does not acknowledge dissenting opinions. However, according to Ran, there is no dispute between R. Tarfon and the *mishna*; therefore, one must drink four cups and may – and perhaps even must – drink a fifth. Raavad (in his glosses to *Ha-ma'or*) states, and Rambam implies, that it is a mitzva to drink a fifth cup. *Mordechai* states that the main obligation is to drink four cups, but the Sages made an allowance for those who wish to drink more wine, that they may recite *Hallel* over the fourth cup and *Hallel Ha-gadol* over a fifth. This is what Rema states in 481:1, but SA does not mention a fifth cup at all. According to *Kaf Ha-ḥayim* (*6 ad loc.*), the implication of SA is that drinking a fifth cup is prohibited.

The customary practice is not to drink a fifth cup, though we do pour one, called Eliyahu's Cup. The Vilna Gaon explains how it got this name: when there is an uncertainty that cannot be resolved, we believe that when the prophet Eliyahu returns as a harbinger of the messianic era, he will resolve it. Thus, we pour a fifth cup in his honor, and when he arrives he will tell us if we should drink it.

We can interpret this issue in a deeper way as well. The Sages instituted the four cups to signify the four expressions of redemption used in reference to the Exodus from Egypt: "I will rescue you… I will save you… I will redeem you… I will take you…" (Shemot 6:6-7). An additional expression of redemption is mentioned there: "**I will bring you** to the land" (*ibid.* 8). However, since this does not relate to the Exodus itself, the Sages do not obligate us to drink a corresponding fifth cup. They tell us, however, that there is a mitzva to drink a fifth cup in order to allude to the complete redemption, which begins with our entry into Eretz Yisrael.

It could also be that the uncertainty about the fifth cup stems from the question as to whether it is proper to drink a fifth cup after the destruction of the Temple and during the long exile. Perhaps after the Temple's destruction we can only celebrate with those cups that allude to our Exodus from the Egyptian bondage, since this will forever distinguish us. Even if the nations of the world subjugate our bodies, our souls remain eternally free; ever since the Exodus, it has been clear that we are God's uniquely chosen people, that we received the Torah, and that all the hardships that have come upon us have not broken our faith in God, our Redeemer. Therefore, we drink four cups of wine corresponding to the four expressions of redemption from Egypt. The fifth cup, though, does not correspond to our emancipation alone; rather, it alludes to the complete redemption, which depends on our entry into Eretz Yisrael, where the word of God is revealed in all spheres of life, through the Torah and prophecy, and through God's blessing, which inheres in the building of the nation and the land. This notion of the Temple is that it joins heaven and earth and reveals the divine unity that nourishes everything. Indeed, the number five alludes to the inner, unifying point at the center of the four compass directions. And so perhaps at the source of the uncertainty about the fifth cup lies the question: is it fitting, in light of the Temple's destruction, to drink the fifth cup, which alludes to the complete redemption?

The solution is to pour a fifth cup but not drink it as part of the Seder until Eliyahu appears. His very appearance will show us that the time has come to drink the fifth cup, celebrating our complete redemption.

The custom is to pour Eliyahu's Cup after drinking the third cup; when we pour the fourth cup for everybody, we pour a cup for Eliyahu as well. The custom is to leave Eliyahu's Cup covered until morning, when we pour the wine back into the bottle and then use it for the morning *kiddush*.[33]

37. DRINKING COFFEE OR JUICE AFTER THE SEDER

We have learned that the Sages ordained the *afikoman* at the end of the Seder to commemorate the *korban Pesaḥ*, which was eaten "while satisfied." Just as it was forbidden to eat any other food after the Paschal sacrifice, so that its taste lingered, so too the Sages forbade eating after the *afikoman*.[34]

It is also forbidden to drink wine after the *afikoman*, for several reasons. If one has not yet finished reciting the Hagada, he might become intoxicated and be unable to finish reciting *Hallel* properly; furthermore, by drinking an additional cup of wine, one will appear to be adding to the number of cups instituted by the Sages.

---

33. Some have the custom of pouring the wine from Eliyahu's Cup back into the bottle right after the Seder (this is the custom of Chabad). Others have the custom to add the wine from Eliyahu's Cup to the fourth cup; see *Piskei Teshuvot* 480:1.

Regarding the symbolism of the fifth cup, my ideas echo what Maharal writes in *Gevurot Hashem* at the end of a brief section on the laws of Pesaḥ. He cryptically states that the fifth cup symbolizes livelihood that comes from God. See R. Goren's *Torat Ha-Shabbat Ve-hamo'ed*, pp. 145-154, where he explains that the fifth cup represents the mitzva of settling Eretz Yisrael, a mitzva that requires total devotion on our part. R. Goren states that the fifth cup is not an obligation because it is on a higher level than ordinary obligations. He encourages drinking the fifth cup nowadays, since we are actively involved in settling Eretz Yisrael.

34. If one accidentally ate after the *afikoman*, as long as he did not recite *Birkat Hamazon* he should eat another piece of *shmura* matza for *afikoman*, as per MB 478:1. If he already recited *Birkat Ha-mazon*, he need not re-wash his hands and eat another *afikoman* (MB 478:12), as explained in R. Harari's *Mikra'ei Kodesh* ch. 9 n. 50.

It is even forbidden to drink wine after the Seder, because there is a mitzva to delve into the laws of Pesaḥ and the Exodus story until one is overcome with sleep, and if one drinks wine or some other intoxicating beverage, he will not be able to do so (Rabbeinu Yona, Rosh). Furthermore, even though the Seder is over, if one drinks additional cups of wine he may still appear to be adding to the cups instituted by the Sages, or starting a new series of cups (Ramban, Ran).

Some *poskim* maintain that it is even forbidden to drink coffee or juice after the *afikoman* until one goes to sleep, because any flavored food or drink weakens the taste of the *afikoman* in one's mouth, so just as it is forbidden to eat after the *afikoman,* so is it forbidden to drink anything flavored. To be sure, we drink two more cups of wine after the *afikoman,* but since these are part of the mitzva, they are not seen as weakening the taste of the mitzva. According to this, only water may be drunk after the Seder.

However, in contrast to these *poskim,* many other *poskim* permit drinking coffee or juice. They maintain that beverages are not included in the prohibition, because only food is seen as weakening the taste of the *afikoman.*

In practice, if one wishes to drink coffee or juice after the Seder, he may, as this is the opinion of most *poskim*. But preferably one should be stringent and avoid drinking anything except water. If one wishes to drink coffee so that he will be able to continue delving into the laws of Pesaḥ and the Exodus story, he may, even *le-khatḥila.*[35]

35. According to *Ha-ma'or* and several other Rishonim, once the Seder has ended there is no reason to refrain from drinking wine, even if it will cause one to become intoxicated. Conversely, *Mordechai* and *Hagahot Maimoniyot* state that even drinking water is forbidden. Most Aḥaronim follow the opinion of Rosh and Ran that either out of concern that one will become intoxicated and will not be able to continue delving into Pesaḥ topics, or out of concern that he will appear to be adding on to the four cups, one may not drink any alcoholic beverage, including *ḥamar medina* (see section 13 above, n. 10). Some *poskim* follow Rif and Mahari Weil, who maintain that one is only permitted to drink water, since water has no taste and will not ruin the aftertaste of the *afikoman.* Accordingly, *Knesset Ha-gedola* and *Ma'amar Mordechai* prohibit drinking coffee or other flavored drinks after the Seder. On the other hand, some Aḥaronim, including MA (481:1), reason that even according to Mahari Weil one may drink a beverage with a weak taste, and the prohibition is only on drinking

38. RECOUNTING THE EXODUS AND STUDYING THE LAWS OF PESAḤ ALL NIGHT

Some have a custom to read Shir Ha-shirim (the Song of Songs) upon completing the Hagada, as it alludes to the love between God and Israel.

Though we have fulfilled our obligation to tell the story of the Exodus by reading the Hagada, there is a mitzva to continue embellishing the story and telling of the miracles and wonders that God did for our ancestors throughout the night of the fifteenth, until one is overcome with sleep. This mitzva includes studying the laws of Pesaḥ (SA 481:2;

---

beverages that have a strong flavor. According to this, the status of coffee requires clarification. Regardless, according to most Rishonim, one may drink coffee or juice, since these drinks are not intoxicating and it does not appear that one who drinks them is adding to the four cups. It is told that Ḥatam Sofer would drink coffee after the Seder every year. *Ḥazon Ovadia* 1:50 discusses this topic at length and rules leniently that one may drink coffee. According to SAH (481:1), MB (481:1), and *Ben Ish Ḥai* (Tzav 35), one should preferably be stringent and refrain from drinking coffee and flavored drinks, but they permit it when there is a great necessity. As I have written, if by drinking coffee one will be able to study Torah, he should certainly drink coffee, even *le-khatḥila*.

According to *Ḥok Yaakov* 481:1, since the main reason not to drink strong beverages is to avoid drowsiness, once one is drowsy he may even drink alcoholic beverages. Many Aḥaronim cite this view. SAH (481:1) also quotes this opinion, and adds that according to those who prohibit drinking because the beverages ruin the taste of the *afikoman*, the prohibition applies all night. Accordingly, it is clear that one may not eat throughout the night, since that would certainly ruin the aftertaste of the *afikoman*. In an extreme situation, one may be lenient based on the opinion of *Avnei Nezer* (OḤ 381), which maintains that according to R. Elazar b. Azarya, since the time for eating the *korban Pesaḥ* (and the *afikoman*) ends at midnight, the prohibition against eating afterward ends at midnight as well. Therefore, in extenuating circumstances, since this is only a rabbinic injunction, one may rely on *Avnei Nezer*'s explanation of R. Elazar b. Azarya's view.

According to the custom of the Sephardim, who do not recite a *berakha* on the fourth cup of wine, one who wishes to drink water between the third and fourth cups does not recite a *berakha* on it (provided that he had in mind to drink water or the water was in front of him), since the *berakha* on the third cup covers the fourth cup and any other beverage. According to Ashkenazic custom, the *berakha* on the third cup does not cover the fourth cup; therefore, one cannot drink water without a *berakha* between the third and fourth cups, even if the water was in front of him, since we assume that when he drinks the water he is no longer thinking about the *berakha* he made on the third cup.

Gevurot Hashem ch. 2), but it does not include "*pilpul*" (talmudic casuistry) (*Derashot Ḥatam Sofer* p. 265).

It is best not to spend a lot of time on the portion of the Hagada that precedes the meal, because we want the children and all of the participants to remain alert until the fourth cup. But after finishing the Hagada, there is a mitzva to continue discussing the Exodus as much as possible.

If one fears that by staying up late he will be unable to pray *Shaḥarit* properly, it is better that he goes to bed earlier (*Sidur Yaavetz*). An effort should nonetheless be made to continue relating the story of the Exodus until after midnight (*Kaf Ha-ḥayim* 481:11).

Before going to sleep on Pesaḥ night, it is customary to recite *Shema* and the *berakha* of *Ha-mapil*, but not to read the other verses that are read on all other nights. These verses are recited as a protective remedy against harmful forces, but this night is safeguarded against such forces and opportune for redemption (Rema 481:2; and see *Ben Ish Ḥai*, Tzav 38).

May it be God's will that just as we have merited to study the *halakhot* of the Seder, so may we merit to fulfill them.

Glossary

afikoman – lit. dessert; the portion of matza eaten to conclude the Seder meal

aḥshevei – a principle whereby one's actions indicate that he assigns subjective significance to an otherwise insignificant object

al ha-sova – while satisfied

Amora'im – Sages of the Gemara (c. 200-500 CE)

bal yera'eh – the prohibition against *ḥametz* being seen in one's possession on Pesaḥ

bal yimatzei – the prohibition against *ḥametz* being found in one's possession on Pesaḥ

Badatz – *Beit Din Tzedek,* an independent rabbinical court that provides kosher certification amongst other services

basar be-ḥalav – the forbidden mixture of milk and meat

batei midrash – Torah study halls

batel be-rov – rendered insignificant by the majority

batel be-shishim – rendered insignificant as less than one sixtieth of a mixture

be-di'avad – a level of performance that *ex post facto* satisfies an obligation in a less-than-ideal manner

bedika – search; often used as shorthand for *bedikat ḥametz*

bedikat ḥametz – the mitzva to search for *ḥametz* in order to eliminate it from possession before Pesaḥ; see chapter 4

beit din – rabbinical court

beit knesset – synagogue
ben yomo – less than 24 hours (the time it takes for absorbed taste to become foul) removed from last use
berakha – a formal blessing recited before eating or performing a mitzva, and on other occasions
berakha aḥarona – a blessing recited after eating or drinking
berakha le-vatala – a blessing in vain
Birkat Ha-mazon – known as the "grace after meals"; the *berakha aḥarona* consisting of four *berakhot* recited after a bread-based meal
bitul – nullification
bi'ur ḥametz – the elimination of *ḥametz*
bli neder – a verbal caveat that ensures that an undertaking does not acquire the status of a vow
de-Oraita – biblically mandated
Eretz Yisrael – the Land of Israel
Erev Pesaḥ – lit. the eve of Pesaḥ; the day preceding Pesaḥ, on which Israel is obligated to offer the *korban Pesaḥ*
gebrokts – see *matza sheruya* and section 8:2
Gemara – the part of the Talmud that interprets and expands upon the Mishna; compiled during the 3rd-6th centuries CE
Ge'onim (sing. Gaon) – the leaders of the Babylonian yeshivot and authoritative interpreters of the Bavli during the latter part of the first millennium CE
Ḥag Ha-matzot – the Festival of Unleavened Bread; the biblical name for Pesaḥ
Hagada – the central text of the Seder, the central part of which retells the story of the Exodus
hagala – immersion in boiling water; see chapter 10
halakha – the collective body of Jewish law; an individual Jewish law
ḥalla – the mitzva to give a part of a large batch of dough to a *kohen*
Hallel – chapters 113-118 of Tehilim, all of which are thanksgiving psalms, recited on Jewish holidays
Hallel Ha-gadol – Tehilim chapter 136; the "Great *Hallel*"
ḥametz – cereal grain that leavened; see chapter 2.
ḥametz gamur – absolute *ḥametz*, in which the leavening process has been completed

ḥametz nuksheh – "hardened *ḥametz*"; see section 2:5
ḥametz she-avar alav ha-Pesaḥ – *ḥametz* that belonged to a Jew during the holiday
ha-motzi – the *berakha* over bread
ha-motzi leḥem min ha-aretz – "Who brings forth bread from the earth"; the formula for the *berakha* on bread
ḥaroset – a sweet paste made of fruits and nuts eaten at the Seder to commemorate the clay mortar our forefathers made when they were enslaved in Egypt
hasava – reclining; see 16:10-11
hatarat nedarim – the annulment of vows before a rabbinical court
heavy *libun* – see *libun*
hefker – ownerless
hefsek – a problematic interruption between two acts or recitations that must be performed or recited together
heteira bala – it absorbed permissible matter
Ḥol Ha-mo'ed – the intermediate days of Sukkot and Pesaḥ, on which certain weekday activities are permitted
ḥozer ve-ne'or – "reawakened"; the reversal of nullification in which a nullified ingredient regains its former status; see sections 7:2-3
ḥutz la-aretz – countries outside of Eretz Yisrael
irui – "pouring"; one of the ways taste is transferred; an intermediate phase between *kli rishon* and *kli sheni*
isura bala – it absorbed forbidden matter
karet – extirpation, the most severe biblical punishment
karpas – the vegetable eaten at the beginning of the Seder
ke-bole'o kakh polto – taste is released from a vessel in the same manner that it was absorbed; see section 10:3
kezayit (pl. *kezeytim*) – an olive's bulk, a standard halakhic measure of volume or weight; see sections 16:23-24
kiddush – the invocation of the sanctity of a holy day with blessings over a cup of wine
kinyan – an act that effects an acquisition or another change in status
kitniyot – non-*ḥametz* species that may not be eaten on Pesaḥ according to Ashkenazic custom; see chapter 9
kli rishon – the vessel in which food was cooked; see section 10:8

kli sheni – the vessel into which hot food was transferred; see section 10:8
korban – a sacrificial offering
korban ḥagiga – a sacrifice offered at each of the three pilgrimage festivals
korban Pesaḥ – the Paschal offering
korekh – matza and *maror* eaten together to commemorate the practice of Hillel the Elder in Temple times; see section 16:28
kos shel berakha – a cup of wine linked to the performance of a mitzva
kvisha – "pickling," or the absorption of taste through prolonged soaking; see section 10:14
leḥem mishneh – the two whole loaves of bread/matza over which the *berakha* of *ha-motzi* is recited at Shabbat and Yom Tov meals
leḥem oni – "poor man's bread"; how matza is described in Devarim 16:3
le-khatḥila – *ab initio* a level of performance that satisfies an obligation in an ideal manner
le-shem matzat mitzva – "for the sake of the matza of the mitzva"; the required intention one must have when baking matza to be used for the mitzva
libun – heating a vessel by fire to the point that absorbed taste is incinerated
light *libun* – heating a utensil by fire to the point that a piece of straw or thread placed on the opposite side of the utensil becomes blackened from the heat
Ma nishtana – "Why is this night different?"; a series of questions that the children ask at the Seder
Ma'ariv – evening prayers
Magid – the part of the Seder in which the story of the Exodus is recounted
Makat Bekhorot – the Plague of the Firstborn
marit ayin – "appearance"; an action that must be avoided because it may give a false impression of being a violation
maror – the bitter vegetable that must be eaten at the Seder
Mashi'aḥ – the Messiah; the restorer of the Davidic dynasty
matza – unleavened bread eaten by Jews on Pesaḥ
matza ashira – matza that was kneaded in a liquid other than water, colloquially known as "egg matza"; see section 8:1
mayim she-lanu – water drawn before nightfall and kept overnight in a cool place, later to be used in matza

mekhirat ḥametz – the sale of *ḥametz* to remove it from Jewish possession before Pesaḥ; see chapter 6

melakha – productive work of the type prohibited on Shabbat and Yom Tov

melakha gemura – full-fledged work; see section 13:2

melo lugmav – a measure of liquid; enough to fill the drinker's mouth with one cheek inflated

Men of the Great Assembly – a group of sages and prophets from the beginning of the Second Temple era (c. 500 BCE) who instituted several enactments that shaped the course of *halakha* and Jewish tradition

mezonot – food that is made from grain but is not bread, or the *berakha* recited on such foods

mikveh – a ritual immersion pool

mil – a unit of distance; it takes 18 minutes (22.5 according to some, and 24 according to others) to walk a *mil*

Minḥa – the afternoon prayers

minḥa gedola – 5.5 seasonal hours before sunset; the earliest time to recite the afternoon prayers

minḥa ketana – 2.5 seasonal hours before sunset

nat bar nat – taste that has been absorbed into a medium twice removed from its origins

nat bar nat bar nat – taste that is thrice removed from its origins

netilat yadayim – ritual hand washing

Nisan – the first month of the Jewish year

notar – uneaten portions of a sacrifice left over until the morning, which must be incinerated and may not be eaten

noten ta'am bar noten ta'am – see *nat bar nat*

noten ta'am li-fgam – something that imparts foul taste

olat re'iyah – a burnt-offering sacrificed in honor of one of the three pilgrimage festivals

pagum – befouled

pidyon ha-ben – the mitzva of redeeming the [firstborn] son

plata – a warming tray used to reheat foods on Shabbat

posek (pl. *poskim*) – a halakhic decisor or authority

pras – half a loaf of bread; see section 16:25

reshut – voluntary, optional
responsa – a genre of rabbinic literature that consists of rabbinic responses to halakhic queries
revi'it – a liquid measure equal to a quarter of a *log,* calculated by most to be c. 75 ml
Rishonim – Jewish sages and halakhic authorities from the medieval era (roughly 1000-1500 CE)
safek – a case of uncertainty or doubt
safek de-rabanan – an uncertainly about a rabbinic ordinance
se'or – a leavening agent that one uses to make dough ferment
se'uda shlishit – the obligatory third Shabbat meal
se'udat mitzva – a festive meal celebrating the fulfillment of a mitzva
Seder – the banquet on the first night of Pesaḥ that includes several special recitations, customs, and *mitzvot*
sefirot – mystical "emanations" through which God created and sustains the world
sfek sfeika – a double uncertainty
sha'ah zmanit – a seasonal hour; one-twelfth of the time between sunrise and sunset (or between sunset and sunrise)
Shabbat Ha-gadol – the Shabbat immediately before Pesaḥ
Shaḥarit – the morning prayers
shali'aḥ – proxy or agent
she-heḥeyanu – "Who has given us life"; a *berakha* recited at specific significant occasions
Shekhina – the divine presence in this world
shi'ur – a standard halakhic measurement for weight, distance, or volume
shi'ur akhilat pras – the time it takes to eat half a loaf of bread; see section 16:25
shmura matza – matza that has been guarded from becoming *ḥametz;* see section 1:2
siyum masekhet – a *se'udat mitzva* occasioned by the completion of a tractate of the Talmud
Ta'anit Bekhorot – the Fast of the Firstborns; see section 13:3
Tanna'im – the rabbinic authorities in Eretz Yisrael during the first two centuries CE
tefaḥ – a handbreadth; a halakhic measurement equal to c. 8cm

tefillin – phylacteries; black leather boxes and straps containing parchment scrolls, worn during weekday morning prayers

teruma – a priestly gift contributed from one's produce

Tosefta – A 3rd century CE tannaitic collection of halakhic material related to the Mishna

tum'a – ritual contamination/impurity

Tzafun – the part of the Seder in which the *afikoman* is eaten

tzeit ha-kokhavim – the appearance of three distinct stars, marking nightfall for various halakhic purposes

yad soledet bo – hot enough to cause the hand to recoil, somewhere between 45°C and 71°C

Yaḥatz – the part of the Seder in which the middle matza is broken and the larger part designated as the *afikoman*

Yom Tov – the festivals of biblical origin during which *melakha* is prohibited

yom tov sheni shel galuyot – the extra day of Yom Tov observed in the Diaspora

zeh ve-zeh gorem – an effect produced by multiple factors

zero'a – a piece of roasted or boiled meat or poultry, preferably a shank bone, placed on the Seder plate

List of Sources

Abba-Shaul, R. Ben-Zion – 1924-1998, Jerusalem; a leading Sephardic *posek* and yeshiva head

Aderet – R. Eliyahu David Rabinowitz-Teomim (1845-1905), a noted *rosh yeshiva* and rabbi in Lithuania and then Eretz Yisrael

Aguda – A compendium of halakhic rulings compiled by R. Alexander Suslin Hakohen, in 14th century Germany; the compendium was deemed definitive by later Ashkenazic scholars

Agur – A concise summary of halakhic rulings, authored by R. Yaakov b. Yehuda Landau (d. 1493) of Germany and later Italy; cited extensively in *Shulḥan Arukh*

Aḥaronim – Halakhic authorities from c. 1500 CE until the present day

Alter, R. Yitzḥak Meir – 1799-1866; the first rebbe of Ger (Gora Kalwaria, Poland) and author of *Ḥidushei Ha-Rim*

Ama Devar – A collection of responsa on matters of *kashrut* by R. Mordechai Eliyahu (see entry)

Amram Gaon, R. – d. 875; Gaon of Sura best known for writing down the Jewish liturgical tradition, thus creating the first *siddur*

Arizal – R. Yitzḥak Luria Ashkenazi (1534-1572, Jerusalem, Egypt, and Tzefat), an influential mystic and founder of a major school of kabbalistic thought

Arugat Ha-bosem – A collection of responsa by R. Moshe Greenwald (1853-1911), rabbi of Chust, Hungary (Khust, Ukraine)

Arukh Ha-shulḥan – A comprehensive halakhic code which follows the order of *Tur* and *Shulḥan Arukh* and is known for its efficient reorganization of each topic; by R. Yeḥiel Mikhel Epstein (1829-1908, Greater Lithuania)

Arukh Le-ner – A commentary on the Talmud by R. Yaakov Ettlinger (1798-1871), a leading German rabbi

Atzei Ha-Levanon – A collection of responsa by R. Yehuda Leib Tsirelson (1859-1941), the rabbi of Kishinev from 1908 until his death during the German bombardment of the city

Auerbach, R. Shlomo Zalman – 1910-1995, Jerusalem; a major 20th century Israeli *posek* and author of several halakhic works

Avi Ezri – A compendium of halakhic essays and rulings by Raavya (see entry)

Avigdor, R. – An Austrian Tosafist of the 13th century

Avnei Nezer – A collection of responsa authored by R. Avraham Bornstein (see entry)

Bayit Ḥadash – A commentary on *Tur* by R. Yoel Sirkis (see entry)

Bedikat Ḥametz U-vi'uro – A halakhic work on the mitzvot and prohibitions associated with owning *ḥametz* on Pesaḥ and eliminating it beforehand; written by R. Ḥayim Mikhel Linder

Be'er Yitzḥak – A collection of responsa by R. Yitzḥak Elḥanan Spektor (see entry)

Beit Ephraim – A collection of responsa by R. Ephraim Zalman Margolis (1762-1828) of Brody

Beit Meir – A commentary on *Shulḥan Arukh* by R. Meir Posner (1735-1807) of Danzig (Gdansk, Poland)

Beit Shlomo – A collection of responsa by R. Shlomo Drimer (1800-1872, Galicia)

Beit Yitzḥak – A collection of responsa by R. Yitzḥak Yehuda Schmelkes (1828-1906, Galicia)

Beit Yosef – R. Yosef Karo's monumental summary of the halakhic positions of the Rishonim; formulated as a commentary on *Tur*, it is from this work that *Shulḥan Arukh* was distilled

Bekhor Shor – A small talmudic commentary by R. Alexander Sender Schorr (1673-1737, Poland), appended to his classic work *Tevu'ot Shor* on the laws of kosher slaughtering

Ben Ish Ḥai – A compendium of laws of everyday halakha, interspersed with kabbalistic ideas and customs and arranged by weekly Torah portion; based on the addresses of R. Yosef Ḥayim of Baghdad (1832-1909)

Bereishit Rabba – A 5th century classic midrashic compilation on Bereishit

Binat Adam – A small collection of responsa by R. Avraham Danzig (1748-1820, Poland), a *posek* best known as the author of *Ḥayei Adam*

Binyan Olam – A collection of responsa by R. Yitzḥak Isaac Ḥaver (1789-1853, Greater Lithuania), a disciple of the Vilna Gaon

Binyan Shlomo – A collection of responsa by R. Shlomo Hakohen (1828-1905), a *posek* and rabbinical court judge in Vilna

Binyan Tziyon – A collection of responsa by R. Yaakov Ettlinger (1798-1871), a leading German rabbi

Birkei Yosef – Ḥida's (see entry) commentary on *Shulḥan Arukh*

Birur Halakha – An edition of the Bavli envisioned by Rav Kook that seeks to reunite the study of *halakha* and Talmud

Bi'ur Ha-Gra – The Vilna Gaon's (see entry) commentary on *Shulḥan Arukh*

Bi'ur Halakha – One of the three commentaries on *Shulḥan Arukh Oraḥ Ḥayim* authored by R. Yisrael Meir Kagan ("Ḥafetz Ḥayim," 1838-1933) and included in *Mishna Berura*; this commentary contains lengthy discussions of halakhic issues

Bornstein, R. Avraham – 1838-1910, a *posek* and the Rebbe of Sochatchov (Sochaczew, Poland), author of *Responsa Avnei Nezer* and *Eglei Tal* on the laws of Shabbat

Cohen, R. She'ar Yashuv – b. 1927; Israeli rabbi and author of halakhic essays and responsa, city rabbi of Haifa

Da'at Torah – A commentary on *Shulḥan Arukh Oraḥ Hayim* by R. Shalom Mordechai Schwadron (see entry)

Dagul Mei-rvava – A commentary on *Shulḥan Arukh* by R. Yeḥezkel Landau (see entry)

Darkhei Moshe – Rema's (see entry) commentary on *Tur* and *Beit Yosef*, which supplements those works with other, mainly Ashkenazic halakhic rulings

Darkhei Teshuva – A compilation and catalog of the responsa literature, following the order of *Shulḥan Arukh*; by R. Zvi Hirsch Spira (1850-1913), rabbi and Ḥasidic rebbe of Munkacs, Hungary (now Mukacheve, Ukraine)

Derashot Ḥatam Sofer – A collection of sermons by Ḥatam Sofer (see entry)

Derekh Pekudekha – An exposition of the 613 mitzvot by R. Zvi Elimelekh (1783-1841) of Dinov (Dynow, Poland), a Ḥasidic rabbi best known for his work *Bnei Yisaskhar*

Devar Yehoshua – A collection of responsa by R. Yehoshua Menaḥem Ehrenberg (1904-1976) of Hungary and later Tel Aviv

Di Trani, R. Yeshaya – See Rid

Divrei Ḥayim – A collection of responsa by R. Ḥayim Halberstam (see entry)

Divrei Malkiel – A collection of responsa by R. Malkiel Zvi Tannenbaum (1847-1910) of Lomza, Poland

Duran, R. Shimon b. Tzemaḥ – See Rashbatz

Eger, R. Akiva – 1761-1837; rabbi of Posen, Prussia (Poznan, Poland), influential commentator on the Talmud and *Shulḥan Arukh*, author of the collection of responsa bearing his name

Eliya Rabba – An influential Ashkenazic halakhic work by R. Eliyahu Spira (1660-1712) of Titkin (Tykocin, Poland) and Prague

Eliyahu, R. Mordechai – 1929-2010, Jerusalem; a prominent *posek*, Sephardic Chief Rabbi of Israel, and head of Yeshivat Merkaz Harav, authored several halakhic works and upheld the customs of Iraqi Jewry

Emek Halakha – A collection of resposa by R. Zev Wolf of Zhetel, Poland (now Dzyatlava, Belarus), 19th century

Encyclopedia Talmudit – An encyclopedia, begun by R. Meir Bar-Ilan in 1942 and initially edited by R. Shlomo Yosef Zevin, consisting of 28 volumes thus far, summarizing halakhic topics of the Talmud

Eretz Zvi – A collection of responsa by R. Aryeh Zvi Frumer (1884-1943), known as the Kozhiglover Rav, who perished at Majdanek

Eshel Avraham – Part of *Pri Megadim* (see entry) and a supercommentary on *Magen Avraham*

Even Ha-ezer – One of the four sections of *Tur* and *Shulḥan Arukh*, dealing primarily with marital law

Feinstein, R. Moshe – 1895-1986, Uzda, Russia (now Belarus) and New York; the outstanding *posek* of 20th century America, author of *Responsa Igrot Moshe* as well as commentaries on the Torah and Talmud

Frank, R. Zvi Pesaḥ – 1873-1960, Kovno (Kaunas, Lithuania) and Jerusalem; a *posek* and rabbinical court judge, author of *Responsa Har Zvi* and other works

Gevurot Hashem – A series of expositions on the Exodus from Egypt, by Maharal (see entry)

Goren, R. Shlomo – 1917-1994; former Ashkenazic Chief Rabbi of Israel and Chief Rabbi of the Israel Defense Forces; authored several works addressing the intersection of *halakha* and modern state-building

Gra – The Vilna Gaon (see entry)

Hagahot Beit Yosef – A part of *Shiyarei Knesset Ha-gedola* (see entry)

Hagahot Ha-Tur – A part of *Knesset Ha-gedola* (see entry)

Hagahot Maimoniyot – Glosses on *Mishneh Torah* by R. Meir b. Yekutiel Hakohen (13th century Germany), reflecting Ashkenazic halakhic tradition

Hagahot Sefer Mitzvot Katan – Glosses on *Sefer Mitzvot Katan* by Rabbeinu Peretz (see entry)

Hagalat Kelim Le-Pesaḥ – A contemporary halakhic compendium on *hagalat kelim* for Pesaḥ, by R. Zvi Ben-Dov Cohen, published in 1980

Hai Gaon, R. – 939-1038; the long-serving Gaon of Pumbedita, author of numerous responsa and halakhic monographs, most of which were lost; considered to mark the end of the geonic era

Ḥakham Zvi – A collection of responsa by R. Zvi Hirsch Ashkenazi (1656-1718, lived in numerous places all over Europe); the nom de plume of R. Ashkenazi

Halakhot Gedolot – A systematic summary of talmudic law from the geonic era; commonly known as *Behag*, its date and authorship are subject to dispute

Halberstam, R. Ḥayim – c.1793-1876; founder of the Ḥasidic dynasty of Sanz, Galicia (Nowy Sacz, Poland), known as "Divrei Ḥayim" after his collection of responsa

Halperin, R. Levi Yitzḥak – Director of the Institute for Science and Halacha in Jerusalem

Ha-ma'or – Objections to Rif's halakhic code, authored by R. Zerakhia Halevi (1125-1186, Provence)

Ha-mo'adim Be-halakha – Halakhic studies of the Jewish festivals, authored by R. Shlomo Yosef Zevin (see entry)

Ḥananel, Rabbeinu – c. 990-1153, Kairouan, Tunisia; 11th century sage who wrote the first complete commentary on the Talmud as well as other works; helped transform North Africa into a major center of Jewish learning

Harari, R. Moshe – A faculty member at Yeshivat Merkaz Harav and author of *Mikra'ei Kodesh* (see entry)

Ha-Seder He-arukh – A three-volume collection of laws, customs, and ideas pertaining to the Seder, authored by R. Moshe Yaakov Weingarten and published in 1991

Ḥatam Sofer – A collection of responsa by R. Moshe Sofer (1762-1839), the leading rabbinic figure in Austria-Hungary of that era; the nom de plume of R. Sofer and the title of his many halakhic, talmudic, and homiletic works

Ḥavalim Ba-ne'imim – A collection of responsa by R. Yehuda Leib Graubart (1862-1937), Polish Ḥasidic rabbi who served in Stashov (Staszow), Poland and later Toronto, Canada

Ḥavot Ya'ir – A collection of responsa by R. Yair Ḥayim Bacharach (1639-1702), a major German *posek* of his era

Ḥayei Adam – A digest of *halakhot* pertaining to daily life, intended for use by laypeople, authored by R. Avraham Danzig (see under *Binat Adam*)

Ḥazon Ish – The name of numerous halakhic, talmudic, and ideological works by R. Avraham Yeshaya Karelitz (see entry)

Ḥazon Naḥum – A collection of responsa by R. Naḥum Weidenfeld (1875-1939) of Dombrova, Galicia (Dabrowa Tarnowska, Poland)

Ḥazon Ovadia – A 21-volume series on the *halakhot* of Jewish festivals, by R. Ovadia Yosef (see entry)

Ḥelkat Yaakov – A collection of responsa by R. Mordechai Yaakov Breisch (1896-1976), head of the rabbinical court in Zurich, Switzerland

Ḥelkat Yo'av – A collection of responsa by R. Yoav Yehoshua Weingarten (1845-1923) of Poland

Henkin, R. Yehuda Herzl – b. 1945, United States and Israel; author of *Responsa Bnei Banim* and other work in Hebrew and English, notably on halakhic issues pertaining to women

Ḥessed Le-Avraham – A collection of responsa by R. Avraham Teomim (1814-1868), rabbi of Zborow and later Buczacz, Galicia

Ḥida – R. Ḥayim Yosef David Azulai (1724-1806) of Jerusalem, a prolific author on a variety of rabbinic genres who traveled throughout the Jewish world

Ḥidushei Ha-Rim – Commentaries on biblical, rabbinic, and halakhic works by R. Yitzḥak Meir Alter (see entry)

Hilkhot Ḥag Be-ḥag – A concise summary of the *halakhot* of Jewish holidays by R. Moshe Mordechai Karp, a contemporary *posek* from Kiryat Sefer, Israel

Hirschprung, R. Pinḥas – 1912-1998, Polish rabbi of a Ḥasidic background who served as chief rabbi of Montreal, Canada during the last three decades of the 20th century

Ḥizkuni – A Torah commentary by R. Ḥizkiya b. Manoaḥ (c. 1250-1310) of France

Ḥok Yaakov – A commentary on *Shulḥan Arukh Oraḥ Ḥayim* by R. Yaakov Reischer (1661-1733) of Prague and later Germany

Ḥoshen Mishpat – One of the four sections of *Tur* and *Shulḥan Arukh*, dealing primarily with civil law

Ibn Attar, R. Ḥayim – 1696-1743, Morocco, Livorno, and Eretz Yisrael; a kabbalist, *posek*, and saint best known for writing *Or Ha-ḥayim*, a commentary on the Torah

Ibn Ezra – R. Avraham b. Meir ibn Ezra (1089-1164) of Spain, who traveled in Christian Europe and wrote works on astronomy, poetry, and linguistics; best known for his Torah commentary

Ibn Gi'at, R. Yitzḥak – See Ritz Gi'at

Igrot Moshe – A collection of responsa by R. Moshe Feinstein (see entry)

Imrei Shefer – Netziv's (see entry) commentary on the Hagada

Itur – A 12th century work on several areas of *halakha* by R. Yitzḥak b. Aba Mari of Marseilles (1122-1193)

Kaf Ha-ḥayim – A 10-volume halakhic compendium, covering *Oraḥ Ḥayim* and part of *Yoreh De'a,* by R. Yaakov Ḥayim Sofer (1870-1939) of Baghdad and Jerusalem

Karelitz, R. Avraham Yeshaya – 1878-1953, Lithuania and Bnei Brak, Israel; a major 20th century *posek* and a massive influence on Israel's Ashkenazic Ḥaredi community; also known as Ḥazon Ish

Karo, R. Yosef – 1488-1575, Spain and eventually Eretz Yisrael; author of the authoritative halakhic codes *Shulḥan Arukh* and *Beit Yosef* as well as *Kessef Mishneh* and other works

Kessef Mishneh – R. Yosef Karo's commentary on *Mishneh Torah,* which provides talmudic sources for Rambam's rulings

Kinyan Torah Ba-halakha – A collection of responsa by R. Avraham David Horowitz (1911-2004) of Grosswardein, Hungary (Oradea, Romania) and later Strasbourg, France

Kitzur Shulḥan Arukh – A concise handbook of Jewish law by R. Shlomo Ganzfried (1804-1886) of Ungvar, Hungary (Uzhorod, Ukraine)

Kluger, R. Shlomo – 1783-1869; chief dayan of Brody, Galicia

Knesset Ha-gedola – A commentary on *Shulḥan Arukh* by R. Ḥayim Benveniste (1603-1673) of Turkey, analyzing halakhic opinions rendered during the 16th and 17th centuries

Kol Bo – An unsystematic halakhic work of unknown authorship from the period of the Rishonim, which also contains miscellaneous nonlegal material

Kol Mevasser – A collection of responsa by R. Meshulam Roth (1875-1963) of Tchernovitz, Galicia (Chernivtsi, Ukraine) and later a member of Israel's Chief Rabbinical Council

Kook, R. Avraham Yitzḥak (1865-1935), the first Ashkenazic Chief Rabbi of Eretz Yisrael, author of numerous halakhic, philosophical, and mystical works; the spiritual giant of religious Zionism

Kook, R. Zvi Yehuda – 1891-1982, Eretz Yisrael; son and successor of Rav Kook, head of Yeshivat Merkaz Harav, central religious Zionist ideologue, and mentor of an entire generation of religious Zionist rabbis and yeshiva heads

Ktav Sofer – Commentaries on talmudic and halakhic works by R. Avraham Shmuel Binyamin Sofer (1815-1871) of Pressburg, Hungary (Bratislava, Slovakia), son of Ḥatam Sofer

Landau, R. Yeḥezkel – 1713-1793; renowned *posek* and rabbi of Prague and author of *Dagul Mei-rvava, Noda Bi-Yehuda,* and *Tziyun Lenefesh Ḥaya*

Leḥem Ḥamudot – A commentary on Rosh's halakhic work, by R. Yom-Tov Lipmann Heller (1578-1654, Bohemia and Poland), best known for his commentary on the Mishna, *Tosafot Yom Tov*

Lev Ḥayim – A collection of responsa and comments on *Shulḥan Arukh Oraḥ Ḥayim* by R. Ḥayim Palachi (see entry)

Levush – Short for *Levush Malkhut,* a 10-volume halakhic code by R. Mordechai Yoffe (1530-1612, Bohemia and Poland)

Lior, R. Dov – b. 1933, the rabbi of Ḥevron and Kiryat Arba and an influential religious Zionist rabbi and *posek*

Ma'amar Mordechai – A commentary on *Shulḥan Arukh* by R. Mordechai Karmi (1749-1825, Provence); alternatively, a collection of responsa by R. Mordechai Eliyahu (see entry)

Ma'aseh Nisim – A commentary on the Hagada by R. Yaakov Lorberbaum (1760-1832) of Lissa (Leszno, Poland), who also authored *Netivot Mishpat* and *Ḥavot Da'at,* commentaries on parts of *Shulḥan Arukh*

Ma'aseh Rav – A collection of customs and practices of the Vilna Gaon (see entry), compiled by his disciples

Magen Avraham – A classic commentary on *Shulḥan Arukh Oraḥ Ḥayim* by R. Avraham Abele Gombiner (1635-1682, Poland)

Magid Mishneh – A classic early commentary on *Mishneh Torah,* by R. Vidal of Toulouse (1283-1360)

Maharal – R. Yehuda Loew of Prague (1520-1609), a major kabbalist, thinker, and author

Maharalbaḥ – A collection of responsa by R. Levi ibn Ḥabib (1480-1545, Spain and Jerusalem)

Maharam Ḥalawa – R. Moshe Ḥalawa (14th century Spain), whose surviving writings consist of some responsa and a well-known commentary on *Pesaḥim*

Maharam of Rothenburg – R. Meir of Rothenberg (c. 1215-1293), a Tosafist who authored numerous responsa; considered a major figure in the Ashkenazic halakhic tradition

Maharam Schick – R. Moshe Schick (1807-1879, Austria-Hungary), a leading pupil of Ḥatam Sofer and a strong advocate of Orthodox separatism; author of a collection of responsa and other works bearing this name

Maharash Engel – R. Shmuel Engel (1863-1935), rabbi and rabbinical court head in Kosice, Hungary (now Slovakia), and a fierce opponent of Zionism

Mahari Aszod – R. Yehuda Aszod (1796-1866), a leading Hungarian *posek* in the mid-19th century, his responsa were published as *Yehuda Ya'aleh*

Mahari Ben Lev – R. Yosef ibn Lev (c. 1505-1580); served in Ottoman Salonica (Thessaloniki, Greece) and Constantinople (Istanbul, Turkey); penned responsa known for their independent-minded and uncompromising stances

Mahari Brin – R. Yisrael Bruna (1400-1480, Brno, Moravia), a leading Ashkenazic *posek* whose rulings, collecting in his responsa, served as an important source for Rema

Mahari Weil – R. Yaakov Weil, a leading German *posek* of the early 15th century and author of the responsa that bear this name

Maharik – R. Yosef Colon Trabotto (c. 1420-1480) of Savoy (southeast France/northeast Italy); author of the collection of responsa bearing this name, which became an authoritative source of French/Northern Italian tradition and had a major influence on general Ashkenazic tradition

Maharil – R. Yaakov Segal Moelin (c. 1365-1427), compiled an authoritative description of Ashkenazic custom and synagogue rite (*Minhagei Maharil*) and authored the collection of responsa that bear this name

Maharim Padua of Brisk – R. Yaakov Meir Padua (1796-1865), head of the rabbinical court in Brisk (Brest, Belarus); author of a collection of responsa bearing this name, as well as other works

Maharitz – R. Yiḥya Tzalaḥ (1713-1804), a leading halakhic authority of Yemeni Jewry who sought to clarify the community's original custom, often based on Rambam's rulings; author of *Respona Pe'ulat Tzadik* and other works

Mahariz Enzil – R. Yekutiel Asher Zalman Enzil (d. 1858), rabbi of Staro (Stryj) and Pshemishel (Przemysl), Galicia; author of the collection of responsa that bear this name

Maharshal – R. Shlomo Luria (1510-1573, Poland); opponent of halakhic codification; author of *Yam shel Shlomo,* a halakhic commentary on the Talmud, and *Ḥokhmat Shlomo,* glosses on the Talmud

Maharsham – R. Shalom Mordechai Schwadron (1835-1911), a Galician *posek* who authored responsa, a commentary on *Ḥoshen Mishpat,* and a commentary on the Torah

Maḥatzit Ha-shekel – A multivolume commentary on *Magen Avraham* authored by R. Shmuel Halevi Kelin (1720-1806) of Boskowitz, Moravia (Boskowice, Czech Republic)

Maḥzik Berakha – A commentary on *Shulḥan Arukh Oraḥ Ḥayim* and *Yoreh De'a* by Ḥida (see entry)

Manhig – A collection of responsa and halakhic citations by R. Avraham b. Natan Hayarḥi (c. 1155-1215, Provence and Spain)

Marḥeshet – A collection of responsa by R. Ḥanokh Henich Eigis (1863-1941, Vilna), a leading Lithuanian *posek* who was murdered by the Nazis

Matza Ashira – A halakhic work devoted to the *halakhot* of *matza ashira,* by R. Ido Alba (Kiryat Arba, Israel), published in 2003

Matzot Mitzva – A halakhic work devoted to the mitzva of matza, by R. Moshe Uri Linder, published in 1992

Meir of Rothenburg, R. – see Maharam of Rothenburg

Meir Simḥa of Dvinsk, R. – 1843-1926, Dvinsk, Greater Lithuania (Daugavpils, Latvia); communal leader and author of the Torah commentary *Meshekh Ḥokhma* and *Or Same'aḥ,* a commentary on *Mishneh Torah*

Me'iri – R. Menaḥem Me'iri (1249-c. 1315) of Perpignan (then associated with Catalan Barcelona, now in southern France); author of *Beit Ha-beḥira,* a restatement and elucidation of the entire Bavli

Mekhilta – An early tannaitic commentary on Shemot, which includes the derivations of numerous halakhot

Mekor Ḥayim – A halakhic work on the laws of Pesaḥ by R. Yaakov Lorberbaum (see entry for *Ma'aseh Nisim*)

Melamed Le-ho'il – A collection of responsa by R. David Zvi Hoffman (1843-1921), a major German *posek* and Torah commentator; head of the Hildesheimer Rabbinical Seminary in Berlin

Messas, R. Shalom – c. 1909-2003, chief rabbi of Morocco and later Jerusalem; considered the greatest 20th century Moroccan *posek* and upholder of that community's customs; authored several halakhic and other works

Mikra'ei Kodesh – A series of contemporary halakhic books on the Jewish holidays, by R. Moshe Harari

Min-Hahar, R. Shlomo Zalman – 1911-2000, Jerusalem; rabbi of the Bayit Vegan neighborhood, teacher, and author of several halakhic works for popular audiences, mainly pertaining to conditions specific to life in Israel

Minḥat Ḥinukh – An encyclopedic work on the 613 commantments by R. Yosef Babad (1801-1874, Galicia), organized as a commentary on *Sefer Ha-ḥinukh*

Minḥat Yitzḥak – A multivolume collection of responsa by R. Yitzḥak Yaakov Weiss (1902-1989) of Austria-Hungary, Manchester, and Jerusalem

Mishbetzot Zahav – Part of *Pri Megadim* (see entry) and a supercommentary on *Turei Zahav*

Mishna Berura – The most central of the three commentaries on *Shulḥan Arukh Oraḥ Ḥayim* authored by R. Yisrael Meir Kagan ("Ḥafetz Ḥayim," 1838-1933); this commentary summarizes the opinions of Aḥaronim and offers practical rulings

Mishneh Torah – Rambam's magesterial, comprehensive, and highly organized restatement and codification of *halakha*

Mor U-ketzi'a – A collection of responsa by R. Yaakov Emden (see *She'elat Yaavetz*)

Mordechai – An influential halakhic commentary on the Talmud and a key source of many Ashkenazic halakhic rulings and traditions; authored by R. Mordechai b. Hillel (c. 1250-1298, Germany), who was martyred in the Rintfleisch massacres

Naeh, R. Ḥayim – 1890-1954, Eretz Yisrael; a *posek*, Lubavitcher Ḥasid, and Ḥaredi publicist best known for converting halakhic weights and measures into metric values

Natronai Gaon, R. – 9th century, Gaon of Sura; authored responsa addressed to communities throughout the Diaspora

Netziv – R. Naftali Zvi Yehuda Berlin (1816-1893), head of the Volozhin Yeshiva and author of commentaries on the Torah, Talmud, and other classic rabbinic works, as well as responsa

Nishmat Adam – Part of *Ḥayei Adam* in which the author (see *Binat Adam*) introduces his halakhic novellae

Noda Bi-Yehuda – A collection of responsa by R. Yeḥezkel Landau (see entry)

Olat Re'iyah – A commentary on the Jewish liturgy by Rav Kook (see entry)

Olat Shabbat – A commentary on *Shulḥan Arukh Oraḥ Ḥayim* by R. Shmuel Orgeler (c. 1645-1700) of Krakow, later a rabbinical court judge in Altona, Germany

Olat Shmuel – A collection of responsa by R. Shmuel Leib Kauder (1766-1838) of Bohemia

Oneg Yom Tov – A collection of responsa by R. Raphael Yom-Tov Lipmann Heilperin (1816-1879), the rabbi of Bialystok, Poland

Or Le-Tziyon – A collection of responsa by R. Ben-Zion Abba-Shaul (see entry)

Or Same'aḥ – A commentary on *Mishneh Torah* by R. Meir Simḥa of Dvinsk (see entry)

Or Zaru'a – A halakhic work and Talmud commentary on Jewish ritual law by R. Yitzḥak b. Moshe of Vienna (c.1200-c.1270)

Oraḥ Ḥayim – One of the four sections of *Tur* and *Shulḥan Arukh*, dealing primarily with liturgy, daily routines, Shabbat, and festivals

Oraḥ Mishpat – A collection of responsa by Rav Kook (see entry)

Orḥot Ḥayim – A halakhic compendium on the liturgy and festivals by R. Aharon Hakohen (13th-14th century Provence and Majorca)

Ovadia of Bertinoro, R. – c. 1445-c. 1515, Bertinoro, Italy and Jerusalem; an influential communal leader in Jerusalem, best known for his commentary on the Mishna and, to a lesser extent, for his travelogues

Palachi, R. Ḥayim – 1788-1869; a rabbi, *posek,* and prolific author from Smyrna (Izmir), Turkey

Peretz, Rabbeinu – R. Peretz of Corbeil (d. 1295); a Tosafist who produced a collection of *Tosafot* and authored glosses on *Smak*

Perla, R. Yeruḥam Fishel – 1846-1934, Poland; author of an encyclopedic commentary on R. Saadia Gaon's *Sefer Ha-mitzvot*

Pfeuffer, R. Aharon – 1949-1993, London, England, Johannesburg, South Africa, and Israel; *posek,* especially on matters of *kashrut,* who wrote several concise halakhic works for popular audiences

Piskei Teshuvot – A series of contemporary halakhic works that collect rulings from responsa to supplement those of *Mishna Berura,* by R. Simḥa Rabinowitz

Pri Ḥadash – A commentary on *Shulḥan Arukh* by R. Ḥizkiya da Silva (1659-1698, Livorno, Italy and Jerusalem) that often critiques and disagrees with earlier authorities

Pri Megadim – A set of classic supercommentaries on *Siftei Kohen* (*Siftei Da'at*), *Magen Avraham* (*Eshel Avraham*), and *Turei Zahav* (*Mishbetzot Zahav*), by R. Yosef Teomim (1717-1792) of Galicia and Germany

Pri Tzadik – A Ḥasidic commentary on the Torah and the Jewish calendar, compiled from the oral discourses of R. Tzadok Hakohen Rabinowitz of Lublin (1823-1900)

Ra'ah – R. Aharon Halevi, 1235-1290, Catalan Spain; commentator on the Talmud and major disputant of Rashba

Raavad – R. Avraham b. David, c. 1125-1198, Provence, France; prolific author of numerous responsa, commentaries on the Talmud, obscure parts of the Mishna, and halakhic midrashim, and objections to the halakhic codes of Rambam, Rif, and *Ha-ma'or*; opponent of codification and of Rambam's rationalism

Raavan – R. Eliezer b. Natan of Mainz (1090-1170); an early Tosafist, liturgical poet, and author of the halakhic compendium *Even Ha-ezer*

Raavya – R. Eliezer b. Yoel Halevi of Bonn (1140-1225), a German Tosafist and author of *Avi Ha-ezri,* a halakhic compendium

Rabinovitch, R. Naḥum – b. 1928 in Montreal, Quebec, Canada, served in several communities, including Charleston, South Carolina and London, England, before moving to Israel to head Yeshivat Birkat

Moshe in Maale Adumim; author of several volumes of responsa, a highly regarded commentary on *Mishneh Torah*, and other works

Radbaz – R. David ibn Zimra (1479-c. 1573), chief rabbi of Egyptian Jewry and author of the collection of responsa bearing this name

Rama Mi-Fano – R. Menaḥem Azariah of Fano (1548-1620, Italy), talmudist and kabbalist who authored the collection of responsa bearing this name

Rambam – R. Moshe b. Maimon (1135-1204, Cordoba, Spain and Fostat [Old Cairo], Egypt); leading rabbi, physician, and philosopher; author of *Mishneh Torah* (see entry), *Moreh Nevukhim*, a commentary on the Mishna, and several other classic works

Ramban – R. Moshe b. Naḥman (1194-1270, Gerona, Spain and Eretz Yisrael), classic commentator on the Torah and Talmud, kabbalist, and author of several halakhic works

Ran – R. Nissim of Gerona (1320-1376, Catalan Spain), commentator on the Talmud and Rif, author of halakhic responsa and other works

Rashba – R. Shlomo b. Aderet (1235-1310, Barcelona), talmudic commentator and author of numerous responsa and other halakhic works

Rashbam – R. Shmuel b. Meir (c. 1085-c. 1158, Ramerupt, France), a grandson of Rashi, a Tosafist, and a major talmudic and biblical commentator

Rashbatz – R. Shimon b. Tzemaḥ Duran (1361-1444), Spain and Algiers, a prolific author of various types of religious works

Rashi – R. Shlomo Yitzḥaki (1040-1105, Troyes, France), the most influential biblical and talmudic commentator, whose interpretations have become an integral part of the texts they elucidate; additionally, his halakhic rulings were collected and disseminated by his students

Rema – R. Moshe Isserles (1520-1572, Krakow, Poland), author of glosses that have become an integral part of *Shulḥan Arukh* (*Mapa*) and *Tur/Beit Yosef* (*Darkhei Moshe*), which present Ashkenazic rulings

Ri – R. Yitzḥak b. Shmuel the Elder (c. 1115-c. 1184), a major French Tosafist

Ri'az – R. Yeshaya di Trani the Younger (d. c. 1280), author of a collection of halakhic rulings

Rid – R. Yeshaya di Trani the Elder (c. 1180-c. 1250), an Italian Tosafist who, alongside extensive talmudic commentaries, also recorded halakhic rulings

Rif – R. Yitzḥak Alfasi (c. 1013-1103, Fez, Morocco), a towering halakhist best known for his summary codification of the Talmud

Rinun Yitzḥak – A commentary on the Hagada by R. Yitzḥak Meller (early 19th century) of Stanislav, Galicia (now Ivano-Frankivsk, Ukraine)

Ritva – R. Yom-Tov b. Avraham of Seville (c. 1250-1330), author of a major commentary on the Talmud

Ritz Gi'at – R. Yitzḥak ibn Ghiyyat (c. 1038-1089, Lucena and Cordoba, Spain), author of several liturgical poems as well as a halakhic compendium on the Jewish festivals

Rivash – R. Yitzḥak b. Sheshet (1326-1408), Spain and Algiers, a student of Ran who authored numerous responsa

Rokei'aḥ – A halakhic and ethical work by R. Elazar of Worms (c. 1176-1238), the last major member of the German pietist circle

Rosh – R. Asher b. Yeḥiel (c. 1250-1327), leading Tosafist in the Rhineland (Western Germany) and later Toledo, Spain; author of a practical summary of the Talmud, similar to that of Rif, but with the inclusion of later Sephardic and Ashkenazic authorities, especially the Tosafists

Ru'aḥ Ḥayim – A commentary on *Shulḥan Arukh* by R. Ḥayim Palachi (see entry)

Saadia Gaon, R. – c. 882-c. 943, Egypt and Iraq; Gaon of Sura, linguist, Torah commentator and translator into Arabic, halakhist, philosopher, and polemicist; considered a pioneer of the rationalist school of Jewish philosophy and exegesis that subsequently became dominant in Spain

Salant, R. Shmuel – 1816-1909, Jerusalem; Ashkenazic chief rabbi and leader of Jerusalem; did not author major works, but several halakhic positions were preserved by his students

Sdei Ḥemed – An encyclopedic collection of responsa by R. Ḥayim Ḥizkiya Medini (1833-1904), who served in several communities in the Ottoman Empire, most notably Karasubazar, Crimea (Bilohirsk, Ukraine) and Ḥevron, Eretz Yisrael

Sefer Ha-ḥinukh – An important 13th century Spanish work on the 613 commandments, of uncertain authorship

Sefer Ha-mitzvot (R. Saadia Gaon) – A liturgical poem on the 613 commandments by the influential Babylonian authority Saadia Gaon (see entry)

Sefer Mitzvot Gadol – A halakhic code by R. Moshe of Coucy (13th century, France)

Sefer Mitzvot Katan – A halakhic code by French Tosafist R. Yitzḥak b. Yosef of Corbeil (13th century)

Seridei Esh – A collection of responsa by R. Yeḥiel Yaakov Weinberg (1884-1966), head of the Hildesheimer Rabbinical Seminary in Berlin; moved to Montreaux, Switzerland after WWII

Sha'agat Aryeh – A collection of responsa by R. Aryeh Leib Gunzberg (1695-1785, Greater Lithuania and Metz, France) and the author's *nom de plume*

Sha'ar Ha-tziyun – One of the three commentaries on *Shulḥan Arukh Oraḥ Ḥayim* authored by R. Yisrael Meir Kagan ("Ḥafetz Ḥayim," 1838-1933) and included in *Mishna Berura*; this commentary contains references to halakhic positions

Sha'arei Teshuva – A compilation of responsa arranged as a commentary on *Shulḥan Arukh*, by R. Ḥayim Mordechai Margolis (1780-1818, Dubno, Ukraine)

Shakh – *Siftei Kohen*

She'arim Metzuyanim Be-halakha – A talmudic commentary that highlights connections between the Talmud and *halakha*, by 20th century American R. Shlomo Zalman Braun

She'elat Yaavetz – A collection of responsa by R. Yaakov Emden (1697-1776, Altona, Germany), a rabbi and prolific author in several genres

She'iltot – A geonic collection of halakhic homilies, attributed to R. Aḥa of Sabha (8th century CE) and organized on the weekly Torah portion

Shema Shlomo – A collection of responsa by former Sephardic Chief Rabbi of Israel, R. Shlomo Amar (b. 1948)

Shevet Ha-Levi – A collection of responsa by R. Shmuel Wosner (b. 1913, now of Bnei Brak), a major contemporary Israeli *posek*

Shibolei Ha-leket – A systematic halakhic compilation by R. Tzidkiya b. Avraham Anaw (1210-c. 1280), an important talmudist from Rome and later Germany

Shiyarei Knesset Ha-gedola – A commentary on *Tur* by R. Ḥayim Benveniste (1603-1673) of Turkey, analyzing halakhic opinions rendered during the 16th and 17th centuries

Shlah – *Shnei Luḥot Ha-brit*, an encylopedic compilation of Jewish law, ethics, and mysticism by R. Yeshaya Horowitz (c. 1565-1630), rabbi in Central Europe and later Eretz Yisrael

Shlomo of Vilna, R. – 1828-1905, Vilna (Vilnius, Lithuania); *posek* and rabbinical court head, author of several volumes of responsa, and an early supporter of religious Zionism

Sho'el U-meishiv – A collection of responsa by R. Yosef Shaul Nathansohn (1808-1875), rabbi of Lvov, Galacia (Lviv, Ukraine)

Shulḥan Arukh – The most authoritative halakhic code, authored by R. Yosef Karo (see entry) and organized according to the four-part structure of *Tur*

Shulḥan Arukh Ha-Rav – A halakhic code by R. Shneur Zalman of Liadi (1745-1812), founder of the Ḥabad/Lubavitch Ḥasidic dynasty

Sidur Pesaḥ Ke-hilkhato – A comprehensive collection of laws relating to Pesaḥ by the contemporary R. Shlomo Zalman Grossman (Elad, Israel)

Sidur Yaavetz – R. Yaakov Emden's (see *She'elat Yaavetz*) prayerbook, containing his version of the prayers and the associated rites

Siftei Kohen – A major commentary on *Shulḥan Arukh Yoreh De'a* and *Ḥoshen Mishpat* by R. Shabtai Hakohen (1621-1662, Poland and eventually Moravia)

Sirkis, R. Yoel – 1561-1640, Poland; known for his commentary on *Tur* and his glosses on the Talmud (both called *Bayit Ḥadash*)

Smag – *Sefer Mitzvot Gadol*

Smak – *Sefer Mitzvot Katan*

Soloveitchik, R. Ḥayim – 1853-1918; a lecturer in Talmud at the yeshiva in Volozhin and later rabbi of Brisk (Brest, Belarus); famous for developing an analytic approach to studying the Talmud and Rishonim, known as the "Brisker *derekh*" and exemplified by his novellae on *Mishneh Torah*

Spektor, R. Yitzḥak Elḥanan – 1817-1896; rabbi of Kovno (Kaunas, Lithuania) and world-renowned *posek*

Ta'anit Bekhorot – A recent collection of laws relating to the Fast of the Firstborns

Tam, Rabbeinu – R. Yaakov b. Meir, 1100-1171, France; grandson of Rashi and brother of Rashbam, a leading *posek* and a founder of the Tosafist school; considered a great halakhic innovator, also authored responsa and a halakhic work called *Sefer Ha-yashar*

Tanḥuma – A post-amoraic midrash on the Torah

Tashbetz – A collection of responsa by Rashbatz (see entry)

Taz – *Turei Zahav*

Teḥumin – A Torah journal published by the Zomet Institute and devoted to the intersection between *halakha,* technology, and modernity

Terumat Ha-deshen – An collection of responsa central to the development of Ashkenazic *halakha* by R. Yisrael Isserlin (1390-1460, Austria)

Teshuva Me-ahava – A collection of responsa by R. Elazar Fleckeles (1754-1826), head of the yeshiva and rabbinical court in Prague

Teshuvot Ve-hanhagot – A collection of rulings on *halakha* and custom by the contemporary *posek,* R. Moshe Sternbuch

Tiferet Yisrael – A commentary on the Mishna authored by R. Yisrael Lifschitz (1782-1860)

Torat Ha-Shabbat Ve-hamo'ed – A work about the laws of Shabbat and Yom Tov by R. Shlomo Goren (see entry)

Torat Ha-yoledet – A modern work on the laws pertaining to parturient women by R. Yitzḥak Zilberstein and R. Moshe Rothschild

Torat Ḥessed – A collection of responsa by R. Shneur Zalman Fradkin (1830-1902), a Ḥabad Ḥasid and rabbi of Lublin

Torat Kohanim – A tannaitic midrash on Vayikra

Tosafot – Medieval Ashkenazic critical and explanatory glosses that appear on the standard page of the Talmud

Tur – Shorthand for *Arba Turim*; the four-part halakhic code by R. Yaakov b. Asher (1270-1340, Spain) on which *Shulḥan Arukh* is modeled

Tuv Ta'am Va-da'at – A collection of responsa authored by R. Shlomo Kluger (see entry)

Tzemaḥ Tzedek – A collection of halakhic responsa by R. Menaḥem Mendel Schneersohn (1789-1866), the third rebbe of the Lubavitch Ḥasidic dynasty

Tzitz Eliezer – A collection of halakhic responsa by R. Eliezer Yehuda Waldenberg (1915-2006, Jerusalem), a major Israeli *posek*

Tziyun Le-nefesh Ḥaya – The Talmud commentary of R. Yeḥezkel Landau (see entry)

Tzlaḥ – *Tziyun Le-nefesh Ḥaya*

Vilna Gaon – R. Elijah of Vilna (1720-1797); the towering rabbinic figure of the 18th century; penned authoritative annotations to classic Jewish texts and established a set of customs still observed today

Weitman, R. Zev – Rabbinical supervisor of Tnuva, a major Israeli dairy food producer, and former rabbi of Kfar Etzion

Yabi'a Omer – The most significant collection of responsa authored by R. Ovadia Yosef (see entry)

Yad Yehuda – A commentary on *Shulḥan Arukh Yoreh De'a* by R. Yehuda Leibish Landau (1823-1900), head of the Sadigura (Sadhora, now part of Chernivtsi, Ukraine) rabbinical court

Yalkut Yosef – The halakhic code compiled by R. Yitzḥak Yosef, current Sephardic Chief Rabbi of Israel, based on the rulings of his father, R. Ovadia Yosef

Yaskil Avdi – A collection of responsa by R. Ovadia Hedaya (1889-1969, Jerusalem), a noted kabbalist and rabbinical court judge of Syrian ancestry

Yeḥaveh Da'at – A collection of responsa by R. Ovadia Yosef (see entry)

Yeḥiel, Rabbeinu – d. c. 1264, Paris; leading Tosafist, tried to defend the Talmud in a major disputation in 1240, in the wake of which 24 carriage loads of talmudic manuscripts were burned

Yerei'im – A work on the 613 mitzvot authored by the Tosafist R. Eliezer b. Shmuel (c. 1115-c. 1198) of Metz, France

Yeruḥam, Rabbeinu – c. 1290-1350, Provence and Spain; a disciple of Rosh, his halakhic compendia served as a key source for *Shulḥan Arukh*

Yeshu'ot Yaakov – A commentary on *Shulḥan Arukh* written by R. Yaakov Meshulam Orenstein (1775-1839), rabbi of Lvov, Galicia (Lviv, Ukraine)

Yisraeli, R. Shaul – 1909-1995, Slutsk, Belarus and Jerusalem; a renowned religious Zionist rabbi, rabbinical court judge, member of the Chief Rabbinate Council, head of Yeshivat Merkaz Harav, and author of halakhic and philosophical works

Yona, Rabbeinu – R. Yonah Gerondi (d. 1263, Gerona, Spain), commentator on the Talmud and Rif and author of influential works on Jewish ethics

Yoreh De'a – One of the four sections of *Tur* and *Shulḥan Arukh*, dealing primarily with ritual law

Yosef, R. Ovadia – 1920-2013, Jerusalem; the leading Sephardic *posek* of the 20th century, upholder of the rationalist and moderate Syrian halakhic tradition, Sephardic Chief Rabbi of Israel, and author of dozens of volumes of responsa and halakhic works

Zekher Yehosef – A collection of responsa by R. Yosef Zecharia Stern (1831-1904), rabbi of Shavel (Siauliai, Lithuania)

Zekhor Le-Avraham – An alphabetically arranged halakhic work authored by the 19th century Sephardic rabbi Avraham Alcalay

Zevin, R. Shlomo Yosef – 1888-1978, Belarus, Soviet Union, and Eretz Yisrael; a Ḥabad Ḥasid and influential Religious Zionist rabbi who authored *Ha-mo'adim Be-halakha* and was the first editor of *Encyclopedia Talmudit*

Zohar – The central work of the Kabbalah; the collection of esoteric biblical interpretation and mystical speculation attributed to the tanna R. Shimon b. Yoḥai

Index of Halakha

C

G

H

I

N

O

P

Q

R

S

T

U

W

Y

Z

Index of Jewish Thought

About the Author

Rabbi Eliezer Melamed is one of the most widely read Torah educators in Israel today. He learned in the Merkaz Harav Yeshiva in Jerusalem under the personal tutelage of Rabbi Zvi Yehuda HaKohen Kook *zt"l*. For twenty years, he taught Gemara and classes in *maḥshava* at the Bet-El Yeshiva. Invited to become the rabbi of the settlement Har Bracha, he established the Har Bracha Yeshiva, which he has headed since 1991. Under his leadership, Har Bracha has grown dynamically and become an example of an idealistic, Torah-based community, which is also integrally involved in the leading social, economic, military, and educational issues of the day.

Besides being one of the founders of, and the spiritual force behind, the weekly newspaper *B'sheva*, he writes the "*Revivim*" column which has garnered wide exposure and generated impact nationally. A partner in the establishment of the radio station Arutz 7, his daily halakha broadcast gained high listener ratings, and brought the light of Torah to a diverse listening audience throughout Israel.

His popular series of books, *Peninei Halakha*, written in a clear, concise, and in-depth fashion, in a language accessible to all, is part of his vision to familiarize the entire Jewish nation with the basics of Jewish law and faith.

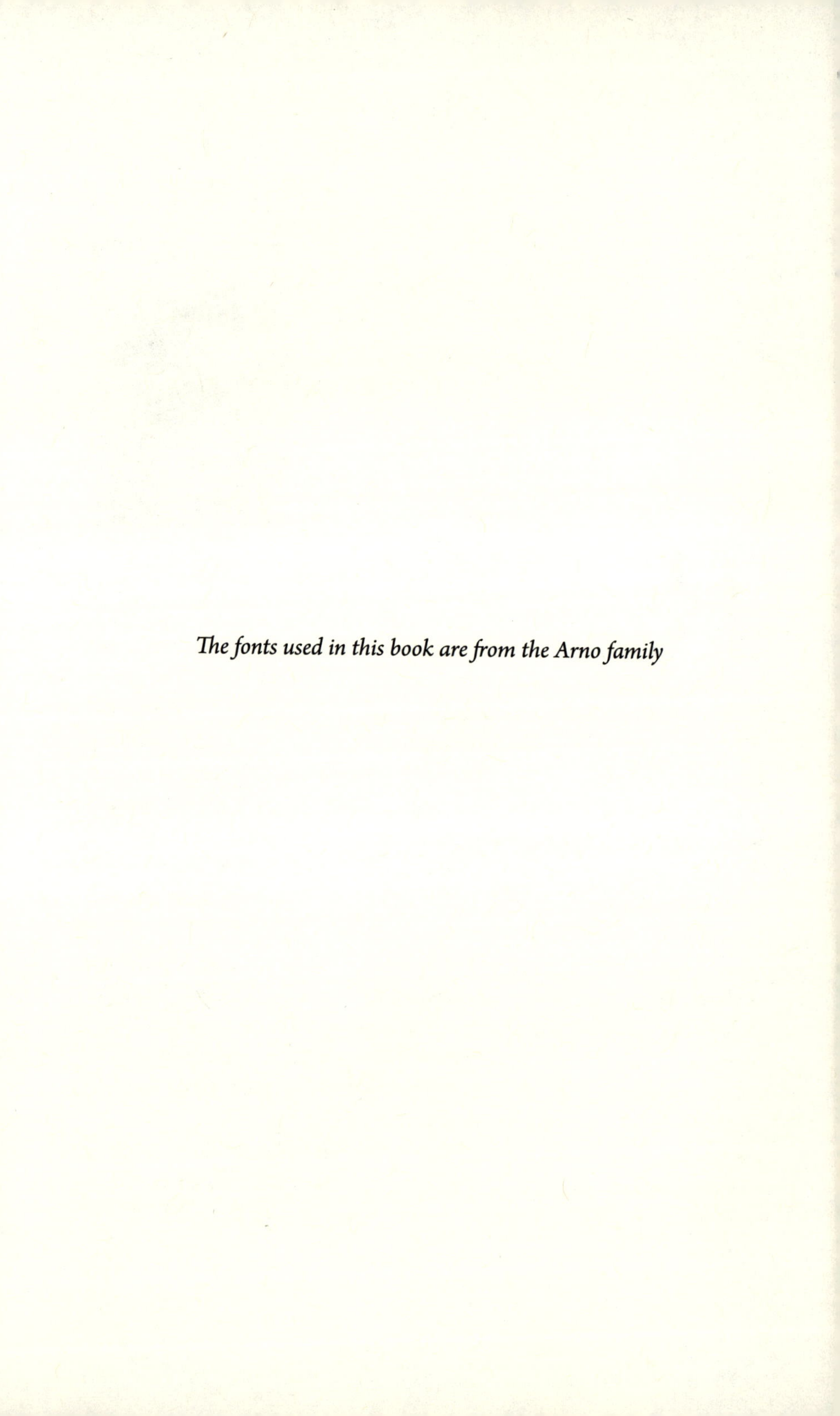

The fonts used in this book are from the Arno family

Maggid Books
The best of contemporary Jewish thought from
Koren Publishers Jerusalem Ltd.